Modern Europ
and the Art

UNGAR FILM LIBRARY
Stanley Hochman
General Editor

Academy Awards: An Ungar Reference Index,
edited by Richard Shale

American History / American Film: Interpreting the Hollywood Image
edited by John O'Connor and Martin A. Jackson

The Classic American Novel and the Movies,
edited by Gerald Peary and Roger Shatzkin

The Blue Angel / *the novel by Heinrich Mann and the
film by Josef von Sternberg*

Costume Design in the Movies / *Elizabeth Leese*

Faulkner and Film / *Bruce F. Kawin*

Fellini the Artist / *Edward Murray*

Film Study Collections: A Guide to their Development
and Use / *Nancy Allen*

Hitchcock / *Eric Rohmer and Claude Chabrol*

Loser Take All: The Comic Art of Woody Allen / *Maurice Yacowar*

The Modern American Novel and the Movies,
edited by Gerald Peary and Roger Shatzkin

On the Verge of Revolt: Women in American Films
of the Fifties / *Brandon French*

Ten Film Classics / *Edward Murray*

Tennessee Williams and Film / *Maurice Yacowar*

OTHER FILM BOOKS

The Age of the American Novel: The Film Aesthetic of Fiction between
the Two Wars / *Claude-Edmonde Magny*

The Cinematic Imagination: Writers and the Motion Picture /
Edward Murray

A Library of Film Criticism: American Film Directors,
edited by Stanley Hochman

Nine American Film Critics / *Edward Murray*

MODERN EUROPEAN FILMMAKERS AND THE ART OF ADAPTATION

Edited by

ANDREW HORTON

and

JOAN MAGRETTA

Frederick Ungar Publishing Co. New York

Copyright © 1981 by Frederick Ungar Publishing Co., Inc.
Printed in the United States of America
Designed by Jacqueline Schuman

Library of Congress Cataloging in Publication Data

Main entry under title:
Modern European filmmakers and the art of adaptation.

   Bibliography: p.
   Filmography: p.
   Includes index.
   1.   Film adaptations—Addresses, essays, lectures.
2.   European literature—Film adaptations—Addresses,
essays, lectures. I. Horton, Andrew. II. Magretta,
Joan.
PN1997.85.M66   791.43′02   79–48073
ISBN 0–8044–2403–9
ISBN 0–8044–6277–1 (pbk.)

Acknowledgments

Each of us has individual debts of gratitude to express. From Andrew Horton: To the University of New Orleans Liberal Arts Division for awarding me release time to work on the book during the Fall, 1979, and to Raeburn Miller, the Chairman of the English Department for his enthusiastic support. To my film students who over the past few years have helped me see familiar films in new ways. To Willard Manus, Lou & Judy Efstathiou, Jim Holte, Jim Pierce, Ariane Cotsis, Peter Brunette, Luciana Bohne, Hans Geisendorfer and Michael Goodman for their insights and suggestions. And finally to Jean Renoir who, more than any other filmmaker, through his films taught me that "everybody has his reasons."

From Joan Magretta: I wish to thank Dean Walter Emge and Transylvania University for generously supporting my work. Neil Friedman of Films Incorporated helped by arranging special screenings. Bertrand Tavernier's conversation was as generous and enlightening as his films. I appreciate the good counsel and encouragement of Helen Irvin and Ruth Prigozy. Bill Magretta not only wrote for this volume, but he participated actively in every stage of the project. I thank him for his patience, his critical judgment, and his unfailing good taste: he is the uncredited third editor of this book. And finally I would like to acknowledge a special and very personal debt to the late Marvin Felheim, friend and teacher.

Together we wish to thank John Montague of New Yorker Films, an important source not only of films but of information about them; our editor Stan Hochman for his unflagging commitment to this project; and Colleen Karimi for her dedicated assistance in preparing the manuscript.

Lastly, and most importantly, we thank the authors of the essays, for this is ultimately their book.

To Bill Magretta and Phil Horton

Contents

Modern European Filmmakers
and the Art of Adaptation

Introduction

The essays in this collection examine closely more than twenty of the most interesting films made in Europe since World War II. What these films have in common is that they have all been adapted from literary works, and the essays themselves consistently approach adaptation as an *art*.

Our basic premises—that adaptation can be a lively and creative art, and that attention to this art will enhance our understanding of film—are not shared universally. Most adaptation studies have shown, rather disdainfully, how great books become inferior movies. In fact, Hollywood has been notoriously crass and shameless in its commercial exploitation of serious writers and their work. But if we want to learn about the rich possibilities of film *art*, very little will be gained by studying the worst that has been accomplished.

Anyone with the most rudimentary literary training should be struck by the perverse backwardness of the adaptation-as-betrayal approach: The study of adaptation is clearly a form of source study and thus should trace the *genesis* (not the destruction) of works deemed worthy of close examination in and of themselves. Knowing how Fellini has reshaped Petronius in *Fellini Satyricon* helps us understand his art, just as knowing how Shakespeare used Plutarch helps us appreciate *Antony and Cleopatra*. However, since there is nothing to admire in Joseph L. Mankiewicz's *Cleopatra* (1963), it would be a waste of time to examine its indebtedness to either Plutarch or Shakespeare. All too often, the study of similarly mediocre films has been carried out under the aegis of adaptation.

One of the goals of this book, then, is to put the horse back in front of the cart. The essays, all of which have been written expressly for this collection, examine the genesis of fine films, and they demonstrate that the study of adaptation can and should be as useful a methodology for film scholarship as source study has been for comparative literature. In both cases, the goal is not only a better appreciation of a particular work but also a fuller comprehension of the creative process of filmmaking. The rationale is essentially the same as that offered by Vlada Petric as justification for what he calls "A Close Cinematic Analysis" (*Quarterly Review of Film Studies*, November 1976): "By discovering the 'creative road' through which the author 'traveled' in making his film, the analyst becomes capable of defining the cinematic strategy by which a film is conceived and realized." Although we are not proposing adaptation as a separate class in film taxonomy—that is, an adapted film is not necessarily different from a film based on an original screenplay—adapted films can provide a privileged map of the "creative road" a filmmaker has "traveled." Collectively, the essays in this book illustrate the virtues of an approach that deserves greater attention from film scholars.

Taken as a whole, these essays have implications for film theory as well. The prevailing trend of beginning with fine books that have yielded indifferent films has led to a highly suspect body of generalizations about adaptation and the generic differences between literature and film. These generalizations, then, are solemnly intoned in each new study: Films can't handle complexities in point of view, films can't abstract or generalize, good films come from bad books, and so on. Although these generalizations may apply to the numerical majority of film adaptations, do they really define the limits and possibilities of the form any more than the latest Harlequin Romance tells us what literature can do? It is surprising to realize that the book about adaptation most often cited in scholarly work, George Bluestone's 1957 *Novels Into Film*, analyzes only six adaptations, all of them Hollywood productions made between 1935 and 1949. Bluestone's pioneering work was (and is) most valuable, but his theories, based on such a limited and now dated sample, invite reexamination. Film has evolved significantly in the past three decades, and Europe has always allowed greater artistic freedom to its filmmakers than Hollywood has.

By focusing on European films since World War II we pick up, in a sense, where Bluestone left off. Such cutoff points are always artificial and frustrating: there are many worthy European adaptations of the 1930s, for instance. But the postwar period witnessed new developments in film, and we believe that our focus will help

draw attention to a development in film history which has generally been neglected by Anglo-American critics. In an important
book that regrettably has not been translated into English, *De la
Littérature au Cinéma: Genèse d'une Écriture* (1970), Marie-
Clare Ropars-Wuilleumier argues that film has gradually evolved
from a dramatic to a narrative aesthetic. In the course of this
evolution, and particularly after World War II in Europe, film has
developed the kind of expressiveness that French critics like Christian Metz and Roland Barthes refer to as *écriture* (writing). For
Ropars-Wuilleumier, not only is film comparable to literature as
an *écriture du mouvement* ("writing of movement"), but it has
been specifically *through* film's confrontation with literature, and
especially with the problems posed by adaptation, that film has
matured as a narrative art. In the pair of essays which appear early
in this volume, Dudley Andrew discusses the polemics of adaptation in postwar French cinema. He describes the dominant French
"quality tradition" in which all adaptations resembled each other
more than they did their literary sources, and he goes on to discuss
the new direction taken by Robert Bresson, who, in his own words,
has insisted on cinematography as "a writing [*écriture*] with
images in movement and with sounds."

The conception of cinema that animated the best work of the
postwar period was most flamboyantly expressed by Alexandre
Astruc in "Manifeste de la Caméra-Stylo" (*L'Écran Français*,
March 30, 1948). Emphasizing *écriture*, Astruc urged that cinematic writing should be as flexible, free, and expressive as literary
writing; the camera should be to the filmmaker what the pen is to
the writer. Susan Sontag is even more positive about film when she
drops the comparison with literature and states that cinema
"presents us with a new language, a way of talking about emotion
through the direct experience of the language of faces and gestures" (*Against Interpretation*, 1966). Certainly the explosion of
New Wave talent in France, Sweden, and Italy in the 1950s, in
Eastern Europe in the 1960s, and in Switzerland, Germany, and
Greece in the 1970s is testimony to the fulfillment of such hopes
for the potential of cinema. If film adaptation at first produced
"filmed literature" that was commercially important but aesthetically uninteresting, it has become, as the essays in this volume
attest, a lively and creative art.

For the most part, Hollywood has made of adaptation a commercial process, a kind of industrial recycling which turns one product (a best-selling book) into another (a box-office success). For the best of the European directors, adaptation has been and is an activity of an entirely different order, essentially artistic and personal. Just as Berlioz's *Romeo and Juliet* is the personal response of one artist to another, so is Eric Rohmer's *The Marquise of O . . .* (1976). This kind of adaptation reflects a serious engagement with the source, but at the same time reflects the independence and self-assurance of the second artist. Borrowing a lyric from Cole Porter, that most European of American songwriters, the directors considered in this volume tend to be "always true" in their own "fashion," in their own "way."

In part, such a spirit of creative adaptation reflects the close ties between literature and film since the early days of cinema in Europe. It is not uncommon for filmmakers themselves to be novelists, dramatists, or essayists, like Pasolini and Fassbinder in our collection but also like many others such as Jean Cocteau, Alain Robbe-Grillet, Marguerite Duras, and Peter Handke. Even those who are primarily filmmakers tend to be clearly attuned to the artistic and intellectual rhythms of their times. Ingmar Bergman, for instance, is fond of saying that film has nothing to do with literature, and certainly, except for *The Magic Flute*, he has not ventured into the realm of adaptation. Yet as one of Europe's leading theatrical directors as well, Bergman brings to filmmaking the rich legacy of Western theater. *Smiles of a Summer Night* is an "original" script, but one doubts that Bergman could have written it had he not been immersed in the traditions of romantic comedy and farce. Similarly, we see that even those directors such as Godard, Truffaut, and Antonioni who have not moved directly in "literary" circles have, nevertheless, read voraciously and worked as critics before standing behind a camera.

The "literary" quality of a film, and especially of an adapted film, should not be taken as a betrayal of the medium. In the mad scramble to stake out the boundaries of film study (who will teach? what will be taught?), there has developed a hostility in certain camps to anything that might be considered "literary." Unfortunately, this has in practice often meant a dogmatic insistence on action and the visual to the exclusion of structural-narrative complexities and the verbal. The films discussed in this volume are characterized by an aesthetic richness that makes detailed source study a rewarding effort. Certainly each film has its sociological and political implications as well, and these are discussed appropriately. But the texture, richness, and complexity of these films, traits that are shared with the best of literature, mean that a thorough "cinematic" appreciation of these works must include an understanding of those qualities which are usually thought of as "literary." In fact, as adaptation studies help define the limits of each medium, they will, we expect, expand our understanding of the nature of *narrative*—a more inclusive category which embraces both the "literary" and the "cinematic."

The "twice-told tales" of this volume support Ropars-Wuilleumier's contention about the development of a narrative aesthetic in European film. In fact, the preoccupations of many filmmakers have become over the years the preoccupations of novelists and writers: the fragmentation of narrative and the destruction of psychological cause-and-effect (*The Goalie's Anxiety At the Penalty Kick*, 1971; *Blow-Up*, 1966; *Le Mépris*, 1963; among others); the self-conscious exploration and manipulation of the film medium labeled the "triumph of artifice" in Neil Isaacs's essay on Antonioni (*Zazie dans le Métro*, 1960; *Effi Briest*, 1974; *Wrong Movement*, 1974; for example); the broadening of the original text's sociopolitical implications (*The Decameron*, 1971; *The Conformist*, 1971; *The Clockmaker*, 1973)); and also the development of a fluid *écriture* as in the films of Bresson and Buñuel, where character and situation are conveyed with ease, simplicity, directness, and economy. In short, many of the filmmakers represented in this collection have realized the ability of film to destroy, expand, and rearrange time and space for the narrative aims of the filmmaker.

Écriture is finally a living dimension of a filmmaker's vision that incorporates but goes beyond the technical possibilities of cinema. In the best adaptations, we can view such a process at work. Our "twice-told tales" suggest that a creative filmmaker can bring the spirit of the original text to life in a different medium at a different time and, as a result, produce a work with a clear life of its own.

Andrew Horton
Joan Magretta

DUDLEY ANDREW

ICE AND IRONY
Delannoy's *La Symphonie Pastorale (1946)*

from the novel by André Gide

Literature has often come to the aid of cinema, but never so dramatically as in postwar France. From 1945 to 1948, that country was beset with ugly internal strife including industrial *épuration* (the barring of personnel on the basis of the merest suspicion of former relations with the occupying regime), beleaguered from without by the threat of 1,800 American films beginning to pour onto the Continent, and constrained by economic and production woes which made the financing of a film difficult and the creation of a product uncertain.

The French response, proclaimed in the first issue of the official *Le Cinéma Français* in 1945, was contained in a single word— "quality"—and France's literary past was invoked as both a model and source for the "quality" films which would dominate the industry until well into the fifties.

A fully ideological term, "quality" was opposed to Hollywood's "quantitative" industry based on a huge number of films and immense budgets for certain pictures. The French system, it was felt, could survive only by exploiting the good taste, intelligence, and ingenuity of its personnel—attributes common to well-bred citizens and fostered by a production mechanism modeled not as in Hollywood on the assembly line but on the image of an *équipe* of artists and artisans working in a revered tradition and on a revered project. No project was better-suited to this conception of film art than adaptation, for here the project was by definition honorable and a market was already prepared. Dependent for solvency on foreign interest, the French found that it was only good business to draw on their internationally renowned literary past. Perhaps more important, the values, both aesthetic and moral, of that literary past promised to grant an economically weak cinema some veneer of maturity.

The maturity and good taste of the cinema of quality were fabled even to the point of complacency and self-satisfaction. Graphically these films looked like perfectly dressed store windows. Narratively they were tidy: an abstract moral problem translated into a perfect dramatic equation solved without remainder. Theatrically trained actors, sporting costumes by Christian Dior and other tasteful but trend-setting *couturiers*, delivered pithy and formal dialogue in voices meant not for the other characters but for an audience paying to see spectacle, performance, and culture—in short, paying to see quality.

The stodgy studio look of these films, their conservative editing styles, and their cold impersonal appearance have turned the world's opinion against them since Truffaut's devastating attack of 1954, "A Certain Tendency in French Cinema."[1] If this era still calls to us at all, it is only through its relation to literature; while we today may decry public and showcase cinema in favor of personal and spontaneous works, nevertheless most of us are ready to acknowledge that the treasure chest of literary classics might demand a different sort of treatment. Privileged to live in the present as remnants from the past, great novels seem to call for reverential treatment, for vellum bindings and quality adaptations. In this period of such adaptations, few seem worthier than Jean Delannoy's version of André Gide's *La Symphonie Pastorale*, a film which took first place at Cannes in 1946.

Jean Delannoy was born to direct this film. Protestant and circumspect, he has always been considered a "cold" director obsessed by moral and metaphysical questions, yet one who invariably finds success at the box office. His first films date from 1938 and show immediately a facility in many genres. Yet it is only with *L'Éternel Retour* (1943), which he directed in close collaboration with Jean Cocteau, the scenarist, that Delannoy's style and preoccupations became clear.

[1] François Truffaut, "A Certain Tendency in French Cinema," in Bill Nichols (ed.), *Movies and Methods*, Berkeley, University of California Press, 1976, pp. 224–236. The original essay appeared in *Cahiers du Cinéma* No. 31, January 1954.

La Symphonie Pastorale suited his temperament perfectly and, because of its literary fame and the renown of the cast, was the subject of tremendous publicity. The critical and popular success enjoyed by this film secured Delannoy an unshakable position in the French film industry and tempted him to risk other abstract subjects. Immediately afterward, he directed Jean-Paul Sartre's first original script, *Les Jeux Sont Faits* (1947), and later directed his other masterpiece, *Dieu a Besoin des Hommes* (1949), from the celebrated novel by Henri Queffélec.

Critical opinion began to turn against him in the fifties because of the predictability of his treatment and the lifelessness of the acting in his films. By the time Truffaut excoriated him in 1954, he was at best a reliable studio director, cranking out too many films a year, the most ambitious of which were historical or literary spectaculars like his 1956 remake of *Notre Dame de Paris*. After 1950 little new could be expected of Delannoy, but in 1945 the whole film community of France anticipated a work of genius or at least of exactness and propriety, presumably the qualities perfectly suited to the adaptation of a work by André Gide.

To watch *La Symphonie Pastorale* today, then, is to perform a complex interpretive task. On the one hand, we can only be impressed by the rigid precision and care of the film's production values. It is a beautiful film to look at, and yet it is apparently self-restrained. For example, we shall see that its mountain scenery forms a structural, not decorative value. *La Symphonie Pastorale* lets us appreciate a kind of film which, owing to its pomposity and deep-voiced seriousness, we often have difficulty listening to today. The name André Gide doubtless forces our attention and indulgence.

But it is this same André Gide who will, I think, ultimately make us share Truffaut's unfavorable judgment of the film. While the overall style of the cinema of quality may render the tone of the novella with uncanny purity, the rigidity of that style was inadequate to the subtleties Gide built into his discourse, particularly in relation to point of view. And so we have in this film a wonderful example of a type of film worth looking at, but a type which, though especially dependent on adaptation, was not supple enough to do justice to the literature it celebrated. The film historian may find himself wholly satisfied, while the literary scholar may be profoundly disappointed, as in fact Gide was. All will agree, however, that if *La Symphonie Pastorale* was ever to be adapted, this was the epoch in film history prepared and eager for the task. Gide saw this at once. Having created a novella which is at once lean and richly coded with traditional imagery, he knew he couldn't have obliged Delannoy further. The intricacies of the plot form a moral equation which the French cinema had learned how to present and solve. The brevity of the original (some seventy pages) reduced immediately the inevitable complaints about editing and expurgation. Finally, Gide's classical style and the elegant structure of the book were eminently suited to the cultural voice of quality cinema, a voice at once elevated and correct.

The moral equation is not the least of Gide's achievements in this work. A Calvinist pastor, happening upon a blind wild child (Gertrude), devotes his energy and life to her bettering, bringing her into the light of the intellect even while he neglects his own wife and children. The Christian love in which he instructs her is complicated by the erotic love he obviously feels and only partially represses. The crisis comes at the moment of her cure, when, seeing life to be discordant and murky, she throws herself suicidally into the river, leaving the pastor alone, his family disconsolate and dispersed.

The exquisite mixture of anticlerical and erotic material in Gide's *La Symphonie Pastorale* (1918) was perfectly suited to the temperament and ideology of postwar French culture, particularly the subculture in control of the film industry. As Truffaut was to point out, the "liberal" sentiments of this group were self-righteous in the extreme. Toying with the blasphemous as well as the titillating, cinema of quality preached in film after film a progressivist, even Freemason attitude toward life.

As a matter of fact, the adaptation shies away from the theological subdrama of the novella (including Gertrude's conversion to Catholicism) and presents the pastor's relation to Gertrude as more chaste than had Gide. But this is only one more indication of the sort of decorum sought after in this era, a decorum rent apart a decade later by such sexually explicit films as Vadim's *And God Created Woman* (1956) and Malle's *The Lovers* (1958). It was enough in 1946 to suggest the erotic and to ridicule the seriousness of religion without treating either of these subjects in a thorough fashion.

Instead, the energy of the adaptation was poured into the dramatic rendering of these themes via a symmetrical development of characters. While the novella continually stretches back in time to give weight to its action, and modulates all action through the eyes and thoughts of the pastor, the film spreads our interest across an entire field of characters. Indeed, a new character, Piette, is invented for this very purpose, embodying a choice for the pastor's son, Jacques, analogous to the role the pastor's family plays for him. As the pastor rejects his family in favor of Gertrude, so does Jacques relinquish Piette for her. The film takes note of the consequences of these decisions by inserting several key reaction shots and even a couple of point-of-view shots of the betrayed parties. In all fairness, it must be noted that in his original adaptation of the novella (spurned by Delannoy), Gide too had added a female character for Jacques, but she played a lesser role.

The balancing of the dramatic equation has its counterpart in the regularizing of the dramatic rhythm of the original. Indeed, it was this aspect which frustrated Gide and ostensibly caused his break with Delannoy. The novella, Gide claims,

> makes sense only in terms of its artistic construction. It is, in sum, a tragedy in five acts which takes on its final value only through the long night of the first four acts. The young blind girl recovers her sight only in the last pages—to her detriment as it turns out. Everything resides in this sudden rupture. They explained to me that the necessities of the screen warranted a new conception of the tale, that it had to be translated into another language.[2]

Delannoy gives Gertrude her sight at the end of the second reel, some two-thirds of the way through the film. This is, as Gide notes, entirely consistent with dominant film narrative practice, but it has the effect of softening and stabilizing that which originally was frighteningly abrupt. But Delannoy worked within his rights here; having taken the tale out of the hands of the pastor and spread it among a whole field of characters, he must make the decisive reversal of Gertrude's blindness affect everyone in turn. Gide's original delivers the experience of such a reversal through

[2] André Gide in *Écran Français*, No. 65, September 25, 1946. Gide's script and some discussion of the circumstances under which it was written appears in Gide's *La Symphonie Pastorale*, édition établié et présenté par Claude Martin, Paris, Minard, 1970.

the mind of the drama's most passionate character, and the brutally swift conclusion is consonant with the overall ironic effect which has repeatedly overturned the pastor's thoughts and desires throughout at least the entire second half of the novella.

Delannoy's decision to incorporate Gide's irony entirely within the plot rather than in the telling of the tale was, I'm certain, quite unconscious. It was sheer instinct, the unquestioned work of a certain conception of film. On the one hand, French cinema at this time was hardly capable of subtle narrational strategies; on the other, an invisible pressure assured the presentation of a clean and balanced picture of events: Every tale and every style was, in effect, turned into that "other language" Gide spoke of—the language of the cinema of quality.

In practice, aside from deletions, additions, and dramatic restructuring, what does this mean? Primarily, it concerns the construction of a totally satisfying picture of dramatic tensions and releases, a picture which, either in one shot or built up through a relation of a few adjacent shots, symmetrically holds the film's values in place. For example, a single powerful shot culminates the tension within and between father and son in their attempt to possess the unseeing Gertrude, a tension ascribed to the possessiveness of sight itself. Vision distances them from each other and from her. In her world of touch (the shots of hands) and sounds, she alone is happy. Delannoy sums up this situation at the end of a quarrel between father and son, when both characters walk to a window and gaze out from their dark foreground to Gertrude sitting in the garden. This shot is the apotheosis of the first half of the drama, and it gains in appeal by mimicking the spectator's own situation, looking through a glass toward an object he can see but which can't see him—the luminous film itself and the blind sexuality at its heart.

The next act of the drama is inaugurated by the operation which restores Gertrude's sight. Her emergence from the hospital after the cure is given to us in three shots: her light cape and dark hair set her off against the two dark-clad nuns with white veils who support each of her arms in a frontal midshot. She frees herself from them, and as she breathes in her first vision of the world, a cut to an extreme long shot both liberates her in a thrilling way and contains her. The liberation results from the distance of the

She is loved . . . she's happy . . .

In *La Symphonie Pastorale*, director Delannoy sums up the tension between father and son for possession of Gertrude in a shot which suggests how vision distances them from each other and from the blind girl.

Her sight restored, Gertrude frees herself from the support of the dark-clad nuns. Delannoy's cut to an extreme long shot thrillingly suggests both her liberation and her containment in this snowy scene.

shot, expressing the sudden expansion of her horizons; it comes as well from the puffy flakes of studio snow which both bless her cure from above and recall the snowy origins from which she was snatched. But simultaneously she is caught in a perfectly composed shot which serves almost to enclose her in a glass-ball paperweight. The church behind her, the signs of nature before her, and the dark nuns on her sides lock her in a pleasing position. She is radiant at the center of this configuration, yet she is trapped within its artificial structure. Delannoy can then move in for a final big close-up of her face amazed at the spectacle of life before her. Her pleasure in seeing compounds our pleasure. Her gratitude to God is simultaneously our gratitude to this film. For a moment the world and the film are glorious visual symphonies, harmonious arrangements of physical and moral properties.

When the dramatic tension does not reside within a single character but is suspended between two or more characters, compositions and lighting are opposed in almost comic-book fashion. Arriving at the church, Gertrude finds her way to Amélie's side, all eyes looking at her eyes. Amélie signals to her that the man in the pulpit is the pastor, and we are then given, predictably enough, an exchange of glances between her and the pastor which derives its impact in large part from the fact that she can now actually glance at him. From her point of view he looms above the congregation, almost ready to pitch forward from his perch. He is dark and severe, a bit ridiculous in his assumed authority. The reverse-angle shot encloses Gertrude in a web of compositional lines formed by the other members of the congregation. Her light cape is highlighted by a key light. In this sea of forms before the pastor, she stands out as an object choice. A second reprise of this pair of shots is dramatized when the pastor breaks the stunned silence of the moment by invoking a prayer of thanksgiving, spreading his arms as he does so. This theatrical gesture carries connotations of crucifixion from Gertrude's point of view, but in cutting behind him for the reverse angle, we see him suddenly as a bird of prey ready to swoop down on Gertrude, who is caught in the center of the frame and nearly blotted out by his backlit figure in the foreground.

This hieratic style retains vestiges of realism even while it continually shapes its reality into tableaux and set pieces. Indeed, the formality of the adaptation can be seen to accord with the literary source being treated. Gestures and views are constructed meticulously in the manner of a literary scene. The frozen effects of cinema of quality seem justified in general by the past tense within which all literary works can be said to exist and in particular by the journal structure of this novella, which carefully dates each entry. The style of the film, then, is appropriately a memorializing one. Even its slight attempts at dramatic camera work, such as the cocked angles and the frequent track-ins on faces, have an academic feel which vitiates any immediacy they might otherwise have attained.

In Clouzot's *Le Corbeau* (1943) or even Carol Reed's *Odd Man Out* (1947), such angles and camera movements strive to involve the viewer corporally in the drama. But Delannoy insists on structure over experience, solidifying dramatic tensions through camera work which we are asked to note and appreciate but which doesn't demand our participation. There is a glass between the viewer and this film: the glass of the store window barring us from the action and asking us to hold it visually in place, to understand it, but certainly not to enter it or to help construct it ourselves. The cinema of quality descends to the viewer from on high, from some seat of visual taste and elegance which graces the movie theater, and from a memorable literary past which is beyond normal experience even as it treats of such experience.

The haughty coolness of Delannoy's personal brand of quality direction has earned him the scorn of progressive film critics, but it did allow him to achieve some remarkable effects in *La Symphonie Pastorale*, effects which placed it among those postwar adaptations singled out by André Bazin as daring and innovative.[3] For Bazin, Delannoy discovered in the omnipresent snow of his decor a visual equivalent for Gide's simple preterite sentences. Both are clear and chilling. Both set off the moral drama crisply. Both connote fatality and a certain spiritual dryness, an emotion (or lack of it) with which Gide, employing an ironic geographical reversal in his imagery, closes his tale: "I wanted to pray but I felt my heart to be as arid as a desert."

---

[3] André Bazin, *What is Cinema?* translated by Hugh Gray, Berkeley, University of California Press, 1968, pp. 66–68.

Bazin's disciple, Amédée Ayfre, writing years later, was even more exuberant about the snow.

> There is a secret correspondence between physical and moral blindness so that this snow which blocks vision and softens the edges of forms, reduces all oppositions and fills in crevices returning the world to its state of primeval cloudiness beyond good and evil. Thanks to the silent consonance between a human visage and a snowy landscape, there is thus instantiated the creation of certain values which cast the metamorphosis of Fate across this tragedy of passion and feeling.[4]

The snow is part of the crude symbolism with which the pastor organizes his experience, and this the filmmakers were quick to make use of. The dualism of the sense of touch—Gertrude's primary way of knowing the world yet also the seat of sensual and sexual engagement—is exploited through continual close-ups of hands. The clarity which distinguishes sight among all the senses is shown to be an alienating knife—not only through the calculated looks the characters give to one another and the more calculating look of the camera which isolates characters, but by the placid nonlook of Michele Morgan as Gertrude. To insist on this effect, Delannoy has recourse to frequent shots of characters before mirrors: Gertrude "looking past" this other sort of window, the pastor arrested by the sight of himself and his protégée. Gertrude senses light by feeling the heat pouring through the windows. She has a tactile relation to vision, which vitalizes her and paradoxically unites her with the world.

Delannoy's determination to insist on these paradoxes and symbols only amplified his native instinct for the handling of actors, an instinct which does not wear well and which was abhorred even in its day.[5] Aside from Michele Morgan, who is quite literally a blind vision and who is photographed in her natural beauty, the other actors present their characters to us in melodramatic fashion. One can almost see them thinking through their spiritual state before locating the precise tone or gesture to convey that state to us. The parts are conned in advance, carefully weighed and heavily ex-

[4] Amédée Ayfre in Henri Agel and A. Ayfre, *Le Cinéma et le Sacré*, Paris, Éditions du Cerf, 1961, p. 169.
[5] Pierre Leprohon, *Présences Contemporains (Cinéma)*, Paris, Éditions Debresse, 1956, pp. 312–313, 318.

pressed. Delannoy exaggerates this pretentious seriousness by reducing the indoor decor to a minimum in most scenes, by toning
down the lighting to an effective modulation of the middle gray
scale, and by playing the dialogue to the audience through cutting
to front shots when the actors stray too far from their 45 degree
open-shoulder deliveries. Cocked angles and expressionist shadow-
ing punctuate the truly "significant" scenes as visual exclamation
marks.

The extent to which abstract character interrelations dominate
this film is made apparent whenever a highly concrete object or
image appears. The pastor clinking the steaming bowl of broth
with a spoon while calling *"Petite, petite, petite"* and the Bach
prelude Jacques plays are good examples. They suggest as well the
slight attention given by Delannoy to the sound track, a strange
inattention especially in view of the film's title and the overt opposition Gide created between aural harmony and visual hetero-
geneity. True, Gertrude becomes the church's organist, but we
don't experience her world of sound. She exists entirely within a
web of speeches and ideas. Her blind sensuality, present as an
unconscious horizon in Gide's novella, is tamed by Delannoy until
we feel that she knows everything about the world except its visible
properties, properties which surprise her but don't alter her fundamental relation to life. In Gide, of course, the impossibility of
correlating sight and sound becomes a key analogy in suggesting
the impossibility of correlating the worlds of experience and morality.[6] Furthermore, Gide's pastor senses Gertrude as an altogether
primitive and foreign quantity which erupts in his life and causes
him to pit Jesus against Saint Paul. Delannoy more discretely and
weakly suggests that the pastor must choose between two women,
one attractive, and one to whom he owes a duty. Gertrude's blindness becomes in the film merely the dramatic precondition of a
conventional temptation.

The conventionality of the film is increased by the background
music of Georges Auric, which exchanges one of Gide's key elements (the use of Beethoven) for ordinary film music. The dic-
tates of the conventional filmgoing public were also responsible for
the introduction of M. Castelan, a wealthy burgher, and his care-

[6] Zachary T. Ralston, "Synesthesia in Gide's *La Symphonie Pastorale*,"
The Citadel Monograph Series, No. 15, Charleston, SC, 1976.

fully appointed bourgeois home. It is as if the filmmakers became afraid that audiences would clamor for their money back if they didn't get a glimpse of well-lit living rooms with lots of crystal. Castelan further obliges the popular taste by playing a broadly comic role. Far from setting off the austere presbytery and its morally wracked inhabitants, Castelan and his daughter, Piette, spread out the dramatic forces of the plot and allow the spectator to enter it from wherever he feels comfortable.

Here we encounter the most serious breach in adaptation, for Gide's novella attains its interest by refusing to allow the reader a comfortable entry into the tale. We are rigorously restricted to the tortured conscience and consciousness of the pastor. While he is self-deceived, his own gradual awareness of that self-deception redeems him before us and, in any case, does not permit us to judge him in any easy fashion. The notorious Gidean irony was never more far-reaching and complex than here. By making the pastor merely another character (even the most important character), the filmmakers have displayed a story before us objectively and have given us the means to judge. The pastor is guilty! The film is a mere exposé of hypocrisy, and the "normal" characters of Piette and Castelan are shown to be duped by a sanctimonious cleric. In Gide there are no "normal characters" and certainly no normal perspectives.

In contrast to the novella, the storytelling of this film knows no bounds and is tied to no principle save expediency and clarity. Its feeble effort to replicate the pastor's hindsight occurs through the cascade of *cahiers* which dissolve into one another and mark the growth of the little blind girl into Michele Morgan. But at the same time, the camera feels free to elaborate scenes at which the pastor is absent (most notably the silent meeting of Jacques and Gertrude at the hospital) and generally to observe the reactions of all characters. The effect of the knot of the plot is thus generalized among the characters and laid out in all its simplicity before the audience.

Surely this did have the effect of popularizing Gide's novella, but at the expense of its real interest, the interplay between action and reflection. The symbols of snow, symphony, mirrors, hands, light and dark, and so forth are potent but naive. Gide, who could never present them in his own name, takes pleasure in allowing the pastor to consider life through them. The inadequacy of such symbolization is the major irony of the tale. And yet, by taking the tale out of the pastor's hands, the filmmakers perpetuate the very simple-minded symbolism that the novella questions. Thus, through its self-righteous style, a style insisting on total narrative command and the urbane presentation of its material, the cinema of quality has been duped by a novella which almost seemed too simple for it but which escaped it by means of the calculated limitation of its presentation. In a very real sense the filmmakers, who have confidently gone beyond and judged the moral blindness of the pastor, are unequal to the complications of his style. Their own eminently public style showcases the situation but cannot reflect upon it. Gide's book has been put forever in a store window through this adaptation, but it has not thereby been read by those who gaze at it. A coffee-table vellum version, Delannoy's adaptation was most valuable for sending some of its millions of viewers back to the pastor's untidy *cahiers*—back, that is, to read Gide.

DUDLEY ANDREW

DESPERATION AND MEDITATION
Bresson's *Diary of a Country Priest* (1951)

from the novel by Georges Bernanos

If adaptation was the saving grace of the French postwar quality tradition and its most ample source of inspiration, it was also, along with the short film, the means and locus of challenge to this tradition. The ethos, the very value of French cinema was never more directly questioned than in Robert Bresson's 1951 *Diary of a Country Priest*, a film which, because of its austere and spiritual subject matter as well as its "diary" format, one cannot help comparing to *La Symphonie Pastorale*.

"After Bresson, Aurenche and Bost are but the Viollet-le-Duc of cinematographic adaptation."[1] With this killing sentence, indicting the scenarists of *La Symphonie Pastorale* and the architects of the cinema of quality by reference to one of the most notorious architectural restorers in history, Bazin concludes his essay "*Le Journal d'un Curé de Campagne* and the Stylistics of Robert Bresson*," an essay called by its translator, without hyperbole, the "most perfectly wrought piece of film criticism" ever written.[2]

This image of Jean Aurenche and Pierre Bost as the prettifiers and popularizers of literary classics was to be taken up, with infinitely more malice, by Bazin's young protégé François Truffaut in his first major essay, "A Certain Tendency in French Cinema."[3] Once again *Diary of a Country Priest* becomes the cause célèbre,

---

© copyright 1981, Dudley Andrew

[1] André Bazin, *What is Cinema?* translated by Hugh Gray, Berkeley, University of California Press, 1967, p. 143.

[2] Ibid., translator's "Introduction," p. 7.

[3] François Truffaut, "A Certain Tendency in French Cinema," in Bill Nichols (ed.), *Movies and Methods*, Berkeley, University of California Press, 1976, pp. 224–237. The original appeared in *Cahiers du Cinéma*, No. 31, January 1954.

the literary masterpiece wrested from the overweening hands of these "professionals" and given over to a true man of the cinema, Robert Bresson. With delectation, Truffaut recounts the humiliating reception Aurenche and Bost's script was given by the novel's author shortly before his death in 1948 and the joy thereafter in the world of letters as well as the world of cinema when Robert Bresson's version was accepted enthusiastically.

What had Aurenche and Bost done? They had done what they always did! They had cinematized a trenchantly literary work by balancing characters and tightening dialogue into pithy maxims; they had dramatized small scenes with flamboyant acts and gestures, reshaping the novel into a cinematic experience. In particular, Truffaut notes, they had eliminated Dr. Delbende because (so Aurenche claimed) "Perhaps in ten years a scenarist will be able to retain a character who dies midway in the film, but as for me I find myself simply unable to do that."[4] They had rearranged key speeches, going so far as to conclude the film with a minor character's despairing cry, "When you're dead everything is dead," instead of Bernanos's "What does it matter, all is grace." And, in their most flamboyant act of "clarification," they had turned Bernanos's delicate dialogue between Chantal and the curé in the confessional into a scene both farcical and blasphemous, in which the girl spits out a consecrated host. This was especially outrageous because Bresson, in his version, would follow precisely the cues in the novel ("her face began to appear little by little, by degrees"[5]), not only expressing the incident with classic purity but also painting one of the most haunting scenes in the history of the cinema.

Truffaut's indiscretion in publicizing this sordid failure by the cornerstones of French cinema did not go unnoticed. He was, as is well known, ostracized from the French film community and forced to build his reputation upon spite and disgruntlement. Even today much of that community has not forgiven him. The script-writer Henri Jeanson grows livid recalling the incident, detailing how Truffaut sweet-talked Bost out of a copy of the rejected script by telling him he adored his work, only to scribble down every

[4] Cited by Truffaut, ibid., footnote 3, p. 236.
[5] Georges Bernanos, *The Diary of a Country Priest*, translated by Pamela Morris, Toronto, Macmillan, 1937, p. 118.

scene or line with which he might later embarrass Bost.[6] But actually Truffaut adds nothing new to the store of examples detailed by Bernanos himself in a 1948 article about the problems with the adaptation.[7] Bernanos was displeased not only with the Aurenche-Bost submission but also with Aurenche's published account of his difficulties negotiating with the famous author. Nevertheless, while excoriating the liberties taken with his novel, Bernanos encouraged other scenarists to try their hand at "dreaming his novel over again in the language of the cinema," for he had been genuinely excited by the idea of the adaptation, especially since Jean-Louis Barrault wanted the lead role desperately, and Bernanos had loved him in *Children of Paradise* (1945).[8]

Bernanos was not unfamiliar with scriptwriting. Indeed, at that very time he was composing his last work, a screenplay called *Dialogue of the Carmelites*. His close friend Raymond Bruckberger, a Dominican priest, was putting this production together with the noted cameraman Philippe Agostini. Bruckberger had previous experience as a producer and had, in fact, been responsible for Bresson's first feature, *Les Anges du Peché* (1943). Agostini had photographed that film as well as *Les Dames du Bois du Boulogne*. Even with this experience, and even with the best wishes of Bernanos, their efforts this time failed, and the shooting was canceled. Later, of course, Albert Béguin resuscitated this script and produced it for the stage with great success. It became the basis for Francis Poulenc's 1956 operatic masterpiece and was finally brought to the screen in 1960 by Bruckberger and Agostini, although with a great many alterations and little subsequent praise.

It was only natural for Bruckberger in 1948 to take up Bernanos's challenge regarding *Diary* while they were working on *Dialogue of the Carmelites*. Bruckberger could not keep himself from rewriting the novel in the atmosphere of the Occupation, for he had been the chief chaplain of the Maquis, entering Paris at de Gaulle's elbow. While the tone of sordid collaboration in the parish which he invented doubtless clarified and tightened the curé's

[6] Henri Jeanson, *Soixante-dix Ans d'Adolescence*, Paris, Stock, 1975, p. 422.
[7] Bernanos, in *Samedi-Soir*, November 8, 1947.
[8] Robert Speaight, *Georges Bernanos*, London, Collins and Harville, 1973, p. 261.

anxiety, this moral specificity couldn't have been more false to the "general" condition of spiritual loneliness which Bernanos had so forcefully created in 1934 by setting the curé's tribulations in the pastoral indifference of a quiet village. This modernization was unacceptable to Bernanos.

It was also in 1948 that Bresson began to compose his version at the behest of an ambitious young producer, Pierre Gerin. With Bernanos's death in July 1948, however, and after a perusal of Bresson's austere and unconventional script, Gerin pulled out and sold his rights to Bresson. When Bernanos's literary executor, Albert Béguin, editor of *Esprit*, accepted Bresson's proposal, the French national production agency, Union Général du Cinéma, agreed to back the film as a special one-time venture.

The story of the making of the film has been recounted often.[9] Bresson chose for his hero a young Swiss actor from among a great many candidates, all practicing Catholics. For over a year Bresson and Laydu met each Sunday to discuss the role. Claude Laydu lived for a time in a monastery to accustom himself to priestly gestures so that he would, in Bresson's formulation, no longer be an actor but a model, a pure form, unconscious and instinctive, to be sculpted by light and camera.

Most of the other actors were nonprofessionals, usually acquaintances with whose faces Bresson felt familiar. The shooting, which lasted from March through May 1950, took place in the precise area of Bernanos's ancestral home, the north coast of Calais. Plagued with uncharacteristically sunny weather, Bresson worked endlessly on the minutiae of the indoor sequences, all of which were shot in the buildings of the area.

The French press covered the making and premier of the film with awe and pride.[10] They helped guide it to a new audience consisting of intellectuals and the pious—people who seldom went to the cinema. They also encouraged cinephiles to see this particular film more than once. In this way *Diary of a Country Priest* opened up new options in the conception, realization, and exploitation of a film, options which would be occasionally exercised only a decade later by the directors of the New Wave.

---

[9] See especially Pierre Leprohon, *Présence Contemporaines (Cinéma)*, Paris, Éditions Debresse, 1957, pp. 363–365; and Michel Esteve, "Bernanos et Bresson," *Archives Bernanos*, No. 7, 1978, pp. 39–52.
[10] See, for instance, *Unifrance*, May 1950 and September 1951.

By insisting on his rigorous conception and by refusing the slightest compromise, Bresson knew he was flying in the face of the tradition of quality and specifically its premier scenarists, Aurenche and Bost. He felt justified, and the French press justified him on the basis of the precious subject which he had chosen and which in a way had chosen him. It was, in other words, the special status of adaptation which allowed this break in standard film practice. In a sense, because of Bernanos, Bresson was given license to attack everything *La Symphonie Pastorale* stood for, and he implicitly recognized the politics of the situation. Later, in 1953, he uncharacteristically brought this struggle into the open by exchanging a series of semipublic letters with Jean Delannoy over the rights to Mme de La Fayette's *La Princesse de Cleves*, certain that the punctilious Delannoy would deaden this treasured classic and personal favorite as he had Gide's novella. Bresson lost the dispute, and Delannoy eventually made a predictably forgettable film, predictable because, as his scenarist Pierre Bost admitted: "After all, authors live with their novels for a lifetime, while we are with them only for a moment."[11] Bresson, who could never accept such lack of ambition, found this attitude consummately unacceptable in regard to adaptation; he wanted to serve literature by allowing it to compel a cinematic style worthy of the original. *Diary of a Country Priest* is perhaps the first adaptation fully forged under such a compulsion.

Although the adaptation of an important literary work provided Bresson with the occasion to challenge the aesthetics of the French filmmaking industry, his challenge in fact involved far more than the single issue of fidelity. Essentially, Bresson's film overturns the notions of the "cinematic story" and the "primacy of the image." Whereas French quality cinema is architectural, theatrical, public, clear, gaudy, and conventional, Bresson's *Diary of a Country Priest* is, on the contrary, fluid, musical, interior, obscure, ascetic, and idiosyncratic.

Nor can these differences be attributed entirely to the genre within which Bresson was working—the spiritual film—although undoubtedly the film industry could applaud his work while dis-

---

[11] Bost, quoted in Jeanson, op. cit., p. 422.

missing its challenge by cataloging it in that way. In fact, as we have seen, *La Symphonie Pastorale* would have to be classified together with *Diary*, and with numerous other postwar French films. No, Bresson's *Diary* goes to the heart of the question "What is cinema?" by implying that the French quality system, including all its varieties and subjects, forms but one overworked genre itself, morally and aesthetically innocuous but pragmatically lethal in its power to choke out other options.

Bresson had always exhibited the self-righteous strength which energized this vaster conception of cinema. His first two features, both shot during the Occupation, were considered rigorous and demanding, even though they utilized quality actors, decorators, and technical personnel and even though they epitomized the studio approach to filmmaking. In these early days he seemed to be an aberration within the system, one which the system could readily handle and from which it could reap a measure of prestige among artists and intellectuals.

But *Diary of a Country Priest* marks a nearly total rejection of the system and the birth of a new system. One can see this from the published *Notes on Cinematography*, the first entries of which date from 1950. This new system would be based, he claims, not on a notion of the construction of a film but on *écriture*, on cinematic writing. The potency of this term cannot be underestimated.

It is a term which gained some measure of common usage after the war and was, perhaps unconsciously, thrown up against "quality." Alexandre Astruc's famed 1948 essay "Le Camera Stylo" fully polemicized the concept, handing it over to filmmakers like Bresson and Resnais and giving them a recognizable alternative to the dominant theatrical film.[12]

Écriture carried with it a special notion of *auteur*, a notion different from the legal denotation of "those responsible for the realization of the film." For Astruc, for Bresson, and a bit later for Truffaut, an auteur was a man of the cinema engaged in forging a personal style adequately responsive to his situation as an artist in history. This Sartrean terminology came via Astruc's reverence for and friendship with the famous thinker whose articles were shaping a whole generation's vocabulary as they appeared month

[12] Alexandre Astruc, "Le Caméra Stylo," in Peter Graham (ed.), *The New Wave*, Garden City, N.Y., Doubleday, 1968, pp. 17–24.

after month in *Les Temps Modernes*. Sartre's crucial essay "What is Literature?" is dated 1947.

Bresson, being neither a man of letters nor an intellectual, took up the vocabulary of Astruc, and through him of Sartre, only because it provided him with the critical resources he needed in his internal battle with the film culture of the day. The vast majority of Bresson's published notes are negative in tone as he warns himself over and over against falling to the temptations of theatricality, solidification, and compromise. But his notes insist on positive programs as well, on ways of working that could release new powers from himself and the world by activating the atrophied limbs of cinema.

Bresson is concerned to rethink completely the notions of the actor, the shot, and the sound track. More important is his strategy of total discipline and control put at the service of discovery, that is, at the service of the spontaneous revelations which grace the making of a work of art. Conventional films are a matter of realizing a clean preconceived design; Bresson warns himself to be prepared for the unexpected and to bend with it so that it can be incorporated into the living texture of the work. Let no classic or even perfect images draw attention to themselves; let no editing structure rationalize and clarify motivations; let not the actor think through his part. Rather, all should happen with the smooth unrolling of a natural gesture, but a gesture acquired only after infinite, patient practice. And may this gesture be prepared to seize whatever sparks of life or truth emerge from the encounter with the subject. This is the attitude with which he made *Diary of a Country Priest*.

Critics have responded to this film with trepidation. Given Bresson's working methods and conception of the work of art, standard film analysis seems ludicrously inappropriate. Bazin was fully aware of this when he offhandedly outlined a conventional iconographic overlay on the film, treating it christologically as a series of Stations of the Cross[13]: the curé's falls, the wiping of his face by Seraphita, his glorious ride on the motorcycle which delivers him to the city where he will die. In Lille he has his Gethsemane in a

[13] Bazin, op. cit., p. 135.

small cafe and his Golgotha in an attic room where he expires amid two outcasts.

Bazin outlines but refuses to pursue this approach, finding it at best trivial, for *Diary of a Country Priest* succeeds not as an allegory of spiritual experience but as a direct exemplification of such experience. It is not, Bazin implies, a film to read so much as one to directly feel. If we must interpret it, we must do so as we interpret a song cycle by Poulenc or a group of paintings by Rouault. Though their subject matter may be conventional, all three artists are out to do something quite different from delivering a subject. They hope instead to create an experience inspired by the subject.

Obviously, from this aesthetic, fidelity to the subject dwindles in importance and Bresson could, without any sense of irony and in full good faith, chop forty-five minutes from his movie to satisfy the distributor. The sections cut invariably involved additional space and characters: more contact with the parishioners, the tense meeting early on with the curé's superior, the extensive and grotesque consultation with Dr. Lavigne during which, amid ravings about God and morphine, the curé learns of his cancer. Bresson could cut these scenes in good faith because the essence of the film was an interior drama and rhythm, something pulsing like the diary itself beneath every image. This he produced most prominently in the least spectacular, least "cinematic" episodes. The only necessary image, as Bazin pointed out, was the final one, the cross toward which a life had aimed. How that life reached its final passion was not a product of tightly interlacing actions but was achieved instead by an orientation (progressively intensified, to be sure) within each episode. Albert Béguin claimed that this orientation

> from its first image to its last is the austerity of an exclusively supernatural drama. Everything in the film takes on power through the supernatural. Even the rapport between characters becomes meaningful only in terms of salvation and perdition and in terms of a community of hope.[14]

Bresson doesn't argue for the presence of the supernatural in his

[14] Albert Béguin, "Bernanos dans le Cinema," *Esprit*, Vol. 19, No. 2, pp. 248–252 (my translation).

film, nor does he demonstrate it as the logical result of his intrigue. It simply is there as an effect of the text, produced, critics seem to agree, by an accumulative method which couldn't be further from conventional dramatic plotting. There is no equation whereby the accidents of appearances are transformed into the necessities of plot. Rather, through repetitions of scenes, gestures, sounds, lighting, and decor, a musical rhythm invades the images, producing a meditation, with themes and variations, on the supernatural. The themes are constant and well known; the variations include dialogues, monologues, landscapes, gestures, scenes of action, scenes of writing, natural sounds, and composed music. In this way Bresson reproduces Bernanos's stunningly innovative compositional principles. For *Diary of a Country Priest* is a novel whose intense unity of concern and effect is achieved without chapters and by an amalgamation of brief acts, reflections, speeches, and descriptions. Bresson could afford to exclude and reduce the episodes because he had matched the diary form, a heterogeneous form in which tone and direction obviously take precedence over logic and completeness.

Bresson's *Diary of a Country Priest* is a meditation which forces us to reevaluate experience. It refuses conventional values (what counts as success in life or in cinema) and concentrates new facts and events, overdetermining them until they form a spiritual economy. The currency in this economy has many denominations (light, speech, sounds, facial expressions, simple objects, simple actions), but all are based on the same standard: the soul of the curé of Ambricourt.

In this regard the actual diary is both the film's capital and its ledger, where mundane events are invested and calculated. Or, to change to an image favored by Henri Agel, here is the heart of the film circulating the images like blood which flows into and out of it.[15]

The diary is represented in three different ways in the film: as written pages on the screen, as a voice which situates the actions we see on the screen, and as those actions themselves when, through fades, ellipses, and the like, we realize that what is represented is a reflection upon an event, not the event itself.

[15] Henri Agel, *Le Cinéma et le Sacré*, Paris, Éditions du Cerf, 1961, p. 34.

Generally, Bresson alternates action and reflection, image and script, or image with voice. Toward the film's end, however, he insists more than ever on the interiority of all action by doubling and even trebling the signifiers of meditation. Sitting bereft at the cafe in Lille, trying to fathom the enormity of the death sentence he has just received, the curé turns to his diary. We watch him write. We hear him say "I must have dozed off for a while" as we see him lean back and close his eyes. A dissolve to a minutely different camera angle embodies the startled displacement he experiences in voice-over: "I must have dozed off a while. . . . [dissolve] When I awoke; Oh God, I must write this down. . . ." And as he bends forward once again over his diary, we realize he is writing the very episode we have just seen. It is a daring layering of all three modes of reflection in a single moment, concentrating our imagination with his as he conjures up the past and tries to give it a place in the story of his spiritual life.

> I think of those mornings, those last mornings of mine this week, the welcome of those mornings—the cocks crowing. That high window, so peaceful, full of night as yet, but one pane, always the same one, the right one, would begin to light up.[16]

This is his Gethsemane, and in it his face goes pale. His diary has cost him his blood, abstracted his life, and converted its acts and times to a final time—the climbing of the attic steps, the inevitable death.

By treating the diary as one object among other objects (lamps, wine bottles, prayer books, furniture), Bresson capitalizes on cinema's indifferent attachment to the physical world, only the better to set off the task of the spiritual—the transformation of physical appearance into interior value, into writing and reflection.

The method and goal of this process become most visible in those moments when this sublimation runs into difficulty, failing to transform or abstract certain events. Both the curé and the film find moments of death especially indigestible. As a limit to life, death is a limit to reflection as well.

Dr. Delbende's suicide is an event so difficult for the priest to absorb that he nearly destroys his diary in reflecting upon it. Death arrests him elsewhere too. A slow tilt down his desk to the open

16 Bernanos, op. cit., p. 225.

diary shows the ink still wet over the words "The countess died last night." Meanwhile, we hear his feet clattering down the steps and away into the night. In the final episode, of course, it is the dropping of the diary and the pen which signals the hour of his death.

It is at this final moment that Bresson daringly sublimates, in a single gesture, the entirety of his film. As Bazin notes, the transmutation of the diary into the image of the cross at the end, "as awkwardly drawn as on the average memorial card, is the only trace left by the 'assumption' of the image, a witness to something the reality of which is itself but a sign."[17] To return to the analogy of economics, the cross is the film's ultimate reward, a life's reward after its images, accumulated and invested with such care, have been cashed in to redeem their share of the spiritual standard which gave them value.

Bresson's task was not to explain the cross, or even the curé's relation to it, but to embody the experience of a life which terminates with the cross. Bresson here has purified the project of the novel by becoming as meek and single-purposed as its hero. Whereas Bernanos gleefully sets up a dialectic between the curé and the "dead souls" of his parishioners, a dialectic brought into focus by the curé of Torcy, Bresson never modulates his tone. The parish is judged obliquely if at all by the curé's "faithful eyes," illuminated in their turn by the secret of prayer and poverty, a "lost secret" which surfaces time and again on his face.

Diary of a Country Priest has appealed to believers and unbelievers alike because it doesn't set belief in a larger context (sociological, psychological, historical). The cross, the measure of the priest's life, is itself left unmeasured. The secret may be lost for us and the cross totally discredited in our own lives or culture; nonetheless, it can be received as the only proper end to the film and the life of this country priest.

The film's nonsectarian success testifies to the consistent and radical interiority attained by Bresson. From first to last (from the image of the diary to that of the cross), we are locked within a particular sensibility, a state of being, a soul. Bernanos struggled to render this soul, succeeding only by contrasting its meekness

---

[17] Bazin, op. cit., p. 141.

with the powerful, garrulous curé of Torcy, the cantankerous spokesman (so like Bernanos himself) of the public church, of politics, and of survival. Bresson, as we have seen, pared down the novel by cutting off its public half. He bored straight to the center of the curé, where he was temperamentally at home, and from there he refused to budge. His earlier films had balanced an obsessive moral concern with (and within) a brittle and abstracted social world, but *Diary of a Country Priest* sees the world from a changeless point of view. There is no dialectic; all is soul.

Stylistically, this is more than the transformation and abstraction of the cinema-of-quality approach which had distinguished Bresson's earlier films. *Diary of a Country Priest* is subjective cinema throughout; in true Sartrean fashion, the style is the soul, a particular way of being in the world, a particular world settling in the soul.

Bazin always claimed that style is primarily a pattern of selection. In Bresson, what pattern produces the interiority we feel? What style becomes a *particular* interior? First of all a rigorous delimitation of means permits only certain forms and objects to be put into play: the brows, the eyes, the hands, and the feet of the characters; the thin roads and barren trees of the Calais landscape; the fireplaces, doors, windows, and lamps of the dwellings; the chairs, books, and wine bottles within those dwellings. A simple iconographic deciphering of these items succeeds all too quickly in abstracting a spiritual universe while failing to touch the body of the film which these elements help constitute. It is not so much the restricted number of photographed things as the obsessive quality of the photography itself which makes of these surfaces an inner economy as well as the actual pieces of the curé's world.

One critic[18] has gone so far as to compare Bresson's photography to the Port Royal paintings of Philippe de Champaigne, with their precise hierarchy of visage over context and their spiritual clarification of authentic landscape. The inadequacy and wrongheadedness of this comparison results from Bresson's fully modernist conception of space and symbol. Space is something only suggested in his films. It is without solidity or boundaries; it

[18] René Briot, *Fiche Filmographique*, No. 117, p. 4.

expands and contracts in response to the diary. It is a fully interior space. Similarly, if symbolism is an excess of signification over the presentation of an object or scene, Bresson's film is rife with a symbolism of the second degree. We must go not only beyond the surfaces of the visible but beyond all conventional symbolic readings to attain a sense of the possibilities of the objects and events presented.

Bresson's style is haunting because it is more than a documentary of a spiritual situation and more than a cultural interpretation or presentation of such a situation (in the manner of the cinema of quality and the paintings of Philippe de Champaigne); it is in fact an *unstable* image he gives us, in which the visible seems on the verge of rendering the invisible.

The dialogue with Chantal in the confessional is emblematic in this regard. In a single shot we move in from the opposition of two faces to concentrate on a single face in the darkness. Three shot-reaction shot couplets (each tightening in on the curé's brow) lead to the crisis of the letter. A single shot drops from Chantal's face to her hand, which pulls an envelope out of the darkness and joins the curé's hand in exchange. Refusing to cut, Bresson then pulls back to the initial composition of the scene and from this vantage point frames Chantal stepping forward and then out of the frame. The curé's face, on which both trauma and thanksgiving can be seen, immediately dissolves into the flames of the fire which consumes the sealed note. We can read through this style—we can in fact directly experience within it the drama of two strong souls in moral combat—but far more striking is the quality of the images on which this drama rests: the darkness couching a suicide letter, rendering up a document of hate, and the luminosity of two faces and two hands in a space where voice and intention are all that count.

Similarly, the cloudy wine, particularly when it runs in pools on the floor, immediately recalls the blood of Christ, but far more interesting is its graphic relation to the "spongy" atmosphere of the landscape in general, to the mud in the fields where Dr. Delbende is found shot to death, to the mud and blood spattered on the curé's face after his hemorrhage. In other words, the physical sensation of the wine flows beyond its symbolic denotation to become part of the spiritual landscape of the present—literally what he

You know quite well all I ask is justice.

In this confessional shot from *Diary of a Country Priest* Robert Bresson captures the luminosity of two faces. This film version of Bernanos's literary masterpiece met with approval from critics of both film and literature.

sees and senses as he acts and reflects. The moist thickness of that background retards clear vision, slows locomotion, leaves traces and stains. This graphic quality is equivalent to Bernanos's thickly adjectival style, and it operates in the film to sully any impulse to easy moral and graphic clarity.

The objects which delimit the scope of the curé's interior world are thus inseparable from the light which renders the quality of that world. Light is an explicit metaphor in the curé's discourse as he passes fearfully dark nights and comes into the sweetness of dawn. He is sensitive to the special luminescence or umbrage on each countenance he meets, and he is drawn to the warmth of fires, lamps, and windows.

Even when light is not the subject of his reflections, it colors the events he records in a formative way. At the countess's wake, for instance, mourners and family members pass him on the stairs like fleeting shadows. They form an indistinct backdrop against which he kneels by her brightly lit and flowered deathbed. More often, the subdued interiors of large flat gray walls and darker rectilinear woodwork and furniture are brightened only by areas of moderate but solid light cast by a lamp or window. The curé's face is then the site of a diagonal border between light and gray, even while it stands out against its somber context. Nothing could be further from the cinema-of-quality style with its penchant for mirrors, crystal, and a delightful mottling of a high key style. The interiors of *Diary of a Country Priest*, on the contrary, seem to absorb much of the available light, creating a continuously dull atmosphere broken up by objects or the shadows of objects.

If the night and dawn sequences are "metaphoric" and the general flat grays are "atmospheric," we must apply the term "dramatic" to Bresson's use of source lighting. Lanterns, lamps, and flickering fires suggest at key moments the soul's resources in a dark universe. In contrast, lighted windows in the night suggest the homelessness of this soul. Altogether, then, Bresson paints with several styles of lighting, but none of them is conventional. By quality standards, the ubiquitous gray geometry of light is dull and abstract while the sensual use of source lighting, on the other hand, is too stark, especially as it fails to highlight the four corners of the screen or give a halo to crucial faces and objects. Light in these scenes is its own object—not a clarifying medium but a substance surrounded by darkness.

Despite this overall importance of light, only rarely does a single image have full pathetic reverberation, containing the spiritual state of the curé. His fall in the mud with a huge, misgrown tree trunk bisecting the screen and forming an angle with the slanted ground is one such "pictorial" exception. The self-consciously beautiful desolation of this landscape is at odds with the dominant graphic style, a style whose function is to throw the curé and the viewer forward to the next image in the hope of a final satisfying light and composition. That pictorial haven is reached only in the film's final shot—the bare shadow of a cross.

This sense of homelessness, this lack of pictorial fullness, is produced narratively as well by means of the structure of entrances and exits, a structure provided for by the diary format. Episodes commonly begin with an intrusion or expedition, many offering no development other than a repetition of this soul in transit.

The actual style of these entrances and exits is more remarkable than their number. The camera remains properly with the curé as he crosses a threshold or goes to meet a visitor, but the visitor's motion is most often counter to the curé's, producing a glancing effect. Only rarely are two people framed in stable composition: Chantal and the curé in the confessional, the curé and the countess during her confession, Torcy and the curé when the image of his life as a holy agony comes to him. These crucial moments show persons locked in combat. For the rest, the curé travels obliquely through life, and we travel with him.

The knowledge he and we have is thus strictly limited. He peers out windows at a retreating Chantal or catches a glimpse in the film's first instant of the count and his mistress, Chantal's governess, turning away from our view in the sterility of their habitual embrace.

Things are perpetually accelerating away from us in this expanding universe of the curé's consciousness. No establishing shots situate the world around him. Although few subjective first-person shots imitate his optical perspective, the displacement of the images through the diary allows us to consider even the frontal shots of the curé as belonging to his perspective. It is a lonely perspective, perhaps a paranoid one. The film is filled with glance-object shots but almost no glance-glance structures. We seldom see the curé from a human perspective other than his own. Over the course of two hours this develops a most solipsistic effect, particularly for an audience accustomed to standard French films of the quality tradition. In *La Symphonie Pastorale*, for instance, a film also representing the record of events via a journal, the pastor not only looks out on the world but is looked back upon from the viewpoint of every other major character. The interlocking gazes of that film construct brilliant tableaux boxed in a cinematic diorama which the viewer's gaze contains and comprehends. Bresson, in contrast, lets us look out with the curé on the fragments of his world, but when we look back at him it is only to peer more deeply inward, to watch him reflect on his limited experience. Bresson refuses to "place" him either dramatically, sociologically, or theologically. We remain within the curé's point of view or, better, within his point of reflection.

The curé and the film avoid the temptations of paranoia and solipsism primarily through the medium of sound. If our eyes are the organs of possessiveness and clarification, our ears are responsive to the messages and events of a larger world. No sights startle the curé, especially upon reflection. He kneels calmly to retrieve the medallion which the countess has hurled into the fire; he kneels just as calmly by her deathbed. But the limited character we have noted in his visual world—its restricted elements and the alternately abstract and dark light in which those elements stand out—suggests a potentially wider world that the curé cannot or will not attend to.

Sound is the reminder of that wider world, intruding as a gunshot on the curé's familiar walk. Sounds frequently anchor the abstract reflective geometry of the images, particularly in the case of carts whose wheels squeak on the periphery of so many shots, often totally out of view but noted, present to the curé. The natural sounds of feet on cobblestones, of a motorcycle, of people whispering, dogs barking, or a breeze blowing constitute the atmosphere of the existential search for grace, and they contrast to Grunewald's musical score, which seems to wash over the entire film from the effusive moment of its end, testifying throughout that "all is grace." Bresson was soon to divest himself of the luxury of musical scores, no doubt needing to refuse the priority of the final vision over the moments leading up to it. After all, a diary isn't written with a continuous musical feeling. Its past tense (reflecting on the day's actions) is also stringently present (what will be written in tomorrow's entry is unknown today). The Grunewald score bridges all days and announces the continuity of the priest's search—announces it and harmonizes it, but must do so against the competition of the daily sounds and unexpected noises which obstruct a clear and self-possessed rendering of the world.

No other aspect of the film so thoroughly exemplifies the structured dispossession which marks both the curé's life and Bresson's treatment of it. Bresson could rightly dispense with countless episodes from the novel simply because his sound track provided that "otherness" to which the curé, even upon reflection, found it necessary to hearken, an otherness Bernanos could convey in the novel only by means of the multiplication of events and reactions to events. Through its sound track the film found a way synchronically to present, at each of its moments, the structure of the curé's world—its pastness, its responsiveness, its fidelity of attitude, its limitation of vision, its openness to a mysterious otherness, in short, its productive loneliness and suffering.

Thus, despite is apparently hermetic form, *Diary of a Country*

Priest situates itself in a cosmic openness. It is a film written across the pages of a notebook, yet it is set in a field of light and sound. The concentration and discipline of the diary allow the curé to attain in his final hours a breadth of soul explicitly measured against his pathetically liberal defrocked friend. His rigorous instrument of self-knowledge—his writing—has brought him into focus with his image and, therefore, has made him one with Christ. It is through a similar textual discipline, this time of cinematic style, that Bresson can in the end reach beyond cinema and be at one with *his* subject, a novel. By going beyond cinema through cinema, he has achieved a revolution in the ethics and potential of adaptation; he has *performed* a novel in sight and sound, not capturing his subject so much as embodying it.

ALAN WILLIAMS

KEEPING THE CIRCLE TURNING
Ophuls's *La Ronde (1959)*

from the play by Arthur Schnitzler

Max Ophuls's *La Ronde* (1959) was the wandering director's first postwar European film, made after years of Hollywood exile. Ophuls was always choosy about directorial assignments, preferring to amass unrealized projects rather than work steadily on material that did not interest him,[1] and the choice of a Schnitzler play as subject matter doubtless had political as well as aesthetic significance for him. This was, in fact, the second time that Ophuls had adapted a play by Schnitzler, the first being *Liebelei* (1932), the last film Ophuls made in Weimar Germany before his hasty departure first to France and then by a complicated route finally to the United States to escape Hitler's Final Solution. With a narrative symmetry appropriate to one of Ophuls's own films, and with an irony he must have savored, *La Ronde* closes this chapter in the director's career and does so, moreover, with a play denounced in its day (first published privately in 1900) as "Jewish filth" and written by a dramatist with whom Ophuls shared political and moral as well as ethnic affinities.

The symbolic value of adapting Schnitzler aside, Ophuls doubtless had other, less timely reasons for choosing to direct *La Ronde*. The play centers on a theme central to virtually all of the director's work—despite its "scandalous" nature, the Schnitzler work is not so much about sex as what leads up to and what follows it. *La*

An abridged version of this essay appeared in *Max Ophuls and the Cinema of Desire*, Arno Press (1980).
[1] See Georges Annenkov, *Max Ophuls*, Paris, Le Terrain Vague, 1962, pp. 57–62. Annenkov's memoir is also very helpful on costume and set design for *La Ronde* and contains many useful illustrations.

Ronde (*Hands Around* was the first English rendering of *Reigen*, but by now, thanks to the film, the French name seems to have stuck) is not about love or sex, but about *courtship*, the principal subject of such Ophuls films as *Letter From an Unknown Woman* (1948), *Lola Montes* (1955), and many others. Equally attractive to Ophuls must have been the play's obvious, intricate patterns of repetition and rhyme, and its self-proclaimedly "circular" shape —comparable to the complicated systems of surface structuration so evident in *Madame de . . .* (1953), *Caught* (1948), and others.[2] Finally, Ophuls's film has had the effect of keeping "in performance" a play known well enough by reputation but not by production, since *La Ronde* is, in fact, a difficult work to stage effectively for the theater. The playwright himself seems to have conceived the work more as "armchair theater" than as a performance piece; those productions which did occur during Schnitzler's lifetime took place against his express prohibition.

Aspects of the play's text indicate its "literary" nature. Its subtitle is "Ten Dialogues," and though dialogue certainly does occur in the work, I take this reference to be ironic, to indicate the philosophical sort of "dialogue" that seems occasionally an object of parody. The stage instructions not infrequently provide details impossible to stage as written—for example, the content of the letter the Maid is writing at the beginning of Episode Three.[3] Most of these details, given to the reader but necessarily inaccessible to the dramatic spectator, are well suited to the film medium (in Episode Three, Ophuls uses a voice-over).[4] At other points in the original, movements are indicated that would be clumsy at best on the stage (requiring either severe compression or the stage of

[2] For an examination of narrative patterning in *La Ronde* itself, see my "The Circles of Desire: Narration and Representation in *La Ronde*," *Film Quarterly*, Vol. 27, No. 1, Fall 1973, pp. 35–41.

[3] Throughout, I am quoting and consulting the translation of Schnitzler's *La Ronde* by Patricia Newhall and Hans Weigert, in Haskell Block and Robert Shedd (eds.), *Masters of Modern Drama*, New York, Random House, 1962, pp. 247–269.

[4] Ophuls also makes a change, typical in magnitude, here. The play's letter to the soldier becomes a letter from him in the film. The change seems justifiable because it retains the original narrative function of the reference and because there are benefits of audiovisual interest (contrast) and narrational smoothness.

Radio City Music Hall) but which work well in the imagination—or on film, with Ophuls's celebrated long tracking shots. (See, for example, the potential blocking problems in Episode Two, "The Soldier and the Maid," or the proto-cinematic crosscutting in Episode Three, "The Maid and the Young Gentleman.")

In any event, the "Ten Dialogues" of Schnitzler's play are not *dramatic* in the normal sense of the word. One knows what will happen: Two people will come together, make love (blackout in the theater, asterisks in the written text), and then separate or prepare to separate. The question isn't at all *if* this will occur, *why*, nor even *what effect* it will have on the participants. The continuing question posed by the play is, rather, how each particular coupling will play itself out and what variations on the basic pattern will occur. A Prostitute and a Soldier make love, then the Soldier and a Maid, then the Maid and a Young Gentleman, and so on to character number ten, the Count, who obligingly sleeps with the Prostitute and so closes the circle. As the play progresses, the social status of the characters becomes more elevated, and types of behavior change accordingly. In this way, much of the humor of both play and film is class-based since the different social ranks woo in very different ways.

In the opening of Schnitzler's text, the scene is set "At the Augarten bridge." The Soldier comes into view, whistling, and is accosted by the Prostitute, who opens with "Hey there, my beautiful angel." She initiates a banter that culminates in the play's first coupling—not even demanding money for her favors. (The Soldier is momentarily astonished, then says, "Oh, you're the one Huber told me about. . . .") After the deed is done, we witness their reactions: He wants to leave quickly; she wants appreciation and acknowledgment, which she does not get. ("So long!" he says, and she replies: "Tightwad! . . . Pimp!") With crucial and frequently funny variations, this is the pattern of the ten sketches: encounter, lovemaking, separation. Ophuls's adaptation of the text is generally, and at times scrupulously, faithful to it—except that in the film the ten dialogues and attendant action account for only about three-

---

[5] The closest analogue for this character is probably the Stage Manager in Wilder's *Our Town*—except that here, obviously, there is no literal "stage" to manage, only images and sounds. Claude Beylie reports that "In the [shooting] script he is sometimes designated as 'Poldy' (the name of Max and Hilde Ophuls's little basset hound)." See *L'Anthologie du Cinéma*, No. 1, Paris, L'Avant-scène, 1966, p. 283.

quarters of the running time. To this series of (minimal) narrations, the film adds a metanarration, a series of interventions by an additional character whose job, as he tells us, is to keep *La Ronde* "moving." This is the *Meneur du Jeu*, the "master of ceremonies" or (literally) "leader of the game,"[5] played and sung by Anton Walbrook. The opening of the film introduces and explains him (to the extent that this is done) in what amounts to an eleventh mini-sketch. The camera, in one long, sinuous tracking shot, follows him from a misty background to a stage, past theater and movie equipment, and into a set of turn-of-the-century Vienna. Throughout, Walbrook keeps up a running monologue addressed directly to the film audience. *"La Ronde?"* he begins quizzically:

> And what am I in this story? The author? . . . A Passerby? . . . I am, well I could be anyone among you. . . . But where are we? In a theater? In a studio? (*The setting of a street appears; in the background is the Augarten bridge.*) One doesn't know any more. . . . In a street. . . . Ah! We are in Vienna, 1900. Let's change our costume.[6]

Walbrook approaches a conveniently placed coatrack, leaves his raincoat, and dons the evening clothes placed there. He walks to an equally convenient carousel (actually from somewhat later in the film) and starts it turning with a push of his newfound cane. He sings the film's theme song, and as he concludes The Prostitute comes into view, seated on the carousel. He helps her down, and she speaks to him what will be the first line of her dialogue with the Soldier. (Ophuls's version changes the line to "You want to come with me, beautiful blond?"—this said to the very dark haired Walbrook character but later said more appropriately to the Soldier.) He replies, "Ah, no madame . . . I'm not part of the game." He then tells her that *La Ronde* will start with her, that she will stand on the streetcorner and accost the sixth soldier who passes. "He'll be like all the others," she replies. Yes, he says, "but in a minute he will be with you." She leaves the frame, and Walbrook announces the sketch title to the film audience: "The Girl and the Soldier."

---

[6] I translate (heavily abridging) from the script of *La Ronde* published in *L'Avant-scène du Cinéma*, No. 25, 1963. An English translation of this script may be found in John Weightman (ed.), *Masterworks of the French Cinema*, New York, Harper & Row, 1974, pp. 153–225.

Max Ophuls adds to his film version of Arthur Schnitzler's play a Raconteur (Anton Walbrook), whose job it is to keep *La Ronde* "moving." Here he informs the Prostitute (Simone Signoret) that he is "not part of the game." *Photo courtesy Museum of Modern Art*

So ends the film's non-Schnitzlerian introduction (and also its first shot!), which is followed by the play's first dialogue with comparatively few emendations. I have described this scene at some length because it demonstrates most of the characteristics of the metanarration. Walbrook employs direct address to the film audience, speculates about the meaning of the play, and refers openly to the fact of film production. He sings the song, which will return periodically with verses appropriate to the different sketches. He speaks directly to a woman from the narrative level of the film (and not to a man—the men only meet him disguised as various minor characters) and gives her instructions on her part. He is aware of the film audience, but she is not (and she seems to misperceive him physically as well—as least to the extent of his hair color). The set of the episode to come is explicitly placed, shown to be surrounded not by "more of the same" but by theatrical and cinematographic paraphernalia. The filmic style of this opening is flamboyant and obvious—a long take gone haywire, showing not spatiotemporal continuity but discontinuity, arbitrariness (the coat rack that just "happens" to be there), and *theatricality*.

The other intrusions of metanarrative material, generally between episodes (sometimes during the act of lovemaking), are in much the same vein. Filmmaking, for example, although absent as a preoccupation in the sketches themselves, is a recurrent *topos* in the added material. Walbrook begins one episode with a clapboard (the name of the sketch written on it), and he interrupts a sex scene in another by a shot in which he is seen cutting supposedly offensive footage with a scissors. He leads the Maid from Episode Two to Three through a stylized, out-of-time-and-place decor, telling her to "be brave." (As with the Prostitute, the extent to which she understands or clearly perceives him is not clear.) At one point he comments to the film audience on changing courtship styles in the "circle." And so on. There is, of course, nothing at all like this in the Schnitzler play, and the additional material may be viewed either as a massive assault on the integrity of the original text or (as I will argue) as a way of systematically contextualizing and foregrounding it. Before addressing this question, however, it will be useful to consider briefly the extent to which the dialogues themselves have been altered in Ophuls's adaptation.

If one ignores the metanarrative instances, the film is, in fact, reasonably faithful to the play. There are comparatively few changes in Schnitzler's "Ten Dialogues," and these all fall into three basic categories: First, some, but by no means all, of the sexual references have been toned down (though not enough to prevent the film from being received as "scandalous" or "obscene" on its release). Gone, specifically, are several clear references to the fact (or not—Episode Five) of erection. Most of these cuts occur toward the beginning of the film since it is in general the lower-class characters who speak their minds on such matters. (Some of these lines seem to have been cut more in the interest of pacing than from fear of censorship. In all cases, what is going on is abundantly clear.)

Second, Ophuls and Natanson (co-scenarist and author of the

film's dialogue) have reworked the last three sketches extensively, changing locale in Episode Eight, cutting some pseudointellectual double-talk in Episode Nine (the seduction is left intact), and shortening Episode Ten and adding a brief flashback with voice-over). These alterations—the only really major ones in the film—reveal, I think, an attempt to improve the weakest portion of the original text, which begins to ramble and repeat itself in these sections. I must admit that I do not find the attempt particularly successful (these scenes always strike me as the weakest in the film), but I refer the reader to the play for a look at what the adapters were up against.

The third type of change in the Schnitzler original is much more symptomatic of Ophuls's style of adaptation and of his general interests as revealed in *La Ronde* and his other work. The film makes small, regular, but important *additions* to the dialogues. These exploit and intensify patterning already at work in the play; the film takes a highly patterned text and makes it even more structured. An implicit system of parallelisms of and variations on bits of action, dialogue, and circumstances in the play develops into an even more intricate web of internal references in the film. The most thematically significant of such patterns, in the context of both Schnitzler's and Ophuls's *oeuvres*, is the series of references to time. For both dramatist and filmmaker, it is always "too late": Time is passing, and the characters wonder how much of it remains, what they have to do next, why the moment of love can't be extended (female characters), why it has to be protracted after climax (male characters), and so on. Ophuls takes this concern of the play and regularizes it, adding additional references and forming an explicit pattern.

He does this by making the often vague time of the play more specific. In its narrative portions, the film has an obsessive "real" time measured in hours and seconds, recalled by strategically placed clocks, and evoked by the repeated question "What time is it?" Episodes One and Two take place in evening, Three and Four in late afternoon, Five and Six and also Seven and Eight at night, and Nine and Ten in the morning. The pattern is drawn from the play, but Ophuls and Natanson add lines that emphasize and make it more specific. In Episodes Seven and Eight (the Young Woman and the Poet, the Poet and the Actress), the film goes so far as to interpolate exactly matching scenes in which the rejected former partner (the Husband waiting for the Young Woman, who does not come to the cafe, then the Young Woman waiting for the Poet) asks of a third party:

> What time is it?
> A little past eleven
> Oh? I have five to midnight . . .
> (Consolingly) Ah! So do I . . .

This is but the most explicit example of such additions; there are many more. Their effect is, first, to emphasize the theme of time passing, and second, to pair episodes much more explicitly than in the play. This pairing is reinforced by a relation of complementarity between narration and metanarration. One aspect of this complementarity is sex-based: It is the male characters who in each case are common to the paired sketches, and it is the women who change at each boundary. This occurs in the play, of course, as a result of its structure, but Ophuls emphasizes the pairings by having the women who "bridge" the pairs of episodes speak directly to Walbrook in his role as Leader (as noted, the men only see him disguised as minor characters).

But a more general relation between the two levels is adumbrated here. The women's access (which is limited since they are not aware of the film audience and do not fully understand the Leader's role) to the metanarration is an aspect of their relatively greater self-awareness and reflexiveness in the film; it is, symbolically, partial access to the very *generality* that the metanarration represents. (This privileging of women characters is certainly more Ophulsian than Schnitzlerian, even if it is a latent possibility in the play.) A result of the emphasis on specific times in the narrative level is an emphasis on the metanarration's complementary *timelessness*. The characters' time is that of specific days, hours, and minutes in turn-of-the-century Vienna; the Master of Ceremonies' time is that of the film and its progress. (The distinction is reinforced by the periodic references to filmmaking mentioned above.)

This relationship between the general and the particular is also evident in another set of references taken from the play but emphasized and played within the film: motifs of *recurrence*. Schnitzler's characters seem to have a sort of repetition compulsion disguised as romantic nostalgia. The Count is reminded of a past love by the Prostitute; the Married Couple recall their honeymoon in Venice; and the Young Man recalls not previous experiences of impotence but literary precedents for it. Ophuls adds a bit here, too: The Young Woman admits to having previously been to a private dining room, then later comments on the Poet's desire to go to one, using the same words as with her previous partner; the Married Man insistently queries her as to her past sex life (this out of a concern, apparently, with disease); and so on. The metanarration generalizes this theme; its principal subject, in fact, is repetition. Ophuls concretizes this quintessentially Schnitzlerian concern with a brilliant metaphor: the carousel that, like *La Ronde*, "turns and turns." If the characters repeat models known to them, in the metanarration the repetitive nature of the whole, already implicitly stressed by the additions cited, is given embodiment—though also made im-personal (calling into question the self-centeredness of the characters). In the words of the theme song:

> Turning, turning, my characters are turning
> The earth turns too, both night and day
> Water from rain turns into clouds
> And the clouds turn back to water again.

Schnitzler's circle has been given motion. The "circle" of the title is no longer simply a spatiotemporal pattern linking the characters; it is also the expression of their own unknown circling in their own lives.

The metanarration reacts with and upon Schnitzler's "Ten Dialogues," contextualizing and commenting upon them in ways such as these. Ophuls's film takes an elaborate, highly structured text and makes it even more elaborately patterned, adding a metadiscourse situated in an alternate narrative and conceptual space. One way of describing the result would be to compare the interaction of the two levels of the film to those ambiguous drawings beloved of Gestalt psychologists—such as the figure that can be seen either as two faces or as a vase. The two levels of the film alternate as figure and ground—each serves (temporarily) as invisible background to the workings of the other. When a "sketch" is on-screen, it is the metanarration that is "off," and not "more of the same"—and vice versa. The ultimate result is to deprive the narrative episodes of the *sui generis* quality of transparent film narrative and to give them an absent but nevertheless functional point of origin not in some continuous "reality" but in *spectacle*.

Thus, the theatricality of the sketches need not be either rationalized or denied since their point of origin (or at least the source of their meaning) is given as *elsewhere*, continually behind and outside of the things that we see. An immediate result is dramatic irony: The characters act as if their world were continuous and sensible, and indeed it appears to be. But lurking 'behind" the scenes is Anton Walbrook and that turning merry-go-around; unbeknown to the characters, their lives are ruled by patterns that can be seen only *en ronde*, from all sides. Thus, the relentless irony of the Schnitzler play is preserved from the threat of cinema's celebrated "impression of reality." Fidelity to the spirit and the letter of the play is facilitated by the metanarration since the issue of the work's theatricality has been both acknowledged and displaced. The characters need not be "fleshed out"—and they are not. The claustrophobic feel of most of the sketches need not be "opened out." The repetitive, relatively unjustified actions need not be made answerable to questions of verisimilitude. Only the *characters* need "believe" in the reality of their existence; we, as spectators, not only need not believe in it but are prevented from believing. It is all simply part of La Ronde—the circle, the pattern, the dance. The flatness of the characters becomes not a defect but a weapon of an ironic discourse; the in-and-out-of-closed-spaces pattern of the episodes is not troubling because it is given as the temporal playing out of the figure of the carousel.

What is clear from this strategy of adaptation is that issues quite important to the director are at stake, that the abstract, *flat* quality of the Schnitzler text must have been of primary interest to Ophuls for its functioning to be maintained by such an elaborate set of procedures. In this way, *La Ronde* reveals an important aspect of Ophuls's particular approach to filmmaking. Roy Armes has given a clear statement of what is *least* important in Ophuls's work in his negative report in *French Cinema Since 1945*:

> Max Ophuls is virtually a test case of one's approach to the cinema. For those whose concern is purely visual and whose ideal is an abstract symphony of images, Ophuls has the status of one of the very great directors. For spectators and critics who demand

> in addition to the images the sort of human insight and moral
> depth that a play or a novel can give, he is merely a minor master,
> maker of exquisite but rather empty films. . . .
>   For Ophuls, the essence of the cinema lies in the play of light,
> the juggling with surfaces. . . . But never does he use his camera
> to probe beneath the surface.[7]

Ophuls's version of *La Ronde* demonstrates the left-handed
justness of this observation. The film consistently chooses theatricality over "moral depth." In fact, it is in this area that it is most
true to the spirit of Schnitzler's play. Both works display surfaces
while mocking sentiment—Schnitzler fiercely, Ophuls almost
placidly. (It is worth noting that Ophuls's surfaces—visual, verbal,
and musical—are, as Armes indicates, elegant indeed. This is another noteworthy result, largely, of the metanarrative intrusions,
which allow extravagant employment of the director's celebrated
moving camera in the midst of what might otherwise have emerged
as closet drama.) But it seems more appropriate to say that for
Ophuls and for Schnitzler, the point is that there is nothing beneath
the surface, and that the "insights" critics like Armes demand are
not there—are *refused*—because they would be *lies*.

Another adaptation of *La Ronde* might seek implicitly the
"why" of the characters' actions and situations, or at least let one
believe that answers might be conceivable and appropriate. Ophuls
refuses this possibility by answering the question "Why?" formally
within the film (they are moved by the *Meneur du Jeu* and the
unknown forces he represents), but not within the individual narrations (within the characters' "lives"). Our visual awareness of
Walbrook's machinations to keep the carousel turning undercuts
the various explanations and introspections of the characters. It is
not just that "moral depth" is absent; it is denied as a possibility.

Speaking of his father and his father's film work, Marcel Ophuls
has said:

> My father was not at all a Romantic. He didn't do period films
> because of nostalgia or *La Belle Epoque* or because of aestheticism.
> He was a very tough cookie, certainly not a sentimentalist. I think
> he was a moralist. I think what he was interested in were the work-

[7] Roy Armes, *French Cinema Since 1946*, 2d ed., London, Zwemmer, 1970,
pp. 62–63, 65.

ings of society and the contradictions between couples, between sex and love. Very moralist attitudes.[8]

By this I take Marcel Ophuls to have meant not merely moralist in the general sense but also in the French literary tradition as personified by Chamfort or La Rochefoucauld. The latter once gave a formula that almost sums up the generalizing, antipersonal attitude of the *moraliste*: "Most people would never fall in love had they not read about it." Statements like this (or "Our virtues are only our vices in disguise"—again, La Rochefoucauld) are characteristic of the attitude of the *moraliste*, whose object of study is human behavior stripped bare of pretensions of "depth" or hymns to "sentiment." Whether Max Ophuls's work should be characterized in its entirety as "moralistic" in this sense is not immediately clear (in an interview, he denied the label).[9] It seems to me, though, that the stance of the moralist is what Ophuls and Schnitzler share, at least in *Reigen* and the film Ophuls made from it. Or, one might rather say, Ophuls interprets the Schnitzler play as a moralistic text.

The moralistic stance is difficult to maintain, however, when combined with narrative realism, as in *La Ronde*. It demands that we experience the characters simultaneously as characters and as *examples* of patterns of behavior of which they are unaware (as witness the brutal sexual chauvinism of several males in the early parts of the play and film). Ophuls's adaptation of *La Ronde*, by splitting the work into two levels that correspond to these two attitudes, seems to have been conceived with this balance as its primary goal. But does this procedure make Ophuls's work less fierce, less bitter than Schnitzler's? The polished kindness of the *Meneur du Jeu* and the moments of genuine comic relief that he introduces (at one point, the Young Man is momentarily impotent, and we cut to Walbrook confronted with a breakdown in his carousel) might lead one to think so. But we can also read this kindness, these moments of genteel vaudeville, as casting the limitations and pettiness of Schnitzler's characters into an even harsher

[8] Transcribed from tape of an interview with James Blue, March 7, 1973, Rice University Media Center.
[9] Jacques Rivette and François Truffaut, "Interview with Max Ophuls," in Paul Willemen (ed.), *Max Ophuls*, London, British Film Institute, 1978, p. 27.

light. My own reaction is that the film is more demoralizing than the play, precisely since one has no fixed, reliable reference point from which to judge and evaluate. Walbrook's very kindness, his refusal to judge "his" characters, makes this responsibility solely the spectator's. (In the play, on the contrary, there is no doubt as to the author's contempt for his creations; the spectator may agree or possibly disagree.)

Ophuls's irony is at least potentially more demoralizing than Schnitzler's because it is never *sure*, never grounded or positioned. The basic structure of the film posits dramatic irony: The Master of Ceremonies sees all; the characters see only parts. The viewer must choose either to read the film's dramatic irony as dramatic irony and nothing more or to read it as the most apparent manifestation of a broader attitude of detachment or even moral condemnation. To take the former attitude leads finally to a *sentimental* reading of the film since the characters' fictional world is, properly speaking, a sentimental one. Thus, John Weightman can judge that Ophuls's tone is "appreciably lighter than in Schnitzler's play" and that the *Meneur du Jeu*'s function is "to remind us that it is love that makes the world go round."[10] If one reads the metanarration's ironic relation to the fiction more broadly, however, one can think of the Leader's possible reply: "Goes round, yes, but *in circles*—and smaller ones than we think."

[10] "Introduction" to *Masterworks of the French Cinema*, op. cit., p. 14.

JOHN L. FELL

THE CORRESPONDENTS' CURSE
Vadim's *Les Liaisons Dangereuses* 1960 (1959)

from the novel by Pierre Choderlos de Laclos

Movies required celluloid strips, light-sensitive emulsions, and a Maltese cross before making their appearance. Likewise, the epistolary novel needed a postal service. London's Penny Post appeared in 1680, and *Pamela* followed sixty years later; Paris organized the Petite-Poste in 1758, and *Les Liaisons Dangereuses* appeared in 1782. In fact, a mother in Laclos's novel[1] is fore-warned that she may obstruct temptations to her daughter by spiriting the young woman away from mail routes.

Les Liaisons Dangereuses (known in translation as *Dangerous Acquaintances* or *Dangerous Connections*) rapidly became a best-seller. Ironically represented in a "Publisher's Note" (written by Laclos) as a false and misleading picture of contemporary manners, the novel constitutes a witty, biting satire of amours among a closed society of aristocrats whose acquaintances and pawns include occasional military officers, the clergy, and servants. The book's subtitle is "Assembled Letters from One Society Published for the Edification of Some Others."

The Novel

Les Liaisons Dangereuses is composed of exchanges between thirteen characters—five minor and one anonymous. Their mutual

[1] Pierre Choderlos de Laclos commanded troops under both the Directory and Napoleon. His activities were varied and sometimes irregular. They included a published attack on contemporary military notions about fortification, an unpublished treatise on women's education, a time in prison, and marriage two years after the birth of his son to the boy's mother.

subject is sexual intrigue, whether they know it or not, and the final effect constitutes a multiperspectived overview on events that germinate in seduction strategies and conclude tragically for almost everyone. Three relationships and five figures prove essential:

> The Vicomte de Valmont and the Marquise de Merteuil
> The Vicomte de Valmont and Madame de Tourvel
> Cécile de Volanges and the Chevalier Danceny

Confined to the central characters (there are various minor dalliances), the plot may be simplified as follows:

Once lovers, Valmont and Merteuil now correspond regularly, recounting their seductions. Sometimes the marquise suggests and even facilitates Valmont's exploits, but it is rather against her wishes that Valmont settles on Madame de Tourvel (la Présidente de Tourvel), the pious wife of an absent lawyer.

The Marquise de Merteuil has enjoyed an affair with Danceny, a friend of Valmont. Stung by his new attraction to Cécile de Volanges, she plans to punish him by "giving" Cécile to Valmont. During his lengthy pursuit of Madame de Tourvel, Valmont succeeds with Cécile, a naive if potentially sly girl recently withdrawn from her convent education. Unknowing, Danceny continues his innocent suit for Cécile's hand.

Valmont finally seduces Madame de Tourvel. He and the marquise have agreed that they will share one more night together as a reward for his success. They measure success by sexual consummations that are quickly, dispassionately severed. Perhaps Valmont genuinely falls in love with Madame de Tourvel; at any rate, he mails her a cruel dismissal dictated by the marquise. The rejected woman retreats to a convent and lapses into madness.

Valmont returns to Paris to find Danceny with the Marquise de Merteuil at an hour he believed reserved for himself. The tone of his indignation infuriates the marquise, and their dispute leads to an angry breach. Valmont arranges Danceny's liaison with Cécile in order to embarrass the marquise, who had planned an evening with Danceny herself. In retaliation, she discloses to Danceny that Valmont has seduced Cécile. Danceny challenges Valmont to a duel and kills him. The marquise loses her fortune in a lawsuit; she is then rebuffed by society because her intrigues have been publicized. Finally she contracts disfiguring smallpox. She flees to Holland.

Laclos's novel is distinguished by clever characterizations betrayed by the separate writing styles and implicit in the thought processes of each correspondent. Because the plot parallels seduction strategies as well as the contrived sentiments assumed by the vicomte and the marquise, the two emerge as a pair of complicated personalities whose relationship constitutes the book's core. In a real sense, it is a story of two criminals falling out.

Their discussions of seduction often employ a military nomenclature.[2] The marquise is inclined toward theatrical images.[3] Occasionally, she tells a mildly bawdy anecdote, but Laclos's language is decidedly nonprurient. Furthermore, it is nearly absent of description. The discussions about emotions, often clinically dissected, so invest sex with ego that the result is coldly to de-eroticize nearly every coupling. The ultimate fates of Valmont and the marquise intrude so abruptly, their stories conclude in so peremptory a fashion, that the novel's ending seems pervaded by irony, because of its heavy-handed moralizing.

The Film

Titled *Les Liaisons Dangereuses 1960* (1959) (and unfortunately known here also as *Dangerous Love Affairs*), Roger Vadim's film followed three previous successful features, in particular *And God Created Woman* (1956). Vadim entered film through scriptwriting and ten years of assistant directing, most often for Marc Allégret. His later films look increasingly mannered (*Pretty Maids All In a*

[2] Pierre Choderlos de Laclos, *Dangerous Acquaintances*, translated by Richard Aldington, New York, New Directions, n.d., Letter 125: "The Vicomte de Valmont to the Marquise de Merteuil," p. 279:
> I departed in no respect from the true principles of this war, which we have often remarked is so like the other. Judge me then as you would Frederic or Turenne. I forced the enemy to fight when she wished only to refuse battle; by clever manoeuvers I obtained the choice of battle-field and of dispositions; I inspired the enemy with confidence, to overtake her more easily in her retreat . . . finally, I only joined action when I had an assured retreat by which I could cover and retain all I had conquered before.

[3] Letter 81: "The Marquise de Merteuil to the Vicomte de Valmont," p. 165: "Then I began to display on the great stage the talents I had procured myself."

Row, 1970) and programatically erotic (*Barbarella*, 1968), in a style previously parodied by Godard in *Alphaville* (1965). Nonetheless, Vadim's first features both exploited and helped establish the beachhead of the New Wave. Vadim displayed to French financing the commercial potential of productions whose innovation rested less in revolutionary narrative forms than in documenting contemporary sexuality. Their freedoms titillated the very audience whose mores were being held up to ridicule; Louis Malle's *The Lovers* (1958) is another case in point.

For his new film, Vadim worked in concert with writer Claude Brulé, and later Roger Vailland, who created (or transposed) most of the dialogue. After experimenting with attempts to counterpoint Laclos's eighteenth century with the time of Premier Mendes-France and Ferrari 250s, the script settled on an altogether modern setting. The central characters and much of the plot are retained, if sometimes altered in their intentions. The narrative shifts to straightforward exposition. Valmont writes only two letters; Here voice-over sometimes punctuates his descriptions, which otherwise appear "live." The marquise, now Juliette, mails no correspondence, although the film is threaded with telephone, telegraph, and tape-recorded messages. In Vadim's version, correspondence withdraws largely to the function of a plot-furthering agency alone.

Through gossip at a Left Bank cocktail party, we are introduced to Valmont (Gérard Philipe in his last role) and his wife Juliette (Jeanne Moreau). Well-to-do, Juliette descends from nobility; she and Valmont connive to secure a post for him with the United Nations. Cécile's engagement to one of Juliette's lovers, Jerry Court, an American, is announced. Actually Cécile (Jeanne Valérie) loves Danceny (Jean-Louis Trintignant), a poor mathematics student. Angry that Court broke their relationship before she did, Juliette proposes that Valmont seduce Cécile.

In consequence, Valmont goes skiing at Megève, where Cécile is vacationing with her mother and friends. There he meets Marianne Tourvel (Vadim's new wife, Annette), a Danish woman whose lawyer husband is attending a distant conference. With her young daughter Caroline, Marianne is visiting her husband's aunt. Basing his campaign on limited candor, Valmont confesses to Marianne

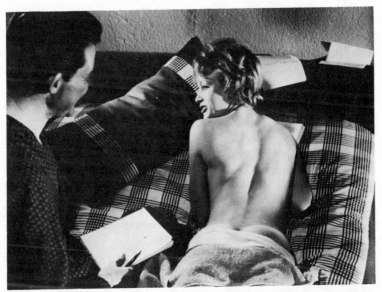

Updating Laclos's epistolary masterpiece to 1960, Roger Vadim replaces most of the letters with telephone, telegraph, and tape-recorded messages. Valmont (Gérard Philipe) carries out his assignment to seduce Cécile (Jeanne Valérie). *Photo courtesy of Museum of Modern Art*

his pact with Juliette: Each is to operate with absolute sexual freedom, seeking every pleasure and recounting their adventures to amuse one another.

Unsettled by Valmont's descriptions of Marianne, Juliette arrives in Megève for the New Year's celebration. Valmont seduces Cécile and accepts Juliette's edict that he conquer Marianne quickly and reject her brusquely.

Marianne returns to Paris with the aunt; Valmont follows and consummates their relationship. While Juliette is in New York, the pair vacations in Normandy. Valmont's UN post secured, Juliette returns. She discovers that Cécile is pregnant. After arguing with Valmont because he has fallen in love with Marianne, Juliette sends a vicious telegram of dismissal to Marianne in his name. Valmont is enraged to learn that Juliette now schemes to seduce Danceny before joining him with Cécile. Combined with the telegram, this causes a break between Valmont and Juliette.

At Juliette's expense, Valmont unites Cécile and Danceny during a party. In retaliation, Juliette discloses to Danceny that Valmont has seduced Cécile. Returning to the party, Danceny fights with Valmont, who is now very drunk. Valmont is killed accidently. Having told everything to her husband before receiving Juliette's telegram and learning of Valmont's death, Marianne becomes insane. Juliette tries to destroy her compromising letters; in the process she burns herself severely. Outside the Palace of Justice after a court hearing, Juliette appears, disfigured. Cécile's mother calls out, "Look at her! . . . Her face is the image of her soul." Juliette confronts a crowd, "proud, defiant, scornful, and cold."[4]

Enlisting fewer characters and working with less incident, the film forsakes Laclos's parallels between Juliette and Valmont. While equally "major," the figures emerge less alike, a condition underlined by the presence of Moreau and Philipe. Vadim drops certain densities from the novel, such as the class relationships spelled out in correspondences between aristocrats and servants. In compensation, the iconography of set, design, and costume contributes an additional atmosphere of wealth and ennui. (Laclos is parsimonious of descriptive detail, to say the least.) In the film, characters are as emotionally isolated from one another as they are separated in the luxuriant space of Vadim's upper-middle-class locales. Even together, the principals are incomplete; Cécile's passage from indignation to submission to self-recrimination never has a moment of modulating transition, never connects with Valmont.

By refining, somewhat simplifying some motives, and altering the ending, Vadim overlays a melodramatic patina of credibility. The intention surfaces in a script notation concerning Juliette's burn, a "great brown spot that disfigures her without, however, making her horrible."[5] As Juliette emerges even more villainous than the marquise, she must endure punitive consequences stemming more literally from the action instead of escaping the plot by disappearing in Holland.

Valmont's death more closely enlists the tongue-in-cheek didacti-

[4] Roger Vadim, *Les Liaisons Dangereuses*, New York, Ballantine Books, 1962, p. 255.
[5] Ibid., p. 254.

cism of Laclos, probably unintentionally because of inadequacies in the sequence itself. The wild party is Vadim's most awkward sequence. An effort to intensify apparent frenzy by fast intercutting between dancers and jazz drumming, and to imply decadence by having women dance together (horrors!) proves ineffectively clumsy. Danceny's blow to Valmont poorly matches tempos and camera angles when Vadim cuts from medium to close shot. Valmont staggers too long, as if looking for the andiron to fall against. Additionally, the party's failure stems from the music. It is intended to incite, even more than to reflect, the guests' moods. Unfortunately, the drum solo reappears at the picture's end. The convention of equating jazz with delinquency never transcends this clichéd employment.[6]

Eroticism in the Film

Elsewhere, Vadim's calculated stagings of heterosexual love-making—usually as it approaches consummation—works, although twenty years' perspective may lead a viewer to wonder anew at the film's reception. *Les Liaisons Dangereuses 1960* was a *succès de scandale*, with admission in France limited to customers over sixteen. Distribution overseas was withheld for three years. It now carries something of the charm of an old *Playboy*, with stylistic overtones of *Vogue*. Probably the film's most remembered moment originates in the book's own recounting of Valmont's quickie with a former love, Émile.

> This complaisance on my part is the reward for one she has just granted me, that of acting as a desk for me to write to my fair devotee; I thought it amusing to send her a letter written from the bed and almost in the arms of a girl, interrupted even for a complete infidelity, in which letter I give her an exact description of my situation and my conduct. Émile, to whom I read the epistle, laughed extravagantly, and I hope you too will laugh.[7]

[6] The French used American jazz to special effect in *Ascenseur pour l'Echafaud* (1957) with Miles Davis, *Murmur of the Heart* (1971) with recordings by Charlie Parker and Sidney Bechet, and *Autour d'un Recif* (1959). The last is an out-of-the-ordinary documentary made by Jacques-Yves Cousteau. Its juxtaposition of tropical fish with the tenor saxophone of Don Byas produces uncanny, surreal sensations.

[7] Letter 47: "The Vicomte de Valmont to the Marquise de Merteuil," p. 88.

Gérard Philipe completes his negotiations on the handsome, bare buttocks of Jeanne Valérie, whose adolescent sexuality Vadim emphasizes clearly by having her puzzling over a geometry assignment while her lover seeks to reach Marianne by phone.

Overall, Vadim leans toward the nuances of sexual behavior. Sexual relationships are telegraphed very skillfully by glances or by touch, as when Valmont first grabs hold of Cécile when he skis to a stop at Megève. In contrast, Laclos veers in the direction of sex as predetermined strategy, like variations on Kierkegaard's *Diary of a Seducer.*

Syntagms and Syntax

Epistolary novels connive a narrative frame unlike other fictional forms and different from film, yet in broad outline Laclos's pages translate easily to Vadim's screen. In some respects, juxtapositions of letters are not unlike film editing. Radical shifts of mood, ellisions of time, and even time overlaps become possible by simple shifts of correspondence and dates. In some ways they are even more successful on paper; the ironies of the correspondents' contrary moods may be abutted with less interference from other elements like speech and setting.

As an equivalent, Vadim joins contrasting sequences in stark adjacency. The technique appears early in the film. Juliette and Valmont plan Cécile's seduction, and we shift abruptly to a picture-postcard composition of Valmont skiing gracefully down a slope toward the chalet from which Cécile and her friends are watching him. Even better is an earlier transition commencing with Cécile and Danceny in his little room. Cécile has vowed into Danceny's tape recorder to wait for him ("But I'm counting on you not to make it too long"). Cut to boxers in a ring. The unexpected crowd noises jar us. The context hints that love games are not without victors and victims. Cutaways to individual spectators include one middle-aged man who seems particularly excited. Back to the ring. Then the camera pulls away to disclose that the image has come from a television set. We have been misled; the spectator is Jerry Court, Juliette's lover, seated in his living room.

Another expository strategy—the introduction of multiple perspectives—lends complexity to novels made up from intimate thoughts and emotions, privacies that are better exposed through the Petite-Poste than they are evidenced in dialogue or gesture. The epistolary structure allows an author to penetrate innermost thought without playing god with his characters' minds.

In this respect, the media simply differ. A letter that describes premeditated social maneuvers operates on several levels. Performance itself is recounted in such a way that the reader seeks to distinguish accurately both past events (what really happened) and the teller's relation to them. He may learn to distrust both teller and tale. The writer's relation to his correspondent figures, too, both in the inflections of his discourse and in dispositions of style that, like gesture or intonation, betray as easily as they illuminate.

Comparison between the two forms can be located in Valmont's representation of his encounter with Madame de Tourvel-Marianne. In the book he writes:

> The word "love" I have not yet spoken; but already we have got to "confidence" and "interest." To deceive her as little as possible and especially to forestall any gossip which might reach her I have myself told her, as if accusing myself, some of my best known exploits.[8]

In the film, this scene appears as part of a sequence that alternates events in Megève, shown lip-sync, and voice-over narration by Valmont, bridged by Thelonius Monk's music (see "Music" below). Separate incidents are linked with the commentary of a letter that Juliette is reading. When we see Marianne and Valmont walking through the snow, Valmont's voice announces, "Against virtue, truth is the most effective weapon. I decided to throw away my mask and I recounted some of my exploits."

After listening with obvious discomfort, Marianne says, "You have a wife, Valmont. Only she can help you." The couple stops. Valmont replies, "Juliette and I—our marriage is abominable." Camera pulls back. Valmont continues, voice-over: "I told her everything about us—our compact to say everything, to permit everything, to dare everything. . . ."

In theory we might consider Valmont's behavior the more heinous for its visible sincerity. In fact, the candor of his words to Marianne about Juliette convinces the viewer equally. Between letter and film, the mixed, shifting levels of discourse prove not to

8 Letter 6: "The Vicomte de Valmont to the Marquise de Merteuil," p. 14.

be strictly comparable. Sound-picture congruences differ connotatively from shifts in tense. Time itself, always *now* in Vadim's as in almost any narrative film's entertainment, separates into three modes (the event recounted, the correspondent's time, and the respondent's time) on paper.

The Marquise and the Vicomte

Laclos's portrait of the Marquise de Merteuil is deft and contradictory, a combination of self-reliant independence[9] and undisguised, vengeful malevolence.[10] Though she speaks of avenging her sex, the marquise ends by betraying every woman she knows. In Valmont's eyes, she seems to combine the body of a woman with the mind of a man, leavened only by a penchant for the unpredictable. "How can I divine the thousands and thousands of caprices which govern a woman's mind, by which alone you are still related to your sex?"[11]

In contrast, the vicomte seems to be moved by a more simple combination of pride and lust that finds its realization in the victimization of women: "But since I intend to avenge myself on the mother, in this case I intend to dishonor the girl."[12] His affection for Madame de Tourvel is recognized as an unexpected vulnerability, a chink in the armor through which a mortal wound is sustained.

Played by Gérard Philipe, Valmont appears more literally subservient to Juliette. The relationship is emphasized by their marital state (she is wealthier and better-born) and underlined by a shift in plot lines through which he pursues Cécile on original commission, meeting Marianne accidently.

More important, the vicomte and the marquise lose themselves in Philipe's and Moreau's handsome images. Philipe's dalliances are reinforced as innocent by a personal history of screen sex

[9] Letter 81: "The Marquise de Merteuil to the Vicomte de Valmont," p. 160: "Those unthroned tyrants now become my slaves," and "I was born to avenge my sex and to dominate yours. . . ."
[10] Letter 159: "The Marquise de Merteuil to the Vicomte de Valmont," p. 342: Her last words are "When I have reason to complain of someone, I do not jest; I do something better; I avenge myself. . . ."
[11] Letter 76: "The Vicomte de Valmont to the Marquise de Merteuil," pp. 140–141.
[12] Letter 66: "The Vicomte de Valmont to the Marquise de Merteuil," p. 123.

farces. His final "rebellion" has the look of supporting screen conventions: *Vive l'amour!* But he is too weak to act. In consequence, the complexity of his role diminishes.

We know Moreau otherwise. Her sensuality has melancholy overtones. Her emotions are unreserved (*The Lovers*), capricious (*Jules and Jim*, 1961), painful (*La Notte*, 1961). She reads Valmont's letters with a characteristically downturned mouth. She watches him with Marianne pensively. Her enticement of Danceny is studied. If Juliette is the victim of injured pride (her husband has fallen in love), her mood and behavior change little in consequence; they only intensify. Ultimately, she has no feminist motives, only the boredom of the *haute bourgeoisie*.

Music

The failure of the drunken-party jazz is belied by the music elsewhere. The film's score begs special consideration. Credited to Jack Murray (a pseudonym), it consists largely of compositions and performance by a Thelonius Monk group and, for the New Year's and party sequences, compositions by Duke Jordan played by Art Blakey's Jazz Messengers (visible on the screen are drummer Kenny Clarke and trumpeter Kenny Dorham instead of Blakey and Lee Morgan).

During the Megève celebration, a Jordan medley shifts from rhumba to Charleston to saxophone ballad back to the rhumba. Each change cleverly modulates a veering emotionality of interrelationships between Marianne, Juliette, Valmont, and Cécile's mother. Uncomprehending, Jerry Court intrudes with the Charleston.

Danceny's innocence is underscored by a romantic swath of Tchaikovsky on his tape recorder. Elsewhere, the music consists of Monk's often recognizable compositions such as *Crepescule with Nellie, Well You Needn't,* and *Rhythm-a-Ning*. The music of Thelonius Monk is imbued with satiric manipulations of conventional phrasing and harmonic progressions. In juxtaposition with Vadim's composed, often picturesque images, the music enforces a kind of ephemeral, ironic perspective, hinting at hypocrisies that lurk beneath the beautiful exteriors. *Les Liaisons Dangereuses 1960* is introduced by Monk's *Off Minor*, which reappears during conversations between Valmont and both Juliette and Marianne. Because the theme is originally identified with the husband-wife liaison and that pair's scheming, it supports our awareness of Valmont as an extension of his wife's intentions. But as intimacy between Valmont and Marianne deepens, a second theme gains prominence. It is a variation on the old hymn "Bye and Bye," still retaining Monk's cold-eyed dissonances. When Marianne loses her mind, the aunt finds her humming the melody.

Narrative Design

Laclos's narrative operates by the accretions of his correspondents' anecdotes. The story mounts in intensity through shifts and, finally, deteriorations of its discourse. *Le style est l'homme*; most of the letters partake of the contrived elegances of Merteuil-Valmont. She notes that "there is nothing so difficult in love as to write what one does not feel. I mean to write it in a credible way. It is not that the same words are not employed; but they are not arranged in the same way. . . ."[13] Yet finally, when "genuine" emotions abrade such syntactical masquerades, the exposition falters. The deterioration of style climaxes in a dictation by Madame de Tourvel to an undesignated addressee. Feeling is unguised, like transcribed agonized speech, and the mood of Madame de Tourvel's anguish shifts direction wildly from one apparent "listener" to another.[14]

Vadim's major accomplishment rests in the performance he elicits from Jeanne Moreau and the skill with which he uses her persona. The director's first sequence prepares our anticipations, introduces Valmont and Juliette, then draws Philipe away to center Moreau in the foreground; it ends on Juliette alone, besieged but undefeated. Vadim is wise to scar Jeanne Moreau, for we all know, all of us who share a history of reading pictures in the dark, that every screen face is an image of the soul. Beautiful faces cannot commit evil deeds without betraying a tic, a wrinkle, a bad angle.

---

[13] Letter 33: "The Marquise de Merteuil to the Vicomte de Valmont," p. 58.
[14] Letter 161: "Madame de Tourvel to. . . . (Dictated by her and written by her waiting-woman)," pp. 343–344. Tzevtan Todorov turns to Madame de Tourvel as a means of illustrating three aspects of basic narrative organization: the effort to elicit love, a character's becoming conscious of a feeling, and a character's changing confidantes when a love relationship has been recognized. Tzetan Todorov, "The Principles of Narrative," *Diacritics*, Fall 1971.

ANDREW HORTON

GROWING UP ABSURD
Malle's *Zazie dans le Métro (1960)*

from the novel by Raymond Queneau

In 1960 when Louis Malle, then twenty-eight, transformed Raymond Queneau's popular novel *Zazie dans le Métro* (1959) for the screen, he had two primary interests in mind. He and co-scriptwriter Jean-Paul Rappeneau were drawn initially to Queneau because his work represented what Malle called "an internal critique of literature."[1] Malle wished not so much to adapt *Zazie* to film as to find an equivalent "internal critique of cinematic language." For Queneau, to critique language meant to play with it, to expose its limitations, and to suggest its vast possibilities for expressing the imagination. The young director was fascinated with the challenge of playing with and thus critiquing the conventions of film in a similar way. Malle also spoke of his awareness that breaking up cinematic language was "the most effective way to decry and to parody a likewise disintegrated and chaotic world." Queneau's *Zazie* thus became a framework to which he remained faithful in spirit, while simultaneously it was a point of departure for his own imaginative and satirical interests.

Queneau's Novel

From the first word of Raymond Queneau's *Zazie dans le Métro*, the reader is caught up in a contemporary Cloudcuckooland where language and reality are the playthings of the author's imagination. *"Doukipudonktan,"* the opening word, is Queneau's contraction

---

[1] Louis Malle, in Philippe Pilard, *"Zazie dans le Métro," Revue du Cinéma*, No. 274, 1973, p. 162. The translation is my own, and all quotations in this paragraph are from this article.

for *D'ou est-ce qu'ils puent donc tant* ("What part of them stinks so much"). Anything is possible after such a beginning. And in a comic, satirical, surrealistic, and even philosophical spirit that reminds us of such diverse authors as James Joyce, Aristophanes, Rabelais, Henri Michaux, and Henry Miller, Zazie's creator proceeds to puzzle, entertain, challenge, and initiate us into Zazie's world. "Literature is the verbal activity of man,"[2] Queneau has explained. In *Zazie*, as in all his works, he expands the possibilities of language and literature by toying with them as if he were a jazz musician with a classical background who is able to create his own music out of the tunes, conventions, and movements of the past.

Zazie dans le Métro resembles *Alice in Wonderland* updated to Paris and thus France of the late 1950s. Alice and Zazie are young girls who share a sense of innocence and curiosity that is never shattered as they wander and, at times, are propelled through an almost surrealistic landscape. But there is a critical difference between them. Whereas Lewis Carroll's nineteenth-century heroine falls into a world of imagination, Queneau's young protagonist travels through the "real" Paris her mother has brought her to for roughly thirty-six hours. The métro that Zazie so badly wants to ride might have been for her what the deep tunnels were for Alice: a means of escape into "Wonderland." But the métro is on strike, and Zazie is "condemned" to pass her time above ground under the half-watchful eye of her uncle Gabriel, a male ballerina and self-proclaimed "artist." Instead of Wonderland, Zazie, a young visitor from *outside* Paris, experiences the chaotic reality of post-World War II France, a reality that appears stranger to us in many ways than eighteenth-century Paris appeared to Montesquieu's Persians. It is a Paris caught between the memories of the Occupation and a sterile Americanized future, populated by a bewildering kaleidoscope of characters in perpetual motion whose identities are tenuous, whose speech is often absurd, and whose collective presence constitutes a crowd or traffic jam rather than a group or "society."

Queneau's vision is one of philosophical laughter: Like Voltaire, he invites us to reflect on as well as laugh at man's follies. According to Jacques Guicharnaud, "Queneau sees the world as a

---

[2] Jacques Guicharnaud, *Raymond Queneau*, New York, Columbia University Press, 1965, p. 26.

vast puppet show—but a puppet show that is worth being meticulously observed and then recreated for the great joy of young and old."[3] Influenced as a youth by Chaplin, Queneau succeeds in creating a female character who maintains Chaplin's sense of wonderment despite the bizarre world that surrounds her. Zazie is neither a sensuous younger Lolita—although sexuality is a major theme in the novel (she continually wants to know if Gabriel is a "hormosexual")—nor a sentimental girl from the provinces.

She is, on the contrary, a completely contemporary girl whose favorite expression, "my ass," sums up the healthy perspective she maintains on the dizzy pace of her Parisian adventures. While *Zazie* reminds us in part of a puppet show, a comic strip, or a silent movie, Queneau establishes a very human depth to Zazie's character. Despite the jokes, puns, and circuslike confusion, there is the general reality of 1950s France and the personal trauma that Zazie had experienced in the past when her father attempted to rape her, only to be discovered and murdered by her mother. In structure the novel is circular—beginning and ending at the train station—and certainly circularity and repetition are major structuring devices in the book. But in terms of Zazie's development, the ending suggests growth, change, maturity. "What did you do?" asks her mother on the train home. "I aged," is the reply. The line suggests a certain amount of self-reflection with a trace of melancholy. Yet Queneau clearly leaves her vitality and innocence intact.

The critique of language (reality) that attracted Malle to the novel can best be seen in a soliloquy Gabriel delivers at the Eiffel Tower. Beginning with a parody of both Hamlet and Jean-Paul Sartre, he goes on to paraphrase and allude to Shakespeare's *Midsummer Night's Dream*, Calderon's *Life Is a Dream*, and other works as he states:

> Being or nothingness, that is the question. Ascending, descending, coming, going, a man does so much that in the end he disappears. A taxi bears him off, a metro carries him away, the Tower doesn't care, nor the Pantheon. Paris is but a dream, Gabriel is but a reverie (a charming one), Zazie the dream of a reverie (or of a nightmare) and all this story the dream of a dream, the reverie of

[3] Ibid., p. 4.

a reverie, scarcely more than the typewritten delirium of an idiotic novelist (oh! sorry).[4]

This paragraph is not a "critique" in any formal sense. Rather, like James Joyce, Queneau makes us playfully aware that language is both a liberating system for expressing the imagination and a gauge of our limitations, our pretentions, and our inability to transcend the self. The opening sentence plays off Sartre and Shakespeare, evoking each yet imaginatively combining both through Gabriel's speech to produce a thought that *is* central to Gabriel and by extension to Queneau, to all writers, and to all people. It is a dialectical view of language and reality: On one hand, man (Gabriel) is *something* and that something is expressed through language, yet man is also a "dream" because, as Ludwig Wittgenstein has made clear in the *Tractatus*, he can never go beyond language to verify "truth" or "reality." Language cannot be formally or *completely* critiqued because one must use language to express that critique. Such is the dilemma of the philosopher but the delight of the writer-creator Queneau. He exposes Gabriel as a character composed of allusions, parodies, half-borrowed lines, and partially understood ideas. He is the language he speaks, and that language has the paradoxical reality of his career: male ballerina. But Queneau's critique is also a celebration. Gabriel is more than the sum of his borrowed phrases and concepts; he is an individual capable of expressing his dream-reality state in an imaginative flow of language that ends with a final wink as the reader acknowledges the presence of the "idiotic novelist (oh! sorry)" as the master puppeteer.

"Talk, talk, talk," pipes Laverdure, the parrot, throughout the novel as if he were a disengaged choral figure. "That's all you can do." And talk is a large part of what any of the characters can do (including Laverdure) to express themselves and establish their identities. From Gabriel's theatrical tirades, to Pedro-Trouscaillon —the fascist cop-sex fiend—and his inability to create any consistent identity or language, to the "gentle" speech of Marceline (Gabriel's bland wife), to the hard-nosed commonsensical talk of Girdoux the cobbler, and finally to Zazie's spunky irreverent slang,

---

[4] Raymond Queneau, *Zazie*, translated by Barbara Wright, New York, Harper & Row, 1960, p. 90. All quotations in the text are taken from this edition and are identified by page number.

In his novel, Queneau invented a contemporary Alice in the wonderland of present-day Paris. Louis Malle found ways to "critique" cinema just as Queneau had challenged language. Catherine Demongeot played the title role in *Zazie*.

language emerges as the true protagonist behind this farce. But, as the end of Gabriel's speech points out, it is language controlled and originated by Queneau as author. Beyond the talk of the characters remains the author, who constantly calls attention to *language* through his puns, his abrupt switches in tense and point of view, and his grammar, punctuation, and sheer invention (he aptly coins the adjective "zazic" to describe his universe).

Malle's Film

Louis Malle transposed rather than translated *Zazie* from fiction to film. He brought Zazie to life on the screen and simultaneously captured the confusion of Paris in 1960 in a film that Pauline Kael described as "bold, delicate, freakish, vulgar, outrageous and occasionally nightmarish."[5] Most importantly, however, he managed

[5] Pauline Kael, *The New Yorker*, November 25, 1961, p. 204.

to find ways to "critique" cinema that paralleled Queneau's concern for verbal language. In the double spirit of parody and celebration of language (visual in this case) that we have examined in Queneau, Malle, like many of the other New Wave directors, reached back to the old Hollywood traditions to make audiences conscious of film-as-film while also imaginatively expanding the potential for those conventions, traditions, and genres to reflect contemporary reality.

The scriptwriter in Jean-Luc Godard's *Le Mépris* suggests that filmmakers should return to the golden days of silent film, to the works of Chaplin and Griffith, in order to relearn their art. Malle's *Zazie* is a direct expression of such a belief, and the traditions from which he draws are those of American silent slapstick farce and the later anarchistic sound comedies of the Marx Brothers and W. C. Fields. His subject matter is Zazie and her contemporary Parisian environment, but his expression is through the "language" of American film comedy. The resulting clash between subject and expression works as a critique by distancing us far enough from the character and "story" so that we are conscious of the illusionary nature of both. Like Queneau's novel, the film is enjoyable for its childlike delight in playing with conventions, forms, and "grammar." But such playful manipulation forces us to go beyond mere pleasure and consider the nature of film as a medium of communication and a means of conveying what Gabriel sees as a dreamlike reality.

A number of other filmmakers have been concerned with such an intentionally self-conscious examination of cinematic language and its relationship to illusion and reality. Think, for instance, of Bergman's *Persona* (1966), with its "framing" opening and closing sequences that remind us that no matter how *real* the drama unfolding between the nurse and the actress may seem, it is, after all, a creation on film run through a projector and seen on a screen. Malle's accomplishment is thus not so much his concept of critiquing cinema as his ability to present that critique in a *playful* tone that approximates and, because of the swiftness of slapstick images, often surpasses Queneau's ability to "frolick" through verbal language.

Queneau does in fact reflect a strong awareness of cinema in the novel. Gabriel predicts that schools will be replaced by cinemas and television. More importantly, Zazie constantly judges the actions of those around her in terms of film. After one adventure she says, "They couldn't do it any better in the movies" (p. 35), and later she informs Gabriel, "I'm as good as Michele Morgan in *Camille*" (p. 64). The Chaplinesque quality of Zazie's innocence and ramblings has been noted. Clearly, the chases through the streets of Paris suggest Mack Sennett, while Gabriel at times speaks with the wry exaggeration of a Gallic W. C. Fields. Furthermore, Queneau's blend of verbal slapstick and social satire echoes Jacques Tati's "silent" comedies. The zippy pace of the novel and the sudden transitions that read like literary "jumpcuts" not only reflect a kind of cinematic structure but also help place *Zazie* as a striking parallel to Godard's *Breathless* (1959), made in the same year the novel was published.

In large part Louis Malle simply amplified and developed these elements, with the result that his *Zazie* is both a homage to cinema and a parody of it and more particularly of its comic traditions. In fact, the opening sequences establish Malle's intention to critique cinema in the same spirit that Queneau manifested with his "invented" word. As the credits roll by, the screen is filled with a speeded-up view of the suburban train tracks taken from an onrushing train while a lighthearted Western score plays on the soundtrack. The rapid pace which is to characterize the film—a pace that is, of course, much more immediate and driving than is possible in Queneau's novel—is set. But the music also prepares us for a Western. Malle has explained that Zazie's arrival in Paris is "like a good guy in a Western arriving in a small town infested with bandits."[6] This segment, which does not appear in the novel, makes it clear that Malle is beginning with *his* version of *Zazie*, employing what cinema can do best: create motion and a sense of immediacy. As we switch to the station and Gabriel waiting for his niece, the dialogue is Queneau's. But Zazie's arrival is staged as a variation on one of Chaplin's favorite gags. We see a woman (Zazie's mother) begin to run down the platform toward Gabriel. There is a cut to Gabriel getting ready to receive the woman in his arms, followed by a shot of the mother's lover stepping out from behind Gabriel to embrace her as Gabriel is left alone to notice

[6] Malle, op. cit., p. 165.

Zazie, in a bright red sweater, appearing behind her mother. The allusion is to Chaplin's missed embrace when he first spots Georgia in *The Gold Rush*, and the effect, like Queneau's opening word, is to wink at the audience, preparing us for a film in which anything is possible.

In general, Malle has condensed and speeded up the novel while adding and elaborating the cinematic possibilities. Malle employs much of Queneau's dialogue with a minimum of rewriting, but he has shortened most conversations and cut out others. The same is true for whole scenes. While the novel contains a number of short scenes, the film focuses primarily on several extended sequences. For example, the scene in which the "sex fiend" cop, Pedro-Trouscaillon, chases Zazie through the back streets of Paris takes up little space in the novel. In the film, this event becomes something of a one-reeler silent comedy as Malle spoofs a seemingly endless number of chase formulas, jokes, camera tricks, and cartoon techniques. In fast motion Zazie and her pursuer hurl bombs with burning fuses at each other, romp across rooftops and through marketplaces, zip along on roller skates, and then fall suddenly into slow motion. Accompanied by suitably bouncy music in the silent-film tradition, the sequence becomes the brightest, most carefree interlude in a film that increasingly suggests an uneasy sense of chaos behind the laughter. This section, totally invented by Malle and his co-writer, most clearly establishes Zazie's buoyant enthusiasm while simultaneously celebrating Malle's ability to play with cinematic conventions.

Queneau creates both tension and perspective by switching continually between an impersonal narrator and Zazie's own thoughts. At one moment we are seeing the world through Zazie's impudent eyes; the next moment she becomes simply one more figure in a frenzied landscape observed by a narrator who, like Gabriel, sees all as a kind of waking dream. Malle makes no effort to capture the young girl's thoughts, but through frequent close-ups of Catherine Demongeot's pixielike features he keeps us involved with Zazie. And, in this comic caper scene, by using a shaky *cinéma vérité* shot to capture the running Zazie in close-up, Malle intensifies our sense of her freedom and enjoyment. But Zazie is not the only exuberant spirit; the playful self-consciousness of the film itself points to Malle's delight in his own cinematic freedom.

"Zazie was very important to me," Malle comments. "It gave me a technical freedom I had never felt before, and made me feel that in film it is perfectly possible to interpret reality, not just to reproduce it."[7]

To understand Malle's ability to transpose Queneau, let us consider the Eiffel Tower scene. The novel is as much about Paris as it is about Zazie, and so it is appropriate that the symbol of Paris should figure prominently in the text. In the novel, Gabriel, Zazie, and Charles, the cabbie, ride to the top for a view of the city. Gabriel then descends to wait for them while Zazie traps Charles in a long interrogation about love, sex, and the nature of language. Queneau follows this discussion with a monologue by Gabriel while he stands alone at the base of the tower.

His speech, part of which we have examined earlier, suggests his tenuous existence and ambiguous sexuality. He is simultaneously in a state of being and nothingness, both an individual and a nonentity, neither overtly gay nor "clearly heterosexual." Queneau's playful critique suggests that confusion of language reflects a confusion of identity and thus of sexuality. As he considers the tower, Gabriel even projects his confusion onto the whole city as he wonders how anyone can think of Paris as a woman "with such a thing like that" (p. 89). He reasons that this metallic phallus has transformed Paris much like women who turn into men because "they are so keen on sports" (p. 89). The sense of ambiguous sexual roles extends throughout the book. Gabriel is a male ballerina; Pedro-Trouscaillon, the fascist cop, is accused of being a sex fiend interested only in little girls; Charles is the confused romantic cabbie who becomes engaged when he is proposed to by the barmaid, Mado P'tits-Pieds; and the widow, Madame Mouaque, is a hopelessly romantic nymphomaniac in love with love. Only Zazie, who was nearly raped by her father, remains beyond the sexual tension. But even she is haunted by memories and becomes curious about her uncle (a "hormosexual"?) and the cop (a "sex fiend"?).

Between the extremes of the attempted rape by Zazie's father and the "artistic" sublimation of sex on Gabriel's part through a nightclub ballet act, there exists no "normal" expression of love, of sex, or of tenderness. All is show, distortion, obsession, repression.

[7] *"Zazie,"* The *New York Herald Tribune*, November 19, 1961, p. 32.

Only Zazie, in her uncorrupted innocence, remains as a hopeful individual who can "age" despite the confusion around her. "My ass," her put-down of the pretense she confronts, is a direct and honest expression of her healthy approach to language and life—an attitude Queneau obviously endorses.

Malle heightens Queneau's interest in the relationshp of language-identity-sexuality in the Eiffel Tower scene while also increasing the cinematic significance of the scene. First he presents a rapid montage of shots from various angles to give us the tower from a variety of perspectives. As Gabriel, Zazie, and Charles rise in an elevator crowded with tourists from around the world, we hear the foreign languages speeded up until they become gibberish. From the observation platform, Gabriel begins a speech, when suddenly Zazie almost falls off. As he grabs her, his glasses fall and land on an old woman reading a magazine at the foot of the tower. In a blind haze he begins to speak of Paris as a dream within a dream as he ascends further up the tower, pursued by a group of Germanic blonds. Meanwhile Malle's camera follows Zazie and Charles as they carry on Queneau's dialogue about sex and love (Zazie being bold, Charles shy and defensive) while they descend the stairs. As Zazie's questions become increasingly bizarre and personal, both image and dialogue are speeded up until they are blurred.

Oblivious to any danger, Gabriel, carried away by his own rhetoric, climbs ever higher up the tower; he is struck by a sea wave and finally by an arctic wind as a polar bear rests in one corner of the tower. Paying no attention to his four lovely followers, who are very sexy and obviously taken by his performance, he grabs a yellow weather balloon from a scientist and floats off into the sky. The scene ends as he drops down beside the woman reading the magazine, retrieves his glasses, and waits for Zazie to return.

Bombastically played by a talented young Philippe Noiret, Gabriel is literally carried away by his own language in what emerges as a form of masturbation. Though surrounded by readily available blonds, he can think of nothing but his own speech as he climbs to the tip of Paris' "phallus" and "climaxes" by floating away, only to descend abruptly after his excitement. I do not mean to suggest that Malle is blatant in his development of this alteration of Queneau's text, for certainly the scene plays as a comic moment on a literal visual level. But given the concern with the themes of sexuality and self-absorption throughout the book, Malle's staging of the tower scene subtly elaborates Queneau's text.

In terms of film-as-film, the scene continues Malle's interest in slapstick and silent comedy as well as his delight in gimmicks such as fast motion. Furthermore, by staging both conversations in motion instead of as static pieces as in the novel, Malle increases our interest in the action and dialogue. Queneau's prose is "cinematic" in its ability to approximate rapid montage. Malle, on the other hand, can create a flow of images and sound directly through film to reflect Zazie's speeded-up world, as in the descent of the tower, giving the audience an even more immediate experience of Zazie's spirit than is possible in the novel. Obviously Malle could have chosen to be more "literary" and thus more directly faithful to the text by, for instance, using a voice-over narrator who would speak Queneau's prose to us as the images became simply illustrations of the text. But the fact that he did not opt for such an approach again suggests how strongly Malle pursued his desire to explore and comment on cinema through cinematic "language."

Malle has also gone beyond Queneau in depicting a Wonderland that becomes a nightmare. More so than in the novel, Paris becomes increasingly surrealistic and absurd. The bright early scenes give way to a gaudy Parisian neon night. The strong focus on Zazie fades into a middle-distance and long-shot view of an enveloping chaos (the nightclub finale) during which Zazie sleeps. Individual action breaks down into mass confusion, and language is replaced by violence and noise.

The nightclub sequence is Malle's most scathing critique of contemporary French society. Queneau's closing chapters, which include a visit to several clubs with time out for onion soup in between, are condensed into two elaborate club scenes. Malle's sequence begins at the nightclub, with Gabriel rehearsing on stage with dancers in a deep-focus shot that reminds us of the newspaper dinner scene in *Citizen Kane* (1941) as Zazie plays piano. And the ending occurs in the remodeled cafe that has become a super-modern restaurant in a parody/variation of the liberating, chaotic conclusion of the Marx Brothers' *Duck Soup* (1933).

Behind Queneau's contemporary Paris of the novel lies the fresh remembrance of things past under the Nazi Occupation. Besides the background indications of the past such as the flea market with its American army-surplus goods and the direct allusions to the war, there is the figure of Pedro-Trouscaillon, who appears under a variety of "identities" as a friendly stranger, a dirty old man, an undercover cop, a storm-trooper leader, and a train conductor, but whose true character, despite his manipulation of language and roles, remains constant: He is an insecure, power-hungry fascist (in the text he is often referred to simply as "the type").

In the film Malle indicates even more forcefully that French society is under attack from two forces: Fascism and modernization (which the French usually refer to as "Americanization"). Pedro-Trouscaillon is not only a fascist "type" in Malle's version, he is dressed specifically to resemble Mussolini as he leads an army into the nightclub to attack Gabriel and his bourgeois artistic friends. Storm troopers pour through doors and windows, machine guns sputter, and bombs explode. As in Chaplin's *The Great Dictator* (1940), comedy gives way to frightening allegory. But the violence done to Paris is made even more bizarre by the futuristic plastic decor in garish colors that we see replacing and covering up the traditional Paris throughout the film.

The final "battle" sequence effectively brings together Malle's critiques of cinema and French society. The pacing, the destruction and confusion, the rapid editing of shots, the use of classical music as a strong counterpoint (a decade before Kubrick's blend of Beethoven and violence in *A Clockwork Orange* [1971]), and the staccato sound of the machine guns build to nightmare intensity as Zazie sleeps undisturbed in the center of the cafe-battlefield. There is even a brief shot of one of the cameramen being caught in the melee filmed by yet another camera. As a film sequence, the scene is meant not only to remind us of famous sequences such as the conclusion to *Duck Soup* in terms of both technique and content, but also to suggest the power of film language to convey an image, a message, an experience that goes beyond time and space. The comic surrealism of the Marx Brothers and of Malle in these particular endings suggests the universality of war and the struggle for power. Yet Malle's "critique" affects us on a level beyond comedy and satire because he is dealing not with a mythical Freedonia but with a contemporary representation

of Paris haunted by Mussolini-like individuals capable of manipu-
lating not only brute force but language—and thus identity and
sexuality as well. The theme of modernization is critiqued more
strongly than in the novel as Malle shows the ultramodern supper
club being ripped apart to expose the original cafe that remains
beneath the cosmetic architecture (Jacques Tati's *Playtime*
[1967] takes this scene and theme to even greater lengths).

The ending is a relief, not a solution. Zazie has managed to
sleep through the cafe-war just as she escaped the horrors of
World War II—because of her youth. Yet she is a war baby and
must inherit the restless confusion that peace and Americanization
have brought. The destruction of plastic decor in one cafe will not
halt the modernization of the rest of Paris, a city of traffic jams,
foreign-speaking tourists, strikes, and neon noise. And although
Pedro-Trouscaillon-Mussolini is carted off at the end of the cafe
sequence, Malle has him return as a conductor on the métro,
which finally reopens, as Zazie is being taken to her mother at the
train station for the trip home. Unrecognized because of his new
"identity", the "type" endures to become a threat on yet future
occasions.

Louis Malle's *Zazie*, representative of the New Wave films of
the time, is both objective and personal. Queneau's text allowed
him an objective framework to build upon, but Malle's elaboration
and intensification of the novel reflect his personal disgust with
French society in 1960. He has stated often that he had become so
depressed with the shallowness of Paris at that time that he wished
to leave the country. François Truffaut's Antoine Doinel in *The
400 Blows* (1959) is more obviously autobiographical than
Malle's Zazie, yet in Zazie's healthy refusal to take seriously the
chaos around her, Malle has invested much of his own critique of
the times. And, ironically enough, he has expressed that critique
through his own recombination of the language of film comedy
created by Hollywood silent and sound comedians.

Malle's Zazie Twenty Years Later

Malle has made a variety of films, but many of his best have
centered on children and young teenagers. Besides *Zazie dans le
Métro*, there have been *A Murmur of the Heart* (*Le Souffle au*

Coeur, 1971), *Lacombe Lucien* (1973), *Black Moon* (1975), and *Pretty Baby* (1978). Why children? He has explained that as a child he was concerned with the trauma of entering the world of adults, and he views this point as a moment of truth. "I see a lot of children at that age have a moment of total lucidity," he has stated, "but the moment you become part of this world of adults, you are just one of them: you start cheating and lying."[8]

The line of development from *Zazie* to *Pretty Baby* is a diverse one, yet Malle's basic concerns have remained remarkably consistent. From the sense of speed and parody in *Zazie*, he has moved on to the warmly comic emotions of *A Murmur of the Heart*, a film that he had to wait to make because it was more closely personal than *Zazie* (he speaks of it as his *400 Blows*). Next, in *Lacombe Lucien* comedy began to fade almost entirely as Malle explored the complicity of the French people during the Occupation and the darker regions of innocence through the life of his young assassin. Most recently in *Pretty Baby*, a film that in its minimalist plot and simplicity of technique appears as the exact opposite of *Zazie*, he has depicted the attractive calm and innocence of Violet, a young teenager in an old Storeyville, New Orleans, brothel.

Brooke Shields's long humorless glances as Violet in *Pretty Baby* may seem far removed from Catherine Demongeot's bouncy performance as Zazie. Certainly the focus of the two films is radically different: *Zazie* goes beyond a postcard view of Paris to expose the comic absurdity of present-day France, while *Pretty Baby*, in Malle's words, attempts to make decadence seem "attractive."[9] But Violet and Zazie are sisters in their innocence and lucidity. Both have observed the violence, sexuality, and confusion of identity that the adults around them reflect, yet both have had the resilience not to be shattered or corrupted by such knowledge. "I aged," says Zazie in her final close-up. Violet does not speak, but her final glance, which becomes a freeze frame as she leaves New Orleans for a middle-class family life in St. Louis, conveys that despite her experiences, she is still more child than woman.

---

[8] Louis Malle, in Andrew Horton, "Creating a Reality That Doesn't Exist: An Interview with Louis Malle," *Literature/Film Quarterly*, Vol. 7, No. 2, 1979, p. 88.
[9] Ibid., p. 92.

Zazie twenty years later? As a cinematic time capsule, Malle's film reminds us how much we have aged since 1960. *Zazie*, considered scandalous by many twenty years ago (the English subtitles softened much of Queneau's original language), now appears more cute than cutting. Yet the film is still remarkably fresh and pertinent. We feel in *Zazie* today the buoyant high energy of Louis Malle as a young director intoxicated with the potential of film for parody and self-expression. And we recognize in Malle's critique of contemporary Paris an awareness of individual and social ills that have merely intensified since *Zazie* was shot.

Robert Bresson, for whom Malle worked as an assistant director on *Un Condamné à Mort S' Est Échappé* (1956), has said that "a virtuoso makes us hear the music not as it is written, but as he feels it."[10] Louis Malle has succeeded in *Zazie dans le Métro* in creating a film that endures on its own merit. He has played Queneau's novel as he felt it.

[10] Robert Bresson, *Notes On Cinematography*, translated by Jonathan Griffin, New York, Urizen Books, 1975, p. 9.

RUTH PRIGOZY

A MODERN PIETÀ
De Sica's *Two Women* (1961)

from the novel by Alberto Moravia

"De Sica's love for his characters radiates from the people themselves. They are what they are, but lit from within by the tenderness he feels for them."[1] André Bazin's description of the special quality of Vittorio De Sica's work suggests at the same time the premise upon which the noted Italian director approached the task of adapting Alberto Moravia's *La Ciociaria* (1957)[2] to the screen. Both novel and film (1961)[3] present war and its effect upon the lives of the ordinary Italian peasantry and petty bourgeoisie. Moravia's, however, is a philosophical statement expressing, through the growing awareness of the narrator, Moravia's conviction that through suffering and compassion for others, the individual can find sufficient reason to go on living in a bewildering, indeed punishing and absurd world. The film, although arriving at a similar conclusion, does so in essentially humanistic terms: The capacity to feel, to love, is ultimately redemptive, and the emphasis is on the purity and tenderness of the love flowing between mother and daughter, a love which ultimately triumphs over their brutalizing experiences. What is in the novel primarily an exploration, with existential overtones, of the meaning of human actions becomes in the hands of De Sica and his screenwriter Cesare Zavattini (a collaboration which Bazin ragarded as the most "perfect example in the history of the cinema of a symbi-

---

[1] André Bazin, *What Is Cinema?* translated by Hugh Gray, Berkeley, University of California Press, 1971, Vol. 2, p. 62.
[2] Published as *Two Women*, translated by Angus Davidson, New York: Farrar, Straus & Giroux, 1958.
[3] The film was released in Rome in 1960 and in New York in 1961.

osis of screen writer and director"[4]) a tender portrait of the misery of a mother and daughter. Their feelings deadened, their own relationship damaged, the two women find through the daughter's love for a young intellectual murdered by the Nazis the sorrow that finally draws them together, renews their love, and heals their wounded spirits. De Sica's selection of scenes and incidents from the novel is consistent with his decision to transmute Moravia's philosophical and political skepticism, as well as his narrowly biological view of human sexuality, into an affirmation of the human capacity for love and endurance. In De Sica's hands, the canvas shrinks as broad implications of the novel are subordinated to the private drama of Cesira, Rosetta, and later—as the focus shifts to a triangular love story—Michele.[5]

For Moravia, the experiences which led to the writing of *Two Women* were intense and unforgettable. In 1943, knowing that his anti-Fascist articles in the *Popolo di Roma* would lead ultimately to his arrest, Moravia tried to escape to Naples. Unable to cross the frontier, he was forced to spend the winter of 1943–44 in Fondi, a little town in the mountains of Ciociaria just north of the front. Moravia lived in a stable, in conditions almost identical to those of his narrator, Cesira; the hardships he endured and the close contact with the Italian peasantry and city refugees formed impressions which he began to fictionalize in Rome in 1944. Because the experience was still too fresh, he put the work aside and did not take it up again until more than ten years had passed. For critics of Moravia, the publication of the novel in 1957 revealed a new writer; his languishing literary reputation was revived by this subtle, powerful novel which had as its narrator the most successful and complex female character he had ever drawn. Indeed, Moravia seemed in *Two Women* to have resolved his earlier problems with point of view, for from beginning to end the action evolves through the consciousness of the petty-bourgeois shopkeeper, Cesira, as she learns that life means more than having money stored under the mattress. For De Sica, the setting of the film—the Ciociaria mountains—would become equally important:

[4] Bazin, op. cit., p. 63.
[5] It is ironic that Moravia, who up to the publication of *Two Women* was regarded as a novelist whose interest was in character, should have his first *social* novel made into a film primarily of character.

To shoot *Two Women* he returned to his birthplace, the province of Ciociaria, where he was raised in the small town of Sora.

The novel opens with Cesira's memories of her girlhood and her loveless but economically advantageous marriage to an elderly, repellent Roman shopkeeper. Cesira's fundamental cast of mind is revealed at once: She is thoroughly materialistic, calculating, selfish, and, until the birth of her daughter, unloving. Because she pours her passion into her home, her shop, and her child, Rosetta, she is uninterested in sex and remains throughout her marriage a chaste wife. Indeed, to Cesira, the idea of sex "almost disgusted me" (p. 4).[6] The years from 1940 to 1942 are the happiest of her life; she has been widowed, and although the war is on, she is profiting handsomely from the black market. She even asks Rosetta to "pray God the war may go on another couple of years, then you'll not only put together a nice trousseau and dowry, but you'll become rich" (p. 9). She knows nothing—and cares less—about the issues over which the war is being fought: "Let them slaughter each other as much as they pleased. . . . my shop and my flat were all I needed to be happy. . . . Germans, English, Americans, Russians—they were all the same to me" (p. 6).

The war reaches Rome, however, and Cesira and Rosetta are forced to leave, for Cesira, in her avarice, has sold all of the provisions that might have saved them from starvation in Rome. They first seek refuge in the filthy, vermin-infested hovel of black-marketeer Concetta and her two sons but leave when Fascist soldiers threaten to take Rosetta as their maid. They find their way, through the help of a shopkeeper with "a mania for making money," to the mountains of Ciociaria, where peasants and evacuees are living in tense expectation of the British invasion. After their welcome at a bountiful lunch served by residents of the little mountain town of Sant'Eufemia, Cesira and Rosetta settle down to months of waiting—months during which provisions grow scarce, the winter cold and rain drive them indoors, and bombing threatens their existence. Paradoxically, to Cesira these months in the mountains—the poorest days of her life—prove the happiest, for she finds here "the profound calm, the complete lack of fear and anxiety, the confidence in myself and in outward things" (p. 180).

[6] All quotations are from *Two Women*, translated by Angus Davidson, New York, Manor Books, 1974.

De Sica's film version of *Two Women* transmutes Moravia's narrow views of sexuality into an affirmation of human love by focusing on the relationship between Cesira (Sophia Loren) and her daughter Rosetta (Eleanora Brown). *Photo courtesy of Museum of Modern Art*

What the women find in the mountains are ties to other human beings, appreciation of the beautiful countryside, and above all, Michele, of whom Cesira would become "as fond . . . as if he had been my own son" (p. 110). Michele, son of shopkeeper Filippo (who shares Cesira's mercantile mentality), is the antithesis of Cesira: He is a committed idealist who detests Fascists and priests (although he has a genuinely religious sensibility) and constantly criticizes the narrow selfishness of the Italian peasant who, by his eternal refusal to relinquish a childish concentration on individual economic survival, by his avoidance of the moral responsibility for his countrymen, and by his unwillingness to recognize the barbarism of the Nazis, has been responsible for the defeat of Italy. Michele touches Cesira's hidden life; he forces her to ask questions that reach beyond the tight spheres of her existence. Michele believes that individuals are not separated from the consequences of their actions. The Italians are paying through their suffering for their passivity in allowing Fascism to flourish. His existential message is that the individual act becomes the meaning. His own death—a martyrdom—is thus consistent with his beliefs. Cesira, through her own experiences, eventually learns the meaning Michele has tried to convey.

Rosetta, herself deeply religious, sees in Michele—despite his anticlericalism—the passion of a true believer. Michele is the catalyst for Cesira. As the three of them walk together on the mountains, Cesira experiences new, unexpected feelings; she reflects that "if there had been a man there who had attracted me and who I could have loved, love itself would have had a new savor, more profound and more intense" (p. 171). Their mountain sojourn ends after Michele, who "had been like a father and brother" (p. 246), is taken off as a guide by some fleeing German soldiers and the evacuees seek to return to their homes newly liberated by British and American troops.

Moravia's novel is episodic; there are eighteen incidents during the time the women spend in the mountains, all serving to develop his philosophical and political speculations. The key episode is undoubtedly the scene in which Michele attempts to read the biblical story of Lazarus to a group of bored peasants and evacuees who would prefer a love story. Infuriated at their inattention, he shouts at them, "You are all dead, we are all dead" (p. 137). Thus, the theme of death—and spiritual rebirth with which the book will end—is directly presented to the reader.

The novel then takes up the journey of the two women after they leave Sant'Eufemia, and Moravia uses it to comment tellingly on the nature of British and American liberating armies. When the two women reach Cesira's birthplace, the deserted town of Vallecorsa, they encounter a convoy of soldiers, including Moroccans, allies of the liberation army. Cesira notes once again how the war forces people out of their native habitations. Wearily, the two seek refuge in a deserted church, where they are attacked by the Moroccans. Cesira's furious defense prevents her own rape, but Rosetta is violated brutally by the barbaric soldiers. The last quarter of the novel details Rosetta's conversion from an "angel" to a cynical, avidly sexual prostitute, as well as Cesira's suicidal despair, which culminates in a vision of Michele telling her, indistinctly but surely, that life is better than death. By the last pages, she and Rosetta, through their sorrow at the news of Michele's death, find the strength to weep, thus releasing their deadened feelings and allowing them to return to life, "a poor thing full of obscurities and errors, but nevertheless the only life that one ought to live as no doubt Michele would have told us if he had been with us" (p. 339).

The novel is rambling and loosely structured, with the rape scene serving as focal point both for dramatic action and—coming as it does absurdly, after the warfare has ended—for philosophical speculation. Perhaps Moravia's greatest achievement in this poignant evocation of the harrowing war years is his narrator, whose direct, earthy voice and determination to comprehend the bewildering events into which she has been thrust make this tale of human endurance and spiritual redemption so powerful.

When De Sica and Zavattini began their collaboration on *Two Women*, they had not worked together for several years. The Moravia work appealed to both men as an opportunity to return to a subject set close to the era when they had begun their fruitful partnership, which had produced *Bicycle Thief* (1948), *Miracle in Milan* (1950), and *Umberto D* (1952). By the mid-fifties, however, neorealism was no longer the dominant force in Italian cinema.[7] De Sica himself had become noticeably more romantic; his love and compassion for his characters, critics felt, lapsed frequently into sentimentality.[8] For De Sica and Zavattini, *Two Women* served, as it had for Moravia, to renew an artistic reputation.

The central problem in adapting *Two Women* to the screen was in the selection of scene and incident that would telescope the loose, episodic novel, provide a dramatic focus, and, without the benefit of a first-person narrator, make Cesira (played by Sophia

[7] See Pierre Leprohon, *The Italian Cinema*, translated by Roger Greaves and Oliver Stallybrass, New York, Praeger, 1972, pp. 125–132. There was, however, a revival of war films in Italy which attempted to demythologize the events of the forties. In *Two Women* the grainy realism of the forties is missing, but the Italian peasants are unheroic, the violators are part of the liberation forces, and the future of Italy is cloudy.

[8] De Sica's films in the period just preceding *Two Women* are *Indiscretions of An American Wife* (1952), *The Gold Of Naples* (1954), and *Il Tetto* (1956).

Loren) the emotional pivot of the action, sufficiently compelling to sustain the viewer's interest throughout the film.

Like the earlier collaborations between director and screen-writer, *Two Women* uses a number of short scenes or vignettes which through careful sequential arrangement acquire dramatic intensity. Up to the rape scene, which artistically and dramatically is the most impressive in the film, De Sica employs a series of carefully framed pictorial images which serve as leitmotifs for the film's multiple meanings. The opening scene—a street in Rome, sirens screaming, airplanes overhead, people running in all di-rections—captures swiftly the chaos and terror of war, the back-ground against which the human drama is played out. The next shot takes us inside Cesira's shop, which is damaged by a nearby exploding shell. De Sica introduces here the first visual symbol, which will recur frequently and will conclude, just as it began, the story of Cesira and Rosetta. Rosetta has fainted from the shock of the bomb (Cesira says she has a weak heart, which is mentioned nowhere in the book), and Cesira cradles her daughter in her arms. As the film unfolds, this image of mother and daughter be-comes the visual analogy for Madonna and Child—the Christian symbol at the center of Rosetta's pure faith, the image which is violated by the war, thus signifying the spiritual loss Italy has sustained under Fascism. The shot of mother and daughter locked in each other's arms will also symbolize the purity of their love, the security which they can find only in each other, and finally, their isolation from a world in which a love like theirs has been ren-dered obsolete. Cesira's protectiveness of Rosetta, her attempts to keep her a child—an "angel"—visually rendered by her proud maternal glances, her efforts to comb and smooth Rosetta's hair, and the tender stroking of Rosetta's cheek become an ironic com-mentary on the girl's vulnerability. In war no one is safe; even Cesira cannot protect Rosetta from the ultimate violation. Indeed, Cesira's fierce sexual protectiveness of Rosetta—she guards her from leering soldiers and keeps her from overhearing married women's sexual jokes[9]—ends in tragic desperation when she can

---

[9] The dialogue in the film is richly colloquial; De Sica captures the colorful tongue of the Italian peasant, just as Moravia had in the novel. Much of the charm of the film is lost in the bland English subtitles and the equally color-less language of the dubbed version. Many Italian-speaking viewers find the peasant dialect the best feature of the film.

no longer prevent her daughter's sexual violation, the most savage wartime casualty.

Visual ironies abound. In the scene where Cesira and Giovanni make love, the darkness in his storeroom and the sunshine outside, the high-angle shot of the lovers on the floor, Cesira looking up at the ceiling, and the close-ups that convey their tenderness and sexual awareness will be duplicated, but as nightmarish inversions of the originals in the rape scene toward which all the action moves. De Sica's emphasis on sexuality is pervasive, but it can be tender as well as cruel in the scenes where the camera focuses on Sophia Loren's body as Michele looks at her longingly. In time of war, however, sex becomes finally a weapon; rape is the ultimate form of dehumanization, as it represents not only a barbaric inversion of love but also (in writers from Homer to Hemingway) the conqueror's rite of subjugation in war.

A second image which conveys the isolation of the two women is the long shot of Cesira and Rosetta, who seem small and defenseless as they walk alone on a road, their steps interrupted by occasional strafing, with nothing ahead of them but the vastness of looming mountains and empty space. De Sica shoots several of these frames from the rear, emphasizing the road which trails off in the distance and the weary backs of the two women whose identities seem to have been swallowed up by mountains and plains.

In contrast, the deep-focus shots up in the mountains of Cesira and Michele with Rosetta in the distance suggest the freedom and possibility of the open spaces that offer a temporary respite from the battles raging below. Nature in the mountains becomes the sheltering setting for refugees who are able to discover human values in the midst of war.

One of the most effective cinematic techniques for De Sica is the close-up. Because his interest as a director is primarily in the feelings of his characters, he focuses on every nuance of sorrow, joy, anger, and despair. Sophia Loren's expressive, mobile face conveys the horror, tenderness, and pathos with which she views the action. Although her Cesira captures fully the ferocity and strength of the novel's heroine, in her extraordinary beauty she is unlike the Moravia heroine, who, ideally cast, would be played by Anna Magnani. Nevertheless, De Sica's use of Sophia Loren is consistent with his purpose in adaptation. It is virtually impossible to make her unattractive; her beauty and sexuality demand the love story which is De Sica's most significant departure from the novel. Whereas Moravia insists upon Michele's asexuality as a condition of his idealism, De Sica's Michele quickly falls in love with Cesira. She finds him too young, but Rosetta loves him from a distance. De Sica introduces an additional element in Giovanni, back in Rome, of whom Michele is intensely jealous. Thus, key incidents from the novel take on a new coloration as they become part of De Sica's effort to demonstrate that love can be a powerful force shaping people's lives. Michele's idealism is perhaps the chief casualty of De Sica's emphasis, for it is unquestionably vitiated by his involvement with Cesira, so much so that his frequent political outbursts seem either eccentric or adolescent. The clearest example of De Sica's alteration is the Lazarus scene. Unlike the novel, the film depicts Michele's anger as stemming not from the inattention of the group but from jealousy over Cesira's reading aloud a letter from Giovanni with asides about the latter's manhood. Immediately afterward, Michele apologizes to Cesira for his outburst and declares his love for her: "I'm the one who's dead. I don't say what I feel. I'm not honest with you." Thus, as the statement becomes a personal outcry, the symbolic value of the Lazarus story is virtually lost.

The many incidents during their nine months in Ciociaria are telescoped, selected, and altered in accordance with De Sica's design. A single confrontation on the mountains replaces several encounters with Italian Fascists in the novel. A trip to town for provisions incorporates three of the many incidents Moravia used to show the effects of war on the average person. The handsome Russian soldier whom Cesira and Michele meet feeds his horse cheerfully, although he knows he faces certain death. The crazed woman whose baby has been killed (in the novel, the woman's baby was very much alive, and she had been "crazy" before the coming of the Germans) offers strangers her mother's milk. The German officer who is entertained lavishly by the Italian lawyer humiliates his host with vicious tirades against Italians. Each of these scenes provides an opportunity for De Sica to express his pity for the war's innocent victims, his anger at the German officer's contemptuousness toward human life, and, in contrast, his tenderness at the delicacy of Michele's love for Cesira. Politically, De Sica softens the novel's treatment of the American soldiers.

Moravia describes the Americans as "indifferent and distant" (p. 255), "slouching along with a listless, discontented sort of air . . . all of them were chewing gum" (p. 252). They throw cigarettes and sweets to the Italians, who scramble in the dust—"an indecent spectacle" (p. 255). To both Americans and Italians, the gifts are unimportant, but they reflect each group's expectations of conqueror and conquered. De Sica's American soldiers are shown singing and waving as the trucks and tanks roll by, and the Italians seem genuinely grateful for the chocolates and cigarettes they throw.

As in the novel, new dramatic tension begins to build after Michele is led off by the Germans and the two women leave their mountain sanctuary. The liberation proves to be a false security, however. The rape scene occurs after an idyllic moment on the road: Soft music plays in the background, they eat lunch, and the beautiful Italian landscape stretches out below. Only a truck carrying strange foreign "liberators" mars the tranquility of the scene.

In the rape scene, De Sica again turns to the visual images which have served as leitmotifs throughout the film: the Madonna before whose picture Rosetta genuflects after they enter the church, and the ceiling, this one a church spire ripped open by a bomb. High-angle long shots reveal once again the isolation of the two women even in the church that ironically serves as the setting for an act of ultimate profanation. The camera work by Mario Capriotti, brilliant as it is throughout the film, is a model of virtuosity in this scene. The camera darts restlessly between high-angle long shots that catch them in the shadows of the invaders, low-angle shots as Cesira and Rosetta look up into the savage faces of the Moors, and point-of-view shots as Cesira sees with wild despair through the legs of her attacker the sight of her daughter set upon by the soldiers. Later, when she recovers consciousness, she looks dazedly at the ceiling (as Rosetta had done *before* the rape) as if to ask where God may be. The ensuing high-angle shot of Rosetta's shocked face creates an emotional bridge between film and audience. The many quick shifts in camera angle and distance are perfect correlatives to the terror and anguish the characters are feeling from moment to moment.

Cesira's first gesture toward her traumatized daughter stretched out like a sacrificial victim before the altar of the Madonna is pathetically familiar: She tries to smooth her dress and, once again, to comb Rosetta's hair. As the young girl staggers to her feet, leaning on her mother, the camera zooms up and we behold the two women, now frail and helpless as the mocking sun streams through the torn church ceiling to the bomb crater in the floor.

The last segment of the film is a clear departure from the novel. Moravia details Rosetta's decline into cynicism and wantonness, portraying her as a young animal released by sexual violation into total physicality. De Sica shows Rosetta's hardness but confines her sexual escapades to one brief adventure in exchange for a pair of silk stockings. He thus focuses on a brief fall which, it is suggested, will be reversed once the young girl has been able to release her pent-up, confused feelings about war, sex, death, and love.[10]

The ending is as visually effective as the rest of the film, but it is finally philosophically reductive. *Two Women* ends in pathos; De Sica eliminates the questions Moravia's heroine raises about the meaning of life after she is faced with the reality of Michele's death. The novel finally transcends pathos through the growing philosophical awareness of Cesira. In the film, when Cesira tells her daughter of Michele's death, Rosetta at last bursts into tears. The mother cradles her daughter in her arms, the camera slowly zooms back, and the figures of the two women weeping on the bed grow smaller and smaller, like a small photograph framed by an old carriage on the left and a bureau in the right foreground.[11]

Two Women, then, is not a literal adaptation of the Moravia novel, but it would be foolish to criticize it on that ground. Despite his rapid, mechanical resolution, De Sica has succeeded in presenting a small, tragic episode of war, a compassionate glimpse at the private drama of two women that becomes emblematic of the suffering shared by millions of innocent victims of that or any war.

[10] Robert Hatch in *The Nation*, 192:487, June 3, 1961, complained bitterly that at the end the work was "brutally truncated from the text of Moravia's novel. The tragic history of these two women is not given time and space to work itself out, so that at the end, they lose their individuality and rich, willful humanity, and become puppets dancing to a production stopwatch."

[11] In an interview held shortly after the film opened, Sophia Loren recalled that during the filming of the last scene of *Two Women*, she saw De Sica out of the corner of her eye, standing by the camera, crying too. "It's so wonderful to have a director who is a perfect mirror. Each time I played the scene, I would see him crying, and each time he was crying in a different way." *Holiday*, 31:143, March 1962.

STUART Y. McDOUGAL

ADAPTATION OF AN AUTEUR
Truffaut's *Jules et Jim (1961)*

from the novel by Henri-Pierre Roché

> The film of tomorrow seems to me even more personal than a novel, individual and autobiographical, like a confession or a private diary.
>
> *François Truffaut, 1957*[1]

In 1956, François Truffaut was browsing in a Paris bookstore when his eyes fell on a copy of *Jules et Jim* by Henri-Pierre Roché. He was immediately drawn to the title and, as he studied the jacket, intrigued to discover that it was a septuagenarian's first novel. At the time Truffaut was twenty-four and supporting himself by writing film criticism for *Cahiers du Cinéma* and *Arts*. He purchased the novel, took it home, and pored over it until, like a character in *Fahrenheit 451*, he knew it by heart. Later that year, in a review of Edgar Ulmer's film *The Naked Dawn*, he wrote:

> One of the most beautiful modern novels I know is *Jules et Jim* by Henri-Pierre Roché, which shows how, over a lifetime, two friends and the woman companion they share love one another with tenderness and almost no harshness, thanks to an esthetic morality constantly reconsidered. *The Naked Dawn* is the first film that has made me think that *Jules et Jim* could be done as a film.[2]

Henri-Pierre Roché received a copy of the review and sent Truffaut a note of thanks. Thus began a lengthy correspondence. Among the subjects discussed was the possibility of filming *Jules et*

---

[1] Quoted in Roy Armes, *French Cinema Since 1946. Volume II: The Personal Style*, London, A Zwemmer; New York, A. S. Barnes & Co., 1966, p. 5.
[2] François Truffaut, *The Films in My Life*, translated by Leonard Mayhew, New York, Simon & Schuster, 1975, p. 155.

Jim. Like many of the *Cahiers* critics, Truffaut was already dreaming of putting his ideas into action.

The following year, Truffaut adapted "Les Mistons," a short story by Maurice Pons about a group of adolescents in the south of France who discover the mysteries of sexuality during the course of a summer. Roché viewed the film and found that it confirmed his belief that Truffaut had the proper sensibility to adapt his novel. However, because of "circumstances and economic arguments,"[3] Truffaut filmed his own work of autobiographical fiction, *Les Quatres Cents Coups* (*The 400 Blows*; 1959), rather than Roché's. During the filming, Truffaut gave a copy of *Jules et Jim* to Jeanne Moreau. She was most enthusiastic about the book and saw a strong role in it for herself. Truffaut mailed her photograph to Roché, who immediately replied: "I absolutely must meet her: bring her to me."[4] Shortly thereafter he died, without meeting the living embodiment of Catherine and without ever seeing Truffaut's first feature film, *The 400 Blows*.

Several years later, Truffaut was able to film *Jules et Jim*. Although Roché's novel forms the basis of his film, Truffaut also draws upon incidents in his own life and in particular his relationship with Roché. *Jules et Jim* becomes both an adaptation of Roché's novel and the "confession of private diary" of its director. This film shows how an auteur can adapt the work of someone else and still make a very personal statement.

In the second half of the film, Jim recounts to Jules and Albert a story about a soldier who meets a girl briefly on a train and begins a correspondence with her. The girl responds to the soldier's letters by sending her photograph. As the weeks pass, the exchange of letters becomes more and more frequent and their relationship becomes increasingly intimate. They decide to marry, and the soldier requests permission from the girl's mother. Then, suddenly, the soldier receives a head wound. He dies in the hospital the day before the armistice, without ever seeing the girl again.

To many viewers this story seems out of place, and yet it is central to an understanding of Truffaut's movie. The soldier was Guillaume Apollinaire, and the incident is related in his letters to Madeleine Pagès, collected in *Tendre Comme le Souvenir*. An ac-

---

[3] C. G. Crisp, *François Truffaut*, New York, Praeger, 1972, p. 58.
[4] Ibid.

complished poet and friend of painters in addition to being a prodigious correspondent, Apollinaire could easily have served as a model for the Jules and Jim of prewar Paris. Apollinaire's story, as Truffaut presents it, leads us in two directions: both inward to the world of the film, and outward to Truffaut's personal experience.

The incident is changed in one significant respect: Truffaut makes the soldier die before being reunited with the girl, and thus his dreams are never tested by reality. Apollinaire did die from a war wound, but at the time of his death he was married to a woman he had met while convalescing, after he had severed his relationship with Madeleine Pagès. By altering the story, Truffaut creates a strong parallel to his relationship with Roché. Like the soldier in Jim's anecdote, Roché died before he could see the dreams of his correspondence realized.

Throughout the film, Truffaut identifies Jim with Roché and Jules with himself. Jim remains close to Roché's characterization in the novel, but Truffaut makes him, rather than Jules, the novelist. Jules is no longer Jewish, as he is in the novel, nor nearly so neurotic as the suicidal character of Roché's creation. Jules shares Truffaut's fascination with language and finds expressions of his own emotions in literary sources (such as Baudelaire and Goethe) at crucial moments in the film. Although awkward with women, he is clearly "the man who loved women," capable of sketching his beloved's face on a restaurant table à la Matisse. His fantasy about writing a novel with insects as characters (and the profusion of metaphors in the second half of the film comparing Catherine to an insect) is less surprising when one learns that Truffaut had used some of the profits from his first films to produce a film on the sex life of insects for none other than the son of Henri-Pierre Roché.[5]

Catherine's character has undergone the greatest change. While Roché's Kate is German, Truffaut has made Catherine French to align her more closely with Jim. Throughout the film, she identifies with Napoleon and therefore *La France*. The many women of different nationalities who surround Jules and Jim in the novel have been dropped, and Catherine's role has been made correspondingly larger. Incidents involving deleted characters (*e.g.*, the burning of the letters or the translation of Goethe's poem)

[5] Ibid.

have been transferred to Catherine. Whereas in the novel two women represent "sacred love [and] profane love" to Jim, Truffaut's Catherine is both sacred and profane, "a woman," in Jules's words, "we all love . . . and whom all men desire." She speaks the first words in the film: The screen is dark and we hear her unidentified voice, intoning lines not from *Jules et Jim* but rather from Roché's later novel, *Les Deux Anglaises et le Continent,*[6] which Truffaut filmed in 1971. The viewer is immediately disoriented since it is impossible to identify either the speaker or the subject, but the lines articulate a major theme of the film as well as asserting the importance of the verbal in a visual medium. In a sense Catherine has the final word as well, since her song ("Le Tourbillon") echoes in Jules's head as the movie ends.

Although Truffaut has simplified Roché's novel, he has retained an astonishingly large amount of its language. Truffaut's love of words nearly equals his love of film, and here his fidelity to Roché is the greatest. Indirect discourse becomes direct speech, and important speeches, like incidents, are transferred from deleted characters to one of the principals or to the narrator. It is a tribute to Truffaut's skill that his characters remain consistent.

Truffaut has retained Roché's narrator, but his presence naturally becomes much more obtrusive in the film than it was in the novel. He distances us from the action and makes us continually aware of the artifice involved in the storytelling. His is a frequent voice in the film—summarizing action, providing transitions, and giving us access to the thoughts of Jules and Jim.

Truffaut is faithful to the general outlines of Roché's novel, but he condenses, selects, and even adds, all the while developing the material in a very personal way. The initial encounter between Jules, Jim, and Catherine is taken from Roché's novel, but Truffaut makes significant alterations and additions. Roché has the pair spend months studying at the Bibliothèque Nationale in Paris before they feel prepared to visit Greece. Once in Athens, they perceive resemblances everywhere between statues and the women in their lives: "The Wingless Victory reminded them of Lucie; a female combatant on a pediment, of Gertrude; and a dancing girl on a vase, of Odile." After a month there, they are joined by Albert, a friend of Jules who is a painter. Among his collection of

[6] Noted in Annette Insdorf, *François Truffaut*, Boston, Twayne, 1978, p. 85.

sketches and photos is one of a "goddess being abducted by a hero." The trio seek out this statue and are captivated by it. Jules and Jim return to Paris "feeling sure that the divine was within human reach." Months pass, and Jules receives a visit from three German girls. One of them, Roché notes, "had the smile of the statue on the island," and Jules falls in love with her immediately.

Truffaut makes the discovery of Catherine symptomatic of the confusion of art and life which pervades his protagonists' lives. The sequence opens in Albert's Paris apartment, where Jules and Jim have come to view a slide show. Truffaut spent his own childhood in darkened cinemas, and it is appropriate that he should have Jules and Jim discover their ideal woman in a similar environment. Her model is revealed through the successive refinements of different artistic media: the photographic reproduction (slide) of an "imitation" (statue) of a woman dead for many centuries. As spectators, we experience this process with them through yet another medium: film. To heighten our awareness of the distances involved here and to emphasize the element of artifice, Truffaut has the second half of the sequence narrated entirely. Jules and Jim pursue this statue at once; Truffaut dissolves directly from the slide of the statue in Albert's apartment to a shot of Jules and Jim on the island, and the juxtaposition substantiates our feelings about their impetuosity. Then, through a subjective camera, we participate in their exploration of the terrain until the statue is located. A series of shots of the statue recapitulates the shots in Albert's apartment, while the narrator assures us that if ever they met such a statue, "they would follow it."

Truffaut adds an important scene before the meeting with Catherine. Jules and Jim are boxing in a gymnasium. Jim offers to read from his novel, which, it becomes clear, is quite autobiographical. Jules listens intently and then declares that he would like to translate it into German. In Roché's novel, Jules is also writing fiction, but without the autobiographical intent of this scene. Truffaut makes Jim the novelist to identify him with Roché; the novel he reads from resembles nothing more than *Jules et Jim*. Jules, like Truffaut, chooses to "translate" the work from one language (or medium) to another. Their activities here contribute to their own characterizations, but also illuminate the life of their creator and his problems in the making of this film.

For the meeting with Catherine, Truffaut takes a scene from

early in the novel, in which Jules proposes a toast to the abolish-
ment of all formalities while drinking with Jim, Lucie, and Gertrude in Munich, and transfers it to Jules's apartment. As the three
women descend the steps, the camera lingers on Catherine's face.
Here is the actualization of the ideal they have discovered in art. A
series of close-ups duplicates the earlier shots of the statue, which
duplicated the slides in Albert's apartment. Once again the viewer
participates in their discovery. To strengthen the visual parallels,
the narrator comments on the likeness, noting that "the occasion
took on a dreamlike quality." The scene is a perfect fusion of the
literary and the purely cinematic.

Truffaut's adaptation of Roché's novel reflects strongly his relationship with Roché, but it is personal for other reasons as well.
Through his use of cinematic allusions and through an extraordinary variety of cinematic techniques, Truffaut presents the viewer
with a cross-section of some of the films in his life: Renoir's *Une
Partie de Campagne* (1936), in the early shot of Jules and Jim
rowing with two women on the river; Welles's *Citizen Kane*
(1941), in the sequence at the theater as well as the use of musical
themes identified with characters; Murnau's *Sunrise* (1927), in the
scene where Jules saws logs on the terrace of his German home;
Ophuls's *La Ronde* (1959), in the scene before the mirror when
Jim and Catherine spend a night at a hotel before his return to
France; Chaplin's *The Kid* (1921), in Catherine's masquerade;
Hitchcock's *Under Capricorn* (1949), in the use of the moving
camera when Catherine tries to seduce Jules after she has taken
Jim for her lover; Hitchcock's *Shadow of a Doubt* (1943), with
the superstition of the hat on the bed; and Griffith's *Intolerance*
(1916); among others. Moreover, there is a production still accompanying both the French and English editions of the film script
showing Truffaut directing in a costume which recalls D. W. Griffith, just as there is a painting within the film of Jules as Mozart.
And Jules, as he is leaving the Left Bank's Cinéma des Ursulines
with Catherine, pauses momentarily before a 1928 cover from the
French periodical *Du Cinéma*, an important predecessor of
Cahiers du Cinéma, which helped support Truffaut as a young
critic. Truffaut has lived his life in and through films, and *Jules et
Jim* chronicles some of these privileged moments.

The tribute to Chaplin builds upon separate incidents in Roché's

In *Jules et Jim* Truffaut's tribute to Charlie Chaplin builds upon incidents in the Roché novel. A mustachioed Catherine (Jeanne Moreau) disguised as "the kid" races her companions as the music recalls that of silent films. *Photo courtesy of Museum of Modern Art*

novel: Catherine's masquerade, and her footrace with Jules and Jim. Truffaut combines a homage to *The Kid*, by dressing Catherine like "the kid," with a homage to its creator, by giving her a mustache like Chaplin himself. In addition, the music helps evoke the period of the great silent films. The scene captures Catherine's need to dramatize and to masquerade. But with all its gaiety, it is filled with ominous undertones. The setting contrasts markedly with the early shots of Jules and Jim frolicking over a bridge in the countryside, where the simple, pastoral beauty of nature was an appropriate metaphor for their relationship. Here the trio passes a barred fence and then enters a totally enclosed industrial bridge with iron girders and chain-link fencing, suggesting confinement and entrapment. Catherine's behavior substantiates the feeling created by the *mise-en-scène*.

Catherine's first leap into the Seine foreshadows the plunge with which the film concludes. Here too, Truffaut takes significant liberties with his text and incorporates several important homages.

Truffaut prefaces the sequence with an original scene at a theatrical performance to which Jim has invited Jules and Catherine. At
the conclusion of the play, Catherine claps with an enthusiasm and
persistence that recall a similar scene in *Citizen Kane* (1941). The
three leave the theater, and Catherine states the reasons for the
heroine's appeal in terms which define her perfectly: "She wants to
be free. She invents her life at every moment." Catherine identifies
with the liberated heroines of Strindberg, an identification which
also points to her propensity to dramatize, and that is exactly what
she does in the scene which follows. Jules and Jim pay little attention to her and instead discuss the play in a cerebral manner, with
Jules quoting Baudelaire on the nature of women. To regain their
attention, Catherine takes a dramatic jump. Truffaut has provided
a motivation for Catherine's action which is lacking in the novel; it
is a protest against both the crippling intellectualism of Jules and
the personal neglect which accompanies it. Roché's woman calls
for help after jumping, but Truffaut's Catherine manages extremely
well on her own. She succeeds by this gesture in becoming once
again the focus of their attention and in inspiring Jim to attempt to
capture this magnificent action in a drawing. Truffaut's characters
continually make art out of the materials of their lives, and model
their lives on works of art.

Truffaut's love of film also reveals itself in his use within *Jules et
Jim* of actual footage from earlier films. Old footage of Paris, for
example, adds an important note of authenticity to his period re-
creation. The lengthy footage of World War I marks a decisive
break between the gaiety of prewar Paris and the more somber life
which follows. The war, which plays a negligible role in Roché's
novel, looms large in the film. Truffaut stretches this footage to the
dimensions of his wide screen, and projects silent footage at sound
speed; as a result, the images become distorted and the movement
of the figures appears mechanized. Not only does this increase our
sense of distance from the war, but it becomes a telling comment on
the futility of combat.

Truffaut also uses the war metaphorically. The war separates
Jules and Jim, who fight on opposite sides, each with the fear of
killing the other. Yet when peace comes, their relationship becomes strained because of Catherine, and their own personal
warfare begins. Tensions are symbolized by the difficulty of com-

munication, and failure by the inability to create. Again, the relationship between art and life is close.

Truffaut makes the different nationalities of the trio serve as bonds and barriers. At one point in the novel, Jim laments that he and Catherine "only communicated in translation," and this becomes the case in the film both with Jules and Catherine and with Jules and Jim. Catherine is capable of translating Jules's recitation of a stanza of Goethe's "Rastlose Liebe" into French for Jim, but she prefers to read Goethe in French and has a copy of *Les Affinités Électives* in Germany which Jim borrows. In Germany, Jules discourses at length to Jim on the difficulty of translation and the importance of this activity for communication: "You will note that the words cannot have the same significance in two different languages as they don't have the same gender. . . ." He then invites Jim to transcend national boundaries and learn "to appreciate German beer," but typically, Catherine interrupts: "Jim is like me, he's French, and he doesn't give a damn about German beer." She follows this by reciting a litany of French wines, which serves as a preface to a quiet taunt: "Catch me," she murmurs to Jim as she flees from the house. Thus, her relationship with Jim begins on a note of linguistic and nationalistic unity. But the importance of translation as an activity with strong parallels to cinematic adaptation has been reaffirmed.

In Roché's novel, the problems Catherine and Jim encounter are principally legal, as they struggle endlessly with the Germanic legal system while she and Jules seek a divorce. Truffaut symbolizes their difficulties by their inability to create a child. Their failure to conceive separates them. When, surprisingly, Catherine becomes pregnant, she suffers a miscarriage. As the narrator notes soberly: "Thus between the two of them, they had created nothing."

For Catherine, having a child by Jim would be a way of transcending time. When she is unable to do this, she steps out of time by committing suicide and taking Jim with her. Like Jules, we bear witness with horror as her car plunges downward in a broken arc. At significant moments in the film, such as this one, Truffaut is able to do what none of the characters can achieve in their lives: manipulate time cinematically by slowing and freezing the moments of descent, just as he had done in Catherine's earlier jump into the Seine, which this scene evokes. In the quickly paced first half of the film, time seems to stand still. Characteristically, Jules records the passage of time with an hourglass, whose form remains the same while the sands shift from one side to another. Neither he nor Jim appears to age during the more than twenty years chronicled by the film. Jim is living with Gilberte and still thinking of getting married, as he was when the film began. Jules attends the cremation in the same striped suit he had worn on his first outing with Jim and Catherine. Jules and Jim live for art and thus seem to be eternally young, as Roché must have appeared to Truffaut. Only Catherine expresses a fear of aging, and her appearance gradually alters from one of romantic lushness to Nazi severity in the more slowly paced second half of the film. Truffaut signals the passage of time not by changes in his characters' appearances but by the presence of works of art which transcend time.

Chief among these are the different paintings by Picasso, which can be dated only by the time of their creation. The other means are the films we see within this film—the newsreels of the war and the burning of books.

Jules and Jim make creation a part of their daily lives: Jim attempts to capture his early experiences by creating the Jim of his novel, Jules sketches the woman he loves on a cafe table, Jim observes Catherine's first plunge into the Seine and desires to make a drawing of it. Catherine shares their continual need to shape the incidents of their lives into anecdotal stories, and few films contain as many narrated stories as this one. But while it is salutary to transform the materials of one's life into works of art, there is a danger in doing the reverse. Jules and Jim's discovery of Catherine is a good example of this, and Catherine herself aspires to model her entire life after works of art. In Roché's novel, Catherine keeps a diary and later achieves some success as a writer and illustrator. Truffaut eliminates this aspect of her creativity and instead shows her attempting to make her life a work of art. Albert's song, "Le Tourbillon" ("The Whirlwind"), is both about her and characteristically performed by her; it is a perfect summation of her enticing and capricious nature. But Catherine realizes that her life, however artful, is transient, and she seeks to overcome this by having a child with Jim.

Within the world of the film, none of the characters succeeds in creating a lasting monument, yet their aspirations are realized by the work of Roché and then Truffaut. We have no way of evaluating Roché's fidelity to his own experience, although his preoccupation with the subject of fidelity in the novel demonstrates its importance for him. It clearly has a bearing on the nature of adaptation, and on this score we are able to assess Truffaut's achievement. Truffaut adheres to the contours of Roché's plot and displays an extraordinary fidelity to the book's language. He also honors his relationship with Roché by creating strong parallels between it and Jules's relationship with Jim. His film resembles a series of reflecting mirrors: a semiautobiographical film creating a work of art out of a semiautobiographical novel which creates a work of art out of the lives of the author's friends, who themselves are engaged in the same process. Truffaut's film is an affirmation of the powers of art to immortalize experience, and it joins the august company of those timeless works which he has incorporated into it.

MARSHA KINDER

A THRICE-TOLD TALE
Godard's *Le Mépris (1963)*

from the novel A Ghost at Noon
by Alberto Moravia

Mᴏʀᴇ than any other film I know of, Jean-Luc Godard's *Le Mépris* (*Contempt*; 1963), is explicitly about adaptation. Based on Alberto Moravia's novel *Il Disprezzo* (*A Ghost at Noon*; 1954), which concerns the adapting of Homer's *Odyssey* to film, *Le Mépris* compares three works, three media, and three cultures and time periods, developing a dialectic view of adaptation.

In this dialectic view, the first premise is that all adaptations try to capture and retain certain qualities of the original, or else there is no reason for choosing that particular source. In this sense, the adaptation is a work of practical criticism which makes implicit judgments about the distinctive nature of the original. Such judgments may range from the crass exploitive view of the movie producer (in both the novel and the film), who is interested only in the sex and violence of Homer's great adventure story, to the more complex views of the writer and director, Moravia and Godard. In *A Ghost at Noon*, the writer Riccardo Molteni wants to retain the simplicity and idealism of Homer's original, while Rheingold, the German director he is collaborating with, wants to update the story with a "debased" psychological interpretation. A caricature of Max Reinhardt, Rheingold is described as "a German director who, in the pre-Nazi film era had directed . . . various films of the 'colossal' type," but who "was certainly not in the same class as the Pabsts and Langs."[1]

[1] Alberto Moravia, *A Ghost at Noon*, translated by Angus Davidson, New York: Farrar, Straus & Giroux, 1955, p. 71. All future references to this edition will be noted in the text.

Not only does Godard reject Moravia's condescending attitude toward cinema and reverse the attitudes of the writer and director, but for the role of Rheingold he casts Fritz Lang playing himself. Lang wants to retain the autonomous natural world of Homer's poem, even though it is missing in our modern age; the writer Paul Javal insists it is no longer viable in 1963 and argues for changing it to a psychological melodrama. *Le Mépris* endorses neither view of adaptation. Although Godard adopts the basic issues, characters, and situations from *A Ghost at Noon*, he uses them to develop his own dialectic views on adaptation and cinema.

The second premise is that any adaptation must necessarily differ from its source if it is to exploit fully the potentialities of its medium. In this sense, every adaptation contains an implicit theoretical comparison between at least two media. Godard compares three, implying that the psychological novel is as obsolete as the classical epic. He claims:

> Moravia's novel is a nice, vulgar one for a train journey, full of classical, old fashioned sentiments in spite of the modernity of the situations. But it is with this kind of novel that one can often make the best films. I have stuck to the main theme, simply altering a few details, on the principle that something filmed is automatically different from something written, and therefore original.[2]

In his *Theory of the Novel*, Georg Lukács argues that the Homeric epic was the only form in which meaning and essence were one, that is, a form in which abstract ideals were completely embodied in concrete particulars. He assumes that this unity is possible "only when daily life is still felt to be meaningful and immediately comprehensible down to its smallest details." This is precisely the unity that Molteni and Lang want to retain in the filmed version of the *Odyssey*. Yet Lukács suggests that by the time tragedy rises as a form in fifth-century Greece, "meaning and daily existence have become opposed to each other." He says "the novel as a form is the attempt in modern times to recapture something of the quality of epic narration as a reconciliation between matter and spirit, between life and essence. It is a substitute for

---

[2] *Godard on Godard*, Jean Narboni and Tom Milne (eds.), New York, Viking, 1972, p. 200.

epic, under life conditions which henceforth make the epic impossible; it is the epic of a world abandoned by God."[3]

In *A Ghost at Noon*, Molteni tries to accomplish this kind of reconciliation in writing the story of his marriage to Emilia, but it results in gross psychological and moral distortions. Brecht also attempted such a reconciliation in his "non-Aristotelian, non-mimetic Epic theater," which relied on construction through montage and focused on political rather than psychological analysis. He argued that film, like his Epic theater, inherently demands "external action and not introspective psychology."[4] Following Brecht's lead, Godard realized that cinema was better equipped than theater or the novel to accomplish such a reconciliation because of its material nature and the concreteness of its visual imagery. Yet Godard knew that the society which produced cinema was still highly fragmented. In *Le Mépris*, he depicts a world which is meaningless to most of its characters and incomprehensible to many of its viewers, although it is manifest in a material form which he analyzes in considerable detail, demonstrating how each separate component manipulates meaning—visual composition, light, color, motion, graphics, music, words, and natural and mechanical sounds. He chooses a story from a psychological novel but boldly strips it of its introspective analysis and focuses instead on the dramatic gestures and exterior signs.

The third premise is that every adaptation must appeal to a contemporary audience in a different time-space continuum from that of its original. In this sense, every adaptation explores the relationship between two time periods and cultures, implying that a work accumulates a variety of meanings through the ages and that no adaptation can escape the particular subjective and cultural biases of the artist. One critic has described *Le Mépris* as a documentary on filmmaking in Italy in 1963. Godard dramatizes the pervasive influence of his own consciousness by playing the role of Lang's assistant director who has the last word. Not only are his main characters Paul (Michel Piccoli), Camille (Brigitte Bardot), and Prokosch (Jack Palance) ironic modern versions of

[3] Georg Lukács, *Theory of the Novel*, translated by Anna Bostock, Cambridge, Mass., MIT Press, 1971, p. 60.
[4] Bertolt Brecht, *Brecht on Theater*, edited and translated by John Willett, New York, Hill & Wang, 1964, p. 50.

Godard chose in *Le Mépris* to reject Moravia's condescending attitude toward cinema by reversing the attitudes of the writer and director. Fritz Lang, playing himself, is flanked by a writer (Michel Piccoli) and a producer (Jack Palance).

Odysseus, Penelope, and Poseidon (as in the Moravia novel), but on an autobiographical level they also represent Godard, his ex-wife Anna Karina, and his producer Joseph E. Levine. Throughout the film Piccoli wears the kind of hat that was Godard's trademark and which we actually see him wearing in the final scene. In the apartment sequence, Bardot imitates Karina's gestures and movements and even dons a black wig. At one point in the film, Jeremy Prokosch, the American producer, receives a phone call from Joseph E. Levine, one of the actual producers of *Le Mépris*, who interfered with Godard's artistic intentions (when the Italian version was entirely dubbed in one language, Godard tried to withdraw his name from the film).

Godard implies that both Prokosch and Levine are part of a fascist system that destroys the freedom of the artist; he and Paul are not the only victims. When Lang fled Germany in the thirties and came to Hollywood to make films, he escaped Nazi domination but was then subjected to economic pressure that was also tyrannical. Godard implies that he, Paul, and to a lesser degree Lang are also guilty because they collaborate with men like Prokosch and Levine. Although Paul criticizes exploitation films that focus on "tits and ass" and Prokosch's lecherous responses to a nude swimming scene are ridiculed, Godard exploits Bardot precisely in the same way—by spending several minutes on her bare ass and by showing her swimming in the nude. Godard identifies himself not only with Paul the corrupted writer and Lang the persecuted director, but also with Prokosch the contemptible producer. *Le Mépris* can be seen as a confession by an auteur of personal films who, on one project, sold out to the Italian-American film industry.

Yet from another perspective, Godard plays Telemachus to Lang's Odysseus, learning how to cope heroically with the greedy monsters who invade their artistic territory. Both are heroic auteurs who have the courage to admit their complicity and to persist in sneaking their radical views past the censors. After Prokosch is dead and Paul resigns from the film, they are the ones who continue filming *The Odyssey*. Although he was later to renounce him as an idol, in 1963 Godard pays homage to Lang without being a slavish imitator. He ironically observes:

> I filmed the scenes of *The Odyssey* which he was supposed to be directing in *Le Mépris*, but as I play the role of his assistant, Lang will say that these are scenes made by his second unit.[5]

Paul tells a story that is relevant to the relationship between Godard and Lang. A young disciple invents a new way of walking on water, which is rejected by his guru, who considers him an "ass"; similarly, Godard invents a new kind of adaptation that is explicitly rejected by Lang. This parable illuminates the famous statement by Lumière that appears in the projection room in Cinecitta: "Cinema is an invention without a future." If one slavishly accepts the vision of earlier filmmakers and gurus without experimenting to find one's own way of walking on water, then this statement would be true. But Godard's approach to adaptation

---

[5] *Godard on Godard*, op. cit., p. 201.

contradicts this homily; his bold experimentation and brilliant originality constantly expand the potentialities of cinema and its future.

These three premises create a dialectic: The first strives for a
similarity between the original and the adaptation, the second assumes that difference is inevitable and valuable, and the third accepts the combination as enrichment. *Le Mépris* implies that it is
impossible to make a film that is faithful either to Homer's autonomous unity or to Moravia's psychological analysis because in
each case the time, medium, and artistic consciousness are different. *The Odyssey, A Ghost at Noon,* and *Le Mépris* all follow the
adventures of a clever storyteller whose actions determine the fate
of the woman he loves and define the world in which he lives. Yet
each of the three works tells a very different story which successfully exploits the expressive potential of its own medium.

Homer's Odyssey

The autonomous harmony of Homer's *Odyssey* that characters
praise in both *A Ghost at Noon* and *Le Mépris* is based on the
central function of the epic—to define what it means to be civilized
within the boundaries of a particular culture. The extended length
and the journey structure ensure that the definition has a compre-
hensive scope. At key points in the narrative, the hero encounters
anarchistic monsters either outside (the Cyclops) or inside (the
riotous guests) the civilization, whose destruction justifies the
temporary suspension of civilized behavior (murder, treachery,
whatever it takes) on the part of the culture hero in order to
preserve the social and moral status quo. Because women lure men
down to the animal level and tempt them to violate their idealistic
culture codes, which the epic defines as the basis of humanity, they
are associated with the counterculture monsters (Circe turns men
into swine, and even Penelope encourages the riotous guests). On
all levels, the epic is an establishment genre rooted in bipolar
rational thought, opposing the disruptive forces of chaos.

The epic requires a highly elaborate, formalized style in order to
give the civilized codes an aesthetic appeal; the poetic rhythms and
figures must be physically and psychically absorbed so that the
rules they convey come to seem like human nature rather than

contrived conventions. The epic contains a large number of characters, a considerable range of behavior and tones, and a compendium of practical knowledge and taste, all of which is subjected to recurring comparison and contrast.

In Homer's *Odyssey* the civilization is controlled harmoniously by the gods who determine the fate of humans, by the poet who shapes the story, and by the clever hero who is never at a loss. The action is ingeniously plotted on all three levels. The work is divided into twenty-four books, organized into six parallel groups of four that move at a carefully modulated pace. The opening book introduces three parallel journeys that demonstrate the unified nature of experience. First, we learn this is the story of Odysseus and his struggle to return home after the Trojan War; his journey of survival has been launched in the past and is now nearing completion. In the present, we watch the journey of Athena from Mount Olympus to Ithaca for the purpose of saving Odysseus from the wrath of Poseidon. She proposes that Telemachus take a third journey in the future to gain knowledge of his missing father and to develop his own manhood. From the outset, we are aware of the tremendous scope of a story that covers past, present, and future and that involves gods and men, the living and the dead.

The comprehensiveness of the scope is enriched by the many inset stories that increase the range of perspectives and demonstrate various methods of narration. The central inset tale (Books 9 to 12) is Odysseus' narrative, in which he tells the court of his past adventures. A highly self-conscious artist, he presents a dual perspective on himself as a lone survivor and as the representative of a civilization. He starts with the end of the story and then moves to the beginning, as if clearly defining the scope of his tale. When he once again reaches the end, he observes that no one wants to hear a twice-told tale, yet this is precisely Homer's technique, particularly in repeating the story of Agamemnon several times. Not only does this suggest a comparison between two kinds of narrative strategy, it also makes us wonder why this particular story is worthy of such reiteration. Ultimately we realize that the story of Odysseus, Penelope, and Telemachus is a comic version of the tragic tale of Agamemnon, Clytemnestra, and Orestes. Both stories belong to the same universe and are subjected to the same culture codes. The reason we may value Homer's narrative beyond

that of Odysseus and the tragedians is because of its greater comprehensiveness.

To reduce an epic like the *Odyssey* to a psychological love story
about neurosis and betrayal, as Moravia does in *A Ghost at Noon*
and as the writer in *Le Mépris* proposes, is to reject the civilization
that Homer defines. The value of invoking the *Odyssey* at all is to
suggest a comparison between the two worlds and all that they
embody, a path that was blazed by Joyce and pursued by both
Moravia and Godard.

A Ghost at Noon

A Ghost at Noon is a psychological novel about the disintegration
of a relationship and of the mind of the man who narrates the
events. This story of how people stop loving each other is told by
Riccardo Molteni, who believes his relationship with his wife,
Emilia, started out perfect, "by which I mean to say that, in those
two years, a complete, profound harmony of the senses was accompanied by a kind of numbness—or should I say silence?—
which, in such circumstances, causes an entire suspension of
judgment and looks only to love for any estimate of the beloved
person" (p. 5). His purpose in writing is to prove that his wife was
to blame; by his own definition, this is an "unloving judgment."

> This story sets out to relate how while I continued to love her
> and not to judge her, Emilia, on the other hand, discovered, or
> thought she discovered, certain defects in me, and judged me and
> in consequence ceased to love me (p. 5).

Molteni tries to use art to accept Emilia's death and to restore his
own peace of mind.

The main question is whether the narrator is reliable. Moravia
exploits fully the formal resources of the novel in order to develop
this ironic dimension of the work and to make us judge the narrator. Despite the rational syntax and logical tone of Molteni's
opening paragraphs, his narrative is soon plagued by contradictions. He is gradually revealed as a man on the point of "reasoned
insanity" who is incapable of distinguishing between inner and
outer experience, intellect and feeling, or dream and reality. We
begin very early to suspect him of lying, for despite his claim that

he never judged Emilia, he sees her as his intellectual inferior and blames her for forcing him to abandon his "serious" writing and accept the degrading screenwriting assignment. Early on he admits that "sometimes I went so far as to reproach myself, with the bitterest remorse, for having been capable of thinking ill of her and judging her to be selfish and insensitive" (p. 23). We begin to suspect that his dogged investigations of Emilia's feelings about him actually destroy her love and become a self-fulfilling prophecy. Despite his detailed explanations, we believe she is justified in suspecting him of using her as sexual collateral to secure a job and please his producer, especially when we examine his choice of images.

> Once she was seated beside Battista, with the door of the car still open, she looked at me with a hesitating glance, a glance of mingled pleading and repugnance. I took no notice of my own sensation, however, and, with the decided gesture of *one who closes the door of a safe*, I slammed the heavy door (p. 7, italics added).

Molteni is obsessed with a fear of the ambiguity that characterizes the twentieth century and destroys the Homeric simplicity he wants to retain in his screenplay and his life. His future is insecure, his finances uncertain. He prides himself on his intelligence and lucidity, which he uses to evade confusion and complexity. He cannot face the fact that his feelings for Emilia are ambivalent, and so he relentlessly "investigates" her behavior and is relieved to reach any conclusion, even if it is negative or inaccurate, so long as it is conclusive. His schematic view of their relationship as a movement from "perfection" to "ambiguity" is based on a false bipolarity which he uses to define and judge all experience. He insists: "The ambiguity which had poisoned our relationship in life continued even after death" (p. 221).

Before discovering she is dead, Riccardo imagines that he sees Emilia at noon. When he speaks to her, he makes "Emilia say all the things I wanted her to say" (p. 216). Although this experience disturbs him because he cannot be certain whether she is a ghost, a hallucination, a dream, or some other illusion, it also brings him great pleasure because it frees him from the complexities of external reality.

Everything had begun and ended with myself; the only difference from what usually happens in such circumstance being that I had not confined myself to a wishful imagining of what I wanted to happen, but, from the sheer force of feeling that filled my heart, had deluded myself into thinking it really had happened. . . . How beautiful Emilia had been, sitting in the stern of my boat, no longer hostile, but full of love; how sweet her words; how disturbing, how violent the feeling I had experienced when I told her I wanted to make love to her and she had answered me with that faint nod of agreement! (pp. 216–217).

At first, Molteni interprets her death as "a last, supreme act of hostility on her part against myself" (p. 220), but gradually he realizes that it allows him to transform her into an ideal form that will no longer disturb his simple view of reality. While alive, she represented the irrational force that threatened to lure him from his cultural idealism. He prefers her dead because in that way she fits more harmoniously into the fixed world of Homer's epic.

Emilia was now, like Ulysses and Penelope, in those great sea spaces, and was fixed for eternity in the shape in which she had been clothed in life. It depended upon myself, not upon any dream or hallucination to find her again and to continue our earthly conversation with renewed serenity. Only in that way would she be delivered from me, would she be set free from my feelings, would she bend down over me like an image of consolation and beauty. And I decided to write down these memories, in the hope of succeeding in my intention (p. 221).

A Ghost at Noon is about a man who yearns for the simple idealized world of Homer's *Odyssey* which no longer exists. The only way he can achieve it is by withdrawing from the woman he loves and from society into a solipsistic universe that converts madness into art. At the end of the novel, he is left alone in his silence, free to create his own world in which he is god, poet, and hero and in which everyone else is reduced to shadows. Although Riccardo thinks he is writing his own story to achieve the idealism and simplicity of Homer's epic, Moravia uses the resources of the novel to develop him as an ironic anti-hero in the tradition of Joyce's Stephen Daedelus and Leopold Bloom.

Le Mépris

Le Mépris[6] is the story of how a man becomes contemptible as both a lover and an artist by making a series of adaptive compromises. The artistic process lies at the center of the tale and controls the structure of the two story lines—the breakup of the relationship between Paul and Camille, and the making of a film based on Homer's *Odyssey*.

Godard rejects Moravia's device of the first-person ironic point of view of a madman trying to play god who controls all perceptions and judgments of the world through his choice of language. He uses instead an omniscient perspective that focuses on external events; embraces past, present, and future; and represents heroes, artists, gods, and machines. This choice is clearly closer to Homer's than to Moravia's.

Yet the world of *Le Mépris* lacks the simplicity of the epic because it is full of false gods who vie to control our vision of the events. Godard claims: "The point of *Le Mépris* is that these are people who look at each other and judge each other, and then are in turn looked at and judged by the cinema."[7]

In the opening shot, a camera dollies down a street; gradually, its huge lens takes over the screen like a monstrous Cyclops. Godard suggests that the camera may also function as epic machinery: "The eye of the camera watching these characters in search of Homer replaces that of the gods watching over Ulysses and his companions."[8]

In the inner film, the gods are represented by magnificent classical statues with painted eyes, posed against the heavens. Godard cuts to shots of Minerva or Neptune whenever Paul is taking an important step toward his salvation or doom, as if these statues were controlling his fate. The film uses the Roman names of the gods rather than the Greek because the adaptation is being produced by an imperialist who is willing to sacrifice the purity of Greek classicism to create a spectacle on a colossal Roman scale.

---

[6] Some of this material is adapted from the discussion of *Le Mépris* in Chapter 6 of Marsha Kinder and Beverle Houston's *Close-Up: A Critical Perspective on Film*, New York, Harcourt Brace Jovanovich, 1972.
[7] *Godard on Godard*, op. cit., p. 201.
[8] Ibid.

In his Roman villa, Prokosch shows Paul a book on Roman art which he plans to use for the art direction of the film; when Paul reminds him that the *Odyssey* is Greek, Prokosch admits he prefers the Roman vision.

Athena and Poseidon are also transformed into human characters—Camille and Prokosch—who similarly try to direct Paul's actions. In one shot, Godard cuts from the divine statue to Camille, wearing dark sunglasses and standing in a boat against the sea and sky; as she stares at Paul, she silently tries to use her powers to prevent him from again passing her off onto Prokosch. In the apartment sequence, she adopts various disguises toward the same end but fails repeatedly, even when she plays Venus. Prokosch is also linked with a classical statue in the screening room, where he imitates the discus thrower by tossing cans of film he disdains. Outside, he struts on a platform like a tyrannical god, pompously quoting homilies from his little red book. Although he is primarily identified with Poseidon (Odysseus' archenemy), he also doubles as Pluto, the God of the underworld, who steals Camille from her artist husband, just as Eurydice was taken from Orpheus. This is foreshadowed the first time the three characters come together; Prokosch races between Camille and Paul in his red sports car, which ultimately drives her to a violent death.

The film is also full of artistic gurus and gods who are evoked in stories and allusions, either verbally or visually. When Paul and Camille go to the theater, we see posters of *Psycho* and *Hatari* that pay homage to Hitchcock and Hawks. In the bathing scene, Paul imitates Dean Martin in *Some Came Running*. There is explicit praise for *Rio Bravo* and *Rancho Notorious*. Though he himself is an idol, Fritz Lang adoringly quotes Dante, Hölderlin, Heine, and Brecht and defends the supreme wisdom of Homer. In the epilogue, after the false gods Camille and Prokosch are dead and Paul leaves Capri, we return to the filming of the *Odyssey* as directed by the real artists, Lang and Godard, who emerge victorious like Odysseus and Telemachus. It is the scene in which Odysseus finally sights Ithaca, his homeland. Raising a megaphone to his lips, Godard shouts, *"SILENCIO!"*—the word that Molteni used as a mantra to evoke an artistic world of perfection. Then the Cyclops lens of the camera rests at last on the "great sea spaces" that provide "an image of consolation and beauty."

Le Mépris has a classical five-act structure, with prologue and epilogue, that gives it a linearity rare in Godard's films; however, this structure is superimposed on self-reflexive, fragmented images that are typical of his work. The prologue and epilogue are dominated by the camera and the filmmaking process. In the prologue, Raoul Coutard, Godard's actual cinematographer, is riding the camera down a street in Cinecitta. He is accompanied by Francesca (Giorgia Moll), who doubles as Prokosch's production assistant and mistress and who has no counterpart in Moravia's novel. Throughout the rest of the film, her primary function is translating the dialogue—a mixture of French, Italian, German, and English. (In the dubbed Italian version, she is assigned trivial dialogue to substitute for her translations; this outraged Godard.) Just as Coutard's camerawork alters the meaning of what is seen, her translations reinterpret what is said, offering a running verbal adaptation which accentuates the ambiguity and parallels Godard's own artistic process.

The first act is confined to a bedroom where Paul and Camille are making love, still under the influence of Venus. Paul is the worshiper adoring her perfect naked form. She asks him to reaffirm verbally his love for each part of her body. As Paul anatomizes his love, Godard begins to anatomize his film technique, switching from one colored filter to another and introducing riffs of romantic music, as if demonstrating how such components alter the tone. By calling attention to these processes of fragmentation, Godard detaches us from the love scene and the erotic feelings it would normally arouse.

The second act takes place in Cinecitta and in Prokosch's Roman villa. This is where the adaptation begins on every level: In the love plot, Paul encourages Camille to ride alone with Prokosch and evokes her contempt; in the realm of art, he agrees to work on the film and to support Prokosch's crass perspective, even though it interferes with the artistic judgment of Lang, whom Paul admires greatly; in the international film industry, Francesca fulfills her function as translator and is exploited not only by Prokosch, who uses her ass as a desk as well as a sex object, but also by Paul, who uses his casual flirtation with her as a decoy for Camille's anger.

The third and central act takes place in the Roman apartment of Camille and Paul, the purchase of which has supposedly motivated his selling out to the movie industry. Godard uses this one long sequence to collapse the two years of marriage covered in Moravia's novel. Despite its spatial confinement, the perspective of the sequence is very expansive, for it contains subjective interludes, a flashback to the earlier bedroom scene, and a flashforward to Capri. Although the primary function is apparently to delineate the dynamics of the love plot, the style in which this sequence is shot draws our attention to the aesthetic issues. Godard never lets the audience forget the presence of the godlike camera, which controls the tone whether it is pacing restlessly through the rooms like the husband and wife or standing still before three rooms through which the characters move freely, creating a marvelous sense of the space beyond. Its presence is most obvious in the scene in which Paul and Camille are arguing about their relationship. Suddenly we find ourselves more interested in watching the playful movements of the camera and seeing whether the lamp between them is switched off or on than in listening to the characters' accusations. Again, we are detached from the love story and the feelings it would ordinarily evoke, so that we are better able to judge the process of adaptation.

The fourth act continues to foreground the aesthetic issues and background the love story, as Paul and Camille join Lang, Prokosch, and his entourage at a theater where they are considering a dancer for the role of Nausicaa. Although this vulgar pop star couldn't be farther from the innocent Nausicaa, they conclude that she is perfect for the part. In this scene there is also literally a great distance between Paul and Camille as she sits on one side of the aisle with Lang and he sits on the other with Prokosch. As in their previous argument, a flashing light in the aisle between them distracts us from the emotional situation. This time it is provided by the flashing bulbs of a photographer, which remind us that cinema relies on a camera, light, and persistence of vision to create its illusions. Combining photography with the theatrical spectacle of song and dance, this sequence underlines the components of cinema that are not shared with the novel or the epic.

The fifth act takes place in Capri, which, as the location for the crisis in both the inner film and the love triangle, provides spectacular vistas that are far superior to the action. Godard claims: "Rome is the modern world, the West; Capri, the ancient world, nature before civilization and its neuroses."[9] He has described his film as the "story of castaways of the Western world, survivors of the shipwreck of modernity who, like the heroes of Verne and Stevenson, one day reach a mysterious deserted island, whose mystery is the inexorable lack of mystery, of truth that is to say."[10]

As Camille grows increasingly contemptuous of Paul, and as he is forced to admit that he knows why, he considers melodramatic resolutions. At one point he postures with a gun, as if contemplating killing Prokosch, even though he himself is the riotous guest; Godard introduces a rush of dramatic music to exaggerate the emotions and parody Paul's gesture, which seems more appropriate to a murder mystery than to an epic. The parallel between Odysseus and Penelope and the modern neurotic couple is made explicit by both Lang and Paul, who, as they walk through the glorious landscapes that have retained their ancient beauty, debate their theories of adaptation and views of how the film should end. Rather than murder or suicide, Godard chooses a modern, absurd death in a car crash. Instead of seeing her ghost at noon, Paul receives a farewell letter from his dead wife; the magnified words fill the screen, forming beautiful abstract graphics. Godard demonstrates that he is able to convert even the written word into cinematic images.

Unlike Molteni, Godard does not fear ambiguity; rather, he cultivates it in the plot he borrows from Moravia and in his visuals and sound track. He assumes that any adaptation must reflect the present as it is filtered through the individual artist and the society that shaped him. As in all his adaptations, Godard expresses boldly the originality and brilliance that his anti-hero sorely lacks.

[9] Ibid., p. 200.
[10] Ibid., p. 201.

IRA KONIGSBERG

CINEMA OF ENTRAPMENT
Rivette's *La Religieuse (1966)*

from the novel by Denis Diderot

Jacques Rivette's film *La Religieuse* (1966) begins with a long prologue that passes before our eyes and tells us that the film is based upon Denis Diderot's important novel, which accurately portrays convent life in the eighteenth century and which had a major influence on the struggle for freedom in both France and the world in general. The use of such a prologue raises issues concerning the impact of both the book's existence and of history itself on our reaction to the film.

Few people in an audience would have read Diderot's novel previously, even in France, but most viewers would have heard his name and accepted the importance of his work. Therefore, the film is to achieve significance from the significance of the author and his book—we are not to consider the film an autonomous creation. It does not matter whether we have read the novel—and the film's prologue gives sufficient information about the book to suggest that it was written for viewers who knew little about it. If we have not read the book, we must simply create in our minds some abstract and general notion of the work and see the film in the context of this hypothesized work of fiction. Indeed, even if we have read the novel, I doubt if our memory of it is expected to be more detailed or specific than the hypothesized version of readers who have not. In either case, the novel itself is absent. Thus, we are called upon to react to something that is present through something that is absent and probably unknown or, at best, scarcely remembered.

The second issue that the prologue raises—the impact of history upon our viewing of the film—is very much related to the impact of the book upon our viewing. Rivette makes two important points here. The first is that Diderot's novel, in its attack on convent life, is based upon actual case histories, especially that of Margaritte Delamerre. But Diderot's novel is based upon actual case histories in only a superficial sense.[1] The novel was the result of a grand ruse, and to some degree must be seen in that context.[2] Both Diderot and his friend Grimm wanted their acquaintance, the Marquis de Croismare, to return to Paris. In order to lure him back, they pretended that a nun, who had recently failed to break her vows and in whose case the marquis had shown interest, had actually escaped her convent and was now imploring Croismare for help. Diderot wrote most of the nun's letters to the marquis, and was so fired by the entire enterprise that he wrote her memoirs. In other words, the memoirs themselves are a fiction, and they are a fiction that was part of a joke.

But even if one admits that Diderot became quite involved in these memoirs, and there is much that rings true in them, the second point Rivette makes about the novel—that in "pillorying these excesses, Diderot's novel helped set the stage for the historic upheaval which forever changed the power structure of France and the world"—must be seen as an outright fabrication. Diderot wrote the novel in 1760 and revised it on three separate occasions, but it was not published until 1796, twelve years after his death and seven years after the French Revolution. The novel was scarcely known before its publication,[3] and it could hardly have had any impact on the course of French history, let alone world history. It is inconceivable that Rivette did not know this and was not aware that he was fictionalizing the actual history of the book.

I have already denied that the actual book has any meaningful influence on viewers' responses to the film, even if they have read it. By discussing this work in his prologue, Rivette forces the viewer to fictionalize it and hence makes the novel into a fiction which is

[1] Georges May, in *Diderot et "La Religieuse,"* Paris, Presses Universitaires de France, 1954, especially Chapters 3 and 4, argues for a closer affinity between the novel and actual cases than I will allow. This matter has been much argued ever since the book's publication. See Arthur M. Wilson, *Diderot*, New York, Oxford University Press, 1972, p. 387.

[2] May, op. cit., pp. 37–40.

[3] Wilson, op. cit., pp. 383–384; and Francis Birrell in his introduction to his translation of the novel, *Memoirs of a Nun*, London, Elek Books, 1954, p. 7.

part of his larger fiction: the film itself. Furthermore, by emphasizing a serious and factual basis for the work and giving it a historical impact, Rivette himself has made a fiction of Diderot's real novel. Since the entire film itself is a fiction—nothing of what we see is happening in the real world, nor are the episodes based directly upon real events—the fictionalized Diderot novel fits entirely into this larger fictional context for the viewer. In other words, everything is fictionalized. I will enlarge this point and claim that any film's appeal to another work is itself a fiction and must be seen as part of the entire fictional nature of the cinematic work—there is simply no appeal to anything that exists outside the movie theater; the film is always a closed and fictionalized entity. Films like Whale's *Bride of Frankenstein* (1935) and Minnelli's *Madame Bovary* (1949) both acknowledge this fact and exploit it by presenting the author of the source book in the film itself in a highly fictionalized way.[4]

The film of *La Religieuse* is not adapted directly from the novel but is based on the play adaptation by Jean Grualt which Rivette staged in 1963. The play script itself is very close to the novel, and Rivette clearly had the novel in mind when making the film. Yet the play script was more than a film scenario of the novel; it was an important intermediary step in Rivette's creation of an independent work of art. But to understand how Rivette's film differs from the actual book and how the film is a separate and independent fiction, we must first establish the similarities of the two works.

Both book and film seek to expose eighteenth-century convent life in France and, by doing so, explore the subject of human freedom—convent life for Diderot and Rivette is seen as a denial of human nature and the source of repression and suffering. In both works, the heroine is not the child of her legal father and so is forced by her mother into convent life. In both works, much of the action is divided into three segments, each dealing with Suzanne's relationship with a mother substitute—her mother superior at the

---

[4] In 1966, Rivette's film was banned for being irreligious both in France and for international distribution by the French government. There is nothing that is explicitly irreligious in the film, nor in the novel for that matter. Indeed, religion is a dominant and positive force in the film. The fictionalizing process itself was extended by the French government, which made another fiction of Rivette's fictionalized film.

time. The progress of both works emphasizes the denial of nature in convent life by showing the deterioration in the heroine's relationships. The first segment, which shows normal Christian love, deals with her relationship with the good Madame de Moni; the second, which shows the denial of Christian love, deals with her persecution by Sister Sainte-Christine; and the third shows corrupt love through Suzanne's incipient lesbian attachment to Mme de Chelles. Rivette's work, then, seems very close to the novel. The plot, individual episodes, and characters are highly similar to those in Diderot's work.

The film begins almost fifteen pages into the book.[5] It omits Suzanne's rapid narration of her background and years as a novice, instead beginning with the heroine's refusal of her vows. From this point the film seems to follow the book, presenting every major scene and, for continuity, dramatizing briefly some events that are only mentioned in the novel. Sometimes the film collapses several scenes into one, but nothing in the work is changed substantially. Equally significant is that for long stretches of the film, the dialogue seems lifted entirely from the novel. Both the book and the film are episodic in nature, and both seem to recount the same episodes, in the same order, with the same dialogue and with the same concerns about convent life, individual freedom, and the repression of human nature.

But the experience evoked by the book is quite different from that evoked by the film. Diderot's novel is an extended psychological exploration of the heroine—Suzanne's internal world is as much created as the external world in which she lives, and the external world is always seen the way Suzanne sees it and reacts to it. The technique of first-person narration directs point of view for us and limits everything to a creation of Suzanne's mind. Note, for example, part of the episode where Suzanne is tortured by Sister Sainte-Christine and three nuns:

> The Superior came into my cell. She was accompanied by three Sisters. One brought a stoup of holy water, the second a crucifix, and the third some ropes. The Superior said to me in a loud and threatening voice: 'Get up . . . kneel down and commend your soul to God!'

[5] Denis Diderot, *La Religieuse*, Paris, Librairie Armand Colin, 1961.

'Madam,' I answered, 'before I obey you, may I ask what is going to happen to me, what you have decided to do to me, and what I must ask God?'

A cold sweat stood out all over my body. I trembled, and felt my knees give under me. I regarded her three inevitable companions with terror. They were standing in a row, with sombre visage, tight lips, and closed eyes. I thought from the silence which was observed that I had not been heard. I repeated the last words of my question, for I had not got the strength to repeat it all: so I said with a feeble, expiring voice:

'What grace must I ask of God?'[6]

In the stylized presentation of this scene in the film,[7] Suzanne exists out there for us, on the screen. We are privy to neither her inner thoughts nor her feelings. These we must surmise from what she says and the way in which she behaves. The entire scene exists as a visual and concrete entity, and Suzanne remains one of the external figures that we see. In Diderot's novel we see the scene through Suzanne's eyes; everything that the heroine describes is in the context of her own reactions. The constant flow of Suzanne's words throughout the novel and the endless procession of her thoughts pass through our minds in the act of reading and take the place of our own thoughts—her experiences seem to become our own experiences, and we undergo a partial identification with the heroine.

Diderot's novel, then, is a work that dramatizes for us the internal world of character and forces us to see and respond to everything in the context of the heroine's thoughts and feelings. Rivette's film, however, limits the dramatization of Suzanne's inner world to her external words and behavior only and keeps her constantly in the context of the entire scene as one of the elements in a highly stylized and spatialized composition. The apparent objectivity of the camera leaves the scene to our own point of view, not to that of the character.

Rivette's *La Religieuse* belongs to a subgenre of cinema which I shall call "entrapment films," a group of works which deal with characters incarcerated in some way. A number of novels also deal with this theme, but not pervasively and evocatively enough to call

6 *Memoirs of a Nun*, p. 86.
7 See below, p. 127.

attention to themselves as a specific group. Since the medium of fiction is verbal language and not visual images, and since it is more adept at creating the internal thoughts and reactions of characters than the external situation, it can communicate to us the sense of spatial entrapment less effectively than film.[8] Films have created such an experience with striking frequency. One need only think of the many successful films dealing with prisoners of war— Jean Renoir's *La Grande Illusion* (1939) and John Sturges's *The Great Escape* (1963), for example—or the many successful prison dramas from George Hill's *The Big House* (1930) to Alan Parker's *Midnight Express* (1978). Film viewing itself is claustrophobic, with the viewer trapped in the dark within the enclosed walls of a theater. The screen is also limited spatially, with the picture being cut off abruptly at each end. Characters are closed into the circumscribed, rectangular scene on the screen. The sense of entrapment, then, is intensified by the enclosure of both the viewer and the characters. Even the flattening effect of the two-dimensional image—the fact that the background is brought forward and seems to surround the characters—intensifies this effect. It is this sense of entrapment which Rivette creates in a far more intense and vivid way than Diderot. Diderot's novel is a work that explores the psychology of an entrapped character, but Rivette's film creates for us the experience of entrapment itself. In Diderot's novel, we involve ourselves with the character when her thoughts and reactions pass through our minds as we read and momentarily become our thoughts and reactions. In Rivette's film, we are not privy to this internal world; we watch the character from outside and experience along with her the experience of incarceration.

We feel entrapment internally, then, when viewing Rivette's film, but our experience is external to that of the heroine. She is always outside us, and what she experiences is communicated to us by a series of spatial images. The space of the scene draws us into it, alongside the character but never inside her. The acting of Anna Karina is always competent, it seems to me, but it is neither complex nor individual enough to create the full sense of drama and

[8] The novel which most influenced Diderot in his writing of *La Religieuse*, Richardson's *Clarissa* (1747–48), depicts the heroine's entrapment first in her family's home and then in a brothel, but Richardson's work achieves its success largely through the internal dramatization of the heroine and not through its external dramatization of incarceration. Indeed, Richardson's work is considered the first masterpiece of psychological fiction in English.

enclosure that we feel.[9] Both the drama and the sense of enclosure are communicated effectively to us by the total scene—the way in which Rivette arranges his characters, objects, and setting, and the way he manipulates the spatial dimension of each *mise en scène*.

Rivette's film has the same episodic structure as Diderot's novel, but whereas Diderot's episodes are without great specificity and flow together in a continuum of time, Rivette's are generally discrete units, individual blocks of action staged in a highly dramatic and even theatrical manner. Here the influence of the stage production is quite clear. Rivette himself said of the film: "At first, I felt like doing it only as an adaptation, in order to get people to know the book; then there was directing the play, and I felt like filming the play and sometimes wanted to see passages of it become a film while still remaining in a theatrical performance."[10] Rivette uses the space within each scene to maximize dramatic effect and communicate to the viewer the psychological state of his heroine and the psychological interplay between characters. There are few films which so successfully exploit the spatial dimension of cinema and do so in such a highly stylized and ritualized manner without ultimately destroying the verisimilitude and reality of the characters and action.

Let me explore this technique by first discussing the series of grille scenes which appear throughout the film, each of which defines spatially the situation of the heroine and, at times, some other character. The grille is a sign of both separation and entrapment—it separates the monastic figures from the outside world and encloses them in the convent walls. In the opening episode of the film, the grille is also a window through which we are allowed to observe the chapel and within it the ritual of Suzanne's vows. Throughout much of this sequence, the characters remain in a careful arrangement while the archbishop unsuccessfully encour-

[9] Karina has a remarkable face, and she uses it to great advantage. But the fact that we are always aware of this beautiful and suffering face suggests that we are constantly on the outside of her, watching her. Novels can never create for us such a visual sense of a heroine's appearance. No matter how many details are given, readers still imagine a character's appearance in vague and personal ways. More significantly, we are generally inside the major characters of the novel, experiencing with them and seeing through their eyes. We no more look at them than we look at ourselves when involved in an intense experience.

[10] In *Rivette: Texts and Interviews*, Jonathan Rosenbaum (ed.), translated by Amy Gateff and Tom Milne, London, British Film Institute, 1977, p. 29.

Grille scenes throughout Rivette's *La Religieuse* define the situation of the heroine and others. Through a grille in the opening episode we observe the ritual by which Suzanne (Anna Karina) takes her vows.

ages Suzanne to participate in the ceremony. On screen left are two priests in white tunicles and black shirts, and balancing them on screen right are two kneeling nuns in black habits with white wimpels; in front of the priests, on the left side of the figure of Christ, is the archbishop in his blood-red robe and white mantle; and in front of the nuns, on the right of the cross, is the kneeling Suzanne in her spotless white gown. The cross separates Suzanne from the archbishop as her view of Christianity is separate from that of the monastic order;[11] his red garment suggests the extreme

[11] In a number of scenes, Rivette places a cross on the wall between characters, not ironically but as a positive symbol of religious faith and as an indication of the conflict between two opposing views of the Christian life—the monastic and the natural. At the same time, throughout the film we are made to associate Suzanne with the suffering Christ. In the final shot, we view Suzanne from above, dead on the pavement below with her arms outstretched like the crucified Christ.

sacrifice and suffering she must undergo if she is to give up the freedom and innocence symbolized by her white gown and accept the black habit of the nuns, who kneel behind her. The shot is straightforward, and the characters are full-length.

Throughout the film, Rivette rarely angles his camera and often uses full-length shots to emphasize the spatial arrangement of the characters. He also has the camera stay with the same shot for a relatively long time to emphasize these arrangements. In the above scene we have three spatial separations: The male figures on the left are separated from the female figures on the right; Christ's figure separates Suzanne from the archbishop; and the grille separates the spectators who view the ceremony and the audience of the film from Suzanne. By pledging herself to be the Bride of Christ, Suzanne will pass into the blackness behind the altar forever. But she refuses her vows and comes toward the grille, comes toward the spectators and us to state that she is inside the convent under duress. She holds onto the bars, pleading, but the nuns grab her, and a curtain is pulled in front of her, separating even her image from our eyes.

The next scene with a grille occurs when the family priest comes to tell Suzanne, who by now has taken her vows and is a nun, that her mother is dead. But on this occasion it is the priest who is on the other side of the grille, though he belongs to the outside world, and we view him, with Suzanne, from inside the grille. Suzanne has not passed through the grille to our world, but rather we have passed through the grille into her world of entrapment and are now with her, looking out. We have been able to do so because she has been sufficiently established for us as the major character, the figure with whom we must associate and with whom we must experience entrapment. Our movement into her world has not been sudden: After her refusal of her vows in the opening scene, Suzanne left the convent and we watched her in a series of scenes with her family; then we accompanied her to the present convent and entered it with her. We are now with Suzanne in her prison. The fact that we are in the convent with her, that we are no longer given a view of her from the outside world, brings her separation closer to us and incarcerates us along with her.

Later in the film, Suzanne has two scenes with her lawyer and one with his messenger; in all of these, the camera stays with her as she views these characters from the other side of the grille. Our sense of her entrapment and our own intensifies, but there is an interesting reversal in the last part of the film. The scene of Suzanne's confession to Don Morel begins after she has told him of her strange relationship with her present mother superior. In this case it is Suzanne whom we view through the grille. Her incipient lesbian attachment is something we cannot be involved in, and we see her trapped behind the bars, trapped in her own innocence, trapped in her own body. When Suzanne confesses to her new confessor, Monsieur Hébert, she is still behind the grille, still trapped in her "perverse" situation. But this priest will be her means of escape, the man with whom she will run off; we wait with him on the outside, looking at Suzanne, who will soon join us on our side of the grille. In the final scene which employs a grille, the camera cuts a number of times between Suzanne and Monsieur Hébert, suggesting rhythmically her approaching departure. The grille, the space on both sides of it, and the point of view of the camera, then, function throughout the film to emphasize the heroine's situation and control the audience's involvement within the film.

Highly stylized spatial arrangements are evident throughout *La Religieuse*. Rivette employs a minimum of cutting and camera movement in order not to interfere with the careful arrangements of his scenes.[12] His scenes are stable, slow, and at times even static. His shots range mostly from full-length to medium so that we do not get too involved with his characters or fail to see the entire scene. His characters themselves remain relatively still throughout long sequences. We are often made to feel the solid weight of the real physical world, the still reality of the convent walls, the surrounding enclosure of his space, and within this space the relationships of his characters.

All of Rivette's group shots are staged remarkably. Figures relate spatially one to another, and the grouping itself dramatizes the heroine's situation. Such scenes are highly ritualistic, and the ritual

[12] "There was an attempt to make a film with extended takes or even one-shot sequences, with a flexible camera and rather stylized performances. So for me it was a deliberately theatrical film." From an interview with Rivette in *Film Comment*, September–October 1974, and cited in *Rivette*, op. cit., p. 93.

element fits in well with both the religious calling of the characters and the religious themes of the work.[13] More significantly, Suzanne seems to move through a whole series of ritualized dramatic actions which emphasize her Christ-like suffering and sacrifice. She is brought before the vicar in the chapel by two nuns, her head covered by a black hood and her right shoulder bare. When the hood is removed and she drops down before the vicar, we have one of the most staged yet dramatic and effective scenes in the film. The seated and standing nuns on screen left form a triangle which opens up to Suzanne, the vicar, and, behind him, his assistant on the right. In his white robe, the vicar stands above the heroine and the other figures, suggesting not merely his superior rank but the higher moral order he represents and the possibility of salvation from her present duress which he offers Suzanne. The nuns on the left stand opposed to the vicar and threaten to pull the heroine back into their triangular wedge. Suzanne, kneeling, has her shoulder bare to suggest both her vulnerability and the flesh which has been hidden and repressed beneath her convent garb. In this scene and throughout the film, Rivette effectively plays his dramatic action against the massive convent walls, heightening our sense of enclosure, and employs a large pillar in the center of his scene both to separate conflicting groups and to suggest the heroine's moral strength.

When Suzanne plays the harpsichord in her new convent, the characters are arranged spatially in a highly pictorial and suggestive way that tells us a good deal about the present convent but also foreshadows future action. Suzanne sits on screen right, and over her stands the mother superior, whose secular dressing gown and bare head contrast sharply with the heroine's ecclesiastic costume. To the left of these two figures a nun strokes a young novice's hair. Here, the costuming of the two major figures is reversed, with the nun wearing ecclesiastic garb and the young novice looking attractive in secular clothing, a reversal which seems to foreshadow a possible change in roles and deterioration in religious values on the part of the heroine. Behind these figures leans a nun

---

[13] Rivette claimed the film to be "about theatre because the subject deals with Catholicism which is the absolute peak of theatre." From an interview cited in James Monaco, *The New Wave*, New York, Oxford University Press, 1976, p. 316.

The scene in which Suzanne plays the harpsichord stresses relationships and foreshadows events. Note how the secular dressing gown of the mother superior contrasts with Suzanne's ecclesiastic garb.

in ecclesiastic habit; balancing her, a young novice, with her hair bare, leans rapturously over the instrument on screen right. For much of the film we see the characters in their nun's habits and with their hair hidden. On a few occasions we see Suzanne's hair as a symbol of her femininity and independence, but in the last part of the film, which demonstrates the perversion caused by the monastic repression of nature, hair appears as a symbol of sexuality. The scene is split in the middle by a pillarlike strip of wall, against which stands the dominant figure of the lesbian mother superior in her ornate peignoir and with her rich head of hair. A triangle of the three hooded figures is broken by the rhythmic line of the three figures with bare hair, as if the religious seemed to be encroached upon and broken by the secular and sexual.

Even in confrontations between two characters, Rivette minimizes cutting and plays the characters off, one against the other, in the spatial dimension of his scene. In such episodes he is especially fond of using the extremities of the screen, often placing antagonist figures on each side. The space between often suggests the gulf that separates them. Perhaps the best-acted episode in the film is the argument between Suzanne and Sister Sainte-Christine, which begins in the heroine's cell, continues as they walk along the cloister, and concludes in an interior room marked by its massive walls and pillars. The characters not only play off one another but are orchestrated against the very lines of the room. In this shot, Rivette places his characters on opposite ends of the screen, using the space between them to emphasize their personal separation; but this time he dwarfs Suzanne on screen right, putting her in the rear of the shot and placing her against a pillar. The scene itself is highly symmetrical and highly stylized, with the two perpendicular figures separated by the lines of the brick and the bench, which culminate at the rear of the screen in the perpendicular pillar. Space is used here dynamically, as part of the movement and force of the scene. Sister Sainte-Christine and Suzanne are pushed apart by the lines on the wall and the massive pillar, which Suzanne holds onto for strength.

When Suzanne is tortured by Sister Sainte-Christine, Rivette again places his major figures on extreme sides of the screen, with the mother superior standing and the heroine kneeling, but this time he places three nuns in a line between them. As in a number of the episodes throughout the film, the cross separates major figures, but this time it is held by one of the nuns, and on each side of it, held by another nun and ironically commenting on the perversion of Christianity, is a rope for bondage and a censer supposedly for purification. Even in these highly dramatic scenes which manifest Suzanne's extreme suffering, the characters are placed in a stylized and symmetrical arrangement which ritualizes the action and emphasizes the heroine's Christ-like experience.

Surrounded by the other sisters, Suzanne is still isolated. This isolation can be emphasized even in a screen filled with characters, where the arrangement of figures—the very composition of the scene—tells us far more than any verbal language. In one such scene, Suzanne clutches her habit, facing us in a three-quarter shot on the front of screen right. Behind her, and stretching back to screen left, a row of five nuns stare at her. By her place on the screen, by her frontal position, by the movement away from her of the line of nuns, we have her isolation communicated evocatively to us. The row of figures, including Suzanne, almost forms a direct line across the screen, but the heroine's slightly different position and larger figure set her off and mark the beginning of her intense separation and suffering.

Rivette is true to the visual nature of his medium through his emphasis upon spatial composition; he is also true to the religious nature of his subject by ritualizing his action spatially. This visual and religious focus of his film may partly explain one of the film's most significant deviations from the novel: its avoidance of explicit sex. The book virtually culminates with three explicit lesbian encounters for Suzanne; once her nature has been corrupted, Diderot ends her life quickly. Rivette keeps Suzanne far more chaste. She is beseiged by the lesbian mother superior, but their relationship culminates in a scene where Suzanne leaps out of bed on screen right and faces Mme de Chelles, who stands on the other side of the bed on screen left. In this scene it is the bed rather than the cross which separates the characters spatially and places them on opposite extremes of the screen. Suzanne will have no physical contact, about which she already has confessed to know nothing—the moral gulf between the two characters is now wide. In a scene added by Rivette, Suzanne's travail ends in an elegant brothel, where rather than submit her body to defilement, she leaps to her death from the window.

It seems to me that Rivette avoided sexual explicitness in order to avoid any attack which would draw attention from his concerns with entrapment and freedom, and in order not to involve the viewer in such a way that the externality of his scenes would be ignored. Diderot was explicit because, ironically, novels in the eighteenth century were less vulnerable to censorship than films in the twentieth century, but also because he was working with a form that encouraged the reader to identify with the heroine—both psychologically and emotionally. Explicit sexual scenes in a film, unless they are highly stylized with a mobile camera and complex cutting—neither of which techniques Rivette uses throughout his film—involve us erotically in a way that destroys the distance between us and the screen necessary for us to react to a highly stylized visual dimension. Rivette wants us always to see and not to lose our perspective by any vicarious association.

But this emphasis on composition, which controls our involvement in the film, also is responsible for some of the work's defects. The very techniques Rivette employs create a work that is episodic, slow, and sometimes even static. Even such scenes as Suzanne's refusal of her vows or her appearance before the vicar are staged so symmetrically that their credibility is momentarily lost. Often we yearn for more versatility with the camera, for more rhythm and variation in the individual scenes and in the film's general movement, and for a larger variety of emotional responses within ourselves that only a larger variety of cinematic techniques can create. For a film that deals with so much suffering, that stays almost continuously with its distressed heroine, the relatively infrequent use of close-ups is, I believe, a mistake. Frequent full and three-quarter shots almost make us feel that we are watching a staged drama.[14] Karina, who is an appealing actress, seems to work at the same emotional level for much of the film because we never get close enough to see otherwise.

Despite all these factors, the film does succeed. It succeeds because it is true to the very visual nature of its medium, because it compels us to watch, and because it communicates so much in such an implicit and often subtle way. Rivette can communicate more through a single *mise en scène* than more versatile and better-known directors. His scenes both impress us and absorb us into them. His spatial arrangements make us react and draw us forward. Space is the basic dimension of film, and Rivette's use of space is thematic and dramatic. Because he is so true to his medium, because he is so little a showman, his film has a seriousness and an integrity that make it one of the impressive treatments of human incarceration in cinema.

[14] Compare this cinematic treatment of persecution and suffering with Carl Dreyer's extended and moving use of close-ups for the same themes in *La Passion de Jeanne d'Arc* (1928).

NEIL D. ISAACS

THE TRIUMPH OF ARTIFICE
Antonioni's *Blow-Up (1966)*

from the short story by Julio Cortázar

Four elements cohere in a dominant mode of contemporary narrative which I call the "triumph of artifice."[1] They are: (1) central concerns with the artist as protagonist and the creative process as plot, (2) technical experimentation and advances in point of view, (3) the theme of appearance versus reality, and (4) life and art conceived as thesis and antithesis in a dialectical construct. Some of the leading narrative artists in this mode are Nabokov, Barth, Borges, Fellini, Bergman, Pynchon, Durrell, Coover, and García Márquez.

The triumph of artifice may also be defined as the self-conscious use of art as play. Art is a game, and the players explicitly announce their awareness of the rules.[2] By "self-conscious" I mean both self-reflexive (novels about the writing of novels, movies about the making of movies) and unselfconscious in the sense of unembarrassed and self-confident.

Among Argentine artificers, Borges is of course preeminent. He has gone *past* the central concerns of artist as protagonist and creative process as plot to an outrageous extension of that conven-

---

[1] The phrase is taken from the late Stanley Edgar Hyman, who applied it specifically to Nabokov's novels in "Nabokov's Gift," *New Leader*, Vol. XLVI, October 14, 1963, pp. 20ff.

[2] According to José Ortega y Gasset:

All modern art begins to appear comprehensible and in a way great when it is interpreted as an attempt to instill youthfulness into an ancient world. Other styles must be interpreted in connection with dramatic social or political movements, or with profound religious and philosophical currents. The new style only asks to be linked to the triumph of sports and games. It is of the same kind and origin with them.

From *The Dehumanization of Art*, Garden City, N.Y., Doubleday, 1956, p. 47.

tion. The exploration, the intrigue, becomes a cerebral puzzle in which the protagonist is the solver, the analyst, the critic, and the refined audience of a construct that may be explicitly or metaphorically a work of art.

But Borges is not alone. Adolfo Bioy Casares has reworked the metaphor of the labyrinth of art in "The Invention of Morel" and several other stories from *La Trama Celeste*.[3] In "The Perjury of the Snow," for example, the intricacies of layers and inversions may distract the reader to delight or to despair. At the outermost frame, the story enunciates an outrageous irony: The highest act of creation takes place in the critic's eye, in the collaborative imagination of the audience.

The audience as artist (the focus on art in an extreme form of the convention) is a major element in Julio Cortázar's "Blow-Up," a short story that epitomizes the form's achievements while challenging its conventions in a compressed dramatization of theme. Cortázar, though he does not share with his countryman Bioy Casares an admiration of Borges, nevertheless shares some of his fellow Argentine master's methods. In "The End of The Game"[4] and "Bestiary" he has conducted two of the finest experiments in point of view in all of contemporary fiction. Both stories examine at one or two removes the nature of appearance and reality in the dialectic of life and art—the first in symbolic tableaux that become metaphors for the meaningful drama of the story, the second in a dramatization of allegory that is subtly reminiscent of Charles Williams's novels.

"Blow-Up," from the same collection, has gained great notoriety as the source for Antonioni's film. But it is far more accurate to call it (as the screen credit does) an inspiration than a source, though the film and story share certain thematic concerns and a few details. In its own right, Cortázar's story exemplifies the triumph of artifice. The protagonist himself wrestles with the prob-

---

[3] *The Invention of Morel and Other Stories* (from *La Trama Celeste*), translated by Ruth L. C. Simms, Austin, University of Texas Press, 1964.
[4] Originally the title story of the collection in which "Blow-Up" appeared in English translation. The volume has been reissued as *Blow-Up and Other Stories*, Collier Books, New York, 1969, translated by Paul Blackburn. All citations made parenthetically in text are to this latter edition. Cortázar's story, however, was named "Las Babas del Diablo" and appeared in 1964 in the collection *Las Armas Secretas*.

lem of point of view, and the resultant pronominal confusion is a deliberately outrageous experiment. He also wrestles with the problem of his own identity—grappling for sanity actually—in the context of appearance versus reality and in the framework of the life-art dialectic.

The protagonist is Roberto Michel, translator and amateur photographer, who speaks of himself in both the first and third persons as he wonders how to tell this story. "It's going to be difficult," he says, "because nobody really knows who is telling it, if I am I or what actually occurred or what I'm seeing . . . or if, simply, I'm telling a truth which is only my truth . . ." (p. 101). This is as concise a description of basic narrative problems as I can imagine. He then goes on to describe his walk on a Sunday morning in Paris that leads him to a small square on the Quai de Bourbon, where he sees a couple: a teenage boy and a young woman. Still wondering about the mechanics of telling his story (he uses "now" as a conjunction, and immediately says, "what a word, *now*, what a dumb lie" [p. 103]), he remembers conceiving and revising a scenario for the couple.

Then he begins framing a picture to shoot out of the scene. "Strange how the scene (almost nothing: two figures there mismatched in their youth) was taking on a disquieting aura. I thought it was I imposing it, and that my photo, if I shot it, would reconstitute things in their true stupidity" (p. 107). It is at this point that he discovers another witness to the scene: a man in a parked car. He decides to include the car in the shot, waiting until he could "finally catch the revealing expression, one that would sum it all up, life that is rhythmed by movement but which a stiff image destroys, taking time in cross section, if we do not choose the essential imperceptible fraction of it" (p. 108).

He closes his eyes, imagining where and how the immediate scene would be resolved in subsequent scenes, and then he stops himself, saying with mock objectivity: "Michel is guilty of making literature, of indulging in fabricated unrealities" (pp. 108ff). And then he snaps the picture, realizing that his subjects are aware of it. The woman begins arguing with him about taking unauthorized photographs, demands the roll of film, and is rebuffed by Michel, who has determined to be whimsically perverse. Meanwhile, the boy has run away. The man in the car comes toward them, he and the woman "consult one another in silence" (p. 110), and Michel walks off.

Days later, having forgotten the incident, Michel develops the roll, finds the negative to be very good, enlarges it, and then blows it up to poster size. He tacks it up and gazes at it, "comparing the memory with the gone reality" (p. 111). He thinks with satisfaction that his snapshot had saved the boy from a seductive woman. Then suddenly he perceives a new reality in the scene.

The picture comes alive—the dry leaves shake on a tree, and Michel impotently realizes that the woman is seducing the boy not for herself but for the man in the car. The man approaches the pair—Michel sees the scene as a "horrible . . . reality" (p. 113)— while Michel feels himself a "prisoner of another time" (p. 114). But then he saves the boy once more as Michel, who is now identified with his camera, enters the scene again, allowing the boy to run away. The focus keeps shifting, extraneous figures of birds and clouds enter the field of the camera's vision, and Michel closes his eyes again. When he opens them, the picture has become his life, tacked up on the wall of his room, presenting now a clear sky, now clouds, now one enormous gray cloud with splotches of rain, and once in a while some birds.

Is he dead, as he said in the story's second paragraph? Killed by the raised hands of the man? Or do we accept the parenthetical denial ("I'm alive, I'm not trying to fool anybody" [p. 100]), and search for a less facile explanation? The answer is that we should not seek conclusive packages. The story raises the problems of art and offers dramatizations of them, not solutions for them. Life and art are dialectically tensive; appearance and reality do contradict each other and paradoxically replace each other. The photographer-as-artist encapsulates the whole issue, the whole pattern, as he frames his picture, becomes his camera, becomes part of the camera's subject, and ultimately becomes the involved audience of his own involving artifact.

From the photographer-as-artist in Cortázar, it is but a small step to the filmmaker-as-shaman in Antonioni. And yet it may seem a great leap, particularly in the context of movie conventions, outrages of those conventions, and an infant art form that is unusually self-reflexive.

For the world of art, in the triumph of artifice, the great illusion is life itself. And this is the subject of Michelangelo Antonioni's *Blow-Up*, one of the masterpieces of fiction films.[5] Antonioni has gone straight to the heart of the matter by adopting the photographer-as-artist for his protagonist. But where Cortázar's Michel is a translator by profession and worries about the insufficiency of literary modes to tell the story involving his blown-up picture, Antonioni's Thomas (David Hemmings) is a high-fashion, a portrait, and a "decisive moment" photographer[6] who is confronted directly with the issue of appearance versus reality. Narrative *syntax* is a problem for the short story, narrative *image* for the movie.

Antonioni's visualization for the film begins and ends with a group of mimers or revelers, whose presence announces the entire duration of the action as a dramatic Dionysian period of misrule or disorder—presumably between Appollonian periods of stasis and controlled order. Even as early as the first draft of the script, these figures are described as "a group of students in bizarre clothes and with white powdered faces" (scene 1) and "a group of strange people . . . in bizarre clothes . . . all covered in white powder" (scene 90, the last scene).[7] In analyzing the process of the artistic development of *Blow-Up*, it is instructive to look back to this draft—a valuable record of a presumptive first conception —to see what has been retained, what has been changed, and what

---

[5] In one of the few genuinely illuminating essays on the movie, Marsha Kinder says, "I do not mean to imply that *Blow-Up* is solely about art, but rather that it is the main focus. As in the earlier [Antonioni] films, there is a very strong relationship between art and life—and it is not at all clear which imitates which." From "Antonioni in Transit," in *Focus on Blow-Up*, Roy Huss (ed.), Englewood Cliffs, N.J., Prentice Hall, 1971, p. 83.

[6] The phrase is borrowed from the title of a collection of Henri Cartier-Bresson (New York, 1952). His foreword defines photography as "the simultaneous recognition in a fraction of a second, of the significance of an event as well as of a precise organization of forms which give that event its proper expression."

[7] The text I cite is the first draft, titled simply "The Antonioni Picture," submitted to MGM prior to production. A friend of mine, who had access to the story department's files and knew of my interest, xeroxed a copy for me. I am very grateful to him, though he will not be named here lest he become involuntarily an underground hero of sorts, a cinematic Daniel Ellsberg. The draft differs in many ways from the edition published by Simon & Schuster in 1971 in The Modern Film Scripts series, and in certain details from what is called "the original script" in notes to that edition, pp. 117ff. My citations will be to the draft because it is probably closest to an "original" written screenplay conception of the narrative.

has been dropped. Indeed, such analysis can approximate part of the accomplishment of a variorum edition of a literary text.

Most strikingly, the evolution of the opening sequence draws attention to the prevailing concerns of the completed film. As released, the movie opens on the mummers,[8] who are driving through a business section deserted (except for one shadowy incongruous figure at an office-building window—a typically inexplicable Antonioni detail) presumably for some holiday. Shots of the mummers are then intercut with shots of Thomas leaving the reception center with the group of derelicts and driving off. Their paths cross at an intersection, Thomas gives money to the revelers, and the camera stays with him from this point on. In the first draft, however (still called first draft, though discrepancies in scene numbers and a handwritten note—"Antonioni Picture Rewrites" —indicate that the opening sequence had been revised), the sequence involves a series of quick cuts introducing all the characters important to the plot later on: the two teenage girls, the antique-shop owner and her helper, Ron the writer, Bill the painter and his wife (Sarah Miles), the models, the rock group, and Jane (Vanessa Redgrave) and her two men—besides Thomas and the derelicts and the white-faced students. And instead of getting money from Thomas, the mimers put the touch on a bejeweled woman in a Rolls-Royce.

The changes indicate clearly the directions Antonioni is moving in this film. The mummers remain, but their significance is enhanced because they are the *only* people other than Thomas on whom attention is focused, and because they are made to cross Thomas's path and awareness precisely at the point where we are

---

[8] The use of this word (which I interchange with mimers and revelers) is insisted upon exclusively (because of their function) by Armando Prats in his chapter on *Blow-Up* in *Cinematic Narrative and Humanism*, forthcoming from the University Press of Kentucky. He insists on *Blowup* (one word) as the title because that's the way it appears on screen. He also refuses to use the names Thomas and Jane because they are never mentioned. Of course he is right. I allow myself the freedom and convenience of using these names because the screenplay (in all extant versions) indicates that Antonioni conceived of the characters as having these names. (I use "Blow-Up" as a point of identity with Cortázar's story. Even Prats refers to the character played by Sarah Miles as Patricia (for convenience) or Bill's wife (for accuracy), thereby dismissing the absurd squabble among reviewers who used "mistress," "companion," and "girl friend" rather than acknowledge the evidence of the wedding band or the authority of script.

led to focus on him. The dropped material shows the falling away of concern with the conventional intrigue of the inner plot and with introducing a central cast of characters à la Fellini, or Welles in *Touch of Evil* (1958). Instead, our attention is drawn directly to thematic concerns and to Thomas as the embodiment of those concerns. Incidentally, Antonioni has also curbed a penchant for automobiles (the draft calls for two Rolls-Royces, a Jaguar, and a Rover during these opening scenes) that had been one of his trademarks for some time. Also, the final long tracking shot of the Dionysian procession has included not only the mummers' incongruous juxtaposition with a beefeater but also the startling image of very black nuns in very white habits. Again, whereas the draft was using this sequence to establish characters and situations, the movie is using the images to establish themes.

The theme of appearance versus reality is thus introduced by way of the mummers and their Dionysian get-up. The period of misrule is characterized by elaborate deceptions that are contrived and enforced; disguises or masks become essential to the meaningfulness of experience. Thomas's disguise among the derelicts and the far-out costumes of his models are other early manifestations of this motif, which is later extended to include contradictions of action and reaction, stasis and movement, violence and stillness, rhythm and arhythm—that is, faces as masks and poses as disguises. Examples are the crowd shots in the rock-club sequence, the slow-motion choreography of groups and individuals at the pot party, Jane moving against the rhythm of the music at Thomas's studio, and the scene between Thomas and the old man in the antique shop.

Dialogue is also used to stress contradictions. Throughout the film it is brisk—never high-powered, high-quality, or highly witty. This seems to me an intentional underplaying and should not be attributed to problems of translation. Sometimes, though, when underlining a central theme, it becomes ponderous or pretentiously cryptic, as when Ron, stoned, denies Thomas's request to go to the park with him for pictures of the body ("I'm not a photographer") and Thomas pompously pronounces an affirmation of identity ("I am," echoing his first words to Jane in the park) that may seem redundant. In the antique shop, however, the heavy dialogue is coordinated with the compositions and subtle pans, tilts, and cuts to supply the needed emphasis on contradictions:

"Pictures."

"No pictures."

Pictures are seen.

"Landscapes."

"No landscapes."

Landscapes are indicated.

"Sold. All sold."

Denials of perceived phenomena here are more important than mere contradictions or ambiguities. The sequence is framed by a pair of shots depicting sexual ambivalence: homosexuals with poodles strolling past the shop, and an androgynous attendant spearing litter in the park (neither one appears in the first draft). But Thomas in the shop is not himself; without camera (or props or car), without the mask of his art, he is stripped of his meaningful identity.[9] It is interesting that on his way to the shop, as Antonioni briefly indulges himself in a moving sequence of and from a weaving car, Thomas is *seen* to be singing, but we hear no sound.

That the reality of Thomas's experience can be perceived only through the mask of his art has been established in an earlier sequence: his shooting session with the high-fashion model Verushka (played by herself). This was shot, as originally written, to be a visual metaphor for fucking. The seductive atmosphere includes music and dancing and wine, and there are actual kisses in the foreplay as Thomas prepares her for the orgasmic shooting. She is wearing feathers and a shimmering sideless gossamer shift; he places her on her back, and as she writhes in a mounting ecstasy, he moves in close, arousing her with erotic murmurs while his camera clicks caressingly on. Finally, he straddles her on his knees, and when he finishes shooting the load in his camera, sighing Molly Bloom's climactic "yes, yes, yes," he rolls over and collapses on the sofa in postcoital exhaustion.

This metaphor is the only actualized sex in the film, and Thomas is never more fully alive than in this sequence. In his romp with the two teenagers he negates himself by taking time out

---

[9] This perception is shared and elaborated by James F. Scott in "Blow-Up: Antonioni and the Mod World," in Huss, op. cit., especially pp. 91–94.

from his life as artist. Yet the interlude may be said to be a cameo of the whole action of Dionysian purgation because, like a sabbatical, it serves to clear his eye (or mind) to perceive a reality in the blown-up pictures that he had missed before.[10] His brief voyeuristic intrusion on Bill and his wife is also empty; he denies involvement with them, and their act of sex with each other seems a meaningless, lifeless thing. Yet the potential traingle among them offers a mirror to Thomas for understanding (recreating?) the triangle of Jane and her two men. Indeed, the identifications between life and art help render both meaningful. The only other sexual activity is the treacherous amorousness of Jane and the victim in the park and the tantalizing, unfulfilled dalliance of Jane and Thomas in the studio. Neither coupling is what it seems to be, and neither comes anywhere near the literal satisfaction of the metaphorical fuck.

The first draft, where the "yes, yes, yes" is punctuated more closely by a ringing telephone, says, "All of a sudden, Thomas is his usual self: cool and cutting." Cold and lifeless would be more accurate, when he is not taking pictures. But he had been fully alive in his erotic act with Verushka, and he is surely "his usual self"—the living artist—as he enters the park for the first time. He is shooting randomly, and he runs up steps and clicks his heels in the air. It is during this enjoyment of life, experienced through the fulfilling mask of his camera, that he first becomes aware of Jane and friend.

Just at this point the remarkable stillness impresses itself on Thomas; the breeze's rustling—a charged peacefulness—makes the audience aware of the sound track. The draft does not record

---

[10] John Freccero, on the contrary, sees "a discovery about himself" as making him "symbolically capable" of discovering the murder. "Lying prostrate on the floor of his studio after his debauch, the photographer looks up and discovers, or thinks that he discovers, the erstwhile older lover lying in the photograph in precisely the same position. He does not as yet suspect what the audience has already grasped: just as Thomas is the metaphoric embodiment of Antonioni's art, so the older man is the metaphoric embodiment of Thomas's art." From "Blow-Up: From the Word to the Image," in Huss, op. cit., p. 121. Aside from the fact that no audience but Freccero ever grasped such a set of analogous equations, the conclusion that (Thomas's) art is a dead end "which cannot be revived by cinematographic sleight-of-hand" runs counter to the evidence in context. Rather one should say that (Thomas's) art has a life of its own.

this element, but its source is Cortázar's original story. There, the "almost furtive trembling of the leaves on the tree" (p. 112) is the first element leading Michel into the world of his blown-up picture, until the whole atmosphere of its scene—clouds, sounds, sense, and ambiance—pervades his consciousness. Here, when Thomas later perceives the "true import" of the drama implicit in his pictures, the identical sound track is played for his and the audience's ear. Thomas, like Michel, reenters the world of his artifact to relive its reality.

The whole process had been anticipated earlier in the interlude between the studio sequence with the models and the antique-shop sequence with the subsequent crucial stroll in the park. Before driving to the shop, Thomas walks into the painter's home, where he is obviously very much at home himself. Though there are undertones of strained relationships here, the beer, massage, and badinage suggest mostly good feeling; this is necessary so that the focus of attention can be on Bill's paintings, his style and method. They are explicated concisely by Bill in dialogue that is retained verbatim from the first draft. The key passages are "afterwards I find something to hang on to" and "it's like finding a clue in a detective story." The movie makes clear what the draft's description implies about Bill's paintings: A medium-close shot of a canvas on the floor shows that its texture and composition, a technique suggesting pointillist abstraction, closely resemble those of blown-up photographs. Much later, when only one meaningless blow-up remains of Thomas's work, his art, and the reality of the park scene, Bill's wife says, "It looks like one of Bill's paintings." If Thomas seems startled by this recognition, he is the only one in the house who is. The audience has long since come to accept and understand the notion of *photography as plot* that is central to the movie.

It is important to ask what happens in the park but even more important to see how Thomas discovers what has happened. In fact, the audience is far more directly involved in Thomas's reconstruction of the sequence of events than in the events themselves. Thomas experiences reality through his art, and he comes to see what happened much differently from the way he saw it when he was there. The point is that his recreation is equivalent to and parallel to the audience's perception. We are led to see what

Thomas perceives in his arrangement of the blown-up photographs as the truth.

We have nothing else to go on. We have seen Jane in the park, upset about having her picture taken, but only with the vaguest sense of a reason. An automatic assumption is that she doesn't want to be caught with the older man. Antonioni has deliberately omitted all background material by deleting from the first draft's opening sequence several shots showing Jane with her young man, Jane with her older man, and Jane aware of the young man following her and the other. Were it not for the recognition of Vanessa Redgrave, who has star billing, as Jane, we would tend to dismiss the scene in the park as readily as Thomas does, when he becomes equally animated over the purchase of an airplane propeller in the antique shop.

In the following scene, Thomas meets Ron for lunch. They discuss their book, and Ron admires the shots of the derelicts. Thomas suggests that the whole collection might end with some stuff he got in the park just that day—"peaceful" and "still," unlike most of the book. The irony here lies not in audience recognition of any violence in the park but only in the discrepancy between Thomas's cool impression of the material from which he framed those shots and Jane's heated agitation over the photographer's uncommitted invasion of *her* concrete reality. And this is where Thomas betrays emotions to Ron, confessing a disillusionment with London (assigned to Ron in the first draft) and also a yearning to be free. "To do what?" Ron asks, but Thomas is distracted by a man at his car and runs out of the restaurant.

The next several short scenes are edited with a series of quick cuts to resemble detective movies. The stranger at the car is gone. Thomas drives off and is blocked by a peace demonstration. Several signs say "NO NO," but one has been put on upside down, reading "ON ON." We can make as much or as little of this as we wish, but Antonioni seems merely to be playing more games of deception and inversion. Nothing is simply what it seems, but nothing counts for much anyway. Thomas's blowing of his horn serves no purpose except to disrupt the normal calm of his street. His phone call, and we never learn to whom, seems irrelevant if not irrational. Then Jane catches up with him at his door, and we are drawn back into the mainstream of narrative-dramatic flow in *Blow-Up*.

The long interior scene between David Hemmings and Vanessa Redgrave is remarkable for its concentration of contradictions. The erotic rapport between them seems based less on a mutually recognized attractiveness than on a mutual acknowledgment of deception—as if they were playing out roles in each other's fantasies. Yet the attraction remains highly charged because of its tenuousness and because it is unfulfilled. Moving against the beat of the music is fascinating for her, but she cannot bear to sustain it. Playing the treasure-hunt frustrations is a challenging game for him. His phone call, with its cadenced contradictions about wife and children, is clearly filled with inventions tried on for effect. But it is not pointless because it puts in perspective Jane's tentative constructions about *her* private life. He is echoing, and mocking, her trial-and-error method of providing a plausible, acceptable scenario. The scene ends not so much in mystery as in the sense of arrant falseness, symbolized by the phony telephone number she leaves behind.

To get to the truth, then, Thomas turns to his pictures, or more specifically to his art—to a recreation of an artistic reality by a process of development, enlargement, and arrangement. This is the dramatic core of the plot—the audience experiencing the artist's reconstruction of what happened. Thomas resees Jane in the park looking over her shoulder; he traces her line of vision (sipping a drink and playing some music as he works it out) and finds the suggestions of a face in the leaves behind the fence. Jane looks angrily at him (Thomas, the camera), and runs toward him as the man stands in the background. Then, in a shot of Jane running back away from the camera, the man is gone. Thomas then works up more precise images of the other man behind the fence. First the face, then a gun. (The first draft is more explicit, calling for the man "to be making strange signs, precisely in Jane's direction, as if he meant to tell her: 'That's it. Stop where you are.' ") In the final shot we see Jane alone, standing at the tree where she had left the older man.

At this point in his working out of the reality, Thomas calls Ron to tell him of the "fantastic" developments from the material in the park. His conclusion, though, is that he saved a man from being killed. The interlude with the teenage girls, with its frolicking use of costume and the colorful photographic backdrops and the free-wheeling physicalness of innocent animality, leaves Thomas with a chance to reconsider his material; then, for the first time, he sees a body. Photography as plot thus has its pattern fulfilled, but it remains for that conclusion to be worked back into the thematic context of the film. The importance of events as subject matter for the artist is established, but what about the event itself? If the artist's reconstruction, which the audience has shared, is accurate, what will be done about it?

The rest of the movie wrestles with these issues and finally resolves them, though not satisfactorily for mystery-oriented audiences. Thomas goes to the park and finds the cold, stiff body with the same face as in his pictures. Alone, frightened, and without a camera, he leaves the park, feeling that he's being watched and uncertain what to do with his knowledge. Bill and his wife, in bed, are no help to anyone, though Thomas's (the camera's) eye is drawn to a painting on the floor. Back home he finds all the prints and negatives gone, except a blow-up of the body that looks like a fuzzy, dotted abstraction. On his way to find Ron, he catches a glimpse of Jane on the street. Elusive or illusory, she disappears. He walks in on the rock scene, the crowd incongruously standing still, one couple coolly dancing, while a frenetic musician kicks an imperfect amplifier, smashes his guitar, and throws its neck to the crowd. Now the crowd comes to life, but Thomas wins the trophy only to throw it down back out on Carnaby Street. Again, this sequence is a dumb show of certain thematic elements of the film —paradoxes of appearance and reality, contradictions of experience and art, and Dionysian suspensions of order.

Thomas is now drawn into the pot party. Despite his affirmation of identity as photographer, his last response to Ron's stoned question, "What did you see in that park?" is "Nothing." In the morning, that *nothing* will become literal and then be resolved in the symbolic *something* that is the film's statement. He has his loaded camera again, but of course the body is gone. Antonioni then uses differential focus to draw our attention to "big publicity signs on top of skyscraper roofs enclosing the meadow." The neon lettering is seen clearly, but it says nothing. It may consist of T or F followed by O and then a lambda or a caret or perhaps an A, but in any case it is a typical Antonioni device to call attention to the *possibility* of meaning. What appears meaningless may be symbolic without prescribed specificity. Whether in life or through art, existing phenomena always contribute to the shape of experienced reality and may therefore contribute to the sense of it as well. But brief abstract considerations as well as unresolved concrete issues are interrupted by the noisy arrival of the mummers in the park.

Their entrance is heralded by bacchanalian shouts, but their performance is silent as they mime a tennis match and gallery. Thomas is drawn into their magic circle of play. He accepts and participates in their illusory tennis game by retrieving their imagined ball, and this is his final reaffirmation of the *I am*. He is an artist, and he has returned to the world of art after a misruled hiatus of ventures into the opposing mysteries of living experience. For most of society, a festival is a venture into the Dionysian spirit, the magic circle of artists; for an artist, a withdrawal from that circle—a setting aside of pen or palette or Pentax—is an equivalent period of misrule. All that is properly put behind Thomas as he picks up his camera before the final frames. As the first draft says, he is "not so different from the other white-faced strangers in the park."

This is the satisfactory resolution of the film if its artifices are read properly, including carefully structured uses of color, music, and scenic design with its striking component of choreographed crowds and parties. It is a resolution that leaves behind such mundane questions as who killed whom, and why, and how and when murder will out. Events are important only as material for art. And in the world of art, in the triumph of artifice, life itself is an illusion, a Dionysian celebration of masked and anonymous revels. In the final shot of *Blow-Up*, these particular revels are properly ended.

Antonioni here, like Bergman in *The Magician* (1959) and Fellini in *Juliet of the Spirits* (1965), has been taken to task by reviewers who object to heavy-handedness and pretentiousness. But it may be that the reviewers have only given epithets to their own posturings.[11] A common denominator in these films is the

[11] I share the dismay of the late Charles Thomas Samuels concerning the state of film reviewing at the present time and the way that serious criticism of a film like *Blow-Up* can magnify the common faults of reviewers. See *Mastering the Film and Other Essays*, Lawrence Graver (ed.), Knoxville, University of Tennessee Press, 1977, especially "The Blow-Up: Sorting Things Out," pp. 119–135. Samuels himself was the most scrupulous of reviewers; witness the way he takes his friend John Simon to task for mistaken views on *Blow-Up*.

playfulness with which they deal with both their serious subjects and their own methods of presentation. And it is the significance of game playing in narrative artifice that is the cornerstone of this contemporary modality.

BERNARD F. DICK

ADAPTATION AS ARCHAEOLOGY
Fellini Satyricon (1969)

from the "novel" by Petronius

Auteurists speak of Orson Welles's *Macbeth* (1948), and theater-goers of Leonard Bernstein's *Candide* (1956). In the arts, one is accustomed to possessives that fuse work and interpreter into a unique kind of authorship. But a solecism like *Fellini Satyricon* seems alien, even pretentious; *Il Satyricon di Fellini* would have been worse, as the director admits. Actually, *Fellini's Satyricon* was the preferred title, but Gian Luigi Polidoro got to Petronius first and produced a quickie *Satyricon* (1969) with Ugo Tognazzi. The courts upheld Polidoro's right to the title (the fact that the film was declared obscene did not seem to matter), and Fellini was forced to call his version *Fellini Satyricon*—hyphenated in Italy, unhyphenated elsewhere.[1]

Yet this juxtaposition of filmmaker and film is curiously fitting. The title, even when hyphenated, is dramatically stark. The possessive denudes it; one thinks of a painting (Frederick Niesler, *Marcel Duchamp*; André Masson, *Heraclitus*), a poem (E. A. Robinson, "George Crabbe"; Walter de la Mare, "Thomas Hardy"; Conrad Aiken, "Herman Melville"), a musical composition (Strauss, *Don Quixote*; Tchaikovsky, *Romeo and Juliet*) or a recording (*Pavarotti Pagliacci*; *Murray Perahia Mozart Concerti*) that juxtaposes the names of source and interpreter, creator and recreator. "*Fellini Satyricon*" is strangely accurate; it is Fellini confronting the *Satyricon*, Catholicism confronting paganism, the present confronting the past. Whether *Fellini Satyricon* is eighty percent Fellini and twenty percent Petronius as the director boasts

---

[1] Eileen L. Hughes, *On the Set of Fellini Satyricon: A Behind-the-Scenes Diary*, New York, William Morrow, 1971, p. 164.

or fifty-fifty as his classical consultant estimates, the film is essentially Fellini's encounter with the world of his ancestors, a world that he must excavate before entering.

Fellini Satyricon is not so much an adaptation as an excavation of Petronius; it is an attempt to uncover the images beneath the novel, images so historically and archetypally charged that they are more apt to appear in the subtext than in the text. It is the subtext, with its shards of history and cracked frescoes, that interests Fellini, not the text, which is only a guide to "the potsherds, crumbs and dust of a vanished world."[2] Petronius' *Satyricon* is like the graffiti-covered wall that opens the film; the work is so overlaid with conjecture (it belongs to the age of Augustus, of Tiberius, of Nero—to the early third century) and so obscured by critical debate (it celebrates-attacks vice, it mocks-champions classicism) that its visual equivalent would be a marked-up wall. But the wall symbolizes not only what the centuries have done to the *Satyricon* but also what they have done to antiquity. Thus, the opening image is central to *Fellini Satyricon*. Against this wall, in the lower left of the frame, a shadow appears—the shadow of Encolpius, the narrator-hero.

The way in which Encolpius' shadow enters the frame represents a recurring type of composition. Frequently a figure will appear in one side of the frame with a wall, an expanse of sky, or simply space constituting the background—rather like the way a figure appears on a mural. In the Villa of the Suicides, a husband opens his veins in the left of the frame; in the Garden of Delights, Ascyltus, left of frame, crouches against a white wall. When Trimalchio rails at the cook, his accusing finger points from the left of the frame. Sometimes one figure complements another spatially. When Ascyltus interrupts Giton and Encolpius as they are making love, Encolpius' face in the left is balanced by Ascyltus' in the right.

The frame is a mural in which the figures have moved out of time and into space; it is as if the prospect of such spaciousness encouraged the figure to seek out a congenial spot for itself within a vast continuum where images do not jostle or crowd each other

---

[2] Federico Fellini, "Preface," *Fellini's Satyricon*, Dario Zanelli (ed.), translated by Eugene Walter and John Matthews, New York, Ballantine Books, 1970, p. 46. Hereafter, all future references to this edition will be noted in the text.

out. Visually, Fellini's compositions have the uncluttered look of Roman wall painting; symbolically, compositions in which the object appears on a block of space call attention to the absence of a specific background and therefore to the gaps in our knowledge of the past. Antiquity is either a sparsely decorated wall or one that has been scarred by graffiti; a Hollywood sound stage littered with ostrich plumes and lamé gowns or something so simple that to understand it we must exorcise the pulp demon that took up residence in our imagination the first time we saw Cecil B. De Mille's *The Sign of the Cross* (1932).

Fellini understands that old ideas die hard, particularly those derived from the movies. Thus, he will occasionally show the Rome that conforms vaguely to the layman's notion of a morally benumbed empire declining and ready to fall: a Rome of bisexuals and sybarites, public sex and private orgies, assassinations and senseless violence. But Fellini's Rome, no matter how much it may flatter the self-righteous by confirming their suspicions about the sins of the ancients, is too stylized for Hollywood paganism. For decadence, Fellini substitutes the rhetoric of decadence; for the familiar, he offers not the unfamiliar but the defamiliarized.

When Encolpius and Giton walk through the notorious Suburra, Fellini defamiliarizes the eternal city, replacing the Rome of the Courtesans with the Rome of the Freaks, in which corpulent whores and pudgy homosexuals wiggle their tongues provocatively —a far cry from De Mille's sleek Poppaea and effete Nero. The Suburra is a freak show, but a stylized one. Similarly, Trimalchio's feast is ritualized grossness, with the camera panning the faces of the guests as they stare vacantly, some of them spastically, into space. In one shot, Fortunata kisses her friend Scintilla in the left of the frame. In the center sit the glazed-eyed guests, and in the right Fortunata's husband, the host Trimalchio, looks longingly at a slave boy. When Trimalchio hurls a dish of sauce at his wife, Fellini paints another fresco: the bespattered Fortunata and her companion in the left, Trimalchio now with two slave boys in the right, and in the center a skeleton that a servant brings in as a *memento mori.*

Obviously this is not the Rome of *The Sign of the Cross, Quo Vadis* (1951), *The Robe* (1953), or *Ben Hur* (1959); the debauchery is too painterly. Nor is it exactly the Rome of Petronius' novel; the debauchery is too dull. It is an archetypal Rome: decadence reduced to tropes and conventions that are general enough to evoke any decadent age but not detailed enough to mirror it with perfect fidelity. For those who saw *Fellini Satyricon* when it was first released, it will always recall the late 1960s. Encolpius and Ascyltus are itinerant students of the first century A.D., yet they behave like dropouts of the sixties: too selfish to be radicals and too unmotivated to be scholars. Styles mingled as freely in the first century as they did in the 1960s, when "one's own thing" was the norm; one's thing could range from granny glasses and overalls to miniskirts and leather.

Fellini also mixes styles, or rather fits the style to the action, which can range from the gross to the noble. In the Villa of the Suicides sequence, for example, most of the shots have a classical simplicity. One shot is especially memorable: In the right of the frame, a husband and wife sit drinking wine in their garden while peacocks stroll in the background. When Encolpius and Ascyltus arrive at the villa, they proceed past the bodies of the couple and into the house; as they do, the classical merges with the modern. The walls are Picasso blue and Pompeian red; a slave girl babbles in an alien tongue, but speech is no problem for those who can communicate in body language. Suddenly one is in a world of groupies and hippies, anonymous sex and nonverbal communication. In short, one is back in the late sixties.

Fellini has achieved his purpose. On the one hand, he wanted to portray "a completely alien world" that had "the enigmatic transparency, the indecipherable clarity of dreams" (p. 26). On the other hand, he wanted to establish parallels between the time of Petronius and the time the film was made: "We can find disconcerting analogies between Roman society before the final arrival of Christianity—a cynical society, impassive, corrupt and frenzied—and society today, more blurred in its external characteristics only because it is internally more confused" (p. 43). Fellini has produced the supreme paradox: a society that is alien but recognizable, seductively transparent but ultimately impenetrable.

It could not be otherwise, for decadence is itself paradoxical. Rome of the Caesars was multilayered and multilingual. It may have been a time of decadence, but decadence is literally a "falling away," a departure from a norm that never existed except in the

An excavation of Petronius rather than an adaptation, *Fellini Satyricon* attempts to uncover the images beneath the text. Guests stare vacantly ahead as Fortunata (Magali Noel) indulges in patty-cake osculation.

noblest writings of the ancients: the norm of classicism. Yet in Petronius, there is a sincere desire for that norm, even from those who would seem to be uncomfortable with standards of any sort. Encolpius, occasional student, murderer, shrine defiler, and legacy hunter, bemoans the current lack of literary standards: "All the literary arts . . . have stunted or died, incapable of whitening naturally into an honest old age."[3] Eumolpus, the pederastic poet, is equally sincere in his attack on the mediocrity of the age: "As for our own times, why, we are so besotted with drink, so steeped in debauchery, that we lack the strength to study the great achievements of the past" (*Sat.*, p. 93). Fellini's Eumolpus echoes those sentiments: "But look at us—between wine and prostitutes we don't even know the masterworks that exist" (p. 125). Clearly,

---

[3] Petronius, *The Satyricon*, translated by William Arrowsmith, New York, Mentor Books 1959, p. 22. Hereafter abbreviated as *Sat.*, with references noted in the text.

the decadents want something more than decadence: They want Golden Age classicism.

But what does one do when the age is silver? Parody the Golden Age, not in the sense of ridiculing it but of inverting it—displacing its genres with antigenres and transvaluating its values. Inversion is the essence of Petronian parody, for just as a Black Mass is the antithesis of a real one, so too is decadence the negative of the norm. Decadence is classicism in reverse. Purge "The Widow of Ephesus" of its cynicism, and genuine feeling pours forth. Strip the rhetoric from Eumolpus' microepics on Troy and the civil war, and the classic line emerges. Replace Petronius' values with Homer's, and one is back in the Bronze Age, for Petronius conceived the *Satyricon* as a parody of the *Odyssey*, with Encolpius treading where Odysseus once strode. But as they stand, "The Widow of Ephesus" is an ironic rejoinder to Book IV of the *Aeneid* and the tragedy of Dido; Eumolpus' miniature epics are bloated poetry; and the *Satyricon* itself turns the epic adventure into a travelogue, reducing the universe to the road.

Fellini can also be a parodist in the Petronian sense. The sequence known as "The Nymphomaniac's Wagon" opens with a perverse *hommage* to the American Western.[4] A surrealistic plain is caught in a dust storm; a clump of tumbleweed rolls like a sluggish hoop; and a lone horse stands by a tent. Nearby is a caravan that resembles a covered wagon, except that it is covered not with canvas but with feathers that give it the appearance of a bird cage. The landscape conjures up the Golden Age of the Hollywood Western refracted through a surrealist lens. However, the caravan does not house a pioneer family; inside is a nymphomaniac, her tongue darting in and out of her mouth—a familiar sign of enticement in the film and one that even old crones make at the young men.

It is in such images as these that Fellini captures Petronius' sense of parody. These shots have genuine wit if one recognizes their source; likewise, Eumolpus' poetry will elicit a wry smile from those who have read Virgil and Lucan. In Petronius, the characters are constantly quoting the classics; in *Fellini Satyricon*, Fellini

---

[4] It may also be a perverse *hommage* to Bergman's *The Seventh Seal* (1957), in which the "holy family" also travels in a caravan. Bergman's film derives from a familiar Western premise: the return of the war hero.

is constantly quoting film, art, literature, and even himself. The white horse that gallops away during the collapse of the Insula Felicles recalls the white horse that saunters past Gelsomina as she sits by the curb in *La Strada* (1954); the chalk-white hermaphrodite resembles Bhishima in *Juliet of the Spirits* (1965); the grotesques are so Felliniesque that they seem to belong to the director's repertory company; and the sight of Encolpius bending over the body of the slain Ascyltus, perhaps the only poignant moment in the film, evokes the end of De Sica's *Shoeshine* (1946), when Pasquale weeps for the dead Giuseppe.

Fellini has left vestiges of his influences throughout the film. The head of the Minotaur may have been inspired by Picasso's *Minotauromachy*, but the hollow eyes are Giacometti's. After reading the ancient sources, Fellini was able to blend details from different texts and invent whole episodes from mere incidents or references. Fellini includes the Lichas episode from the novel but adds certain details that make Lichas more than just an old enemy of Encolpius; Fellini's Lichas is another Nero, who is so infatuated with Encolpius that he wants to join with him in a mock marriage. Petronius does not even hint at this side of Lichas' character, but both Tacitus and Suetonius describe Nero's penchant for legalizing his relationships with male lovers in a ceremony complete with dowry, bridal veil, torches, and marriage bed.[5] The ritual battle between Encolpius and the Minotaur does not occur in Petronius; it is Fellini's invention, suggested by an incident in Book III of Apuleius' *The Golden Ass*, in which Lucius is subjected to a mock trial at the Festival of Risus, the god of laughter. The husband and wife who commit suicide in the film recall Seneca and his wife Paulina, but with a major difference: Paulina survived.

Fellini invents, blends, reworks, and borrows. In Petronius, Encolpius becomes impotent with Circe; Fellini's Encolpius becomes impotent during the Festival of Laughter when he tries to have sex

---

[5] In the first (unfilmed) version of the "Lichas and His Ship" sequence, there was a double wedding: Encolpius and Lichas, and Giton and Pannychis. Fellini transferred the mock marriage between Giton and the child Pannychis in the Quartilla episode of the *Satyricon* to Lichas' ship, where Pannychis was part of a cargo of slaves. Fellini wisely revised the sequence, which would have depicted a seven-year-old's wedding night. Humankind cannot bear very much depravity, to paraphrase Eliot.

with Ariadne and discovers, to his shock and the spectators' disappointment, that he cannot perform. The transposition is effective; the public loss of potency, apart from being the stuff of nightmares, fits into the dreamlike nature of the entire episode in which Encolpius plays a timid Theseus wandering through a labyrinth of ruins, fights a bogus Minotaur, and fails to satisfy his Ariadne—all in view of a noisy audience.

However, the borrowings create a tension between their original form and their new context so that one is forced to compare Giuseppe's death in *Shoeshine* with Ascyltus' or to contrast Picasso's witty Minotaur with Fellini's bearhugging bull-man. But Petronius is also one of Fellini's borrowings. Fellini is faithful to Petronius—in his fashion; he reproduces two of the novel's main features: a blending of styles, and the portrayal of life as a picaresque odyssey or "road" trip. Fellini's narrative structure, however, is quite different from Petronius'. Despite its fragmentary nature, Petronius' *Satyricon* has a recognizable story line but not a *mythos* in the sense of an interconnected series of incidents. The novel as we have it simply recounts the adventures of two young men, and an occasional third, as they roam around southern Italy; Encolpius and Ascyltus are the forerunners of Dean Moriarty and Sal Paradise of Kerouac's *On the Road*, and their lives are just as amorphous. Like the cross-country trips in Kerouac's 1957 novel, the major episodes in Petronius are vignettes that fit into the plot because the plot is loose enough to accommodate them.

Thus, even if one had the complete *Satyricon*, "Trimalchio's Banquet" could be excerpted and read independently, as it is today, because it has a beginning (the introduction of Trimalchio as he is playing ball with a slave), a middle (the banquet), and an end (the music grows so loud it brings out the fire brigade). Because the novel is made up of such causally unrelated episodes, one must keep inserting "and then they did this" between them. The reader must provide the narrative links; the episodes may be self-contained, but they are not autonomous. One would like them to have a cause-effect relationship, but since causal succession is impossible, we invent a kind of temporal succession: "and then" instead of "because." The "and thens" continue to the end: and then Encolpius became a legacy-hunter, and then he became impotent, and then he was cured, and then Eumolpus made a will requiring his heirs to eat his flesh. And then . . . the text breaks off.

Although *Fellini Satyricon* seems to share the same disconnectedness, its structure is much more sophisticated. For all its dreamlike atmosphere, it is not dream narrative. The film has a *mythos*, not merely a plot: a carefully planned nexus of events and images that is apparent from the very first sequence. Both the novel and the film begin with a rhetorical outburst. In Petronius, Encolpius laments the decline of rhetoric, and the rhetorician Agamemnon replies with a tirade against progressive education. In Fellini, Encolpius laments the treachery of his companion Ascyltus and the infidelity of his lover Giton. Fellini obviously knew that even an art film should not open with a debate on classical rhetoric. Thus, he opens with the soliloquy Encolpius delivers later on in the novel (*Sat.*, p. 87). A soliloquy on fickleness is more theatrical than a sermon on the abuse of rhetoric. Encolpius, however, does not practice what he preaches; his soliloquy epitomizes the stylistic affectation he criticizes in others. By making the substitution, Fellini plunges the audience into Rome's Silver Age, in which emotion is bombast and language a nacrèous shell enclosing a void. Encolpius declaims as if he were auditioning for the debating team or, to put it historically, trying to please some *rhetor*. One does not doubt the sincerity of his feelings; one doubts the sincerity of his expression. Yet Encolpius is no different from Petronius, who "even in his exposé of the fatuities of the Roman rhetorical education . . . reveals himself the true product of it."[6]

By opening with Encolpius' lament, Fellini is forced to use conventional narrative for the first few sequences. Encolpius concludes his soliloquy by noting that Ascyltus has fled with Giton; immediately, Ascyltus crawls out of a cubicle in the baths as if he had been hiding from his angry friend. Encolpius does not know Giton's whereabouts, but Ascyltus does—he sold the boy to the mime Vernacchio. A second sequence is required: Vernacchio's theater, where Encolpius reclaims Giton and takes him home through the Suburra to his apartment in the Insula Felicles, which collapses upon their return. Thus far the episodes have been interconnected, but the collapse of the Insula Felicles brings linearity to

[6] P. G. Walsh, *The Roman Novel*, London, Cambridge University Press, 1970, p. 8.

a momentary halt. Is the collapse real or hallucinatory? Are we in
Rome or in Pompeii at the eruption of Vesuvius?[7] Or is linear
narrative collapsing under the weight of the surreal? The white
horse that gallops off may provide the answer. What is a white
horse doing amid the rubble of a toppled tenement except perhaps
to remind us of *La Strada*, in which there was logically no reason
for a riderless horse to trot down a street in early morning, but
emotionally there was every reason in the world? The surreal has
its own way of bringing an action to a close—with a striking image
rather than a conventional mark of punctuation.

One segment ends, and another begins: "Trimalchio's Banquet." Again, Fellini rearranges the original to connect two incidents: the banquet and the visit to the gallery. In Petronius,
Encolpius attends the banquet with the rhetorician Agamemnon,
"and then" visits a gallery where he encounters the poet Eumolpus. Fellini omits Agamemnon, whose presence would make sense
only if he had retained the novel's opening scene. Instead he has
Encolpius meet Eumolpus *before* the banquet. Because they met at
the gallery, the poet brings Encolpius to Trimalchio's.

Sometimes the dream material is too strong for linearity, and the
epidodes merge rather than connect. Shortly after the banquet,
Encolpius, asleep on a beach, awakens to see Ascyltus and Giton,
who have miraculously reappeared. Suddenly Encolpius is mana-
cled, and the three are led aboard Lichas' ship. After Encolpius
kills the robber at the end of the hermaphrodite sequence, he is
driven down a hill into an arena where he plays Theseus to a
good-natured Minotaur. But generally Fellini tries to supply
causal connectives for the episodes. The young men journey to the
Temple of Ceres because the nymphomaniac's slave told them
about the hermaphrodite who dwells there. Because Encolpius becomes impotent, he must seek out the witch Oenothea.

[7] At times one feels the film is Fellini's *The Last Days of Pompeii*. The baths
in the opening sequence recall the *thermae* of Pompeii—a combination Turk-
ish bath and athletic club; the art gallery looks like the *atrium* of a Pompeian
house; the Villa of the Suicides suggests the kind of villa that would be built
along the coastline of the Gulf of Naples; the arena where Theseus fights
the Minotaur is modeled after the amphitheater at Pompeii; Trimalchio's
dining room resembles a Pompeian *triclinium*; and the graffiti-scrawled wall
at the beginning also evokes Pompeii. A reading of Marcel Brion, *Pompeii
and Herculaneum: The Glory and the Grief*, translated by John Rosenberg,
New York, Crown, 1960, will confirm Fellini's debt to Pompeian culture.

Fellini's ability to impart verisimilitude to fragments of narrative is evident in his handling of the best-known part of the novel, "The Widow of Ephesus." Petronius has Eumolpus tell the story on board Lichas' ship; Fellini makes it part of "Trimalchio's Banquet." The filmmaker's reasoning is excellent. After the banquet, Trimalchio and his guests retire to the site of his mausoleum, where the tale is performed as if it were a masque. At first, one does not know if it is a dramatization. It seems more like a flashback: One of the guests starts telling the story, and then, in typical flashback fashion, the spoken narrative is visualized. At the end, when the widow and the soldier walk off like actors after their curtain call, one realizes that the performance was given in the valley *below* the rocky plain where Trimalchio and his guests were sitting. To use a modern analogy, it was as if the cast were in the orchestra pit and the audience on stage. By presenting "Trimalchio's Banquet" and "The Widow of Ephesus" in succession, Fellini is asking us to compare the banquet and the performance, the real and the illusory. However, by putting the spectators on a stage, Fellini is suggesting that the banquet is unreal and the play is the true reality: The one is the acceptance of a ritual that denies life; the other, the rejection of a ritual in order to affirm life.

In "The Widow of Ephesus," a ritual proves futile as a woman learns from an ardent soldier that the only antidote for death is love; thus, she offers her husband's corpse as a replacement for the stolen body of a crucified slave. The banquet, however, is total ritual, with Trimalchio playacting to the end and asking his guests to mourn for him as they would if he were dead. Naturally, they comply. The widow has a real corpse in her tomb, but in Trimalchio's mausoleum the living impersonate the dead and merrymakers pretend to be mourners.

Other episodes also turn into theater pieces complete with audience reaction. Antiquity thus acquires the reality of the stage—its truths those of art rather than history. In Fellini, the ancients are part of their own drama; they watch themselves perform as we in turn watch them. Sometimes it is an actual performance like the one at Vernacchio's theater, but more often Fellini simply has his characters observe each other: In the balcony above the picture gallery, a group of onlookers listen to Eumolpus; at Trimalchio's banquet, the poor relatives dine on the mezzanine and react to what is happening below; Encolpius' combat with the Minotaur is a spectacle witnessed by an audience; and the reading of Eumolpus' will elicits sneers from the youthful bystanders. Sometimes the characters observe us, peering enticingly or lethargically into the lens. Perhaps the ancients are equally curious about the moderns.

All is performance, past and present. But a performance soon becomes a memory; even the drama of antiquity becomes a blur of impressions. Time robs history of its particulars, and soon one is reduced to speaking of "eras" and "ages" whose generalities are more comforting than the ungilded facts. Fellini is not a historian, but in an attempt to infuse his *Satyricon* with the spirit of imperial Rome (which, like all spirits, is atemporal), he appropriates certain historical events, transforming them into images and creating a kind of historical imagery that enjoys the freedom of the archetypal. The albino emperor who stabs himself and is then dispatched by his troops is not based on any one historical model. Perhaps one should say "empress" since the Caesar is clearly female. Yet one's curiosity is aroused, particularly since the Caesar resembles the sacred hermaphrodite who shriveled into a tangle of skin when exposed to the heat of the sun. One thinks of Caligula, who, according to Suetonius, was extremely pale with hollow eyes and thin hair and who often dressed in women's clothes and shoes. Caligula was slain by his officers, but he did not stab himself first. Nero is another possibility; he also appeared on occasion in gown and slippers. But Nero committed suicide by plunging a dagger in his throat, his hand guided by his secretary. The Caesar is an anomaly, and a denatured one at that; the creature is Rome on the brink of exhaustion, a powdery changeling that must be destroyed.

The new Caesar marching toward Rome personifies the physical and moral strength needed to return the empire to its pride of place. If pressed for his name, one might suggest Trajan, Hadrian, or even Constantine. Historically, none of the suggestions fits, but history as such has little to do with *Fellini Satyricon*. One cannot assign a time period to the film other than the general "Imperial Age." In the Villa of the Suicides, the wife is reading Hadrian (A.D. 117–138), although Petronius was, it seems, a contemporary of Nero (54–68). The dignity with which the husband ends his life evokes—and only that—the suicides of Seneca and his nephew Lucan in 65 and of Petronius himself in 66. The film suggests the world of the first century by incorporating certain historically tinged incidents (noble suicides, ignoble emperors) into a fiction that springs loose from history, becoming what everything in *Fellini Satyricon* becomes: images of the other and the self.

The dig is approaching completion. The artifacts have been assembled and numbered like pieces in a special collection. Encolpius is about to sail off to new adventures. We see him in close-up, and suddenly the shot freezes; his face dissolves into the face on a fresco, and his narration ends in midsentence. The camera tracks back, revealing the ruins of a fresco whose jagged pieces are spread across a lonely plain like painted monoliths; Encolpius and his companions are now faces on broken plaster.

Fellini tried to subject Petronius to the rigors of film art, but the order he imposed on the *Satyricon* was alien to a fragmentary work. Such order is illusory, for ruins cannot endure prolonged excavation. Nothing holds, and the *Satyricon* returns to the state in which Fellini found it.

LINDLEY HANLON

THE "SEEN" AND THE "SAID"
Bresson's *Une Femme Douce (1969)*

from the story "The Gentle Creature" by Fyodor Dostoevsky

> Proust says that Dostoevsky is original in composition above all. It is an extraordinarily complex and close-meshed whole, purely inward, with currents and counter-currents like those of the sea, a thing that is found also in Proust (in other ways so different) and whose equivalent would go well with a film.
>
> *—Robert Bresson*[1]

At first glance, how odd that Bresson should choose Dostoevsky as his source for three films: *Crime and Punishment* for *Pickpocket* (1959), "The Gentle Maiden" for *Une Femme Douce* (1969), and "White Nights" for *Quatre Nuits d'un Rêveur* (1971). On the one hand, Dostoevsky—the literary master of hysterical fears, verbal mania, and criminal tortures in his characters—on the other hand, Bresson—the master of the serene surface, unspeakable humiliation, and silent horror. Yet the written works and the films contain remarkably similar visions of human action and thought, passivity and passion. Bresson sifts through the currents and countercurrents of voices in Dostoevsky and siphons off the essence, pure and refined. Bresson shows us the luminous surface beneath which agony festers. Nearly every line of dialogue and every character trait in Bresson's Dostoevsky trilogy can be found in the source. It is Bresson's selection, reduction, and arrangement of these widely dispersed fragments of material which distinguish his vision. A comparison of narration in the film *Une Femme Douce* with narration in the Dostoevsky short story "The

[1] Robert Bresson, *Notes on Cinematography*, translated by Jonathan Griffin, New York, Urizen Books, 1977, p. 63.

Gentle Maiden" (1876) on which it is based will clarify Bresson's revisions of a given narrative structure, revisions in which a multi-plication of narrative perspectives is primary.

The narrative structures of Dostoevsky's story and Bresson's film hinge on a contest of points of view. In the story, our knowl-edge of the young woman is filtered through her husband's self-absorbed and self-congratulatory interpretation of the events of their life together. In the film, the conflict of characters, the divi-sion of spaces, the alliances of objects, the juncture of shots, and the partitioning of time evolve from a fundamental drama of point of view in which the character-narrator—the husband—struggles in his first-person narration with the silence, presence, glances, words, and suicide of his beautiful wife, the gentle maiden. His quest for understanding, his search through their past for the rea-sons for her suicide, engages the reader and the viewer alike, but at important junctures in the narrative we part company with the interpretation of the self-proclaimed narrator to form our own interpretation based on a subtle array of evidence orchestrated by the "real" narrator, the masked narrator, the writer or the film-maker. In the film version, our privileged access to "facts" pro-vided by Bresson's "showing" makes us increasingly skeptical about the husband's "telling." The film declares the eminence of the "seen" over the "said."

Une Femme Douce consists of thirty-four sequences (527 shots). Half those sequences depict the husband walking back and forth around a bed where the body of the young woman lies. Bresson has derived this alternating structure from a minor realis-tic detail in the story. The husband says: "I keep walking and walking about."[2] As he paces in the film, he ponders the meaning of their life together, speaking to Anna, the housekeeper, who listens. The other half of the sequences are flashbacks, direct cinematic representations of incidents in their life. As a transition to and within those sequences, the first-person, voice-over com-mentary of the husband is heard together with occasional dialogue. The alternation of flashbacks begins as follows: (1) flashback

---

2 Fyodor Dostoevsky, "The Gentle Maiden," in *"Letters from the Under-world," "The Gentle Maiden," "The Landlady,"* translated by C. J. Hogarth, London, Dent, Everyman's Library, 1971, p. 205. Future references to this edition will appear in the body of the text.

(suicide), (2) pondering, (3) flashback, (4) pondering, (5) flashback, etc. The film ends with a recapitulation of the suicide. The film's narrative structure consists of these regular alternations between the past (sequences of their life together) and the present (sequences of the husband pacing with Anna and the corpse present). The sequences are bridged by the sound of the husband's footsteps and the words of his voice-over narration.

Since the short story consists of a continuous fabric of language —of words—the change from past to present can be made instantly, suddenly, and subtly in verb shifts. Furthermore, the story takes place in the fluid and chaotic mental space of the husband's world. Bresson as a filmmaker must make Dostoevsky's world of language and passion physically, spatially, and temporally concrete.

Dostoevsky's story begins with a description of the girl's body stretched between two card tables, as the character narrating the story (the husband) beholds her, but the exact nature of her death is not revealed until the end. A major element of the suspense of the story becomes our desire for an answer to the question: *How* as well as *why* did the gentle maiden die? In the short story the character-narrator tells us about his first meetings with the girl immediately, gradually describing her from his point of view, shocking us with a very vivid description of the suicide near the end of the story (Part II, Chapter 4, pp. 201–203).

The four shots with which Bresson begins the film fundamentally reorient the Dostoevsky narrative by showing *how* the death occurred. (See "Shot Analysis" on the following pages.) The shots are sudden and terrifying: A maid nears a door; on a terrace, a rocker and table yank violently from the shock of a jump; a white scarf flutters down from the balcony to the street; we see the body of a beautiful woman on the pavement below, blood streaming near her head. There is no gradual exposition of idea, no establishment of character and location, no build-up of tension and action to this event which forms the more traditional climax of Dostoevsky's story. In Bresson's adaptation, effect precedes cause. In terms of our allegiance as spectators, the husband's verbal narration cannot compete in power with the visual directness and shock of the images of suicide.

In the short story, the first-person "I" of the husband's narration occurs in the second sentence, clearly establishing him as the teller

TABLE 1. Shot Analysis of *Une Femme Douce*

Shot #	Feet 16mm	Distance	Angle	Camera Mov't	Subject	Sound	Transition
1.	6.5	cu	wl		Handle of a glass-paned door. An older woman (back to camera) places hand on handle, opens door, stands in doorway and walks forward, lampvase behind.	(footsteps)	Cut
2.	4	mls	wl		On the balcony outside a rocker yanks back violently; a table falls over, vase and plant fall off. The woman (back to camera) enters frame left.	(clatter) (screach of brakes) → (traffic)	Cut
3.	4.5	ls	ela	td	A white scarf flutters down from above.	(plunk, screach of) (brakes)	Cut
4.	9.5	ms	wl	td pan 1	A car stops, another brakes. A man gets out of front car; a young woman lies on the ground in white blouse and gray skirt, blood streaming near head. Legs of people standing there and circulating.	(siren) (footsteps) (different footsteps) →	Cut

cu = close-up
wl = waist-level
mls = medium long shot
ls = long shot
ela = extreme low angle

ms = medium shot
td = tilt down
pan l = pan left
pan r = pan right
sha = slight high angle
VO = voice-over

TABLE 2. Shot Analysis of *Une Femme Douce* (continued)

Shot #	Feet 16mm	Distance	Angle	Camera Mov't	Subject	Sound	Dialogue (translated below)	Transition
5.	13.5	ms	sha		A man walks forward, back to camera. The older woman w/ one knee on cane chair, rests folded hands on railing of brass bed. He paces forward again.	(footsteps on floor) (silent on rug)	HE: *Elle paraissait seize ans. Anna, tu te rapelles?* ANNA: *Oui.*	Cut
		mcu						
		cu	wl			(light footsteps)		
6.	6.5		sha		White plastic basin in bed w/ cloth in it; girl's knees stretched out on bed. He moves basin with blood in it to chair on l. beside bed and walks to rear of frame.	→		Cut
		ms		pan l				
7.	2.5	cu	sha		Ring with gems in hand.	(footsteps)		Cut
8.	7.5	mls	el	pan r	The young girl enters store, traffic behind, stands in line at counter, behind which Anna is seated. A customer passes in front.	(traffic) (door closed) (light footsteps)	vo: *"Elle venait comme les autres. Je ne l'avait pas re- marquée."* [HE: She seemed to be sixteen years old. Anna, do you remember? ANNA: Yes. * * * * * vo: "She came like the others. I hadn't noticed her."]	Cut

of the subsequent tale. In the film, the suicide is unmediated by the husband's verbal narration. By placing this startling event at the beginning of the film, Bresson first engages our sympathy for and interest in the woman: Who is this beautiful woman? Why did she throw herself off the balcony? The character of the husband and his constant function as the narrator become apparent only after several reappearances in the same room, near the body of the woman, which is tended by Anna, the housekeeper.

In the story, the husband articulates the main question of the narrative:

> How it has happened I cannot tell, I try, again and again, to explain it to myself. Ever since six o'clock I have been trying to explain it, yet cannot bring my thoughts to a focus. Perhaps it is through trying so much that I fail. Perhaps it were better that I should once more recount these events in their proper order. Their proper order, indeed! (p. 155).

This systematic ordering of events is indeed the task which Bresson undertakes to perform on Dostoevsky's narrative. Although the events, details, and order of events are very similar to those of the short story, their restructuring by Bresson into a more clearly organized sequence of cinematic pieces shifts the emphasis away from the husband's psychological tensions and perspective, which were Dostoevsky's main interest, to a focus on the mysterious character of the woman, which we infer from fairly sparse evidence. Bresson's camera—by revealing the young woman's beauty, reactions, actions, spatial imprisonment, and objects which refer to her—contradicts the first-person viewpoint of the husband, which can be maintained only in the dialogue and voice-over narration. Bresson "directs" our attention and sympathies toward her and allows the girl to speak for herself and for him in a variety of ways. The truth of the verbal, literary narration of the husband is undermined by the evidence we find in her dialogue and in the direct visual images of the woman throughout the film. In the short story, the character of the woman is solely a function of the husband's verbal descriptions and reports of her. In the film, we observe the husband and wife alike through the harsh and seemingly objective stare of the camera lens.

Bresson further directs our sympathies toward the woman by

giving her a more prominent ally in the film: Anna, the house-keeper (Lukeria in the short story). Bresson uses Anna's figure as the receiver of the narrative—the listener—to embody a second narrative point of view about the husband. In keeping with this claim, it is interesting to read Dostoevsky's preface to the story, in which he describes specifically the status of the husband as narrator:

> Throughout, the man soliloquises to himself, with only occasional references to some unseen auditor—to some unseen judge, as it were. Always in the realm of actuality it is so. Had I been able to *stenograph* the words of the speaker, they might have issued even more rough and unwrought than I have conceived them: yet, for me, their psychological order would still have remained the same. In this sketch I have tried to imagine myself such a stenographer: and it is to that factor in the work that I have applied the term "fantastic" (p. 154). (Dostoevsky's italics)

In *Une Femme Douce* Bresson rejects the element which Dostoevsky sees as "fantastic"—the rambling, unheard narrator—and documents the story as if it were told to Anna. Although the husband mentions in the story that Lukeria lives with them and listens to his woes (she was originally a servant in the woman's household whom he bribed for information about the young woman), he mentions her less frequently in the story than her frequent appearances in the film would suggest. Not only does Anna witness events—such as the suicide, as she did in the short story—which the husband cannot because he must be shown to be at the wrong place at the wrong time and to be excessively jealous of the gentle woman's moments alone, but Anna also listens to and witnesses his version of the story of their life together. In the film, Anna is present by the woman's corpse as the husband tries to explain the events of their life to himself and to her. She watches and listens as we do and can be interpreted as the viewer's surrogate in the fiction. Using the figure of Anna, Bresson chooses to represent that "unseen auditor," that "unseen judge" which Dostoevsky describes in his preface.

Bresson's camera, however, is the "unseen judge" that passes the final verdict. Bresson establishes a dramatic irony, a conflict between the camera's visual perspective on the husband and the husband's perspective on himself in his verbal narration. In one case, for example, we hear him say: "An indescribable enthusiasm invaded me." In the image, however, we see him cover his face in a look of terrible anguish and torture. The verbal narration seems a subjective, self-interested, although—in comparison with the short story—emotionally understated rendering of the events of their life. The visuals seem an unmediated and objective account of their life since Bresson's role as narrator is masked effectively. In both story and film, the husband becomes an "unreliable" or "semi-reliable" narrator.[3]

In Bresson's subversive filmic fiction, the husband's narrative function is more limited than in Dostoevsky's first-person tale. In the film, the husband appears to "decide" which events in their life will be related and comments on them. Bresson's authorial function as selector is masked by his narrator's supposed freedom of choice. One reason for the fragmenting of narrative incident in both story and film is that the incidents are supposed to appear to be chosen by the husband from his awakening memory in order to justify his story. With illusions about the nature of their life shattered by the suicide, the husband attempts to make sense of what occurred in their life. The incidents are "typical" from his point of view, rather than flowing chronologically from one event to the next. Part of the discrediting of the narrator evolves as we suspect that *other* incidents, chosen from *her* point of view, might explain her position more clearly. For example, in the film the husband finds her in a car with another man, just as, in the short story, he had listened to her conversation from an adjacent room.

While the short story emphasizes the pomposity, verbal cruelty, and tyranny of the husband, "a cheap sort of egoist" (p. 164), as he finally admits in passing, the film stresses his stern coldness and silent domination of the woman. In the story the husband frequently mentions their periods of "silence" and describes her insolent glances, but he, as narrator, must continue to "generate" pages of prose by verbally analyzing the cause and significance of these silences rather than representing them or describing them and mimicking their duration. Bresson has mastered two narrative possibilities of the film medium: the possibility of representing silence through images of severe glances or through what he has termed the "pianissimo" of noises.[4] The connective tissue of the narrative of *Une Femme Douce* is a series of hundreds of footsteps made by the man as he passes from silent room to silent room. The footsteps echo because there is no other living sound to over-power them. Analysis and penetration of the psychological dy-namics of those states of silence are never attempted or considered possible by Bresson. The presence of death is suggested both by this sound vacuum and by the presence of the corpse. Bresson provides a continuous filament of sound and images for Dostoev-sky's striking invocation of the void at the end of the story:

> O void, O nature! Only men dwell upon the earth—and therein lies the calamity of it. "Is there in all the plain a man alive?" cries an old Russian hero. It is *I* who am crying that now—not a hero; yet there is no one to answer to my call. They say that the sun puts life into the universe. He rises, and one beholds him. Yet is not *he* dead also? Everything is dead, and dead men are every-where. Only human beings are here, and over them there broods a silence. *That* is the world. "Men, love one another." Who said that? Whose command was it? The pendulum continues beating insensibly, malignantly. It is two o'clock in the morning. Her little boots stand there by the bed, as though awaiting her. Ah, but, in very truth, when they take her away to-morrow, what will become of me? (p. 207).

The preeminent silence of the film is the silence of the corpse, whose presence in image after image cancels out the verbal articu-lations Bresson allows the husband. No matter what he says to justify his thoughts and actions, the presence of her corpse, the presence of death, constantly reminds us that their relationship failed, that she took her own life. The silence of the corpse is in turn doubled by Anna's silence. It is by the silence of those se-quences near her corpse and by the silence of their hours together that Bresson stresses the deathlike nature of their relationship, her stifling at his hands. The gentle woman's silent arsenal are those icy, daggerlike glances with which Dostoevsky armed her—glances which cut across the space between them in the film—and those few, incisive words which level all his pretensions. Those glances are the very mark of her gentleness. Bresson creates a character

[4] Bresson, op cit., p. 21.

Une Femme Douce is Bresson's adaptation of Dostoevsky's "A Gentle Creature." Focusing narrative sympathy on the young woman, he captures Dominique Sanda's pale beauty framed by her dishevelled hair and grubby raincoat.

remarkably close to the spirit and specifics of Dostoevsky's description.

Still other cinematic means are at Bresson's disposal to focus narrative sympathy on the young woman. Bresson captures all of Dominique Sanda's pale, pure, aquiline beauty in the subtle Vermeer-like tones of his first color film, framing her with carefully disheveled hair which falls out of place seductively and with a grubby raincoat several sizes too small which emphasizes her long hands; a startling combination of innocent girl and passionate woman. She has a natural grace and erect posture which reinforce and convey her self-possession despite all her compromises, illnesses, and humiliations. That so much of her character is revealed in details of clothing, figure, and face means that her presence as a corpse, as an object, is as powerful as her living presence, as if she, like Anna, were a silent witness and judge.

Bresson associates other objects with her in a variety of ways as he recasts Dostoevsky's descriptions into a physically concrete world and medium. These objects can "stand for" her or refer to her as "physical correlatives" when she is absent and become her agents, her surrogates.[5] Repeatedly seen at crucial moments throughout the film, the objects remind us of earlier events in which they appeared, and register changes in meaning and development when they reappear. The bentwood rocker from which she jumps to her death comes to signify "suicide." The white scarf which she wraps around herself as a shroud suggests her spirit in flight. A green bar of soap, which she hurls across the floor in defiance of her husband, will, when later seen alone on the edge of the tub, remind us of that defiance. The white shroud in Dostoevsky becomes the white scarf in Bresson's adaptation; the amber cigarette holder and crucifix are appropriated directly from the source. These objects, which at first appear as mere props in a realistic decor and drama, take on symbolic meaning as they reappear in different dramatic and filmic contexts.

Bresson takes the most important of these objects—the crucifix —from his source, duplicating its form and function. In both story and film, the crucifix unites early and late scenes; in the film, it forms a more ambiguous although important thematic and causal thread in the narrative, the only reference to religion in the film. In an early scene in the film it is the last object she relinquishes to the pawnbroker before relinquishing herself to him in marriage. The husband unceremoniously takes the ivory Christ figure off the gold cross and then weighs the cross, like any other object he buys, to determine its monetary value. His statement and treatment of the object, which to her is sacred, marks the fundamental contrast of their characters, attitudes, and points of view: "It would be better if you kept the Christ and I took the metal." She refuses to keep the dismantled Christ figure and takes the money instead.

In the last sequence of the film, we see that she has kept the crucifix, now together again as one icon, wrapped in a scarf and tucked away carefully in her top drawer. She touches it gently, as she did in the story, lifting it out of the drawer—a gesture which

[5] See Robert Scholes and Robert Kellogg, *The Nature of Narrative*, New York, Oxford University Press, 1966, pp. 196–197, on "physical correlatives"; Angus Fletcher on metonymy and synecdoche in *Allegory: The Theory of a Symbolic Mode*, Ithaca, N.Y., Cornell University Press, 1964; and Roland Barthes, *S/Z*, translated by Richard Miller, New York, Hill and Wang, 1974, pp. 190–191.

suggests that it is to regain the world of the spirit and of freedom that she commits suicide. The object, which had become in his hands a chunk of metal with a commercial value, takes on its appropriate religious signification in her hands. In the story, she takes the crucifix with her to her death; in the film, she wraps herself in the shroudlike scarf.

During the course of the film the gentle woman's dignity increases as she becomes the speaker for what we can infer are Bresson's own ideas about art, contemporary life, and the human condition. Bresson bestows upon her the narrator's most intimate mask: Her voice we can infer to be the voice of the "real" narrator —Bresson himself. The most extensive example of her mediation is the sequence devoted to a rather stiff performance of *Hamlet*, which she watches with full attention. It is she who afterward comments on the lines left out by the performers to allow them to exaggerate gestures and speech, a style the opposite of Bresson's severe understatement. In addition, there are six shots of her leaning forward during the performance, with appropriate parts of the dialogue heard over those shots. These lines from the play become a kind of transplanted voice-over narration referring to her fate and dignifying it by cultural association with Hamlet's dilemma. By indirect reference we remember Hamlet's soliloquy, "To be or not to be," which seems a fitting statement of her dilemma and decision. Dostoevsky had invoked the same precursor:

> Oh, believe me, I understand the matter as a whole: yet it still remains a question why she killed herself. It must have been because she was frightened by my amorousness—because she asked herself seriously, "To consent or not to consent?" and, unable to face the problem, preferred death (p. 203).

Another cinematic form of Bresson's narrative sympathy for the woman can be seen in his systematic use of close frames and framing within the frame, which become spatial emblems of her confinement. For example, hundreds of doors open and close as they walk from shop to office to apartment and out. The sound of closing doors frequently signals a cut and emphasizes her enclosure, her lack of freedom. The husband often spies in on her through the glass-paned doors, through the rearview mirror of the car, and through the car windows. Bresson often moves the camera in very close to the husband to suggest his tendency to crowd his wife. In some shots the husband blocks the camera completely with his back, creating the effect of a fadeout. These close, blocked-off frames reinforce our sense of his rigidity and dominance, which are specifically described in the story: "She could go nowhere without my leave—such was the marriage agreement" (p. 175). The gentle woman's release from this world is depicted in the only extreme close-up in the film: her face is bifurcated momentarily by the window frame, which slowly moves right as she opens it, leaving her free from enclosure before her fall to death.

The fragmentation of the film narrative contributes to the enigmatic character of the gentle woman as we are forced to make inferences and construct possible causal relationships. This is the process through which the husband is drawn in order to comprehend her death: "But why did I go out? And She, why? why?" He restates the question at the end of the film as if still profoundly puzzled by her contradictory behavior: She says she despises marriage; in the next shot they are married. She says that she will be a faithful wife; in the next sequence she commits suicide. As privileged witnesses of Bresson's narration, however, we feel that we have been able to gain a greater knowledge of her character than the husband, although she still remains a mysterious creature.

The last shots of the husband and the coffin reaffirm his attachment to the material as he clings to her body for an answer. The body is then locked up to be put away, a finality emphasized by the loud grating of screws. *We* have seen evidence of her heightened spirituality, her ultimate freedom despite this locking up. *We* feel that she has indeed escaped prior to the closure of the narrative, although her motives are never made explicit.

Bresson's refusal to explain motive is his greatest departure from the source. In the story we are told many more details of the woman's past: her servitude to her cruel aunts who beat her, burn her with tongs, and decide to sell her to a "fat shopman next door" (p. 165). Her decision to leave the household and support herself by working as a governess and by pawning objects of value seems justified and noble in the story. In the film, her decision to marry the husband is unexplained. In one shot she says no to his proposal, after a discussion of the boredom and conformism of modern marriage; in the next shot they are being married in a civil ceremony. She describes her home and family as "sinister," and we see that her hallway is shabby, but Bresson never specifies the physical and mental hardships and servitude of Dostoevsky's heroine. In the story her decision to marry the pawnbroker seems based on her rejection of a more horrible alternative: slavery to a shopkeeper. Her suicide seems based on a realization that her marriage too has been a selling into slavery. Her suicide is an act of independence that enrages her husband, proud as he is of his power to dominate her.

In Bresson's modernization of the story, the woman's actions and passivity may seem in comparison less comprehensible, more irrational, and more maddening to viewers accustomed to characters whose actions flow smoothly and unproblematically from idea, through willing, toward effect. Bresson's work as a filmmaker involves the short-circuiting of such facile patterns of will and action. In Bresson's films cause and effect are often temporally reversed, but more often and more mysteriously we are presented with a series of actions set end-to-end from shot-to-shot with no immediate explanation of motive.

While the multiplication and contradictions of narrative points of view, narrative explanations and meanings, and character allegiances have clear structural value for Bresson, one must emphasize the broader implications of this fragmentation in Bresson's view of human motivation, will, action, knowledge, and understanding. Over the course of the film we are led to make comparisons and contrasts by the repetition of objects, situations, and set-ups from which we infer the development of characters and the changes in their predicaments and attitudes. Yet because of the multiple perspectives from which we view these characters, the process of learning about them is made difficult by a lack of clear-cut information about what they do and feel—the inability and perhaps impossibility of these characters to communicate completely their interior states through visible or audible means. We feel that there is an impenetrable zone of enigma, of mystery which is represented effectively by these multiple and contradictory possible interpretations, by these narrative fragments. These contradictions are central to Dostoevsky's analysis of the strange and incestuous minglings of reason and madness, passion and passivity in human actions, but clearer and more compelling sets of motives are available in the short story. The contrasts between the characters of the husband and wife are much more dramatic in the story than in Bresson's film about a thoroughly modern couple. Bresson's hard-edged, end-to-end placement of shots and sequences compounds the inherent ambiguity of his film images.

In both novel and film, the result of these discrepancies is that we feel that no *one* perspective, no *one* story, certainly not the one told by the husband in the film, can account fully for the complexity and depth of these characters. Nor do facile psychological categories provide a satisfactory explanation. Least of all do Bresson's characters seem to know themselves until just before their final moment of trial, suffering, death, or triumph. This fragmentary relativism, this refusal of final and absolute explanations, this sense of mystery and drift are Dostoevsky's legacy and the mark of Bresson's modernism. These contradictory directions are a challenge to the viewer, which Scholes and Kellogg among others have recognized as the distinguishing feature of the contemporary novel:

> The Renaissance allegorist expected his readers to participate strenuously in his work, bringing all their learning and intellect to bear on his polysemous narrative. Similarly, the modern novelist often expects just such intense participation, but being empirically rather than metaphysically oriented he makes the great question that of what really happened inside and outside the characters he has presented; whereas the allegorists made the question of what these characters and events signified the primary question for their audience.[6]

Bresson poses a double challenge to himself: He is both allegorist and realist, metaphysician and empiricist, in his exploration of the problematics of human existence. As a director, he shows the way in a maze of contrary directions and points of view which define the interpretive quest of the viewer, and he creates some of the most beautiful and powerful images of man and woman in the history of art.

[6] Scholes and Kellogg, op. cit., p. 265.

CHARLES EIDSVIK

DARK LAUGHTER
Buñuel's *Tristana* (1970)

from the novel by Benito Pérez Galdós

In dealing with the films of Luis Buñuel, it is usually safe to begin with two assumptions: First, that at one level or another, Buñuel is joking, and second, that Buñuel's sense of humor is a key to understanding his handling of serious sociopolitical, psychological, and religious issues. That sense of humor is sacrilegious, antiauthoritarian, and above all perversely devious. Thus, to those familiar with his previous work, the most incredible thing about Buñuel's public comments on *Tristana*—a project that had just, in 1962, been stopped by the Spanish censors on the pretext that it "encouraged dueling"—was that Buñuel seemed to expect people to believe his pose of ingenuousness:

> What does one story or another matter? It is the script that is interesting. You know, I could make the life of Christ into a Buddhist film. . . . *Tristana* was a pretext. It gave me an opportunity to deal with some aspects of Spanish life. That apart, like all my films it would contain no social criticism or condemnation of this or that. No thought of it. I limit myself always to showing things without taking positions for or against. People know that, particularly the producers.[1]

Returning to the project in 1969, intent on making a film that unlike most of his others could be shown in Spain, Buñuel resumed his mask of innocence and, despite outbursts of unexplained laughter on the set,[2] made *Tristana* in such a way that no censor could stop the film by claiming that it had hidden subversive meaning.

[1] Quoted in Francisco Aranda, *Luis Buñuel: A Critical Biography*, translated by David Robinson, New York, Da Capo Press, 1976, pp. 217–218.
[2] See Jean-Claude Carriere, "The Buñuel Mystery," *The World of Luis Buñuel*, Joan Mellen (ed.), New York, Oxford University Press, 1978, p. 91.

Buñuel succeeded. His 1970 *Tristana* slipped by Spanish censors, international audiences, and even by critics as a somber, almost humorless study of the decline of two people—a film that is the most classically structured, accessible, and readily comprehensible of his recent works. A quietly gloved social critique of Spanish mores, *Tristana* "reads" on the surface as only a mildly antiauthoritarian and anticlerical study of social realities, a film that contains "no social criticism or condemnation of this or that." But for those familiar with Buñuel's handling of Benito Pérez Galdós's 1892 *Tristana*—a book Buñuel's has called "one of Galdós's worst"[3]—and with Buñuel's penchant for private, darkly sacrilegious humor, the film has an additional, highly subversive level of meaning. Accepting the main characters and basic plot of *Tristana* as a frame, Buñuel quietly reversed the thesis of the novel— that people will adjust happily to just about anything—and thus indirectly attacked the most fundamental assumption of repressive regimes such as Franco's. Galdós built a novel, and Franco a government, on the belief that people can be made to like almost anything. Buñuel's film demonstrates that adaptation to repression leads to perversion and murder. It is an answer to those who wished or feared that Buñuel, given a chance to make a film for Spanish audiences, would behave himself and avoid attacks on the government. Beneath its somber surface, *Tristana*, like Buñuel's other films, shouts for rebellion and may even be, like *Un Chien Andalou* (1928), a "desperate, passionate appeal to murder."

What does one story or another matter? For the wily Buñuel, a rebel perfectly capable of a bird's (or guerrilla's) tactic of deliberately leading attention away from its nest, it may have mattered a great deal. Why, of Galdós's thirty novels, choose one of the worst, a work critically regarded as a "mere tract"? Buñuel had, of course, based his 1958 *Nazarín* on Galdós's greatest novel; it may have given Buñuel perverse pleasure to adapt a bad work of Spain's greatest nineteenth-century novelist. More important, perhaps, Buñuel could assume that Spanish audiences would at least be familiar with three of the novel's basic elements: its thesis that people are totally malleable; its male protagonist, Don Lope Garrido, an aging *hidalgo* who defends all victims except his own and

[3] Ibid., p. 90.

is preoccupied with "honor"; and its female protagonist, Tristana, a young woman enslaved by society, by Don Lope, and later by having her leg amputated. These elements gave Buñuel the framework to make a social, psychological, and political statement, though a statement decipherable only to those who take the trouble to compare Galdós's original with Buñuel's adaptation.

Buñuel's "official" reason for his interest in the novel centered on Don Lope: "Now that I begin to be old myself I feel inspired by this work about old age and decrepitude."[4] Buñuel's sly invitation to equate Don Lope with himself is a perverse, private jest; in both novel and film, Don Lope represents a type of Spanish male Buñuel has always hated. Don Lope is an aristocrat with all the vanities and parasitism of his social class, including a liking for duels and a highly self-serving sense of "honor"—an honor based on public appearances, not on private behavior. In Buñuel's hands, Don Lope's public style and liberal rhetoric (the style and rhetoric of the "intelligentsia" of Buñuel's youth)[5] excite a grudging admiration, while his private piggishness, vanity, and jealousy excite contempt; as Don Lope ages, the victimizer becomes a victim, the object of the viewer's ambivalent pity. In short, Don Lope gives Buñuel the opportunity to force viewers to confront their own complex emotional attitudes toward a symbol of the old paternalistic order. But Buñuel's invitation to regard Don Lope as the center of interest in *Tristana* may also have been a private joke intended to distract attention from Tristana, the title character and center of the film.

Francisco Aranda gives a glimpse of Buñuel's personal sense of humor:

> Buñuel will sometimes tell his friends, with morbid complacency, that when his death becomes imminent he will call a priest to his bed. Thus will he disturb his friends with the doubt whether he will thus have crowned his existence with a cold posthumous sacrilege, or whether he intends to assure his entry into Heaven! . . . The end of *Tristana* is no more than the visualization of this terrible jest.[6]

[4] Aranda, op. cit., p. 218.
[5] Ibid., p. 243.
[6] Ibid., pp. 243–244.

Buñuel's sense of humor allows Don Lope to serve both as a satirical target and as the basis for a private joke in which Buñuel makes light of the expectations that stem from his reputation. Similarly, for the cinema's most notorious student of foot fetishism to make a film about leg amputation could be nothing but a black jest aimed at those who think they know what to expect from Buñuel—that is, unless the subject also provided the opportunity for a bit of private sacrilege. According to Francisco Aranda, the central article of faith in the small town in which Luis Buñuel was raised was the "Miracle of Calanda":

> A man very devoted to the Virgin of the Pilar, having had a leg amputated, dreamed that Our Lady disinterred the member and stuck it back on his stump. The flesh, even though it was already putrefying and worm-eaten, resumed its vital functions. No other miracle can compare with this. To revive a dead man or return sight to one who is blind, can be faked; to see a man who has been without a leg walking with it once more is a proof too absolute to allow a possibility of doubt.[7]

It must have delighted Calanda's most famous son to take up the subject of amputation, make the amputee—Tristana—highly religious, and have the whole business end not in a miracle but in murder. What better way to follow *The Milky Way* (1969), an analysis of heresies, than with a bit of private sacrilege? Thus, Buñuel's interest in Don Lope and Tristana as characters may have stemmed from his love of private jokes that, although they are not likely to be shared by his audience, provide the private amusement and inspiration that has fueled Buñuel's art for a half century.

If Buñuel's interest in Don Lope and Tristana stemmed at least in part from his sense of humor, his interest in *Tristana* probably centered on its thesis. *Tristana* is a case history, "the outline of a story of personality adjustment," that exemplifies Galdós's theory of the "inexorable law of adaptation."[8] As one critic puts it:

> The preponderance of the motive of security over conscience . . . is one element of Galdós's persistent realism. . . . the individual,

7 Ibid., pp. 7–9.
8 Sherman H. Eoff, *The Novels of Pérez Galdós*, St. Louis, Washington University Studies, 1954, pp. 50, 53.

when viewed as a member of society, manifests above all his capacity for arriving at a tolerable way of life. Shortcomings and violations of moral codes are commonly forgotten or subordinated through rationalization, more or less out of the necessity for survival.[9]

Buñuel would probably agree with Galdós's viewpoint as stated in the above terms. Many of Buñuel's films are, in fact, studies of adaptations to reality; one might name *Viridiana* (1959), *Robinson Crusoe* (1952), and *Nazarin* (1958) as three such "studies." But for Buñuel the subconscious always remains a wellspring of revolt; adaptation to repression is always subject to the backtalk of dreams and nightmares. Thus, for Galdós's Don Lope, an unprincipled Don Juan, to become a middle-class husband at the end of *Tristana* might have amused Buñuel, but for Don Lope and Tristana's submission to reality to result in happiness must have aroused a sneer. This is how Galdós's novel ends:

> The old gallant came back to life in his new estate; he seemed less doting, less foolish, and, without his knowing when or how, toward the end of his life he was aware of the birth of inclinations that he had never known before, the manias and longings of the pacific bourgeois. . . .
> [There follows a description of his joy in planting trees and raising chickens.]
> Don Lope was bursting with happiness, and Tristana shared his excitement. At that time the little cripple found a new *afición*: the art of pastry making. An adept teacher showed her two or three kinds of cakes, and she made them so well, so very well, that Don Lope when he tasted them licked his fingers and never ceased praising God.
> Were they happy, each of them? Perhaps.[10]

Galdós's ending is ironic but sympathetic to his characters. At another time, and perhaps in any country except Spain, Buñuel could have taken Galdós's novel as the basis for a satirical study of the ways in which rebels and idealists often succumb to bourgeois feelings in their old age; Galdós's tone is not, after all, that far from Buñuel's in *Viridiana*. But the theory of human adaptability

[9] Ibid., p. 58.
[10] Benito Pérez Galdós, *Tristana*, translated by R. Selden Rose, Peterborough, N.H., Richard R. Smith, 1961, pp. 142–143.

presented in Galdós's novel is almost exactly the psychological basis on which repressive regimes (including bourgeois ones) predicate their survival. Because too many people do adapt to repressive circumstances, the powerful remain unchallenged. For Buñuel, one function of his films is to ensure that "the powerful can never affirm that everyone agrees with their acts."[11] By reversing the meaning of the novel—by making Don Lope miserable and Tristana a monster at the film's end—Buñuel demonstrates the consequences of accommodation to oppressive structures. In Buñuel's view of human nature (which is similar in many respects to the neo-Freudian view that life forces are opposed to death-oriented forces), behavior and its rationalizations may be malleable in the short term, but repressed desires must erupt eventually with destructive force.

For Buñuel, the cinema has two potentials. The first is "to express the world of dreams, of emotions, of instinct."[12] For him, the subconscious is a reservoir of revolt, intractable and powerful. Tristana's hallucinatory nightmare, in which Don Lope's severed head swings attached to a bell clapper in a bell tower that once dictated the movements of all Toledo, expresses perfectly in a single image her suppressed feelings about oppression. By linking this nightmare image with the film's "ordinary" reality, without transition, and by making the nightmare consequential—a cause of perversity and perhaps murder—Buñuel created a simple demonstration of the relationship between oppression and revolt. To provide a context for this image, Buñuel worked with the cinema's second potential—its ability to depict reality.

Buñuel cites Engels on the value of realistic depiction:

> I take for mine the words of Engels, who defined the function of the novelist (understood in this case as that of the filmmaker): "The novelist will have accomplished his task honorably when, through a faithful depiction of authentic social relations, he will have destroyed the conventional representation of the nature of these relations, shaken the optimism of the bourgeois world and obliged the reader to question the permanence of the existing

---

[11] Luis Buñuel, quoted in Carlos Fuentes, "The Discreet Charm of Luis Buñuel," in *The World of Luis Buñuel*, Joan Mellen (ed.), New York, Oxford University Press, 1978, p. 71.
[12] Aranda, op. cit., p. 274.

order, even if he does not directly propose a conclusion to us, even if he does not openly take sides."[13]

Buñuel reconstructed the characters, their relationships, and the story of *Tristana* in accord with Engels's prescription. His reworking of Galdós's novel was radical in both senses of the word.

Some changes, to be sure, were minor. Galdós set his novel in the late nineteenth century; Buñuel changed the date to around 1920, a period in which intellectual liberalism was more akin to our own. The novel takes place in Madrid; Buñuel's film is located in Toledo. Partly this may have been simple expedience: Madrid modernized in the 1960s; Toledo remained relatively unchanged. But partly it may have been a matter of emotional distance: Buñuel vacations in Madrid in winter; he is fond of the place. But Toledo? "I don't like Toledo. It is old and stinks of piss."[14] Buñuel avoided Toledo's main tourist attraction—its El Greco cathedral—and represented the town as an endless succession of grayish-brown stone buildings, streets, and walls, a claustrophobic labyrinth, uninviting and cold, cluttered and dirty. Toledo provided the setting for an unromantic view of "Old Spain."

About all that remains of Galdós's novel are its basic situations. An old *hidalgo* espouses manly honor but makes his ward his mistress; he is her father or husband, as he chooses. He spouts iconoclastic ideas. She rebels and falls in love with a painter, and the old man becomes jealous. She develops a leg tumor; the leg becomes infected and must be amputated. The *hidalgo* cunningly brings the painter and young woman together, knowing that their love affair will fizzle under the circumstances. The young woman becomes ultrareligious. Don Lope and Tristana marry so that Tristana will have an estate after Don Lope's death. The rest of the film—excepting bits of dialogue, odd character traits, the personality of Saturna, Don Lope's maid, and a few minor incidents—is sheer invention.

Buñuel revamped the characters of both Don Lope and Tristana. Don Lope is the less changed of the two. Galdós's Don Lope was a nineteenth-century type; Buñuel's might have been his son. In the novel, Don Lope is vain, jealous, a Don Juan with women,

[13] Ibid., p. 275.
[14] Ibid., p. 241.

In *Tristana*, Buñuel keeps little of the Galdos novel except the basic situation in which an elderly man seduces his ward. Reality slips into dream as Tristana (Catherine Deneuve) sees the phallic clapper as a severed head.

an autocrat, a man who espouses male honor and has dueled frequently in defense of his own. He spends mornings fixing up his appearance, the rest of his time with friends in cafes. He despises commerce as much as he hates marriage and religion; the result is increasing poverty until, just before the novel's end, his nephew, an archbishop, openly "buys" a marriage between Don Lope and Tristana. Don Lope assents merely to assure that Tristana will not end up in the poorhouse. Only then does Don Lope become a bourgeois.

Buñuel made two drastic changes in Don Lope's character. Galdós links Don Lope's financial misfortunes with his sense of honor: Don Lope, at the novel's beginning, spends most of his fortune supporting Tristana's family (her father was his childhood friend). Buñuel drops this "prehistory" of Don Lope and Tristana's relationship, perhaps because it could have led viewers to sentimentalize Don Lope. The second change: Buñuel gives his

Don Lope the attitudes of 1920s intellectuals. Unlike Galdós's character, he is a verbal defender of the poor and the workers, a hater of cops. His liberal and iconoclastic views are gratuitous: He speaks from a position of prestige, from the safety of his position, his house, and his cafe. However, Buñuel kept the bulk of the idiosyncrasies of Galdós's Don Lope, and, by casting Fernando Rey, emphasized Don Lope's charm, quick wit, and aristocratic style.

While Galdós's Don Lope is a character of both good and evil, an egoist matching his wits against adversity, Buñuel's begins as a witty, charming heel. When he falls in love with Tristana, he degenerates into a pathetic old man who loses everything he wants or believes in. Through Fernando Rey's skill, this decline is depicted through physical changes: Don Lope's frame sags, his face goes lax, his walk stiffens, he hunches, he grows colder and speaks more slowly. When he can no longer pretend to dignity, age gives him the manner of a victim. But Buñuel's Don Lope is never really poor. He has a rich sister, and, though they hate each other, she leaves him her money when she dies. Galdós's Don Lope loses the last of his money caring for the ill Tristana. In the film, by the time Tristana becomes ill, Don Lope has his wealth as a tool and source of power. He buys her pianos, sweets, and a country house, attempting to purchase affection with material comforts. Buñuel's Don Lope is a materialistic hedonist, his wealth and weaknesses linked closely.

Buñuel's changes in Don Lope are relatively minor compared to his changes in Tristana. Galdós's Tristana is a spokeswoman for the plight of women in Old Spain; she knows that her victimization and social situation are linked. She is pathetic but perceptive. In reply to Saturna's view that only three careers are open to women —marriage, the theater, and prostitution—Tristana says:

> And what can a woman live on if she hasn't any money? If they could make doctors, lawyers, even druggists or notaries out of us, we could. . . . But sewing and sewing. . . . How many stitches do you have to take to support a household? When I think what will become of me, I feel like crying. . . .
>
> I want to *live*, to see the world and find out why we're here on this earth and what for. I want to live and be free.[15]

15 Galdós's *Tristana*, pp. 19–20.

As a result of the gap between reality and desire, Galdós's Tristana becomes an idealistic dreamer and eventually a hobbyist (the ultimate limbo of the frustrated), unable to accept the virtues of reality. After her amputation, the distance between everyday reality and her dreams becomes so great that she uses religion as an escape, an opiate to make her indifferent to reality. At the novel's end, her only contact with her earlier ideas, talents, and potentials is through pastry making.

Despite Buñuel's sympathy for the oppressed, he dropped Galdós's profeminist analysis of Tristana's situation. Perhaps it was too deterministic for his tastes; perhaps it was too sentimental; perhaps it was too obvious—certainly it was too liberal. Buñuel has always had contempt for liberalism's tendency to sympathize with everything in a weak-kneed way. He retains Galdós's version of Tristana's situation but makes her less a self-conscious victim, a dreamer. At the beginning of the film she is playful, inventing for herself a game 1920s Surrealists enjoyed playing, finding a way to prefer among seemingly identical pairs one grape, one column, one chick-pea. She enjoys everyday life—her companionship with Saturna and Saturna's son, Saturno; her walks around Toledo; a simple meal of fried bread offered her by the town's bellkeeper. All beauty and playful innocence, she has only one problem: a nightmare in which Don Lope's head swings attached to a bell clapper. The nightmare precedes and perhaps predicts her horror of phallic power when Don Lope makes her his mistress. She is a Titian-haired innocent, only mildly irritated when Saturno tries to look up her skirt, and unaware of the effect of her open-necked nightgown on Don Lope.

Under Don Lope's tutelage, she becomes a rebel, accepting his views of marriage and the church. Don Lope beds her; she rebels by falling in love with a painter, eventually leaving Toledo with him. (In Galdós's novel, she does not leave but becomes sick when the painter departs to tend a sick aunt.) She returns to Don Lope's house, sick and wanting to die there. Perhaps unfortunately for both her and Don Lope, she recovers after her leg is amputated. She shuts herself off from the painter; immerses herself in religion, pastries, and music; and becomes increasingly perverse, mean-spirited, and even demonic—the nastiest cripple in Buñuel's films. From here on, her character bears no relationship whatever to Galdós's original.

In this third stage of her character development, Tristana seems to take pleasure in torturing both herself and those around her. She clumps about on crutches with a deliberate clumsiness, often seeming to refuse herself the artifice of a false leg; when she goes out, it is in a wheelchair pushed by Saturno, with whom she is now curt. Reveling in the identity of being a cripple, she uses her infirmity to manipulate Don Lope. When, on the urging of a priest, she marries him, she refuses to consummate the marriage. Instead, she gets pleasure from exposing herself to Saturno from the safety of her balcony. Eventually Don Lope has a heart attack at night. She merely pretends to call a doctor, and opens the window to the cold winter wind to make sure he will die. In a coda, the central images of the film flash by in reverse order while we hear the sound of the winter wind and the reverberation of a bell, its sound distorted and hollow. Tristana's mind, as well as her body, has become grotesque.

To allow social issues and an additional dollop of sexual perversity to enter the film, Buñuel made one additional radical character change. In Galdós's novel, Saturno is a normal boy being raised in a *hospicio* (an orphanage for the children of working mothers). Though there is one scene with deaf-mutes and blind children—one of the most compelling in the novel—Saturno is not handicapped. Buñuel makes him a deaf-mute and brings him into the film as a very important secondary character. Dressed in worker's blue but unable to hold a job because he spends too much time masturbating, Saturno becomes an all-purpose foil for the other characters. He peeks up Tristana's skirt in the bell tower; her reaction reveals her innocence. He runs into Don Lope's house when the police attack a crowd of young workers; although Don Lope's sentiments fall on (literally) deaf ears, Don Lope speaks to Saturno about his sympathy for workers and hatred of work. Saturno becomes Tristana's servant after the amputation. He pushes her wheelchair, unsuccessfully attempts to seduce her, and is voyeur to her exhibitionism. Impetuously sexual and incorrigible, Saturno is an image of mute rebelliousness. The only thing that vanquishes him is Tristana's display of her crippled body. But with that exception, Saturno has been subjected to everything and has internalized nothing.

Typically, Buñuel allows little sympathy for either Tristana or Saturno. In Buñuel's films from *Los Olvidados* to *Viridiana* to

Tristana, infirmity and nastiness are linked, and we are denied nice sentiments about the unfortunate. In his depiction of behavior, Buñuel denies the notion that infirmities make people any nicer; bourgeois pity is but the other face of the bourgeois optimism and escapism that Buñuel's unromantic, cold eye rejects as he depicts "authentic social relations." But if infirmity or ugliness are not grounds for sympathy in *Tristana*, neither is beauty. Once she has lost her playful innocence, Tristana becomes perhaps more beautiful but certainly no more sympathetic. And Don Horacio, the painter with whom she falls in love, is treated as little more than a pretty picture. Played by a matinee idol—Franco Nero—Don Horacio is depicted as a dandy, physically uptight and certainly not very gallant: When Don Lope challenges him to a duel, he simply and unceremoniously slugs the old man. Though he tries to behave decently toward Tristana, Nero's Don Horacio is not a very interesting human being; looks are no guarantor of human depth. And in the atmosphere of emotional gamesmanship in which Don Lope and Tristana exist, naive beauty has little place. In Buñuel's world there are no heroes or heroines. Rather, Buñuel deliberately denies his viewers any chance of romanticizing his characters.

Critics have likened Buñuel's approach in *Tristana* to Brecht's; both Buñuel and Brecht distance their audiences from their stories.[16] It is true that Buñuel keeps his audience at an emotional distance from his characters. Otherwise, however, his technique is quite unlike Brecht's: The swiftness of Buñuel's pacing, the "flattening" of all kinds of actions and dreams into a single level of discourse, and the cold tone of Buñuel's film are all antithetical to Brecht's openly didactic stance. Brecht preaches; Buñuel demonstrates. And the viewer must watch a Buñuel film as if it were a rapidly evolving game in which one's attention is consumed by keeping track of the players, the events, and the ever-changing rules. It is a game in which one cannot choose sides or, for more than a moment at a time, identify with the players. It is enough to keep track of what goes on. Because Buñuel structured *Tristana* as a series of elliptical scenes rather than as a single narrative pro-

[16] Aranda, op. cit., p. 242. See also Raymond Durgnat, *Luis Buñuel*, Berkeley, University of California Press, 1977, p. 158.

gression, concentration is required merely to follow the dramatic action.

The structure of *Tristana* is dialectical. Each scene gives one or two new insights into Don Lope's or Tristana's personalities or into their relationship; it is then effaced by the next scene, the next insight. Altogether, the film has over three dozen scenes, each interrupting the emotional progression of the last and often contradicting its mood. There are few transitions between scenes. A scene usually begins with a close-up; the camera then pulls back to reveal what is happening. It happens, and then the next scene begins—often with another close-up. For example, one scene begins with a close-up of Tristana ironing. The camera pans to a full shot of Don Lope entering the room. He orders Saturna out and tells Tristana to stop ironing. Tristana and Don Lope go to Don Lope's bedroom. Tristana undresses; Don Lope puts the dog out of the room. The scene functions to tell us that Tristana is now Don Lope's mistress. But as quickly as we have grasped that fact, the camera shows young men running in the street with cops chasing them. One of the young men is Saturno. He escapes into Don Lope's house. But now there has been a time shift; Don Lope is sick in bed with a cold. And so on through the film: Each moment breaks the mood of the previous one; just when one thinks one understands, new elements are added with which one must cope. The accumulation of details, each sparely and briefly revealed, adds up finally to a summary of the configurations in which Tristana and Don Lope play out their existences—a summary in which there is little room for optimism about the bourgeois world or the permanence of the existing order. In Buñuel's hands, *Tristana* becomes an essay on the inexorability of impermanence.

What shifts from scene to scene are the power relationships between the characters. A victim in one scene becomes a victimizer in the next—only to become a victim later on. The overall effect is, of course, polemical: All the characters derive their meanness from a world of social relationships based on inequities between people and on the assumption that victimization is both inevitable and a source of pleasure. Eventually, such a social structure makes everyone a victim. The social structure—a repressive society—is the villain. *Tristana* is a condemnation of Spain (and, by extension, of societies like the Spanish one) carried out by a demonstration of what Spain makes people become. Excepting the episode in which Tristana exhibits herself to Saturno, each scene in *Tristana* is a description of relatively "normal" behavior. The effect of the film is cumulative: One becomes repulsed by the endlessness of the power games the characters play; it is finally the game, not the players, that one condemns. In *Tristana*, Buñuel's cold eye becomes his most effective weapon.

Among Buñuel's films, *Tristana* is unique. Its realistic approach resembles most closely that taken in *Los Olvidados* (1950); in *Tristana*, as in *Los Olvidados* and *Land Without Bread* (1932), Buñuel documents dispassionately the effects of powerlessness and oppression. But in *Tristana* this documentation is focused not on the poor or helpless but on the relatively well-off and privileged: In oppressive cultures, the rich oppress not only the poor but each other and themselves. There is an anger, a sense of outrage, in Buñuel's earlier work that is absent in *Tristana*. *Tristana,* like *Viridiana, Diary of a Chambermaid* (1964), and *The Milky Way* (1969), is a deliberate, calculated study of behavior and motivations. Though the nightmare image of Don Lope's severed head is central to understanding Tristana's psychology, *Tristana* is in virtually every other respect a far less fanciful film than anything Buñuel has done since *Belle de Jour* (1966). Neither the warmth nor the droll, surrealistic humor of the later Buñuel is present in *Tristana*.

The reason is simple and obvious. In *Tristana* Buñuel had to keep a straight face. *Viridiana* had caused trouble for his producers and could not be shown in Spain because Buñuel had ended the piece slyly with a scene clearly indicating that Viridiana, her cousin, and the maid would henceforth live in a *menage à trois*. In Mexico and especially in France, Buñuel could indulge his sense of humor openly and revel in ironies. But in Spain, to work at all Buñuel had to avoid the suspicion that he was clowning at the expense of the Spanish government. Thus, he kept his laughter private and left his subversive message for the viewer to infer from the structure of the film rather than from its explicit dramatic content. As with any rebellious filmmaker working under conditions of tight censorship (whether in Spain or Czechoslovakia or Hungary), Buñuel had to hide his meaning behind a mask of benign respectability. Buñuel, the bad boy of Spanish cinema, had to get away with pretending to be good.

And he did get away with it. In *Tristana* there was nothing for a censor to cut. Except for the cumulative effect of the film, there was no possible reason for the censors to prohibit exhibition. Everything subversive—the reversal of the meaning of a novel by Spain's most respected novelist, the private sacrilege, the savage analysis of power and oppression, the unromantic view of Spain— is not obvious to the casual or uninitiated viewer. *Tristana* is a study of the consequences of oppression, a demonstration of the murderous and unhappy results of repressing the subconscious for too long. An attack on the root assumptions of Spain, *Tristana* accomplishes its ends without ever saying what they are.

I can hear Buñuel's laughter when his version of Galdós's *Tristana* was approved for viewing in Spain. It is a dark laugh, a song of rebellion, and a testament to the artist's power to turn a muzzle into an eloquent mask. It is a noise nothing can stop.

PETER BRUNETTE

FILMING WORDS
Wenders's *The Goalie's Anxiety at the Penalty Kick (1971)*

from the novel by Peter Handke

Wim Wenders's 1971 film adaptation of Peter Handke's novel *The Goalie's Anxiety at the Penalty Kick (Die Angst des Tormanns beim Elfmeter,* 1970; English translation, 1972) is especially interesting because of the relative "purity" of the difficulties Wenders confronted in adapting the novel for the screen. Since Handke was an active collaborator on the screenplay (though it's important to remember that he is listed in the credits as collaborating on the dialogue alone), the problem was not one of clashing artistic personalities or ideological differences or—as is most often the case, at least in Hollywood—widely disparate conceptions of art and of what is suitable for mass entertainment. Rather, the problem seems almost exclusively to have concerned the essential differences in the two media themselves.

The plot of Handke's novel is told simply. Bloch, an ex-soccer goalie, almost nonchalantly kills a movie cashier after spending the night with her and then travels to a country inn run by a former girl friend. He meets people along the way, engages in quite a few desultory conversations, and thinks a lot about the nature of reality and his relation to it. On the surface at least, not very promising material for a film.

Complicating matters is the fact that Handke's novel is ultimately about language, about itself. It is an anguished dramatization of the arbitrariness of all sign systems. Bloch, Handke's hero, alienated from the concrete reality which surrounds him and lost in a sea of signs, experiences the breakdown of the "natural" link between signifier and signified. If the novel is indeed about itself—

about its own words, which somehow become shifting realities and "characters" in their own right—how can a film ever hope to capture in visual images the novel's dynamic verbal texture? Wenders could have attempted to convey this drama of unruly signifiers solely by means of the film's specifically verbal component, *i.e.,* the dialogue, but this would have created an awkward and destructive dichotomy between the film's visuals and its sound track. In the book, the verbal gyrations are not limited to the few scraps of dialogue we overhear; rather, they permeate the entire novel so thoroughly that at one point the words even turn into stick-figure drawings of real objects. One is at pains to imagine how this could ever be translated successfully to the screen.

Also involved here is the whole question of the "art film's" absence of overt activity and plot. For even when nothing is "happening" in the novel, *the words themselves* are happening—engendering conflicts, rising up from the page to assert themselves and insist that we pay attention to them for their own sake, and refusing to be limited to their docile role of mere referentiality. This verbal "activity," again, is impossible to translate to the screen, and the film does in fact often seem more static than the novel.

There are additional problems which arise from the particularities of Handke's novel. For one thing, the author is often given to a terse shorthand in describing scenes; he is most unlike Henry James in this regard, almost always, except for key thematic statements, preferring to "tell" rather than to "show" in order to dedramatize the flow of external events. At one point, for example, he writes: "In the evening [Bloch] left the hotel and got drunk. Later he sobered up and tried calling some friends. . . ."[1] Can a film ever imitate this incredibly laconic efficiency? One can imagine Wenders simply cutting to a tipsy Bloch in a new scene without actually having to show him *getting* drunk, but could he show him getting drunk and *then* getting sober with the same brevity found in the novel? In fact, so many small "events" can be packed into one paragraph of Handke's stripped prose that Wenders must omit many scenes that he would otherwise have had to show in all their particularity. The scenes he *does* choose to film, of course,

---

[1] Peter Handke, *The Goalie's Anxiety at the Penalty Kick,* translated by Michael Roloff, New York, Farrar, Straus & Giroux, 1972, p. 4. All further references in the text will be to this edition.

must often be supplied with characters, a dramatic situation, and dialogue that are lacking in the curiously indirect, passive-voice, often personless reportage of the novel.

Wenders's general strategy for approaching the problems outlined above involves two different but complementary paths. On the one hand, he is sometimes able to find cinematic equivalents for the verbal phenomena of the book. On the other hand, he is forced to alter certain aspects of the theme to suit the exigencies of the film medium, while maintaining and translating others. The difficulty here is that his thematic revision cannot help but be somewhat reductive and disappointing. What happens, in effect, is that the book's profoundly disturbing depiction of a man who has become socially, psychologically, and morally unglued because of his sudden and inexplicable detachment from reality, language, and the easy production of (apparent) meaning becomes in the film a more conventional tale of the impossibility of human communication—a favorite Wenders theme, especially in the later *Kings of the Road* (1976). Nevertheless, Wenders does manage to preserve and explore in cinematically appropriate ways (which I will examine later) some features of the novel's theme, most notably its self-reflexivity. In fact, it is largely through *formal* means— specifically the distortion of film language and the manipulation of genre convention—that Wenders is ultimately able to approximate the verbal disturbances of the novel and thus salvage some of its thematic depth.

In many cases, Wenders was able to take things over directly into the film or, more often, translate the terms of the print medium into visual language. One of the more important changes comes at the very beginning of the film, when we see a short scene of a soccer game followed by a purposely stylized medium shot of Bloch the goalie passively watching the movement of the ball even as it is shot right past him into the net. When the novel opens, however, Bloch is a *former* goalie who is presently being fired from a construction job. (Wenders told an interviewer that this "was difficult to explain in the film and so we made him a real goalie. That's the only thing we really changed from the novel."[2]) The first scene of the film, then, seems to be wholly Wenders's inven-

[2] Tony Rayns, "Forms of Address: Interviews with Three German Filmmakers," *Sight & Sound*, Vol. XLIV, No. 1, Winter 1974–75, p. 6.

Wim Wenders in *The Goalie's Anxiety at the Penalty Kick* finds cinematic equivalents for Handke's verbal technique in telling the story of Bloch (Arthur Brauss) who hits the road after committing a casual murder.

tion until one realizes that it is actually a translation of Handke's ten-word *epigraph*, which stands at the head of the novel and sets the tone for everything which comes after it: "The goalie watched as the ball rolled across the line. . . ." Here Wenders has nicely extrapolated an entire scene from a single sentence. His isolation of the motionless, seemingly catatonic goalie in a patently artificial shot sets the tone of the movie, serving a function analogous to the book's epigraph.

Wenders has more difficulty with the perennial problem of screen adaptations—the rendering of thought. He has wisely avoided the most common solution—voice-over—for the constant presence of Bloch's voice would obviously work against our sense of his isolation and distance, bringing him improperly close to the viewer. Often, the thoughts are simply not rendered at all, especially in the case of memories, when the effort of translation to the screen would necessitate awarding them far more importance than they deserve. For example, where Handke has written

Were there ants in the teapot? "Ants?" When the boiling water from the kettle hit the bottom of the pot, he didn't see tea leaves but ants, on which he had once poured scalding water (p. 18).

Wenders contents himself with a neutral close-up of the teapot. At other times, he finds appropriate visualizations, as when Bloch takes a shower in the apartment of the young woman he later murders. The text reads:

> If the pressure of everything around him when his eyes were open was bad, the pressure of the words for everything out there when his eyes were closed was even worse. "Maybe it's because I just finished sleeping with her," he thought. He went into the bathroom and took a long shower (pp. 17–18).

In the film, this is rendered by an extremely slow zoom-in on Bloch's face as he stands in the shower, the water coursing violently down over his closed eyes. Obviously, the precise content of Bloch's thought cannot be conveyed by this camera movement, but a palpable sense of pressure, at least, *is* conveyed, and conveyed much more dramatically and forcefully than it ever could be in the novel. These are the kind of trade-offs, naturally, that characterize all adaptations.

Michael Covino, in an excellent introduction to Wenders's films,[3] has pointed out a few of the director's visual metamorphoses. He mentions, for example, Wenders's use of relatively static shots to indicate Bloch's almost terrifying passivity. Wenders himself commented on his use of camera movement in an interview with Tony Rayns:

> When we started, we thought we could do it without any movement, and we actually did for the first two days of shooting. Then we saw that we could make movements that weren't really movements, that were still very static, and we made a lot of tracks from then on. But always following a moving subject. Except once, with the penalty at the end. I didn't like it.[4]

The tracking shots are often wonderfully expressive; at one point Bloch continually speeds up and slows down while walking along the edge of the road, as if to escape the tracking shot which

[3] Michael Covino, "Wim Wenders: A Worldwide Homesickness," *Film Quarterly*, Vol. XXXI, No. 2, Winter 1977–78, pp. 9–19.
[4] Rayns, op. cit., p. 6.

pins him so tenaciously. One can also add that amid these static shots are often found shots of restless, consciously petty movement which express Bloch's constant need to fiddle nervously with objects in a most annoying manner.

Covino also points out that much of the film is shot at dusk in order to convey to the viewer the gnawing anxiety of which Bloch can never free himself. But what Covino doesn't mention is that the peculiar anxiety-producing aspects of this shooting at dusk come largely because Wenders seems to have underexposed the film stock deliberately. The colors that result remind one of the colors of Polaroid film that has been taken from the camera before the chemicals have had a chance to complete the developing process—the look is consequently highly stylized, unreal, even *metallic*, and this is fully consistent with the stylization we find throughout both novel and film.

Other camera movements and angles which serve as translations of the texture and mood of the novel include the use of unusual camera set-ups to suggest Bloch's feelings of anxiety and isolation. Thus, Wenders uses an occasional overhead shot from the ceiling of Bloch's hotel room, showing him sprawled out and pinned to his bed as though he were a laboratory specimen or Kafka's cockroach, Gregor Samsa. At another moment we cut quickly to a strange, whirling aerial shot high above what seems to be the village and then cut away just as quickly to Bloch lying wide awake in bed. Further similarities with the book include: (1) the refusal to emphasize, emotionally at any rate, one scene over another (so that in both film and novel, murders, muggings, and playing jukeboxes are given exactly equal stress), (2) the lack of continuity shots to connect causally (or any other way) the various episodes that are served up to us, and (3) the infrequent use of an odd camera angle—an exterior crane shot, for example—in which the camera seems to look down upon the action with the eyes of the novel's omniscient narrator.

One of the most difficult transitions Wenders is able to effect concerns Bloch's relationship to objects. In the novel, Bloch is thoroughly alienated from the real world of objects and tends to experience the words which stand for them rather than the objects themselves. Naturally, then, a lot of time is spent in the novel rendering Bloch's peculiar consciousness of external reality, while the film medium can only hint dimly at what is going on. Nevertheless, Wenders is able to suggest Bloch's uneasiness by again underexposing the film stock and by holding the shot a long time. Finally, the objects are seen so intensely that they actually appear to pulsate in the semidarkness, and the audience shares Bloch's experience at least viscerally if not intellectually.

Interestingly, many of the most effective translations of the novel concern not the visualization of its elements but their *aural* rendition. In one of the scenes described above, for example, Bloch is so overwhelmed by the sheer weight of existent objects that he vomits. One of the advantages of Wenders's rendition of this particular scene is that the actual sound of Bloch's hoarse vomiting is naturally much more powerful than Handke's sentence "He immediately vomited into the sink" (p. 57) could ever be. Similarly, the butcher slapping a piece of beef on the counter jars Bloch (and us) more immediately than any verbal indication ever could. The same holds true for the piercing sound of Bloch's upturned glass banging against the beer bottle it accompanies—the effect is like fingernails on a blackboard. Bloch jumps, irritated, and so do we. The records change on the innumerable jukeboxes with a mechanical scraping that serves as a natural prelude to the often harsh American rock 'n' roll which always follows it. Probably the most effective use of sound, though, is Jürgen Knieper's droning, driving musical score that blares out at the most unexpected times; it contains a strong suggestion of a European-style police siren which makes us anxious with its strident insistence and continually reminds us that Bloch is a hunted man.

But the filmmaker must always be visually and aurally inventive in his search for cinematic equivalencies, and in this regard Wenders's difficulties were not especially greater than those faced by most adapters of introspective novels. Rather, the real problem for this adaptation concerns the special nature of Handke's novel, a novel whose basic constituent—language—is also its subject, theme, plot, and ultimately even its central character. Consider, for example, this passage:

> It seemed as though a crowbar had pried him away from what he saw—or, rather, as though the things around him had all been pulled away from him. The wardrobe, the sink, the suitcase, the

door: only now did he realize that he, as if compelled, was thinking of the word for each thing. Each glimpse of a thing was immediately followed by its word. The chair, the clothes hangers, the
key (pp. 57–58).

The film can only show the objects directly, of course, and not
how they are immediately followed in Bloch's mind by the *words*
which stand for them. In the novel, on the other hand, *only* the
words are shown, even before the fact of the words following is
mentioned. As the reader realizes that all he sees is the abstracted,
arbitrary word and not the thing, he suddenly perceives the novel
as participating in and actualizing Bloch's thought process in a self-
reflexive or metalinguistic way that is unique to the printed page.
Another, perhaps clearer example of how the novel itself, as producer of meanings, is tied up with its subject occurs very early in
the book when we read: "Without meaning anything by it, Bloch
lowered his head" (p. 7). The novelist is here able to participate
directly—with the use of words which can explain, qualify, or call
themselves into question—in exploring the problematic aspects of
referentiality, of objects and gestures and fragments of other systems which have, in addition to their own proper "natural" meaning, a meaning which resides *outside* themselves. This, of course, is
one of Bloch's chief problems: To what extent do the things,
noises, and gestures that one encounters in the world have meaning
in themselves, or do they also signify beyond? How is one to tell
when a second system of external signification is in operation and
when it is not?

The difficulty of ever "fully" translating this novel into film is
made even more clear when Handke uses words to contradict
themselves or to flout deliberately the conventional demand for
verisimilitude. At one point we read: "Bloch pretended to be startled, and in reality he was startled" (p. 10). And later: "The
waitress brought the drink Bloch had ordered for her [his ex-girl-
friend]. Which 'her'?" (p. 36). Or again: "The empty mailbox
resounded as [the postcards] fell into it. But the mailbox was so
tiny that nothing could resound in there. Anyway, Bloch had
walked away immediately" (p. 46). Can a film show any of these
verbal contradictions? Can it have us hear, at the same time, a
mailbox resounding and not resounding?

The reason film cannot translate the novel here is because by its very nature film is always *intentional* (in the phenomenological sense of the word); like consciousness itself, a film must always be a film *of something*. With the possible exceptions of animation and films produced by computers, say, or by Norman McLaren, who paints directly on the celluloid, film must always be, and can *only* be, a recording of the reality that is placed before it. Even the most wildly surrealistic films, like René Clair's *Entr'acte* (1924) and Buñuel and Dali's *Un Chien Andalou* (1928), must *begin* at least with real objects that obey the laws of nature and are not pure products of the imagination. Handke can therefore choose to strip language to its barest essentials, ruthlessly eliminating adjectives and adverbs, but film cannot help but show its "adjectives" and "adverbs." It differs from the novel, then, in that words can have form *without content*—without meaning beyond a collection of arbitrary sounds—whereas film can never be contentless. Its very essence is to show *something* which it can embody but which is originally not itself. The special quality of film, of course, is precisely this *presentness* that novels never have.

The height of the novel's "unfilmability" comes when Handke renders Bloch's perceptions of objects in the form of an alternative sign system, that of simple stick figures. Paradoxically, this system stands in a closer relationship to the cinematic system of signification, even though it would be more difficult to render than words, especially in its verbal context:

> He sat down on the bed: just now that chair had been to his right, and now it was to his left. Was the picture reversed? He looked at it from left to right, then from right to left. He repeated the look from left to right; this look seemed to him like reading. He saw a "wardrobe," "then" "a" "wastebasket," "then" "a" "drape"; while looking from right to left, however, he saw ⊓ , next to it the ⊤⊤ , under it the ⊟ , next to it the ⧻, on top of it his ⌂ ... (p. 124).

And so on. Even actions are rendered in this fashion by means of contiguous drawings of a window with the drapes closed and a window with the drapes open, to indicate that Bloch has gone to the window, has opened the drapes, and is now looking out. This is followed by an entire paragraph of these elementary figures which represent what Bloch sees.[5]

In general, then, Wenders has sought to provide visual equivalencies for the novel whenever possible. But, as we have seen, the very subject and theme of Handke's work preclude any "final" cinematic adaptation that can be thoroughly faithful to the text. Ultimately, therefore, Wenders must transcend (or skirt) the novel so that he may treat approximate themes which he can personalize and which are more easily rendered in filmic terms.

What happens, essentially, is that Handke's rich and complex themes dealing with the shifting, arbitrary relationships among man, the world, and language are reduced to a favorite Wenders concern—the impossibility of real communication between human beings. This notion is present in the novel as well, but it is clearly secondary. Wenders has chosen to heighten certain suggestions and episodes contained in the novel in order to underline and explore this concern more fully. While it is perhaps not as fresh and unique an approach as Handke's, it was clearly a wise decision for him to move in this direction, to suggest a core of meaning that is well within the possibility of the film medium to demonstrate.

Throughout the film, Wenders stresses Bloch's difficulties in communicating with others. When he tries to telephone, for example, the phone doesn't work, or he can't reach his party, or the phone has yet to be installed in a new booth. Wenders also "enacts" scenes which are unemphasized in the novel. For example, where Handke has

> When Bloch wanted to talk, she had started in. He wanted to show her that the waitress was wearing orthopedic shoes, but the landlady was already pointing to the street, where a policeman was

[5] Handke himself involves his character momentarily in the problematics of verbal and cinematic depiction of reality. Early in the novel, Bloch goes to a movie theater several times, and at one point we are told that his "feeling of pretense, of playing around . . . went away only when, in the movie, a comic snitched a trumpet from a junk shop and started tooting on it in a perfectly natural way; all this was so casual that it almost seemed unintentional, and Bloch relaxed" (pp. 14–15). Of course, Bloch is mistaken here, as he often is in his highly wrought state, because the objects depicted *in a film* are not real either, just as they are not real when translated into language, but rather referential in a highly complex way that is simply different (and perhaps less arbitrary) than the referentiality of words.

walking past, pushing a child's bicycle. "That's the dumb kid's bike," she said (p. 48).

Wenders, instead, actually shows their cross-conversation, their individual lines of dialogue that clash and end up sounding like nonsense.

An even better example is a "conversation" between Bloch and the maid at his hotel: Misunderstanding follows misunderstanding as they talk at cross-purposes. In the novel, Bloch is merely trying to comment on the fact that the rooms have too much furniture in them; in the film, Wenders gives him an additional line of dialogue at the end of the aborted conversation to the effect that "even talking is hard work in these rooms." The best example, however, is Bloch's encounter with the school janitor while Bloch is out on one of his interminable, aimless walks. Again, this scene is in the novel as well, but as the janitor's important remarks are given only one short paragraph, the reader can easily pass over them without realizing their thematic significance. They are important enough to quote:

> No wonder the children hadn't even learned to read by the time they left school, the janitor said suddenly . . . they couldn't manage even to finish a single sentence of their own, they talked to each other almost entirely in single words, and they wouldn't talk at all unless you asked them to, and what they learned was only memorized stuff that they rattled off by rote; except for that, they couldn't use whole sentences. "Actually, all of them, more or less, have a speech defect," said the janitor.
>
> What was that supposed to mean? What reason did the janitor have for that? What did it have to do with him? Nothing? Yes, but why did the janitor act as if it had something to do with him? (pp. 104–105).

In the film version, the encounter is also short, but Wenders manages to make it resonate so that the viewer understands clearly that these lines form an important thematic statement. The janitor's description, of course, fits Bloch perfectly: Only with the utmost difficulty is he able to form meaningful sentences, in other words to go beyond the objects that appear before him by putting them into some meaningful relationship with one another. The formation of sentences implies the possibility of coherence, a system of arbitrary but useful rules which transcends the objects and interrelates them and by which men can communicate with each other, in some makeshift fashion at least.

But if Wenders is content to stress the more accessible theme of human communication, he is not content to let Handke's subtler themes escape him entirely. Thus, one aspect of the novel that he is able to suggest is its self-reflexivity, which, given our discussion, is obviously important. One good example occurs in the passage quoted above, in which Bloch's word-oriented consciousness actually begins to transform real objects and actions into stick-figure symbols. In effect, Handke is exploring the nature of reading itself, and how reality is "read" as well, especially when Bloch's eyes move from left to right. It is only when he forces himself to move his eyes in the opposite direction that he can see the objects as themselves rather than mediated by words. The same reawakening to reality is effected in the "climactic" scene at the end of the film and the book, in which Bloch forces himself to watch the idle goalie rather than to follow, "naturally," the progress of the ball.

In another place, we read what first seems to be nothing more than narratorial description: "Back in town; back at the inn; back in his room" (p. 80). The sentence which follows, however, brings us up short and forcefully reminds us of the process in which we're engaged: " 'Eleven words altogether,' thought Bloch with relief." Bloch's consciousness has thus seemed momentarily to merge with that of the undramatized narrator, and we have the fleeting impression that Bloch himself is imagining not only his own thought but the whole book. The ontological status of the novel itself is thus cast into doubt, and we are temporarily alienated from it and uncomfortable with it, just as Bloch is with *all* the objects which surround him.

Wenders has made his version equally self-reflexive, but in ways which are particularly appropriate to the cinematic medium. Thus, he challenges us at regular intervals throughout to question the nature of the process we are engaged in, to remember that this work takes its place in a tradition of other films which have conditioned us to see reality and its filmed image in certain specific but arbitrary ways. He does not, however, indulge in the sort of violent *Verfremdungseffekt* that Godard, for example, has adopted from Brecht; Wenders's effects are far more lighthearted and whimsical, sometimes little more than the kind of "in jokes" that the early, prepolitical New Wave so delighted in.

In order to achieve his own brand of self-reflexivity, Wenders has occasionally invented entirely new scenes or, more frequently, added new details to scenes already there. One sequence, for example, shows Bloch paging through a magazine while an American couple finishes their breakfast in the hotel dining room and leaves. We cut to a shot through the dining-room window and watch as a car is started up and driven away. Without being consciously aware of it, we assume, given the film grammar that is so naturally and thoroughly a part of us, that the Americans are in the car. Instead, a second or two later, we see the Americans walk by the window, and we are immediately thrown off balance. We experience momentarily the uneasiness that Bloch feels throughout the film, but more importantly, our conditioned sense of causality in films is challenged and, by extension, *all* systems of meaning are challenged as well. This disturbing shot forces us to consider, at least for a moment, the nature of the activity in which we're involved. Similarly, many shots, like the one described above, are filmed through windows, thereby putting an inside frame around the action, which must necessarily remind us of the exterior frame constituted by the film image itself.

Wenders also spreads little "jokes" throughout the film which play with our expectations. At one point, for example, Bloch looks like he is just about to kick a pumpkin that's in his path, but he kicks a ball instead. The viewer feels a bit chagrined at having been taken in so thoroughly by his expectation. Elsewhere, the waitress in the bar explains the provenance of the elk horns above the jukebox, and though Bloch looks up at them, Wenders refuses to tilt up, as we expect, to show them to us. At another point, Bloch asks someone at a bar what film is showing at the local theater and is told *"72 Hours to Go."* But immediately after saying this, Bloch's informant flamboyantly pulls back his sleeve, and checks what time it is on his watch. Most of these bits are of the variety that Godard uses in *Weekend* (1968) in the scene in which he refuses to tilt down to show us the bare breasts of his heroine while she takes a bath. He then makes fun of our lascivious desires and expectations by including in the shot a small classical picture of a naked woman's torso.

Some of Wenders's jokes are more complex and tie in nicely with Handke's central theme of the disassociation of object and label. For example, Bloch's former girl friend who runs the inn near the border is known simply as Hertha in the novel; in the film, Wenders christens her Hertha Gabler, though I can find little similarity between her and Ibsen's character. Another, more important name change is a signal for Wenders's special preoccupation with America and its "colonization" of the European mind. While the girl whom Bloch kills early on is known simply as "Gerda" in Handke's version, in the film she is called "Gloria" and at one point spells her name in English for Bloch. The obvious, purposely artificial connection is made sometime later when we hear the American rock song "Gloria," in which the name is spelled out, emanating from a jukebox just as Bloch is about to get beaten up.

Probably the most interesting self-reflexive changes concern Wenders's fascination with film history, especially that of the American genre film, which is apparent in nearly all his films. Thus, much of his leg pulling depends not only on our expectations of film language and grammar but on our more specific expectations of genre conventions. At one point, for example, Bloch is looking out his hotel window in a scene which clearly imitates *film noir* conventions. Only the last two letters of a neon light are visible—"EL"—and we subconsciously fill in the "HOT" which is missing. But just at that moment a train comes roaring by—an "el"—which is thus labeled neatly by the two neon letters. We realize suddenly how readily our minds have supplied the missing letters.

Another example concerns Bloch's fascination with American money. Some of this is in the novel, when, for example, he inadvertently leaves a few American coins at the scene of the murder, but Wenders plays up this motif in the film version, even adding bits of stage business with quarters and dollar bills to scenes otherwise taken intact from the book. For one thing, this sharpens Wenders's own theme of "Americanness," and for another, it provides a unifying structuring device, along with other motifs which are taken over from the novel but are much more highly emphasized in the film. Most importantly, though, the coins and dollar bills serve as obvious clues to Bloch's guilt, which, as Michael Covino points out, "make us sit up straighter, for in the conventions of the thriller they foretell his doom. But it is a doom that never arrives."[6] Each time the American money appears, the camera zooms in on it or cuts to a close-up of it, purposely overstressing the genre convention in order to use it, parody it, and alert us to the fact that we are participating in the unfolding of an artifact that is very aware of itself and its origins. Accompanying nearly every obvious camera movement of this sort is a spurt of equally obvious "clue music" on the sound track, which further heightens the parodistic elements and the self-reflexivity.[7]

More examples could be added, but I think the point is clear. Owing to the nature of the film medium itself, Wenders is unable to duplicate (even if he wanted to) the novel's profound study of the relationship of the human mind to external reality, to language, and, by extension, to all signifying systems. More precisely, he is unable to embody this theme in the way the novel does—through the thoughts and emotions of the characters themselves. Rather, what there is of this theme in the film is expressed primarily through the film's form. And just as this theme must necessarily be formally self-reflexive and cause the reader to interrogate the process of reading, Wenders is able to make his film self-reflexive in terms which are most appropriate to cinema's own history and its own possibilities. We thus become more aware of what it means to watch a film, and we realize that the conventions and codes of cinematic meaning are as arbitrary, as "unnatural," and, finally, as complicated as the linguistic codes which make up Handke's brilliant novel. And that, after all, is what it was all about in the first place.

[6] Covino, op. cit., p. 11.

[7] The novel itself participates, in advance as it were, in the film's awareness of genre conventions. Witness the following passages:

She turned on the radio on the kitchen cabinet. . . . When somebody in a movie turned on the radio, the program was instantly interrupted for a bulletin about a wanted man (p. 114).

The headline and the picture looked to him as if they had been pasted onto the paper; like newspapers in movies, he thought: there the real headlines were also replaced by headlines that fitted the film; or like those headlines you could have made up about yourself in penny arcades (p. 127).

BEN LAWTON

THE STORYTELLER'S ART
Pasolini's *Decameron (1971)*

from The Decameron *by Giovanni Boccaccio*

Pier Paolo Pasolini's *Decameron* (1971) is in its own way the most important recent tribute to Boccaccio's masterpiece. Murder, sexual adventures, and graphic scatology appear in Boccaccio's text and in Pasolini's film, but while the former has been legitimized by the passage of time, the latter has been accused of being unfaithful to its literary source, to Pasolini's own cerebral style, and to the cinema itself.[1] These responses were predicated in part upon a justifiable admiration for Boccaccio's *Il Decamerone,* and on the less comprehensible assumption that Pasolini should have attempted merely a mechanical transcription of the fourteenth-century masterpiece.

Having made *The Gospel According to St. Matthew* (1964), Pasolini realized that film will always differ from its literary source because the images inevitably alter the literary text to an extreme

---

The above essay is a reworking of material that originally appeared in *The Decameron: Giovanni Boccaccio,* edited and translated by Mark Musa and Peter Bondanella, New York, Norton, 1977.

[1] For a more extensive treatment of the life and works of Pasolini, see *Bianco e Nero,* Vol. 1, No. 4, 1976, which is dedicated entirely to Pasolini and which contains the most complete bibliography and filmography currently extant. See also, Enzo Siciliano, *Vita di Pasolini,* Milano, Rizzoli, 1978; Adelio Ferrero, *Il Cinema di Pasolini,* Venezia, Marsilio, 1977; *Pier Paolo Pasolini,* Paul Willemen (ed.), London, British Film Institute, 1977; Marc Gervais, *Pier Paolo Pasolini,* Paris, Seghers, 1973; *Pasolini on Pasolini,* Oswald Stack (ed.), Bloomington, Indiana University Press, 1969; Sandro Petraglia, *Pier Paolo Pasolini,* Firenze, La Nuova Italia, 1974; and Réné Prédal, "Pier Paolo Pasolini," *L'Avant Scène du Cinéma,* No. 175, 1976, pp. 27–42, and No. 176, 1976, pp. 16–36. Among the many reviews which attack Pasolini's *Decameron* on these grounds, see Goffredo Fofi, "Qualche Film," *Quaderni Piacentini,* No. 44–45, 1971, p. 258; Guy Allombert, "Contre *Decameron,*" *Image et Son,* No. 255, 1971, p. 108; and Marc Gervais, *Pier Paolo Pasolini.*

degree.[2] He therefore attempted to re-create the past by analogy, and he intended it to be a metaphor for the present.[3] In an interview, Pasolini discussed his film in relation to Boccaccio and compared the author's joyous celebration of the birth of the bourgeoisie with his own depiction of the innocent joy of the lower classes of southern Italy, a world "which is at the limits of history, and, in a certain sense, outside history."[4] Later, during a pause in the shooting of *Arabian Nights* (1974), Pasolini was to tell Gideon Bachmann repeatedly that "no critic has had the imagination to understand" that it is "much more difficult to make films in which the ideology is hidden, indirect, implicit, than to make thesis films, defending a clear point of view."[5] In the "trilogy of life," Pasolini states, he was concerned with the "experience of entering into the most mysterious workings of artistic creation . . . into the ontology of narration, in the making of cinema-cinema." He added: "I find it the most beautiful idea I have ever had, this wish to tell, to recount, for the sheer joy of telling and recounting, for the creation of narrative myths, away from ideology, precisely because I have understood that to make an ideological film is finally easier than making a film outwardly lacking ideology. Outwardly: because every film has its ideology, first of all its intrinsic truth to itself, its poetry, and then its external ideology, which is the more or less self-evident political attitude."[6]

This rejection of the increasingly hermetic tendencies which had characterized his earlier intellectual, externally ideological films was born in part of his desire to reach a broader audience, and in part as a result of his perception that art is valid only when it is "revolutionary," that is, when the artist is on the firing line, breaking the laws of the system within which he operates.[7] Thus, he

[2] See the discussion of *The Gospel According to Saint Matthew* in Stack, *Pasolini on Pasolini*, op. cit., pp. 73–97; and "Pier Paolo Pasolini: An Interview with James Blue," *Film Comment*, No. 3, 1965, pp. 25–32.

[3] Pasolini outlines his theories in "An Epical-Religious View of the World," *Film Quarterly*, No. 18, 1965, pp. 31–45; and "Il Sentimento della Storia," *Cinema Nuovo*, No. 205, 1970, pp. 172–173.

[4] This interview is reprinted in part by Petraglia, op. cit., pp. 15–16.

[5] Gideon Bachmann, "Pasolini Today: The Interview," *Take One*, No. 4, 1973, p. 21.

[6] Ibid.

[7] Pasolini, "Il Cinema Impopolare," *Nuovi Argomenti*, No. 20, October–December 1970, pp. 166–176. Reprinted in Pier Paolo Pasolini, *Empirismo Eretico*, Milano, Garzanti, 1972, pp. 273–280.

rejected both traditional and avant-garde cinemas. The former because their extreme readability does not force the viewer to reflect on what he has seen; the latter because avant-garde filmmakers have charged beyond the firing line and, in his words, have been trapped in a POW camp which they have promptly transformed into an intellectual ghetto. Both, he argues, are consumer products since neither challenges its respective public. Pasolini returned to the firing line by fusing traditional and modernist modes in his "trilogy of life": *Decameron, Canterbury Tales,* and *Arabian Nights.*[8] In the process, while acquiring a broader and more popular audience, he alienated the greater part of the intellectuals, critics, and art-house patrons who had earlier championed his more esoteric works. At the same time, he discovered how accurate he had been when he defined the revolutionary artistic process as sado-masochistic: sadistic in that it destroys the expectations of the public; masochistic because the public will reject the work and attack the artist. Still, he refused to be entirely pessimistic since there is, he said, the "liberated" spectator who rejoices in the freedom of the artist.[9]

Several of the filmmaker's major deviations from Boccaccio's text reveal immediately that the film is intended to be an evolution beyond the original. Of the three social classes portrayed by the Florentine writer, Pasolini depicts only the bourgeoisie and the lower classes, while he totally ignores the aristocracy, a class which might well be said to be irrelevant today. More explicitly, the director tells us that the film is a reinterpretation of Boccaccio's *Decameron* by having the storyteller start to read the first convent story (Day X, 2) from a printed edition of the work: an obvious anachronism since *The Decameron* was written well before the invention of the printing press. The storyteller then pauses and says: "Now I'll tell it to you in the Neapolitan way!"[10] In other words, Pasolini has taken the text reflecting the rising middle class of Boccaccio's world[11] and has rewritten it in terms of the

---

[8] Pasolini, *Trilogia della Vita*, Bologna, Cappelli, 1975, contains the scripts of the "trilogy of life" films.

[9] Pasolini, "Il Cinema Impopolare" op. cit.

[10] All translations of the script of Pasolini's *Decameron* are mine in the absence of a published screenplay in English.

[11] For a discussion of Boccaccio's work as the epic poem of the mercantile class, see Vittore Branca, *Boccaccio Medioevale*, Florence, Sansoni, 1964.

subproletariat, the only class which, in his opinion at the time, retained "mystical features."[12]

The film nevertheless reveals the director to be a perceptive, scholarly reader of *The Decameron,* one who is extremely faithful to the spirit and structure of Boccaccio's collection of *novelle.* On the most superficial level, he deviates from Boccaccio's text no more than the latter deviated from his own sources, which included not only popular tales but also well-known classics. To cite only one example, Boccaccio's version of Peronella's story (Day VII, 2) certainly modifies the original found in Apuleius' *Golden Ass* far more than Pasolini alters Boccaccio's version. Of greater interest is Pasolini's handling of the major literary devices which characterize *The Decameron.* The *novelle* in Boccaccio's work are placed within a general framework and are arranged according to topics determined by the "king" or "queen" of the given day of storytelling. The individual stories are introduced to some extent by their storytellers, and on several occasions Boccaccio addresses his imaginary readers directly to explain his intentions and to counter possible objections. For ten days, ten storytellers—three men and seven women—tell one story each. Boccaccio himself appears as narrator in the introduction to Day IV.

Pasolini alludes to Boccaccio by emphasizing the number ten in several ways. His film contains ten episodes taken from Boccaccio's text and ten original episodes.[13] Divided into two parts, the film includes five of Boccaccio's *novelle* in each part. Furthermore, we find three Pasolini episodes in Part I and seven Pasolini episodes in Part II, respectively, the number of days of storytelling into which the two parts of Boccaccio's *Decameron* are divided by the author's appearance, and also the number of male and female narrators in the original. The total number of Pasolini episodes, like the total of those borrowed from Boccaccio, equals the number of days of storytelling in the original text.

Like Boccaccio, Pasolini designs an elaborate framework for his film. The ten episodes from Boccaccio (B) are framed by two of Pasolini's (P) own invention (P 1 and P 10). The episodes in the film are arranged by topics determined by the "kings" or dominant figures in the two parts of the film—Ciappelletto and the artist,

---

[12] Stack, op. cit., p. 48.
[13] See the detailed chart explaining the structure of Pasolini's film and its relationship to Boccaccio's *Decameron.*

THE DECAMERON
Part I

Pasolini's *Decameron*	Boccaccio's *Decameron*
P1 Ciappelletto commits a murder: his victim screams: "You have understood nothing!"	
B1 Andreuccio da Perugia.	Day II,5: Andreuccio from Perugia, having gone to Naples to buy horses, is caught up in three unfortunate adventures in one night; escaping from them all, he returns home with a ruby.
P2 The Neapolitan storyteller and Ciappelletto as a thief.	
B2 The first convent story, as told by the Neapolitan storyteller.	Day IX,2: An abbess gets up quickly from her bed in the dark to surprise one of her nuns accused of being in bed with her lover. The abbess herself is with a priest in bed, and she puts his pants on her head, thinking that she is putting on her veil. When the accused nun sees the pants and points them out to the abbess, she is set free and is allowed to be with her lover.
P2 The Neapolitan storyteller and Ciappelletto as a pederast.	
B3 Masetto da Lamporecchio and the second convent story.	Day III,1: Masetto from Lamporecchio pretends to be a deaf-mute and becomes the gardner for a convent of nuns, who all compete to lie with him.
B4 Peronella.	Day VIII,2: When her husband returns home, Peronella puts her lover inside a barrel which the husband has sold; she says she has already sold it to someone who is inside checking to see if it is sound. When her lover jumps out of the barrel, he has her husband scrape it and carry it off to his home for him.

*The episodes inspired by Boccaccio's *Decameron* are indicated with the letter B; the Pasolini episodes are indicated with the letter P. All of Boccaccio's *novelle* listed here and included in Pasolini's film are present in the Norton edition of *The Decameron*.

B5   Ciappelletto and Messer Muscià.

P3   Pasolini's tribute to Brueghel's *The Combat of Carnival and Lent* and *The Triumph of Death*.

B5   Ciappelletto's confession, death, and sanctification.

Part II

B6   Pasolini, the northern artist, is not recognizable as "Giotto's best disciple."

P4   The artist arrives in Naples, and the mural is produced as a collective effort; the view of Caterina's family in the marketplace; the painting of Santa Chiara.

B7   Riccardo and Caterina.

P5   The artist eats rapidly with the friars and returns to his work.

B8   Isabetta, Lorenzo's decapitation, and the pot of basil.

P6   The artist sees Don Gianni and Compare Pietro

Day I,1: Ser Cepperello tricks a holy friar with a false confession and dies; although he was a most evil man during his lifetime, he is after death reputed to be a saint and is called Saint Ciappelletto.

Day VI,5: Messer Forese from Rabatta and Maestro Giotto, the painter, make fun of each other's poor appearance as they return from Mugello.

Day V,4: Ricciardo Manardi is found by Messer Lizio of Valbona with his daughter; Ricciardo marries her and remains on good terms with her father.

Day IV,5: Isabetta's brothers kill her lover. He appears to her in a dream and tells her where he is buried. She secretly digs up his head and places it in a pot of basil, over which she weeps every day for a long time. Her brothers take it away from her, and, shortly afterwards, she dies of grief.

Day IX,10: At Compare Pietro's home and casts a spell in order to turn his wife into a mare; but when it comes time to stick the tail on, Pietro spoils the spell by saying that he doesn't want the tail.

Day VII,10: Two Sienese are in love with the same woman, and one of them is the godfather of her child; when he dies and returns to his friend, according to a promise he had made to him, he describes how people live in the next world.

B9 Don Gianni goes to Compare Pietro's home and meets Gemmata, his wife.

P7 A view of the revelry at the peasant wedding.

B9 Don Gianni at the home of Compare Pietro and Gemmata.

P7 The wedding of Zita Carapresa ("All cuckolds").

B9 Don Gianni puts the tail on Gemmata.

P8 The artist paints while his assistants whistle.

B10 Meuccio and Tingoccio; the problem of the sinfulness of sex; and the death of Tingoccio.

P9 Pasolini's tribute to Giotto's *Last Judgment* in a vision of the artist where the Madonna replaces Christ.

B10 Tingoccio returns from the dead to tell Meuccio: "It [sex] is not a sin!"

P10 The painting is finished, and a celebration ensues; Pasolini, the artist figure, asks: "Why realize a work when it is so nice simply to dream it?"

Giotto's pupil. Each of these characters frames one part of the film. Part I opens with Ciappelletto in the rather dark and confusing murder scene (P 1) and closes on him as the peasants crowd around to worship his dead body as that of a saint (B 5). The artist, played by Pasolini himself, opens and closes Part II. Like Boccaccio, Pasolini appears in his own work in what might be described as the introduction to the fourth of the original blocks of storytelling. More specifically, we first see him in B 6 when he and some friends seek refuge from a storm in a peasant's hut, and the last shot of the film in P 10 shows him as he looks at his paintings. In P 1, Ciappelletto's victim screams: "You have understood nothing!" In P 10, Giotto's pupil, having completed his painting, asks himself: "Why realize a work of art when it's so nice simply to dream it?" These remarks seem to suggest that the topics of the two parts concern an error or a failure to comprehend. However, paraphrasing both Boccaccio and Pasolini, we might say that under the rule of Ciappelletto in Part I it is only with his death that an individual can express himself fully, and that under the rule of the artist in Part II it is only the finished work of art which can fully express itself.[14]

All the episodes in Part I, with the exception of the story of Ciappelletto and Messer Muscià (B 5), are open-ended and remain seemingly ambiguous. Pasolini, however, warns us rather explicitly that a more careful reading of the film is essential. The last Ciappelletto episode (B 5) is interrupted abruptly by an insert which presents an odd juxtaposition of life and death, perhaps best illustrated by the shot of the clergymen who play a primitive form of volleyball with a human skull. Almost inevitably, the viewer is disturbed by this painterly montage which seems initially to have no narrative function but which, in fact, is the key to the entire first part of the film. The director has deliberately fused two works of art—*The Combat of Lent and Carnival* and *The Triumph of Death*—by Peter Brueghel the Elder.[15] The closing shot of the

[14] In "La Paura del Naturalismo (Osservazioni sul Piano-Sequenza)," *Nuovi Argomenti*, No. 6, 1967, pp. 11–23, Pasolini argues that the "meaning" of a life can be determined only after death, and that death resembles, in this regard, the montage of the cinema.
[15] The first of these works was painted in 1559 and is located in the Kunsthistorishes Museum in Vienna; the second was completed in 1562 and is in the Prado in Madrid.

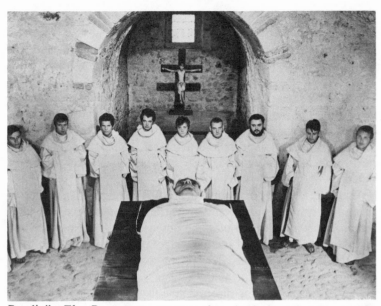

Pasolini's *The Decameron* suggests that death is the only possible synthesis between the primitive urges of Carnival and the repressive tendencies of Lent. Ciappelletto, a scoundrel in life, becomes a saint in death.

skull, which replaces the Christian symbol of the fish in Brueghel's *Combat*, suggests that death is the only possible synthesis in the dialectical conflict between the primitive urges of Carnival and the repressive tendencies of Lent, and that it is from this perspective that all the episodes in the film must be viewed.

As B 5 ends, Ciappelletto is dead and is, hence, defined forever. As Pasolini once remarked: "live and remain unexpressed, or express yourself and die."[16] In life or in film, he argued, it is only with death that one can have a meaningful montage. He expresses this theory concretely through his own montage of the important episodes of the life-film of Ciappelletto. Ciappelletto is a victim of the bourgeoisie who, as his own victim warns him (P 1), has understood nothing. In life he is exploited first by Messer Muscilà and then by the usurers. In death he is used by the Church as a

---

[16] "La Paura del Naturalismo," op. cit., p. 22.

saint. During his death scene, Pasolini speaks directly to the spectators of the film by breaking one of the cardinal rules of traditional filmmaking. A usurer turns directly to the camera and tells us that Ciappelletto is "really a saint!" Pasolini considers him a saint because the montage of his life which culminates in and is defined by his death is a total indictment of the bourgeoisie and of the institutions which represent this class—the Church, the Family, and Business. Even though Ciappelletto may seem to act independently when he appears as a murderer, a thief, and a pederast, he is, and has always been, only a pawn to be used to exploit others.

While Pasolini pays tribute to the first major Italian writer to turn away from the medieval theocentric vision of the human condition, the storyteller episode, the absence of the aristocracy, the visual anachronisms, and the indictment of the bourgeoisie suggest that the director intended to present a more contemporary anthropocentric perception of the human condition. This is underlined in Part II, with the director himself as the "best" disciple of Giotto, the painter whose artistic style went beyond the Byzantine theocentric vision of the world in the plastic arts.

Pasolini's explanations for his presence in the film have bothered the numerous critics who responded negatively to his role. While his statement that the first two choices for the part were unavailable is too facile to be accepted, the reactions of the critics themselves reveal indirectly the success of the device. Pasolini's presence is a clear and self-conscious manifestation of the process of unrealization in narrative.[17] Because of a storm, Giotto's pupil supposedly becomes unrecognizable. But this is only the narrated event, and thus it should cause us to perceive that the director is addressing himself to another issue. The very act of drawing attention to the unrecognizability of Giotto's pupil, if anything, makes Pasolini more recognizable. It is not Pasolini as Giotto's pupil who is potentially unrecognizable, but Pasolini's new style, the "cinema-cinema" which "no critic has had the imagination to understand."[18]

Pasolini in his *Decameron* is no longer explicitly, externally

[17] Christian Metz, *Film Language: A Semiotics of the Cinema*, New York, Oxford University Press, 1974, p. 21.
[18] Bachmann, op. cit., p. 21.

ideological. As we have already seen, however, the film does reveal an ideological stance in its indictment of the three pillars of the bourgeoisie, an indictment which becomes clearer if we juxtapose the Boccaccio elements of Part I with those of Part II. If we compare the episode in which the artist first appears (B 6) to the Andreuccio episode (B 1), we can see strong parallels in the process of unrealization and should thus look beyond the surface of the narrative. When the young servant invites Andreuccio to visit the "beautiful Sicilian lady," the young man's less-than-chaste thoughts are rendered visually by his casting aside a yellow flower. The result of his "sin" seems to be his fall into the feces, a punishment which Tingoccio mentions specifically when he appears briefly to Meuccio after his death (B 10). Is it possible, however, that Pasolini, the apostle of sex as revolution, has come to consider sexual desire a sin?[19] If we reconsider the story of Andreuccio (B 1) in the light of the first episode in which we see Pasolini (B 6), we observe that in both there is an attempt to deny the recognizability of the protagonists.

Giotto's pupil, as we have already observed, is recognizable as Pasolini. And Andreuccio, who supposedly becomes unrecognizable to the servants and the "brother" of the beautiful Sicilian woman because of his fall into the cesspool, is actually recognizable to his newfound "family" as Andreuccio and to the literate spectator as Ninetto Davoli, a well-known star of the Italian cinema who has appeared in several of Pasolini's films. If we look beyond the surface, we observe that the director presents a criticism of himself, as disciple of Giotto (B 6), which might suggest one answer.

Even though the artist dislikes being called *Maestro* and is the only person to thank the peasant for loaning him his rags for protection from the rain (B 6), he nevertheless is part of a class which exploits members of the proletariat such as this peasant. Pasolini, writing about himself, once remarked: "I too, like Moravia and Bertolucci, am a bourgeois, in fact a petit-bourgeois, a turd, convinced that my stench is not only scented perfume, but

[19] In *Pasolini on Pasolini*, op. cit., Stack writes: "In fact, rather than politics, it is sex which Pasolini now seems to see as the main threat to the bourgeoisie" (p. 9).

is in fact the only perfume in the world."[20] Thus, we might argue that the condemnation of Andreuccio is predicated not upon his sexual desire but rather upon his condition as a bourgeois. Andreuccio, having been told that the woman he had planned to seduce is his "sister," suddenly appears holding a red flower to his nose. His "original sin," in Pasolini's order of things, is his unquestioning surrender to the repressive powers of the family.

Pasolini's ideology and his reinterpretation of Boccaccio become more clear when we compare the story of Riccardo and Caterina (B 7) to that of Isabetta and Lorenzo (B 8) and then compare both of these episodes in Part II to the two convent stories from Part I (B 2 and B 3). The two love stories reveal one major difference: Because Riccardo was born a member of the bourgeoisie, his escapade ends happily. Although Caterina's father surprises him naked in her arms, he escapes harm because he is wealthy and a suitable match for the girl. Lorenzo, on the other hand, is murdered by Isabetta's brothers because he is a servant and a member of a despised, exploited class. Pasolini emphasizes this difference by changing Boccaccio's story significantly. Lorenzo (who in Boccaccio's *Decameron* comes from Pisa, a northern Italian city) becomes a Sicilian in Pasolini's film, and his death is thus a result of the antisouthern racism which Pasolini considers to be a characteristic of the Italian middle class.[21] The two love stories thus serve to render specifically the indictment of one of the most important institutions of the bourgeoisie, the Family.

The appearance of the dead Lorenzo to Isabetta in her sleep is the first of Pasolini's *mysteries* in the film, an element which reflects the director's constant attempt to reconsecrate ancient myths and to remystify reality.[22] This mystery is followed by a last shot of Isabetta, gazing upon the pot of basil containing Lorenzo's head, in a position very much like that of various Renaissance

---

[20] Pasolini, *Oedipus Rex*, New York, Simon & Schuster, 1971, p. 7.

[21] In discussing the prison sentence he received for the making of *La Ricotta* (1962), Pasolini remarked: "The Italians are supposed not to be racists, but I think this is a big lie. . . . Public opinion rebelled against me because of some indefinable racist hatred, which like all racism was irrational. They couldn't take *Accattone* and all the subproletarian characters" (Stack, op. cit., pp. 63–64).

[22] Pasolini, "An Epical-Religious View of the World," op. cit., pp. 31–45; see also Stack, op. cit., pp. 9, 83.

adoration scenes. In opposition to the mystery in this scene, we find several other adoration scenes connected with the clergy which are demystified. The first occurs when our view of the peasants' hands reaching up to touch Ciappelletto, now a dead "saint," is juxtaposed with the shot of the richly dressed clergymen flanked by the two usurers. The obvious suggestion is that even in death Ciappelletto is being used to exploit the poor.

The two adoration scenes contained in the story of Masetto (B 3) are thematically related. The first pictures two nuns gazing up at Masetto's sexual organs and is intended as a spontaneous reconsecration of the primitive, instinctive sexual drive. The first moment of worship, however, is coupled immediately with the typical bourgeois process of rationalization and leads inevitably to the exploitation of Masetto, pleasant though it may seem at first, which is revealed in the words of one of the nuns, who addresses Masetto as "animal" ("bestia") just as he is about to lay with her. The second adoration scene in this episode, picturing the nuns crowding around Masetto after the mother superior has told him he will be able to pass for a "saint" because of the "miracle" which has restored his speech, simply culminates and institutionalizes his sexual exploitation. The nuns have managed to channel his services in a direction which serves their purposes, just as Caterina's father was able to use Riccardo's affair with his daughter to his advantage. In both instances, Church and Family reflect their bourgeois foundations, just as Ciappelletto's sainthood and the murder of Lorenzo bear witness to the darker side of this class relationship.

The relationship of Don Gianni, Compare Pietro, and Gemmata in B 9 is analogous to the relationship existing between the Church and the subproletariat. The episode demystifies yet another false miracle planned and performed with premeditated malice by a clergyman. Just as the story of Masetto and the convent was prepared by the tale narrated orally by the Neapolitan storyteller (P 2), here the episode is punctuated by the revelry of a peasant wedding (P 7). At this wedding, an event which is not to be found in Boccaccio's text, the only dialogue to interrupt the picture of the bride dancing with a priest is a drunkard's remark that all present are cuckolds (*"Tutti cornuti!"*). There is, presumably, truth in wine, for this remark foretells the outcome of Don Gianni's visit. As Don Gianni pins the "tail" on Gemmata, he is also pinning the cuckold's horns on Compare Pietro. Ignorance, the belief in miracles (in this case, a false miracle contrived by a churchman to indulge his illicit desires), and greed motivate Gemmata and her husband to submit to Don Gianni's plan. A comparison with the Peronella episode (B 4) reveals a similar theme, for there the cuckold motif is expressed in the familiar gesture of the fingers by one of the neighbors. Here, however, there is a significant difference. While it is the desperate poverty of the one couple which leads them to believe any ridiculous story in order to improve their economic status, Peronella manipulates the greed of her husband, on the one hand, and the sexual desire of her lover, on the other, for her own benefit. For Pasolini, she epitomizes the selfishness of the middle class much as Don Gianni typifies the Church.

The Meuccio and Tingoccio episode (B 10) becomes understandable if we recall the allusion to the two works by Brueghel which are included in the earlier story of Ciappelletto (B 5). While Pasolini included an insert in the earlier story of Ciappelletto which was inspired by these two paintings (P 5), in B 10 he refers to another famous work of art, Giotto's *Last Judgment*.[23] He makes a significant modification in this work, as he had done earlier with those of Brueghel, for he replaces the Christ-Judge figure with a Madonna. While Meuccio is very much caught up in the combat between Lent and Carnival—the subject of the first of the two Brueghel paintings—Tingoccio passes to the side of Carnival with such enthusiasm that the result is the triumph of death —the subject of the second Brueghel work. Those who have not read Boccaccio will naturally assume that Tingoccio is placed among the damned for his excessive lovemaking, but instead we witness the second *mystery* of Pasolini's film as Tingoccio returns from the dead just as Lorenzo had returned earlier to Isabetta (B 8). In response to Meuccio's anxious questions about his punishment in hell for his sex life, Tingoccio announces that he was told in the other world: "You turd! Forget it! Screwing your 'comare' is

---

[23] Giotto's *Last Judgment* covers the entire internal wall above the entrance to the Arena Chapel in Padua and confronts the viewer as he turns to leave. It was painted around 1306.

not a sin here!"[24] Upon hearing this revelation, Meuccio runs to his own "comare" and shouts: "It [sex] is not a sin!" Tingoccio's message from the realm of the dead expresses Pasolini's anthropocentric vision of the world.

After criticizing other directors for not committing themselves to an idea and expressing it in a finished form, for not "dying enough in their films,"[25] Pasolini does just this in his *Decameron*. Tingoccio's death serves to give concrete form to Pasolini's point of view, here thinly disguised as that of Giotto's pupil. By replacing Christ the Judge in Giotto's original with the Madonna-like figure played by Silvana Mangano, who portrayed Pasolini's mother in *Oedipus Rex*, the director is suggesting that this film too is a "kind of completely metaphoric and therefore mythicized autobiography."[26] Pasolini in this manner reveals that he has rejected the "superego represented by the father repressing the child."[27] And while the triumph of death may inevitably follow the combat of Carnival and Lent, in Pasolini's version of the Last Judgment one is no longer punished for sexual transgressions. The oppression and exploitation of the poor will now be considered as the cardinal sins in this anthropocentric, cinematic universe.

Pasolini's *Decameron* is "cinema-cinema," and it takes a well-defined, albeit concealed, ideological stance. It is metanarrative and meta(plastic) art—in sum, metacinema. We have already seen that Pasolini comments on Boccaccio's narrative strategy through a selective adoption of various structural and stylistic devices. We have also mentioned the use that the director makes of the paintings of Brueghel and Giotto. In this context, of greater interest than the "content" of the paintings is the manner in which they are presented. In the depiction of the "Brueghel," the direc-

---

[24] In *Opere di Giovanni Boccaccio*, Cesare Segre (ed.), Milan, Mursia, 1967, Maria Segre notes that "during Boccaccio's times the relationship between 'comare' (the woman whose child one has held during the baptism) and 'compare' (godfather) was considered particularly close, to such an extent that sexual relations between the two were considered incestuous" (p. 979). The more casual use of the expressions *compare* and *comare* in Pasolini's film would seem to suggest that he intended a more general meaning of the words, a form of familiar address which Boccaccio himself uses in the story of Don Gianni, Compare Pietro, and Gemmata (Day IX, 10).
[25] "La Paura del Naturalismo," op. cit., p. 21.
[26] Stack, op. cit., p. 120.
[27] Ibid.

tor's abrupt editing forces the viewer's eye to assimilate apparently unrelated material; in the "Giotto," the sweeping movements of the camera lead the viewer's eye along the major thrusting lines of the work. In both instances, Pasolini draws our attention to the painterly nature of the works in question and demonstrates to us that cinema is not merely a narrative form but one that can focus on and discuss its own spatiality.

The filmmaker's awareness of film as a medium imbued with the expressive characteristics of both the temporal and spatial arts is reiterated throughout the film. Pasolini, the novelist and film-maker, appears as Giotto's pupil, a painter, and more specifically a painter of murals—that art form then most accessible to the masses, much as film is today. In the episode in which Giotto's pupil arrives in Naples to paint Santa Chiara (P 4), Pasolini demonstrates to us that in mural painting, as in filmmaking, there is a collective effort which requires the use of massive machinery under the guidance of an individual: the artists.[28] We next see Pasolini-Giotto's pupil in the marketplace, where he looks at different people and frames them with his fingers. The people he frames are framed individually by the film itself as the director-painter turns to the camera, lowers his hands, and smiles directly at us (and the camera). As we move into the next episode, that of Riccardo and Caterina (B 7), we discover that the people who were framed at the marketplace by the artist are now the protagonists.

In the Pasolini episodes which follow, there is a progressively more explicit fusion of description and narration. Description becomes narration, and narration inspires further description. With the end of the episode of Riccardo and Caterina (B 7), we find the artist who, after eating rapidly with the friars, returns to the mural, wakes his helpers, takes up his brush, and places a dab of blue paint on the nose of one of his helpers. As he does, we pass into the episode of Isabetta and Lorenzo (B 8). Painting, the spectator comes to realize, is narration. The two moments, however, are not

[28] Film criticism is also often a collective effort requiring the use of much machinery. I would like to thank Mr. Donald Krim of United Artists-16 for the use of a print of Pasolini's film, and Professor Peter Bondanella, Professor Anna Lawton, Mrs. Janet Staiger, and Ms. Lauren Mueller for their assistance. I would also like to thank Professor Fredi Chiapelli, director of the Center for Medieval and Renaissance Studies at UCLA, for his help in identifying the paintings cited and others far too numerous to mention in this context.

respectively bound by the Pasolini and the Boccaccio episodes. By painting the nose of his assistant, Pasolini "paints" one of the characters in the film. Thus, in one stroke Pasolini is painting a mural, telling a story, and making a film. In P 6 we return to the marketplace; as Pasolini-Giotto's pupil observes the scene, two of the characters there (Don Gianni and Compare Pietro) move directly into a Boccaccio episode (B 9) from the marketplace of P 6: The objects of the director-painter's interest have appeared directly in the film without the mediating fiction of the mural of the Santa Chiara church. This integration is reinforced through the intertwining of B 9 and P 7. The shots of the revelry at the peasant wedding and the wedding of Zita Carapresa (P 7) two scenes clearly inspired by Brueghel's *Wedding Dance* (1566), *Peasant Dance* (1566), and *Peasant Wedding Feast* (1566)—not only appear in Boccaccio's tale of Don Gianni, Compare Pietro, and Gemmata (B 9), but have become a component of the narrative.

The suggestion that the artist's assistants are to be considered among the manifestations of Pasolini's filmic art (P 6) is reiterated strongly in P 8. This episode consists of a series of close-ups of the assistants as they whistle, work, smile, and laugh, and it ends with a quick long shot of the back of the squatting artist. For the first time, inverting the order employed until this moment, Pasolini shows us first the results of the artist's work and only subsequently the artist at work. As he works, the camera shifts to the outside of the church and then down to Tingoccio and Meuccio and their respective comari, establishing a synchronous parallel to the shots of the assistants. The Pasolini episodes and the Boccaccio episodes, the painting and the storytelling, have become one in the film. With Pasolini-Giotto's pupil's vision of the altered *Last Judgment* by Giotto, Pasolini's disquisition on the relationship between painting, narrative, and cinema is moving toward its climax. Two apparently incongruous perceptions of the divine judgment— Giotto's and Boccaccio's—are juxtaposed in the mind of the artist with results which are greater than the sum of the parts. In the filmic "painting," while the Christ-Judge figure is gone, the torture of the damned remains; in the filmic "story," while the events are essentially unchanged, the impact of Tingoccio's liberating message from beyond the grave is heightened by contrast with the scenes of hellish suffering.

Pasolini's controversial political and aesthetic statements in *The*

Decameron do not ignore the humanistic heritage of Boccaccio's work but seek to preserve it in the contemporary world. After a period of externally political filmmaking, Pasolini came to reject film as a tool for mass communication and remarked that, for him, "the only hope is a cultural one, to be an intellectual . . . for the rest I am consistently pessimistic."[29] Pasolini had not lost all faith in the potential of the cinema, however, and he believed that there still existed a "small space for culture of a humanist tendency" as there was "still a possibility of some sort of relationship of a personal nature, since the film *I* make is seen by you."[30] Within the film Pasolini outlines clearly the limitations of his ideology. Tingoccio's last speech to Meuccio is deeply rooted in an ancient culture and tradition which have changed little from Boccaccio's times in spite of its revolutionary rejection of sexual repression: "Have masses said, and prayers. Be charitable. That helps us a lot." These limits are underlined further by the mural painted by the director-artist in the church. It is an incomplete triptych, composed of a gothic, heaven-directed arch in the first panel, an anthropocentric rectangle whose top line is perfectly horizontal in the second panel, and a third panel which is completely blank. Pasolini, the artistic descendant of Boccaccio and Giotto, has taken a step forward through an imaginative retrieval of the past. He moves back in time to the medieval world which was their point of departure and then, using them as a springboard, vaults into the contemporary world, completely bypassing the implicitly desperate Renaissance opposition of life and death, which in the film is synthesized by the montage of Brueghel's works. He presumes to have done no more than this, and he has no simplistic answers for the future; thus, the blank third panel.

Pasolini's *Decameron* is not without a structure; Boccaccio, Giotto, and Brueghel are not merely occasional sources, nor is the director's choice of episodes random. The film has a discernible ideological posture with both political and psychological dimensions.[31] The magic of Pasolini's film multiplies with each successive viewing as a number of tantalizing possible structures, appar-

[29] Stack, op. cit., p. 124.
[30] Bachmann, op. cit., p. 20.
[31] For a discussion of Pasolini's ideology, see Francesco Dorigo, "Pasolini da Marx a Freud," *Revista del Cinematografo*, No. 4, 1970, pp. 135–141; and Franco Prono, "La Religione del Suo Tempo in Pier Paolo Pasolini," *Cinema Nuovo*, No. 215, 1972, pp. 42–45.

ently contradictory ideologies, and different potential films are discovered beneath the surface. Two phrases frame the film: "You haven't understood anything" and "Why realize a work of art when it is so nice simply to dream it?" The first is a description of the majority of the work's characters and a warning to the spectators. The second reveals the internal contradiction which, according to Pasolini, is proper to both life and art. Neither Ciapelletto's life nor Pasolini's *Decameron* can express itself fully until it is completed. At the same time, the joy of creativity and of narration exists most intensely for the author during the process of creation preceding the work's final form. This awareness has driven the director to force the spectator to participate in his narration, to become not merely the user or the consumer of the work but the co-author of yet another work of his or her own creation.

Pasolini has rejected the limitations of traditional and avant-garde cinema; these types of film have been analyzed. Whether they are produced in Paris, Prague, Brazil, or Italy, their structures, according to him, are identical and have been revealed, and their respective publics treat them as consumer products.[32] Their conventions are obvious, and they have lost their oneiric qualities. Pasolini's *Decameron* avoids such established structures by remaining a process rather than becoming a finished form; this is so not only for the director while he is making the work but also for the individual spectator while he views it. Pasolini tantalizes and delights us by playing with a number of well-known structures from literature (Boccaccio's *Decameron*) and art (the works by Brueghel and Giotto). In so doing he becomes the author of a new masterpiece through his personal reading of art and literature and, thus, gives them new life. At the same time, he refuses to give us a work which we can merely consume. The rectangular shape of the second panel of the artist's triptych, representing the present, does not accidentally reproduce the shape of a single frame of film, nor is it accidental that it is virtually impossible to determine its contents. The second panel stands midway between painting and narrative, between the motionless single frame which belongs to the plastic arts and at most is descriptive, and the moving pictures which through their temporal dimension become narrative.

[32] Pasolini, "La Sceneggiatura come Struttura che Vuole Essere Altra Struttura," *Empirismo Eretico*, op. cit., p. 200.

T. JEFFERSON KLINE

THE UNCONFORMIST
Bertolucci's *The Conformist (1971)*

from the novel by Alberto Moravia

> However the thing might have been, whether it had really hap-
> pened, it was nevertheless a dream because it was not to be ex-
> plained in a rational manner.
>
>

Moravia, "The Dream"

There is a moment in Bertolucci's *The Conformist* (1971) when
Professor Quadri, the Italian anti-Fascist leader in exile in Paris,
asks his former student, Marcello Clerici, to deliver a letter for the
anti-Fascist cause. When Clerici, as a loyal Fascist, refuses,
Quadri unexpectedly thanks him for that refusal and reveals that
the request was a test to see whether Clerici would accept the letter
and then betray its contents. This incident, taken directly from
Moravia's *Il Conformista*,[1] contains a significant deviation emblematic of Bertolucci's entire relationship to the original. Whereas
in the novel Quadri simply thanks Clerici for refusing to take the
letter (p. 260), in the film Quadri shows the letter to Clerici,
revealing it to be a blank page. As we shall see, virtually every
instance of writing in this film is highly charged: Literature functions constantly as a trap, or contains empty, false, or indecipherable writing; in short, it is never reliable.

Texts for Bertolucci are to be approached with suspicion, even
his own:

> often cinema is merely an illustration of a story. That is the biggest
> danger you face when you make a film from a novel. That was my
> problem when I made *The Conformist*. . . . Many filmmakers use

---

[1] Alberto Moravia, *The Conformist*, translated by Angus Davidson, London,
Secker and Warburg, 1953. All references in the text will be to this edition.
(Original edition: Milano, Bompiani, 1951.)

their scripts as if they had started from a novel; they simply make an illustrated film of the script. On the other hand, I, too, start from a very precise script—but only in order to destroy it.[2]

Quadri's letter, then, functions as a gratuitous sign—gratuitous precisely in terms of its relation to the original and of its necessity to the action of the film—of the unreliability of texts. Proffered by the professor whom Marcello feels he must betray in order to establish his own identity, this letter may on one level be interpreted as the Moravia novel itself.

This ambivalence about models is also revealed strikingly in an earlier scene again centering on a text and a betrayal. In Quadri's apartment, Marcello reminds his former professor of his lectures on Plato, and quotes:

> Picture men dwelling in a sort of subterranean cavern with a long entrance open to the light on its entire width. . . . Picture further the light from a fire burning higher up and at a distance behind them, and between the fire and the prisoners and above them a road along which a low wall has been built, as the exhibitors of puppet shows have partitions before the men themselves, above which they show the puppets.[3]

The scene signifies betrayal on a variety of levels. Marcello's "faithful" recollection of Quadri's lectures on Plato appears as a homage to their earlier master-disciple relationship, but is in fact merely an attempt to blind the professor to Marcello's real perversity.

As he quotes this passage from Plato's *Republic*, Clerici moves around the professor's desk and draws the blinds so that Quadri becomes silhouetted as if on a screen against the harsh light of the open window behind him, and consequently loses the illusion of

[2] Amos Vogel, "Bernardo Bertolucci: An Interview," *Film Comment*, Vol. 8, No. 3, Fall 1971, p. 26. Bertolucci said elsewhere:

> To write a script for me is a literary experience . . . when I'm writing, I can't think of shooting because to write is to write. Words are words, not images. . . . I feel very bored to do what is written on the script because I think it becomes sort of an illustration of a literary page, if you do what is on the page. . . . I must be completely free when I'm shooting. I can't follow the script.

"Bernardo Bertolucci Seminar," *Dialogue on Film*, Vol. 3, No. 5, April 1974, pp. 14, 16.
[3] Plato, *The Republic*, in *Collected Dialogues*, E. Hamilton and H. Cairns (eds.), translated by Lane Cooper, New York, Pantheon Books, 1961, Book VII, p. 747.

depth—becomes two-dimensional. By this visual insistence on the link between a darkened cavern and a lighted puppet show, Bertolucci distorts the Platonic text from its allusion to the human condition to a statement about cinema.[4] Two texts are here simultaneously betrayed: Plato's and—since this allusion to Plato does not appear in the novel—Moravia's. There is yet another level of betrayal at work here. The allusion to cinema and the reduction of Quadri to a black-and-white, two-dimensional image suggest that Quadri may symbolize one of Bertolucci's cinematic mentors. Indeed, Quadri's address and phone—given as 17, rue St. Jacques, tel # MED-15-37—belonged in 1971 to Jean-Luc Godard. Bertolucci confessed, in fact, that

> *The Conformist* is a story about me and Godard. When I gave the professor Godard's phone number and address, I did it for a joke, but afterwards I said to myself, "Well maybe all that has some significance. . . . I'm Marcello and I make Fascist movies and I want to kill Godard who's a revolutionary, who makes revolutionary movies and who was my teacher. . . .[5]

As object to be emulated and betrayed, Quadri also may signify Father at the archetypal level. In the Oedipal configuration, the father is to be imitated because he has won the mother—but he functions simultaneously as rival to be eliminated in *fantasy*, not in reality.

In this light, we may appreciate the oneiric, fantastic rendering

---

[4] Bertolucci has himself indicated this interpretation:
They talk about Plato's cave. It was, the first meaning was Italy with the slaves . . . but the second was the cinema because when you read the cave of Plato's, the cave is exactly like the theater and the background is the screen and Plato says there is a fire and people walking in front of the fire and the fire projects the shadows in the background of the cave. It's the invention of cinema.
"Bernardo Bertolucci Seminar," op. cit., p. 21.

[5] "Bertolucci on *The Conformist*: An Interview with Marilyn Goldin," *Sight and Sound*, Vol. 40, No. 2, Spring 1971, p. 66. It is perhaps coincidental that *quadri* means "diamonds" in Italian, for what is difficult for Moravia's Marcello is the combination of political purity and ruthless hardness in the older man. But Bertolucci did not keep all of the original names in his film, and if he did so here, it may have been because *quadri* not only means "diamonds," but sounds like *quadra*—a quadrant (from which the expression in Italian *dare la quadra a qualcuno*, meaning to hold someone up to ridicule); like *quadro*, meaning square (sensible), paintings, or outline; but also like *quadraiao*, a picture seller!

of Quadri's assassination: The entire scene is self-consciously patterned on cinematic versions of the murder of Caesar, and, despite
repeated stab wounds inflicted in an artificial mist and in balletlike
cadence, Quadri spills not one drop of blood. Anna, pursued
through a primeval forest and shot repeatedly in the back, falls,
her face unrealistically smeared with what is unmistakably red
paint. Bertolucci said of this scene:

> I thought that this exaggeration of blood on Anna was sort of a
> compromise with my old meaning, so audiences . . . could think
> . . . it's not true it's not true it's not true. . . . The murder of the
> father (i.e. Quadri) is a fantasy . . . it's imaginary.

And added, "I think the relationship between Marcello and the
professor is a relationship between a son and father, completely."[6]

Of the four explicit references to literature in this film, two
involve Quadri in his author-father relationship to Marcello, and
the other two involve Marcello's real father. In every case, writing
emphasizes the ambiguity of paternal relationships. An anonymous
letter to Giulia claims that Marcello has inherited a syphilitic disease from his father, *i.e.,* that father has betrayed son through
sexual activity. But Giulia guesses that the author of this infamous
letter is "Uncle" Perpuzio, the father figure of her youth who had
raped her and then held her in sexual bondage for years. As signifier, the letter spells betrayal by the father on a variety of levels.
As text, it constitutes an unconscious autodenunciation of the authority of both text and author-parent.

A last example of writing even more clearly establishes Bertolucci's ambivalent relationship to author-ity. When Marcello visits
his father in the asylum, the old man is sitting in a huge forum—
architecture reminiscent of the Fascist minister's office—writing
madly. Moravia's version portrays the son listening rather passively to his father's mad ramblings. In the film, Clerici seizes his
father's manuscript and holds it up, proclaiming, "My wedding
invitation." Marcello thus implies that the father's madness has
forced his son to seek too ardently a normal life with a "middle-
class girl who is very ordinary, full of ordinary and petty thoughts."
He then takes his father's pen hand in his own and guides it in the

[6] "Bernardo Bertolucci Seminar," op. cit., pp. 25, 27.

writing of some words which remain a mystery to the viewer: a symbolic collapse of the paternal relationship, giving the origin and progeny equal author-ity. The implications of this act for the relationship between Moravia and Bertolucci are clear: Bertolucci rejects any hierarchical difference in authority between the two symbolized figures. Finally, Marcello taunts his father with recollections of the father's former crimes of torture and murder while an Italian soldier, goading him until he breaks down and demands to be straightjacketed. Here Marcello unconsciously alludes to his own activities for the Fascists, an autoaccusation he will soon repeat for the church "father" in the confessional. As in the scenes with Quadri, this encounter with his father indicates how Marcello is obsessively driven simultaneously to imitate and to repudiate authority.[7]

Since Moravia constitutes the author-ity being explicitly imitated and implicitly contested in this film, it is crucial to understand in what other ways Bertolucci decided to "betray" the original. Clearly, Bertolucci chose not to follow the chronology or causality established systematically in Moravia's novel, as though the novelist had to demonstrate a particular set of hypotheses leading to a truth.

From Marcello's first sadistically violent games in his parents' garden to his ultimate betrayal of Quadri, Moravia follows the progress of his protagonist with an almost deadening chronological rigor and proleptic foreboding. His parents' neglect of him leads Marcello to the symbolic castration of

> a fine clump of marguerites covered with white and yellow flowers, or a tulip with its red cup erect on a green stalk, or a cluster of arums with tall, white fleshy flowers . . . leaving the decapitated stalks standing erect (p. 7).

Moravia's narrator stresses that it is "inevitable" that Marcello should pass from these symbolic acts to a massacre of dozens of lizards, and from this frenzied agitation to the "murder" of the family cat. In this last act, Marcello perceives "an un-mistakable

---

[7] A theme basic to Bertolucci's *Spider's Stratagem* made in the same year (1970). See my essay, "Father as Mirror: Bertolucci's Oedipal Quest and the Collapse of Paternity," *Psychocultural Review*, Spring 1979, pp. 91–109.

In adapting Moravia's *The Conformist*, Bertolucci started with a precise script "only to destroy it." A cap and a pistol prove to be illusory authority symbols of the pederastic chauffeur (Pierre Clementi) who seduces Marcello.

sign that he was predestined in some mysterious and fatal way to accomplish acts of cruelty and death" (pp. 19–20). These fatal signs of Marcello's abnormality serve as the context for the central psychological moment of the novel. All too willingly seduced by Lino, a pederastic chauffeur, Marcello takes up the pistol constituting and symbolizing the exchange that was to have taken place, and "kills" Lino.

The rest of Moravia's novel painstakingly charts Marcello's misguided attempt to atone for this childhood "crime" through a life of "well-defined, barren, reserved, benumbed, grey normality" (p. 72). He dedicates himself to total conformity by marrying the most apparently ordinary, uninspired, materialistic, middle-class girl he can find, by going to confession in order to be married ("a further link in the chain of normality" [p. 96]), and by joining the Fascist party, "as an abstract whole, as a great, existing army held together by common feelings, common ideas, common aims, an army of which it was comforting to form a part," despite the fact that he finds it "impossible to recognize himself in them and feels at the same time both repugnance and detachment" (p. 77).[8]

It is, of course, heavily ironic that the Fascist party sanctions Marcello's plan to betray (and symbolically to murder) one of his former professors during Marcello's honeymoon in Paris. Rather than anonymity and atonement, Marcello finds within the Fascist ranks an ever-more-murderous destiny so that "the figure of Judas, the thirteenth Apostle, became confused with his own, coalesced with its outlines, in fact *was* his own" (p. 193). Moravia not only exposes Fascism as a barely repressed perversion but also raises a more general question about the nature of conformity. Each time Marcello believes he has espoused normality, he discovers a new form of perversion. His normal bride turns out not only to have been the illicit child concubine of a well-known Roman lawyer but also to have carried on a lesbian affair immediately before their marriage. The priest who hears Marcello's confession rather perfunctorily exacts a few prayers as expiation for the "murder" of Lina but expresses avid interest in the particulars of their sexual encounter. Moravia's Quadri "sacrificed [his anti-Fascist initiates] quite coolly in desperate actions . . . that . . . involved a cruel indifference to the value of human life" (pp. 182–183). Quadri's wife Lina doubles the perverted chauffeur of Marcello's "original sin" not only in name—she repeats Lino's homosexual seduction on Marcello's much-too-willing wife (p. 231). Fleeing this discovery, Marcello seeks seclusion on a park bench and ends up being seduced again by an older man with a large black car. Moravia hammers doggedly away at the overwhelmingly evident message of *Il Conformista*: Normality, as Marcello imagines it, is an illusion. Society is a composite of polymorphously perverse individuals in a

> topsy-turvy sterile world in which merely sensual relationships occurred from the most natural and ordinary to the most abnormal and unusual, [between] ambiguous figures of men-women and women-men whose ambiguity when they met was mingled and redoubled (pp. 233–234).

[8] This basic need to seek in the group relief from feelings of fear and Oedipal guilt is well analyzed by Freud in *Totem and Taboo, Complete Psychological Works of Sigmund Freud*, edited and translated by James Strachey, London, Hogarth Press, 1955, Chapter XIII, p. 1; and in *Group Psychology and the Analysis of the Ego*, Chapter XVIII, p. 67.

Moravia's insistence on this theme reads almost as a repetition compulsion: Virtually every character becomes a distorted double of every other. Lino as homosexual chauffeur with a coveted pistol is redoubled by Orlando (and the Fascist authorities), the mother's lover (and therefore, by extension, the father), the old man in the park, and Lina. Lina is also portrayed as a double of a whore in Ventimiglia (and therefore of Marcello's promiscuous mother) and of Giulia. Quadri doubles not only Marcello's father but Orlando and the Fascists. Moravia singlemindedly builds an enormous but simple equation in which all the characters collapse into a composite image of the bad parent.

This repetitive explicitness, frequently bemoaned by Moravia's otherwise sympathetic critics, is mirrored by the author's overly insistent use of destiny. Moravia repeatedly alludes to Greek tragedy in general and to the *Oedipus* in particular. From his first taste of violence, Marcello discovers in it "an unmistakable sign that he was predestined, in some mysterious and fatal way, to accomplish acts of cruelty and death" (p. 19). Later, Moravia describes Marcello as caught in

> a trap of which you have been forewarned, which, even, you can clearly see, but into which nevertheless, you cannot help putting your foot. Or just a curse of . . . blindness that creeps into your movements, your senses, your blood . . . an intimate, obscure, inborn, inscrutable fatality . . . which stood like a signboard at the opening of a sinister road. He knew that this fatality implied he would kill somebody; but what frightened him most was not so much murder as the knowledge he was predestined to it, whatever he might do (p. 55).[9]

The many allusions to this mysterious yet inevitable fate coupled with the uncanny arrangement of doubles appear merely anomalous in the framework of an otherwise straightforward narrative structure. The novel offers no access that doesn't prove

[9] Other references to fate and Greek tragedy include the following: He is "marked out by a solitary, menacing fate and already launched upon a bloody course in which no human force could arrest him" (p. 20), where "murder seemed to be inevitably awaiting him" (p. 20). Prey to an "obscure, malevolent, cunning, external force, darkly tinged with doom and misfortune" (p. 20), a "circle of foreboding and doom" (p. 30), and "a circle of grim fatality" (p. 55). See also pp. 65, 110, 185, 203, 216, 268, 285, 295.

ultimately problematic: It can be read as a study of the relationship between psychology and politics, in which case the allusions to fate and the series of doubles strain the reader's credibility, or else it can be approached as a surrealist exercise in which most of the traditional narrative elements seem simply out of place.

Bertolucci's other films would suggest that precisely these "anomalous" elements—the doubling, the Oedipal arrangements, the mythic level[10]—attracted him to a novel which was for him like a "memory of my own memory."[11] This particularly significant phrase not only signals the personal relationship he felt to the original text but defines the very form of his film and specifies the particular genius of his adaptation of the novel. Indeed, Bertolucci's *The Conformist* becomes an exploration of what it means to say a "memory of my own memory."

The film opens with Marcello (Jean-Louis Trintignant) sitting on a bed bathed in an eerie blinking red light. A phone call "awakes" him from his silent thoughts, and he rushes from his bedroom to the street below, where he effects a rendezvous with a (heretofore) unidentified driver and begins the pursuit of another car through the mist of a snowy Paris morning. Nothing is explained or will be explained through traditional narrative exposition and chronology. Bertolucci's viewer must garner whatever understanding he can of the situation from a system of flashbacks out of a point in time given as the film's "present" (Marcello in the car in Paris) to a series of moments which appear either as memories or as *memories out of memories*. This use of flashbacks is unusual not only because they do not proceed chronologically once begun, but because Bertolucci frequently uses what we must designate as flashbacks of flashbacks.

In addition, it becomes increasingly clear that these abrupt cuts out of the Paris present are not explanations of the present within an authoritative traditional narrative framework (Bertolucci clearly eschews *any* appearance of narrative authority, further weakening the concept of authority in general)—they are instead

[10] See T. J. Kline, "Orpheus Transcending: Bertolucci's *Last Tango in Paris*," *International Review of Psycho-analysis*, No. 3, 1976, pp. 85–95; and "Father as Mirror: Bertolucci's Oedipal Quest and the Collapse of Paternity" (see footnote 7).
[11] Bernardo Bertolucci Seminar," op. cit., p. 16.

the pure associations of a character who is drifting in and out of sleep.

Indeed, late in the film, Marcello awakes from sleep and reports,

> I just had a strange dream. I was blind. You were taking me to a clinic in Switzerland. Quadri was operating on me. The operation was a success; I got my sight back. Then I ran off with Anna.

Significantly, this dream may be interpreted as castration anxiety (the operation) successfully thwarted ("I got my sight back") coupled with an Oedipal "victory" ("I ran off with Anna"). As such it serves as a structural parallel of every other flashback in the film.

The first of these flashbacks jumps the spectator into a recording studio where Marcello is talking to the blind propagandist, Italo, who proceeds to deliver a talk on International Fascism after broadcasting a popular song and bird imitation—a potpourri of programming which puts a serious strain on the spectator's ability to understand or follow the action. Interspersed in this jumble of elements are shots of Marcello walking through an enormous Fascist structure. It is impossible at the moment to situate these scenes logically or chronologically: Are they memories, imagination, dream, or subsequent action? A sudden cut returns us to the radio station, where Marcello awakes from a doze to find himself opposite a mysterious personage whose entry into the studio we have not witnessed. It becomes evident gradually that this character is a Fascist agent sent to inform Marcello that his plan for a honeymoon in Paris has been approved by the Minister. Another cut projects Marcello just as inexplicably into a different Fascist architectural immensity. Flashes back and forth to and from Marcello in the car further confuse the narrative progression.

In direct contrast, then, to the careful chronology of Moravia's text, the film presents the viewer with a jumble of elements and chronologies which can be described only as oneiric.

Not only does the film begin on a bed and in eerie lighting, but Marcello is repeatedly portrayed as dozing in both the car and the first flashback. These first scenes not only lack causal and chronological coherence, they operate by condensation, displacement, projection, and doubling—all techniques of what Freud has termed the latent dream work.

The clearest example of condensation involves the uncanny, indeed oneiric reappearance of Dominique Sanda in three different roles. She is most prominently cast as Anna Quadri. When Marcello first glimpses Anna, he is clearly smitten by an overpowering desire—within minutes of his arrival at the Quadris', he draws Anna into an empty room, pulls her to him, and kisses her. The reason for this sudden emotional bond, he tells her, is that she reminds him of the whore he'd met in Ventimiglia. But Marcello is unable to explain his immediate and passionate feeling for either of these women. Bertolucci's means of linking Anna and Luisa differs from Moravia's technique of discovering a single physical similarity in the two. Instead, the film introduces an uncanny series of visual doublings. Anna *is* Luisa, for both are played by Dominique Sanda. But Sanda plays a third role in the film: the mysterious mistress of the Fascist Minister.

Bertolucci's handling of this first appearance of Sanda is visually grandiloquent: Marcello is projected by means of a flashback out of a flashback (*i.e.,* a memory of a memory) from the car chasing Quadri to the studio, where Marcello has *fallen asleep*, and from there, projected ambiguously to an immense office building where he is dwarfed not only by the proportions of the building but by the gigantic head and pair of wings that are carried past him as he waits. Next, Marcello quite inexplicably finds himself peering through some curtains, like a naughty child, down the length of an enormous hall where a woman, legs dangling under the table (exactly as Marcello's mother's legs appear under her bed when Marcello fishes out her shoes and the syringe which symbolizes her sexual oppression), glances meaningfully at Marcello and immediately lies full-length on the table while the Minister explores her body. All the elements of this scene indicate a symbolic recurrence of the primal scene. As lost woman at the mercy of a powerful authority figure, Dominique Sanda here doubles the mother symbolically, and physically doubles her portrayal of the whore and Anna. In her role as the Ventimiglia whore, Sanda is portrayed in an architectural space visually analogous both to the Minister's palace and to Marcello's father's asylum. When she cries *"Sono pazza"* ("I'm crazy") from Manganiello's Fascist arms, she evokes both the primal scene previously experienced and the condition of the real father. When Marcello encounters her in

Quadri's apartment, she has already been visually identified as mother-whore-victim, and thus she elicits fantasies of love, betrayal, and rescue consistent with those normally experienced by the child in the Oedipal phase.

According to Freudian theory, the deepest level of the latent content of dream is the Oedipal configuration. Thus, the larger configuration of these elements, the uncanny condensation, the Oedipal triangle, and the displacement of the primal scene can be seen to place the opening moments of Bertolucci's *The Conformist* directly in the realm of dream work.[12]

Similar inexplicable elements (structural and visual) permeate the entire film: When Marcello first visits Giulia's apartment, a confluence of decor, costume, and lighting combine to give the entire scene an obsessive and inexplicable striped effect suggesting either emotional ambivalence or prison bars. In flashbacks to Marcello's first encounter with Manganiello, Bertolucci films with a distorting lens and with the camera tilted at a 45-degree angle, giving the entire scene a sense of being off balance—again an effect which deserves explanation but receives none. During Marcello's encounter with Lino, the camera for the first time takes the child's position and seems itself to run away through the forest of hanging sheets. On the train ride to Paris, Bertolucci himself says that he

> wanted to have two levels. One was the realistic level inside the train and the other one was . . . I wanted a sort of film in the film. A window like a magic lantern. So . . . outside the time is very surrealistic . . . very magic, because in two minutes you have sunset and night, and I also made some dissolves in the window but not in the train.[13]

The decor of the asylum is uncanny: Marcello's father has been given a Roman forum-like space in which to deliver his mad discourses. The decor of the bordello in Ventimiglia imitates the architecture of the Fascist bureaucracy and the asylum. The desk and bookshelves of Raoul's office, for some never-to-be-explained reason, are covered with walnuts. On leaving that office Marcello

[12] Of his working methods, Bertolucci has said, "I do what I'm feeling at the moment and, of course, the result of *dreams* and thinking and ideas." "Bernardo Bertolucci Seminar," op. cit., p. 24 (italics mine).
[13] Ibid., p. 15.

makes three grandiloquent gestures with the pistol, ending in a mock suicide. Quadri's apartment contains an oval, vagina-like door through which special camera lenses make the scene appear distorted and oneiric. Manganiello addresses the birds in a Paris park. A photo of Laurel and Hardy appears on the outside of the restaurant window through which the camera strains to catch a glimpse of Marcello and Quadri. Quadri's death is filmed through clouds of obviously artificial mist. Fantasy (as already discussed) takes over reality. And finally, after Marcello's *Walpurgisnacht* stroll at the end of the film, he is last seen sitting next to a grating, pondering a young man lying in a fully made-up brass bed situated in the open alley.

The fragmented, uncanny, and oneiric quality of the entire film, then, can be understood to be "a memory of my own memory" in its deeper sense: as dream, a structure essential to Bertolucci's entire enterprise. By rearranging Moravia's original chronology to conform to a purely associative process, Bertolucci rigorously situated the film's point of view in Marcello rather than in an omniscient (and all-too-explicit) narrator. In this way, elements in the novel's objective structure which strain the reader's credibility overly can be comprehended (along with a multitude of other uncanny elements) as the mental associations or dream work of a single consciousness.

The Lino incident central to Moravia's novel stands as a logical and fated occurrence in the progression of Marcello's violent tendencies and as the unique and consciously felt explanation for his obsessive conformity. In Bertolucci's dream structure, Marcello's seduction by Lino occurs rather late and then only as an involuntary association produced by an analogous moment during the trip in Manganiello's car.

Only in retrospect can the viewer (interpreter) understand that Marcello has already projected the Lino role onto Manganiello as well as onto his mother's sexually exploiting chauffeur: When Manganiello in his big black car first follows Marcello along the street toward Signora Clerici's house, the scene is distorted by the tilted camera (signifying the oneiric) and Marcello flees and succeeds in closing gates similar to those he had all too willingly passed through as a child in Lino's car. Marcello then suggests that Manganiello eliminate the mother's chauffeur—an act which symbolically condenses revenge on Lino (as chauffeur and original source of guilt), on father (Alberti as mother's lover), and on Manganiello himself (who has just unwittingly doubled Lino). Such uncanny condensations of the Oedipal arrangement occur repeatedly in this film yet never become obtrusive because of the way they are masked in unconscious symbolism.

The Lino affair does of course affect Marcello's conscious behavior, for he tells the priest during confession that he has decided to repay blood (Lino's) with blood (Quadri's)—and yet in Bertolucci's arrangement (as opposed to Moravia's handling of the same problem), this conscious motivation is far from explaining adequately the choice of Quadri. Theoretically, any blood would repay Lino's blood. But Marcello insists (and it is his plan) that he travel to Paris on his honeymoon to finger his former professor. Even the Fascists fail to understand Marcello's motivations. Standing outside the film and with the material provided in an associative way, the viewer has a better understanding. Quadri is an authority figure with a deformation (yet very popular with the girls, Marcello recalls), who had preached the illusion of appearances. Lino's gun and cap mark him as an authority figure too; his homosexuality is an unexpected deformation; and his signs of authority themselves prove to be merely an illusion since his gun is turned against him and his cap is removed to reveal long black tresses of womanly hair. Marcello's gestures of adoration (the spontaneous caress) and subsequent violence are to be displaced onto Quadri in what can only be termed a return of the repressed.

The dream (since that is clearly the structure of Bertolucci's film) reproduces the Lino relationship (seduction, adoration, loss of illusion, betrayal) in so many different forms that it appears to be a repetition compulsion. The most striking occurrence of this repetitive structure involves Anna (whom Moravia heavy-handedly named Lina). In her seduction of Giulia she reproduces with extraordinary fidelity the gestures Lino had used in seducing the child Marcello: She kneels "innocently" between the seated Giulia's legs, head on knee. Marcello watches through the half-open door, and she returns his gaze just as she had done when he had voyeuristically watched her in the Minister's office. Moreover, her exact replication of Lino's gestures itself imitates Marcello's replication of "Uncle" Perpuzio's gestures as Giulia confesses her childhood seduction during the train ride to Paris. Bertolucci effects an extraordinarily rich condensation of levels and characters in this gesture of Anna's, for in this single scene she condenses Lino (as homosexual seducer), mother, whore, and Marcello himself, and indicates Marcello's unconscious tendency to *project* the structure of his early relationships onto all those who surround him. The scene also manifests the dream's tendency toward multiple determinations by engaging in a wish-fulfillment fantasy of seduction (by projecting Anna as Lino, Marcello is projecting himself as seduced!) which is simultaneous with a fantasy of revenge (the betrayal of Quadri).

In the final moments of Bertolucci's film, Marcello recapitulates once and for all this ambivalence. Discovering that the dead man is alive (another wish fulfillment), Marcello immediately displaces his feelings of guilt for Quadri's death onto the blind Italo. In the final shot, we see Marcello looking ambiguously at the bed on which lies a naked boy just seduced by Lino.[14] Another projection? The glance and the relationship are as ambiguous as every gesture undertaken by the conformist, who has never ceased using authority figures as convenient scapegoats for a crime un-committed and a desire unassuaged.

Bertolucci has succeeded masterfully in transforming a novel of uncertain means and dubious distinction into a film of extraordinarily rich texture and meaning. If Moravia's *The Conformist* demonstrates that normality is really a mask for polymorphous perversity, it complicates this demonstration by an inexplicable insistence on fate and retribution.

Bertolucci dismissed Moravia's notions of fate and his final *deus ex machina* (the airplane which strafes and kills Marcello, Giulia, and their daughter) and replaced these classic conceptions with the more psychoanalytic notion of the character's unconscious conformity to certain psychic structures. The film succeeds in unmasking Marcello as a conformist not to some illusory social standard but rather to unconscious desires and structures. The genius of Bertolucci's film is that it succeeds in reincorporating most of Moravia's narrative elements into a new and more meaningful oneiric structure while at the same time subtly but surely

[14] Bertolucci described this scene as "Marcello looking at the guy making a sort of striptease." "Bernardo Bertolucci Seminar," op. cit., p. 20.

addressing the issue of the relationship between original text and film. Ultimately both the psychological and metacinematic levels of the film address the same issue: the relationship between origin /author-ity and imitation.

As Edward Saïd noted in *Beginnings*:

> Each text pushes aside ordinary discourse in order to place before the world a textual composition whose authority derives from two sources: the ancient originals whose style is being copied and the present text's appearance in the form of a preserved duration. To put pen to a text is to begin the movement away from the original; it is to enter the world of the text-as-beginning as copy and as parricide. The Oedipal motif lurking beneath many discussions of the text . . . makes more sense if we regard the textcopy as totem and the making of such a text as the beginning parricidal deed . . . that Freud spoke of in *Totem and Taboo*.[15]

As copy and as parricide, Bertolucci's *The Conformist* not only invites us to reconsider the necessarily ambivalent relationship theorized in *Beginnings*, it extends Saïd's theory to a new and important realm: the relationship between text and image. The film encourages us to imagine Bertolucci standing over Moravia and guiding the novelist's pen, holding up the result as a blank page, a screen, on which is filmed a new and deeper language.

[15] Edward Saïd, *Beginnings*, New York, Basic Books, 1975, p. 209.

WILLIAM R. MAGRETTA
& JOAN MAGRETTA

PRIVATE "I"
Tavernier's *The Clockmaker (1973)*

from the novel The Clockmaker of Everton
by Georges Simenon

Bertrand Tavernier's *The Clockmaker of Saint Paul* (1973) has the paradoxical quality of many of the finest cinematic adaptations of literary works: While achieving an admirable fidelity to the source—here, Georges Simenon's novel *The Clockmaker of Everton* (1954)—the film is at the same time an original, finely wrought work which stands on its own.[1] Tavernier is faithful to the human drama of Simenon's novel—a father's painful search for understanding, when, out of the blue, his teenage son murders a man. But whereas in Simenon's novel this search is private, a psychological drama of introspection and memory, in Tavernier's film it is both private and public at once, gradually revealing the complex relationship between individual psychology and socio-political realities.

In the novel, the apparently uneventful existence of Dave Galloway, a clockmaker in a small town in upstate New York, is destroyed when he learns that his sixteen-year-old son Ben has

[1] Simenon's novel first appeared in French as *L'Horloger d'Everton*, Paris, Presses de la Cité, 1954. All citations will be from Norman Derry's English translation, *The Clockmaker*, New York, Harcourt Brace Jovanovich, 1977. Page numbers from this edition appear in the body of the text. Tavernier's *L'Horloger de Saint-Paul* (1973), released in the United States in 1975 as *The Clockmaker*, is available from Joseph Green Pictures. Tavernier collaborated on the script with veteran screenwriters Jean Aurenche and Pierre Bost.

The above essay was written for this volume but was first published by special permission in *Literature/Film Quarterly* (Vol. VII, No. 4, 1979).

murdered a man, stolen his car, and eloped with an underage girl
named Lillian. "Horrified, as one is by a cataclysm" (p. 69), Dave
begins to review his life, looking for some meaningful pattern in
the past that will explain the present. While Ben is being hunted by
the police, Dave submits passively to the prying of a swarm of
reporters who expect to profit from his grief. But while he goes
through the motions of cooperating with the reporters, the police,
and later Ben's defense attorney, the real drama unfolds within
Dave as he discovers gradually the bond that joins him to his son
and his father. Each of the three Galloways had had his revolt, and
all had "imagined that they were going to set themselves free" (p.
123): Dave's father had defied his wife by staying out all night
one Fourth of July; Dave had defied his family and friends by
marrying an unsuitable woman, the town slut, Ruth; and Ben had
defied all society by committing a senseless murder without feeling
any remorse. The understanding Dave has reached is explained
in a crucial passage near the end of the novel, when he decides
to have separate photographs of himself, his father, and his son
mounted together in one frame:

> Didn't the gaze of the three men reveal a shared secret life . . . ?
> A look of timidity, almost a look of resignation, while the identical
> drawing in of the lips hinted at a suppressed revolt.
>
> They were of the same breed, all three of them. . . . It seemed
> to him that, in the whole world, there were only two sorts of men,
> those who bow their heads and the others. As a child, he had al-
> ready thought it in more literal terms: the whipped and those who
> whip[2] (pp. 118–119).

In presenting this story, Simenon has constructed a narrative
with essentially two strands: (1) the ongoing action of the present,
consisting largely of Ben's crime and the pursuit, arrest, trial, and
imprisonment, all filtered through Dave's consciousness by the use
of free indirect style,[3] and (2) Dave's search for an explanation of

[2] Perhaps a better translation of this last phrase, *les fessés et ceux qui
fessent*, would be "the spanked and those who do the spanking" since Dave
is speaking of his perceptions as a child.
[3] In free indirect style (French, *style indirect libre*; German, *erlebte Rede*),
a character's thoughts and speech appear to be reported by an external narrator, but at the same time they retain the flavor and immediacy of spoken
language. (For example: "What could he do? So much the better if they
blamed him, if the whole world blamed him" [p. 109].)

Ben's act, a process involving the interweaving of memory and introspection with the present action. The real challenge for the filmmaker is to find appropriate cinematic expressions for the abstract mental processes of the latter strand which actually constitute the core of the novel. Rather than resort to the oversimplification of equating cinematic techniques with literary forms (*e.g.*, the kind of literal-minded approach to film "language" that would equate flashback with memory and voice-over with introspection), Tavernier chose instead to recast the story so that Dave's search for understanding would unfold primarily in the present action, not in his meditations on the past. The ability of Tavernier's new form to convey the tone and themes of the original supports Martin Battestin's contention that the key to successful adaptation is not literal fidelity but analogy, specifically the filmmaker's skill "in striking analogous attitudes and in finding analogous rhetorical techniques."[4]

In this case, what is important in the novel is not the past per se, but rather the slow process of discovery and understanding which we are able to share with Dave because of the novel's ability to render consciousness directly. The film is no less subtle or sophisticated than the novel in its treatment of the protagonist's inner life, but in order to achieve analogous effects, Tavernier has devised a number of rhetorical and narrative strategies that externalize the process of intellection which is the focus of the novel.

A comparison of the openings of novel and film reveals clearly the kind of analogous rhetorical strategy that characterizes Tavernier's adaptation. Simenon begins on the night of the murder with a question about the as-yet-unnamed protagonist: "Would he have spent that evening differently, or would he have tried to enjoy it more, if he had foreseen that it was his last evening as a happy man? To this question and many others, including that of whether he had ever been really happy, he would later have to try to find an answer" (p. 3). The narrator teases us with deliberately withheld information, thus compelling us to seek answers (just as Dave will) to a number of mysteries: Who is "he"? What horrible thing is about to happen? Why is there uncertainty about his past happiness? Repeated throughout the novel, this abstract question about

4 Martin C. Battestin, "Osborne's *Tom Jones*: Adapting a Classic," in *Man and the Movies*, W. R. Robinson (ed.), Baltimore, Penguin, 1969, p. 37.

Dave's happiness becomes a central motif, deepening in significance as it is used to reveal his closeness to Ben and his estrangement from the world represented by his mother.

In the film, the opening shot shows a train hurtling toward Lyons through the darkness. As the camera then circles a car burning mysteriously near the tracks, the suspense is heightened by the noise of the train and the music on the sound track. After the credits, the frame is filled by a black-and-white shot of two workers from an earlier era, each with his arm raised in a gesture of revolt. Almost before this image registers, the camera zooms back to reveal that it is merely an old photograph hanging on the wall of a neighborhood bistro. Finally we see the protagonist, Michel Descombes, repairing a clock in the kitchen. The camera, much like the narrator of the novel, has drawn us into the film by dwelling on these mysterious and initially confusing images. The burning car, we later learn, belonged to Razon, the man Descombes's son Bernard murdered. Like the abstract question of Dave's happiness, the burned car, a visual correlative of Bernard's rebellion, becomes a central motif in the film—a touchstone which reveals Descombes's affinity to his son. It is the image which jolts Descombes out of his complacency and forces him to reexamine everything that had seemed secure. Just as we can fully appreciate the resonances of the opening questions only at the end of the novel, it is only at the end of the film that we can properly understand the opening images. The picture of the two workers, men whose appearance is as old-fashioned as the values of Descombes and Bernard, now reverberates with the newfound solidarity of father and son. The final shots of the film show a train arriving at the Lyons station in daylight, suggesting the successful completion of the inner journey of discovery that Descombes has made.

A major element in Tavernier's narrative strategy is the addition of an explicitly political dimension to the film, political both in the traditional sense—focusing on parties and ideologies, and political also in the broader sense, dealing with the mechanics of power, the meaning of personal choices, and the individual's relationship to society. The conflict between Left and Right pervades the film, beginning with the opening scene, in which Descombes jokes with his companions about the French voters' fear of the left. The clockmaker's sympathetic friend, a role taken by an older, apolitical man in the novel, is filled by Antoine in the film, a younger man who is characterized primarily by his interest in leftist union politics. While Ben Galloway's victim is merely an innocent passerby, the man Bernard Descombes shoots is a right-wing *flic d'usine* (a combination thug and informant) who has brutalized the workers in Liliane's factory. The meretriciousness of the reporters in the novel ("Get a picture of it. . . . We'll probably have the whole center spread to fill" [p. 59]) is retained, but Tavernier adds a sensitivity to the politics of communication that Simenon lacks, an awareness that extends from the more obvious examples of distorted media coverage to more subtle questions of how language expresses and confirms power relationships. The former is illustrated by the way the journalist Costes uses Bernard's story to arouse antileftist sentiments, knowing full well that the boy acted on his own; the latter is shown by a wall poster in Bernard's room which reads "Teach the subjunctive to the lower classes."

Bernard's act is political at a personal level, the gesture of an individual against the institutions of power and the rigidity of society. At one point Bernard states that he killed Razon because he was "filth" and because Bernard was "tired of the same ones always winning." This kind of politics adds an external logic to what in the novel is an exclusively internal logic of rebellion. Tavernier makes a similar change in the father's "revolt": Dave's strange marriage to Ruth is replaced by Descombes's insubordination during the war—his refusal to return to a burning building to retrieve a trivial possession for his superior officer. By having both father and son rebel against abusive authority, Tavernier deals more clearly and coherently than did Simenon with the questions raised by an unconventional act in a society where all actions (and even thoughts) seem constrained by convention, questions that focus on the problematic relationship between individual and community.

It is especially significant that Tavernier has moved the story from a small-town setting to an urban one, for in this film, if not in all films, theme is expressed through setting.[5] Tavernier's Lyons is

[5] We are reminded of Henry James's famous dictum about the impossibility of discussing incident or story apart from character in the novel: "What is character but the determination of incident? What is incident but the illustration of character?" "The Art of Fiction," in *Partial Portraits*, New York, Macmillan, 1888, p. 392. There is a similar interdependence here, for what is setting but visualized or embodied theme?

a city of endless traffic jams, malfunctioning telephones, and inces-
santly chattering television sets. Behind the charred remains of
Razon's car, the ugly wasteland factory where Liliane worked
spews pollutants into the air. This Lyons is a place where radio
announcers interrupt tacky music in order to report that "89 percent of all Frenchmen are happy," and where a "man-on-the-
street" says he can easily understand murder but not the burning
of a car.

Everything that we see and hear about Bernard implies a rejection of the values of this mass society. One poster in Bernard's
room proclaims that all cops are enemies; another shows a map
with the title "Polluted France." (Razon's room, in contrast, is
decorated with nude pinups and military souvenirs of Indochina.)
When Descombes apologizes for a radio appeal he recorded, Bernard says that he and Liliane didn't even hear it—they prefer
talking to each other to listening to the radio. As in the novel,
Bernard scornfully rejects the lawyer's conventional defense.[6]

However, Bernard is not characterized only by his dislikes or by
his antisocial act. Tavernier introduces Madeleine, a woman who
cared for Bernard until he was six and with whom he still has close
ties. She is an especially important invention because she enables
us to see—literally, since she and her setting function iconograph-
ically—the values that both Bernard and Descombes embrace, just
as the cityscape defines what they reject. As Penelope Gilliatt observes, "Madeleine is one of modern French cinema's most
poignant examples of French ordinariness at its finest."[7] Her
ramshackle garden seems to be the one island of greenery left in
the city, the kind of haven that children need and that Bernard
loved. The authorities are planning to tear down her house, she
says, in order to build a hospital. For Tavernier, this is yet another
encroachment of mass society; the individual is displaced by more
institutional concrete. The image of Madeleine in her kitchen is,
in its simplicity, eloquent testimony to how irreparable the loss
will be.

Ultimately, the solidarity of Descombes and Bernard depends

---

[6] In keeping with the change in setting, Tavernier has altered the defense in
order to preserve the lawyer's coventionality: The insanity plea is as conventional in the United States as the crime-of-passion defense is in France.
[7] Penelope Gilliatt, "The Current Cinema: Wild Justice," *The New Yorker*,
August 9, 1976, p. 49.

on the added dimension of their common antipathy for the surrounding culture; Tavernier has thus effectively translated the in-
effable family likeness of the Galloways into the realm of visible
action. It is then appropriate that Dave's introspection in the novel
should be replaced by Descombes's investigation of the world
around him in the film. While Dave is passive, waiting for scenes
from the past to appear to him, Descombes is more active, search-
ing like a detective for tangible clues in the present. This is an
especially apt cinematic way of conveying the process of intellection, because we accompany Descombes in his investigation and
participate in his discoveries. Thus, we too can recognize that
Madeleine is, in a sense, one of the clues he uncovers. And when
Descombes sits alone in his workshop, listening over and over
again to a tape of Bernard's interview with his lawyer, we understand that the answer might be hidden beneath the surface of the
boy's words.

In one of the film's most effective sequences, Tavernier uses
quickly changing visual perspectives to mirror Descombes's developing consciousness. Beginning with a shot of Razon's charred car,
the camera then moves to the right, revealing Descombes at the
rear left of the frame, standing in silent contemplation. Almost
immediately, this significant pattern is altered when a white Peu-
geot enters the rear of the frame. A "typical" family of four,
happy sightseers armed with cameras, scampers out to examine the
car, revealing to us and Descombes the frightening vulgarity of
"normal" society. For the children, the car is a playground toy, for
their parents an object of fascination, a cheap thrill to satisfy their
insatiable appetite for the sensational. The fluidity of this short,
one-shot sequence captures perfectly the complexity of Descombes's search for understanding, his gradual discovery that objects and actions have meaning only when seen in context.

Descombes is not only more active than Dave, he is also more
angry, perhaps in part because Tavernier's world is more oppressive and hostile than Simenon's. Tavernier invents a scene in which
two hired thugs from the factory smash the window of Descombes's shop, a shocking lesson for him in the brutal realities of
management-labor relations. Furious, Descombes pursues them,
ordering his friend Antoine to drive through a red light in order to
catch them—a detail which is significant because the law-abiding

Tavernier not only transferred the scene of *The Clockmaker* from America to France, but also developed the role of Inspector Guiboud (Jean Rochefort) as an antagonist to the troubled Descombes (Philippe Noiret). *Photo courtesy of Joseph Green Pictures*

Descombes had earlier refused to cross a deserted street against the light. Descombes and Antoine gives the thugs a good beating and feel much better for it than if they had called the police.

One of Descombes's many angry outbursts in the film is particularly interesting when contrasted to what was most probably its germ in the novel. On a plane, Dave notices a woman with a baby who seems to have recognized him from his picture in the newspaper. "When he met her gaze and glanced mechanically at the child, she shuddered, as though she was making heaven knew what comparison, and clasped the baby more tightly to her" (p. 84). This sets Dave off into memories of Ben as a baby. A similar incident in the film, however, provokes an angry confrontation. In a restaurant, while a television newscast jabbers about Bernard, Descombes senses that a woman in the next booth has recognized him. As he leaves, he angrily thrusts his face at her and shouts, "The Murderer's Father, Madame." Aware now of how the mass media destroy individuals in order to create conventional types, Descombes has begun to feel what Antoine later verbalizes, that they're "suffocating in this country," strangled by the very institutions that were made to serve them.

By far the most effective innovation for externalizing the novel's inner drama is Tavernier's creation of an antagonist for Descombes: a police inspector called Guiboud. The two men meet periodically to discuss the progress of the manhunt, but Guiboud's interest in Descombes is more than professional, for he too is a father who seeks to understand his own children. The complex relationship between the two men provides the dramatic center for the film: Descombes's progress is marked by his gradual awareness that the seemingly sympathetic Guiboud is, in fact, a conflation of all the antagonistic figures and forces against which he and Bernard rebel. By connecting Guiboud to the reporters, to the *flic* Razon, and to Bernard's defense attorney, Tavernier develops what is only hinted at in the novel: The quality shared by all the "whippers" is a rigid conventionalism which, in order to sustain a mass society, must suppress the individual.

The central oppositions represented by Descombes and Guiboud are shown most clearly when they meet, at Guiboud's request, at the monument to the dead in a Lyons park. The camera pans from the stone-carved words "MORTS" to Guiboud as he tells Descombes that, for Bernard's sake, he should have remarried after his wife left him. Descombes replies quietly, "So I've been told," as if he has heard this bit of conventional wisdom many times over the years. Guiboud's ideas are as dead as the backdrop. A few moments later in another part of the park, against a field of young deer, vital and unrestrained, it is Descombes's turn to speak. Shortly after his wife left him, a child he'd never seen before ran up to him, told him he'd changed, and then ran off. For Descombes this was marvelous, an outpouring of the child's love. Guiboud, on the other hand, is irritated by the child's rudeness and annoyed that Descombes approves of it. Tavernier has said that this incident, which actually happened to his co-scenarist Jean Aurenche, contains "the moral of the film; it summarizes the relationship between these two men."[8] What in Simenon is stated as an opposition between "those who bow their heads and the others" here becomes the more explicitly defined conflict between Des-

[8] Interview with Bertrand Tavernier, *Positif*, No. 156, February 1974, p. 46. The translation is ours.

combes's vitality, spontaneity, and rebelliousness and Guiboud's sterility, rigidity, and conventionality. Descombes's eventual dismissal of Guiboud, then, is the dramatic expression in the film of Dave's discovery in the novel.

Simenon ends his story with this discovery and with the narrator's report of Dave's new state of awareness: Though he is now alone, he has found a sustaining closeness to his father and to his son— and perhaps soon to his grandson as well. Although reported consciousness may be a peculiarly novelistic feature, Tavernier's ending shows brilliantly that there are cinematic ways of demonstrating consciousness. Descombes finds it hard at first to communicate with Bernard in jail because it is so noisy in the visitors' room. They must learn to articulate, Bernard says, his face framed but not obstructed by bars. As the two are at last able to talk, the camera moves closer and closer to Descombes, until the restraining grille which had at first obstructed our view of his face seems to vanish. When Descombes leaves the prison, the natural sound of the passing traffic subsides gradually, replaced first by the non-synchronous sound of singing birds and then by the richly moving strains of stringed instruments. After we see a train arriving, the camera pans to reveal the interior of the Lyons station, the emptiness of which suggests repose rather than desolation. Voice-over narration tells us that nothing much has changed, that the current traffic jam is "so bad that you might as well sell your car." But this final image of daylight streaming through the beautiful grillwork of the station roof conveys the sense that, for one man at least, a journey has reached a positive completion.

WILLIAM R. MAGRETTA

READING THE WRITERLY FILM
Fassbinder's *Effi Briest (1974)*

from the novel by Theodor Fontane

> My whole production is psychography and criticism, creation in
> the dark, arranged in the light.
>
> —*Theodor Fontane*

In Samuel Beckett's *Krapp's Last Tape* (1958), Krapp at one
point muses dreamily, "Scalded the eyes out of me reading *Effie*
again, a page a day, with tears again. Effie. . . . Could have been
happy with her, up there on the Baltic, and the pines, and the
dunes."[1] Krapp's deliberate reading pace, his effort to savor every
moment of Theodor Fontane's famous novel, *Effi Briest*, remarkably parallels the measured pace of Rainer Werner Fassbinder's
1974 film, *Fontane Effi Briest*.[2] However, the slow pace is only
one of a complex of formal features which together succeed in
making the film more than just a faithful rendering of the novel,
but an astonishing re-creation of the attitudes of the novel in a
different medium.

The novel, which first appeared in 1894, is familiar to German-
ists as one of the landmarks of nineteenth-century literature and as

[1] Samuel Beckett, *Krapp's Last Tape and Other Dramatic Pieces*, 1958, reprinted in New York, Grove Press, 1970, p. 25. (The spelling "Effie" is a frequent Anglicization of the German original *Effi*.)

[2] Although *Fontane Effi Briest* is the full, formal title of Fassbinder's film,
it is usually referred to simply as *Effi Briest*, a practice I shall follow. Fassbinder himself insists on the appropriateness of using Fontane's name in the
title. Even for those who do not know the novel, he says, "it is completely
clear that it is a film about the relationship between the author and the
story he tells, and not a film based on that story. What interested me was
his approach, the rapport and the distance of the poet, the fabric of what
he writes, and his own world." Daniel Sauveget, "Entretien avec Rainer-
Werner Fassbinder," *La Revue du Cinéma Image et Son*, No. 333, 1978,
p. 47. The translation is mine.

a penetrating depiction of the petty nobility of Prussian society. It has often been compared with *Madame Bovary* and *Anna Karenina*, chiefly because of its basic subject matter: the story of a young woman who violates the rigid social code of her class and era through an adulterous affair. Fontane later revealed that the story was based on actual events, but that the spark which set his imagination going was a single scene:

> The whole story is one of adultery like a hundred others, and as Frau L. told it to me it would not have made any further great impression on me if the scene—in particular the words "Effi, come" —had not occurred. The appearance of the girl at the window overgrown with vines, her red hair, the call, and her ducking away and disappearance made *such* an impression on me that from *this* scene the whole long story was born.[3]

Fassbinder's film maintains a remarkably literal fidelity to the book, even to the point of including the symmetrical occurrence of that poignant call, "Effi, come"—once at the beginning, when Effi's childhood friends attempt to call her away from her first step into adulthood through her engagement to Baron von Innstetten, and finally as her father telegraphs her to return to the family fold and the forgiveness of her parents in her fatal illness. The film also keeps the exact language of the book, using both the speeches of the characters and the narrator's commentary spoken in voice-overs by Fassbinder himself.

What strikes the viewer above all is the extreme stylization of the film—static compositions, long takes, fades to white, intertitles in Gothic script. These devices are not only means of achieving distancing, they also illustrate one or more important themes of the story. Thus, although the slow pace and inactivity may fool viewers into thinking that the film is diffuse, it is actually extremely dense and economical. No gesture, no stylistic feature is wasted; each is endowed with several levels of significance. Like a good book, the film cries out for re-viewing, for re-examining to discover additional subtleties, for the kind of intensive reading which Roland Barthes gave to Balzac's *Sarrasine*. All these devices produce

---

[3] Excerpted from Fontane's letter to Friedrich Spielhagen, February 21, 1896. Quoted in Theodor Fontane, *Sämtliche Werke*, Bd. IV, Walter Keitel (ed.), München, Carl Hanser Verlag, 1963, p. 682, note 18. The translation is mine.

a complex interplay of distancing and involvement which is at the heart of the aesthetic of the film. Fassbinder has stated specifically that he wanted the audience to be actively engaged in a process of imagining, to "read" the film:

> To show the narrative on film is like an author telling a story, but there's a difference. When one reads a book, one creates—as a reader—one's own images, but when a story is told on screen in pictures, then it is concrete and really "complete." One is not creative as a member of a film audience, and it was this passivity that I tried to counter in *Effi Briest*. I would prefer people to "read" the film. It's a film which one cannot simply experience, and which doesn't attack the audience . . . one has to read it. That's the most significant thing about the film.[4]

The act of reading required of the audience is not simply a more intensive and critical effort of interpretation; it is rather an act of producing a text. Although the terminology might seem contradictory at first, the distinction that Fassbinder has asserted is just the one that Roland Barthes makes between the "readerly" (*lisible*) and "writerly" (*scriptible*) text.[5] The readerly text is a "closed" text, the traditional or classic text which a reader approaches as a *consumer*, "with no more than the poor freedom either to accept or reject the text."[6] The writerly text, on the other hand, is marked by the limitless plurality of meanings; in exploring actively the play of intelligibility, the reader becomes a *producer* of the text, in effect rewriting the text in the process of reading it:

> The writerly text is *ourselves writing*, before the infinite play of the world (the world as function) is traversed, intersected, stopped, plasticized by some singular system (Ideology, Genus, Criticism) which reduces the plurality of entrances, the opening of networks, the infinity of languages. The writerly is the novelistic without the novel . . . production without product. . . .[7]

Although Barthes's distinction is typological, he does seem to recognize that these are functional concepts, that most texts—even

[4] Christian Braad Thomsen, "Interview with Fassbinder (Berlin 1974)," in *Fassbinder*, Tony Rayns (ed.), London, British Film Institute, 1976, p. 46.
[5] Roland Barthes, *S/Z*, translated by Richard Miller, New York, Farrar, Straus & Giroux, 1974, p. 4.
[6] Ibid.
[7] Ibid., p. 5.

classics like Fontane's *Effi Briest*—are composed of both the readerly and the writerly. In Fassbinder's film the emphasis is clearly
on the writerly, and it is chiefly through a complex of distancing
devices that he forces the audience to become more deeply involved in experiencing the play of meanings, in producing the
text.

This distancing is, of course, closely related to Brecht's "alienation effect" (*Verfremdungseffekt*), an inheritance which Fassbinder has acknowledged explicitly.[8] The distancing is a way of
controlling the audience's emotional involvement, of preventing us
from identifying too closely with any of the characters, of forcing
us to reject simplifying, subjective attitudes toward the story. Most
importantly, it enables us to experience Fontane's (and Fassbinder's) own ambivalent attitude toward the story and toward
society: Fontane saw and decried the meanness, the pettiness, the
rigidity, and the ultimate inhumanity of the Junker social code, but
ultimately he accepted it as the necessary alternative to chaos.[9] He
can treat with sympathy those who are outsiders or who break the
rules, for they are only trying to break out of a set of stultifying
social attitudes, but at the same time he can recognize that order
must prevail, that "even the most enlightened critic of society's
attitudes cannot in the last analysis cut loose from them."[10]
Moreover, despite his dislike of the constraining Prussian society,
Fontane himself strove for acceptance and recognition within it.
Fassbinder has acknowledged explicitly that he shares these contradictory attitudes with Fontane. But Fassbinder does not want

[8] John Hughes and Brooks Riley, "A New Realism," *Film Comment*, Vol.
11, No. 6, 1975, p. 14.
[9] For more extensive discussions of Fontane's attitudes toward his works
and his society, see A. R. Robinson, *Theodor Fontane: An Introduction to
the Man and His Work*, Cardiff, University of Wales Press, 1976; G. Wallis
Field, *A Literary History of Germany: The Nineteenth Century, 1830–1890*,
New York, Barnes & Noble, 1975, pp. 155–180; Maurice Larkin, *Man and
Society in Nineteenth-Century Realism: Determinism and Literature*, London, Macmillan, 1977, pp. 160–162; Henry Hatfield, "The Renovation of the
German Novel: Theodor Fontane," in *Crisis and Continuity in Modern
German Fiction*, Ithaca, Cornell University Press, 1969, pp. 1–34; and
J. P. Stern, "Realism and Tolerance: Theodor Fontane," in *Re-interpreta-
tions: Seven Studies in Nineteenth-Century German Literature*, New York,
Basic Books, 1974, pp. 301–347.
[10] Larkin, op. cit., p. 162.

merely to present these conflicting attitudes to the viewers of *Effi Briest*; he wants us to explore our own attitudes:

> For me, *Effi Briest* is about Fontane's attitude to society, which is re-created in the film by the distance between the audience and what is happening on the screen. There's explicitly something between the two; it may be the author, or even me as director. Through that built-in "distance," the audience has a chance to discover its own attitude to society.[11]

Thomas Mann described Fontane's attitude toward his work and his society with the phrase "responsible disengagement" (*verantwortliche Ungebundenheit*),[12] and it is this same attitude which the audience is required to take toward *Effi Briest*.

Because the devices for distancing are crucial to the effect of Fassbinder's film, it is revealing to examine them in greater detail. The emphasis on artifice in the film signals that this is a story about belief in forms: good form, outward form, formal honor. The film presents the story in a series of relatively brief sequences punctuated by fadeouts to white and by intertitles taken directly from the novel. The set-ups within the sequences are usually static, giving each shot the quality of a *tableau vivant*—or even a still life—although Fassbinder never immobilizes the characters in a freeze frame. The characters often seem to be caught in frozen poses, caught in long or medium shots that keep them at a distance most appropriate for exhibiting their public, social aspects.

The stasis within the shots also forces us to read them more intensively, to attend closely to the details of characters, objects, and especially compositions within the frame. For example, in the early sequence of the film in which the voice-over narration recounts Frau von Briest's announcement to Effi of Baron Innstetten's marriage proposal, the first shot shows Effi and her mother embracing on the stairs. Effi's activity, which we have seen is a vital part of her character from her first appearance in the film, is arrested for the momentous change which is about to take place. She is, moreover, "caught" on the unstable diagonal of the stairway while the narrator reads Frau von Briest's words, "You look so

---

[11] Thomsen, op. cit., p. 45.
[12] Thomas Mann, "Der Alte Fontane," in *Reden und Aufsätze*, Bd. IX of *Gesammelte Werke*, Frankfurt am Main, S. Fischer, 1960, p. 30.

unready, so completely unprepared" (Chapter 2).[13] Both mother and daughter are captured in long shot so that we are not encouraged to identify with them. In addition, Effi's back is toward us so that we are unable to see her reaction; we thus rely more heavily on the assertion of Effi's state of mind contained in her speech as read by the narrator: "You're making me all scared and frightened" (Chapter 2). The two figures are isolated on the white stairway by the confining frame of dark woodwork and furnishings. There is, finally, a slight distortion in the entire perspective of the room, enough to subtly reinforce the incongruity of this impulsive, immature girl being taken in marriage by a man who is old enough to be her father and who, as we have just learned, had earlier courted Effi's mother.

The stillness of this tableau is broken as Herr von Briest brings Baron Innstetten into the room—and into Effi's previously uncomplicated life. After Effi goes down the stairs and curtsies to the baron, we cut to a close-up of Effi and him. In a shot that fleetingly recalls the famous two-shot of Liv Ullmann and Bibi Andersson in Bergman's *Persona* (1967), we see an extremely compressed two-shot with Innstetten's face toward us but half-obscured by the back of Effi's head with its luxuriant hair. We might expect this to be a reaction shot, but his face is expressionless—perhaps emotionless —despite what should be the joy of the moment. (At the same time, the voice-over narration presents Frau von Briest's reaction to Effi's astonishment at the proposal: "It's not something one would joke about" [Chapter 2].) Effi's face and reaction are, of course, invisible to us. This composition is almost excessive in its emblematic representation of their anticipated union, but it is also

---

13 The problem of translations and editions is somewhat complicated. There are a number of German editions available; I have used the one cited in note 3. The only complete English translation is by Douglas Parmée, Harmondsworth, England, Penguin, 1967. Fassbinder follows Fontane's text exactly. All of the narration, dialogue, and intertitles (with the exception of the film's epigraph) reproduce the language of the novel faithfully. The subtitles in the film, however, do not always match Parmée's translation. Finally, although I find both translations generally admirable, I do not always agree with them in every detail. Therefore, to avoid an unwieldy apparatus for translations and references, I shall employ the following procedure: The translations will be mine (and may or may not coincide with the subtitles and the Parmée translation); I shall include references only to the chapter of the novel in the body of this essay.

part of the continuing visual motif of obscuration—we are not allowed to see the characters too closely, nor can they see themselves fully.

The shot frames and emphatic framing devices within the picture are also important features for our complete reading of the film. The opening shot of the Briest house in Hohen-Cremmen shows the building in bright sunlight, framed by the heavy trunk and foliage of a dark tree in the foreground and by the shadows of the tree. More than just a pretty composition, the shot at once suggests that this will be a story about limitations, about constraints, and about closures. Throughout the film the repeated use of framing objects—doors, corridors, windows, and dark woodwork and furniture—emphasizes the way that people are confined by their milieu, in particular, their social milieu. But the limitations are not only external; they are the internal limitations for those who will not, or cannot, break out of their molds. As Innstetten remarks, "But after all, we are what we are" (Chapter 12).

This framing is accentuated by the use of the stark contrasts available in black-and-white film. Fassbinder remarked that he made the film in black and white "because they're the most beautiful colors I know."[14] Although in the past black and white may have been accepted as the more neutral or "realistic" representation primarily because it was the standard,[15] nowadays color is the norm, and black and white has a subtly archaic flavor—images from an earlier age that have been preserved for us to examine. Fassbinder's choice is thus appropriate not only for a story set in the past but also as a distancing device to deter us from the closer identification we make with the supposedly greater reality of color film.

The limitations of the screen frame are also significant. Our first view of Effi, in the second shot of the film, has her playing on a swing at Hohen-Cremmen. As several critics have noted,[16] swinging (*schaukeln*) is an important leitmotif in the novel: At the

---

[14] Thomsen, op. cit., p. 45.

[15] See, for example, Jurij Lotman, *Semiotics of Cinema*, translated by Mark E. Suino, Michigan Slavic Contributions, No. 5, Ann Arbor, University of Michigan, 1976, pp. 18–20.

[16] See, for example, Field, *Literary History of Germany*, op. cit., pp. 170–172; and Mary E. Gilbert, "Fontane's 'Effi Briest,' " *Der Deutschunterricht*, 11, Heft 4, 1959, pp. 65–66.

Hanna Schygulla in the title role of Fassbinder's *Effi Briest* picnics with Major Crampas (Ulli Lommel). Unable to check on her appearance in mirrors, she risks deviating from socially acceptable behavior. *Photo courtesy of New Yorker Films*

outset it reflects Effi's youthful liveliness and her free spirit as well as her love of danger ("most of all I always like being scared that something will give way or break and fall down" [Chapter 4]). At the end, when Effi swings once more shortly before her death, the associations of vivacity and freedom are brought back, but now only as remembered joys which cannot be recaptured. Fassbinder retains the symmetrical use of the swinging motif at beginning and end, for in addition to showing Effi swinging at the start, he shows her near the end swinging gently and then sitting quietly as she asks Pastor Niemeyer if she will ever get to heaven; in the final prolonged shot of the garden, the swing sits motionless in the foreground, all in shadow except for the seat, while Effi's parents discuss the outcome of her life.

But to return to the initial shot of Effi swinging, not only is she shown in motion in contrast to the stasis of the rest of the composition (and the dominating stasis of most of the film), but the arc of her movement takes her in and out of the frame of the screen—

she is significantly breaking out of the rigid limitations of her world, an action that carries with it the danger of falling: "a strange tingling sensation, a shiver of pleasant apprehension at the thought: 'Now, I'm going to drop' " (Chapter 15).

Another characteristic of the visual style of the film which both distances the viewers from the events on the screen and involves them more intimately in the ongoing enterprise of re-creating the story is Fassbinder's use of fadeouts to white between sequences. As contrasted with the more usual fades to black, these "white-outs" seem more emphatic. Vincent Canby found them suggestive of "the empty space on the page at the end of a chapter."[17] Rather than leaving the nothingness of the black screen—the absence of light and therefore of image—the fade to white, by leaving us in light, sustains our conscious attention. Fassbinder's remarks on this device are most revealing:

> [The white fadeout is] one element of alienation; like books which have white color with black print. According to Kracauer, when it gets black, the audience begins to fantasize, to dream, and I wanted the opposite effect through white. I wanted to make them awake. It should not function like most films, through the subconscious, but through the conscious.[18]

For Fassbinder in *Effi Briest* and his other films, the omission of "key" or "action" scenes is another distancing technique: "Had we made 'action scenes,' we would have asked the audience to identify with the characters. But having decided beforehand *not* to make such a film, we had to reduce the action scenes to a minimum because they got in the way of the argument."[19] But it must be noted that Fassbinder omits "action scenes" only to the same extent that Fontane does. Fassbinder does, in fact, retain all the crucial scenes of the novel, such as Effi's meetings with Major Crampas, Innstetten's discovery of Crampas's letters, the duel, Effi's renunciation of the baron, and her final acceptance of her fate. Although he left out segments that he considered unessential, they are not decisive for our re-creation of the story, and the

[17] "The Decline and Fall of Effi Briest," *New York Times*, June 17, 1977, Sec. C, p. 5, Col. 3.
[18] Hughes and Riley, op. cit., p. 16.
[19] Thomsen, op. cit., p. 46.

interstices that we fill in for the film are much like what we provide for the novel.

The most striking demonstration of Fassbinder's complex technique for distancing and engagement in a key scene occurs in the duel sequence. Because Fassbinder adheres so closely to the chronological ordering in Fontane's text, using straightforward cuts and fades, restricting his stylization, for the most part, to the level of the shot, the one syntactic artifice of the film becomes especially marked. As Innstetten and Wüllersdorf discuss whether any action should be taken six and a half years after Effi's affair with Crampas, and while their voices continue on the sound track, the sequence is broken up first by shots of a train rushing along and later by shots of a carriage moving through the countryside in the early morning light. This parallel montage, at first not easily interpretable, fuses the discussion with its outcome—elements that were clearly discrete in the novel. It is a stunning visual representation of the inevitability of the duel: Even while the two men are debating the necessity of such action, the conclusion is foregone. As Innstetten says near the end of their discussion, "as soon as we had exchanged our first words, there was someone else who knew all about it. And, because there is such a person, I can't go back" (Chapter 27). Innstetten is driven headlong into this act by the prevailing idolatry of the "cult of honor." Despite the unhappiness that must ensue, he must resign himself, as Wüllersdorf puts it, "as long as the idol stands" (Chapter 27).

The duel itself, which follows immediately, is presented with extreme economy: a close-up of a pistol firing, a long shot of Crampas falling, a shot of Innstetten standing by Crampas, a close-up of the fallen Crampas as he raises his head and says, "Will you . . ." and a long shot of Innstetten walking away as the camera tracks to reveal for the first time the fishnets where Crampas and Effi had embraced. This is an action scene, but it is so stylized and sparing that we maintain our distance.

In striving to avoid "predetermined characters" in the film, to free the viewers to make the effort of imagination in creating the characters, Fassbinder has his actors employ a deliberately restrained acting style. The enforced visualization of the characters in film—often observed to be a kind of limitation on the audience's imagination, especially when comparison is made with representations in novels—is here counterbalanced by the underacting which opacifies and only hints at their emotions. This corresponds to what Seymour Chatman calls "enrichments by silence"[20] in modern prose narratives, and it maintains our interest by keeping the characters "open constructs"[21] which we endeavor to understand. This unemotive acting is, of course, appropriate for people in a society which prizes self-control, obedience, and sobriety; Frau von Briest admonishes Effi in the opening sequence: "Don't be so wild and impulsive, Effi" (Chapter 1). But just as importantly, it is a visual representation of the ultimately *passive* relationship of the characters to their social milieu.

As J. P. Stern observed about Fontane's work, "the suggestion is never absent from his novels that private life and morality are one thing and social and political life another, and the relation of the one to the other is a *passive* one. . . . characters . . . exhibit the social forces always only by being their victims."[22] This attitude is most clearly set forth in Fassbinder's epigraph for the film, his one departure from strict fidelity to Fontane's text. The letters themselves are constrained within a long, narrow, vertical column at the center of the screen:

> Many who have a sense of their possibilities and needs nevertheless acquiesce in the prevailing order through their actions, and thereby confirm and strengthen it absolutely.

Effi steps outside the system ("rebels" is really too strong a term) and in the emotional high point of the film even passionately denounces Innstetten for what he has done from a sense of honor, but in the end she quietly acknowledges that he was right to have acted as he did. As the intertitle after the second sequence of the film had announced, "A story of resignation cannot be bad" (Chapter 1).

Part of what enters into the distancing effect of the restrained acting style in the film is Fassbinder's use of dubbed voices. Effi, Innstetten, and Wüllersdorf read their own parts, but the voices of the other major roles are dubbed (in German). Although their

[20] *Story and Discourse: Narrative Structure in Fiction and Film*, Ithaca, Cornell University Press, 1978, p. 132.
[21] Ibid., p. 118.
[22] Stern, "Realism and Tolerance," op. cit., p. 341.

voices are by no means toneless, and most foreign viewers are probably unaware of the dubbing, this substitution is one more element of artifice that ensures that viewers will consciously "read" the film. Fassbinder even intended that "when it [the film] was to be shown abroad it should be synchronized in that language, including the intertitles. This film already works through two levels of alienation, and that would make it a third level."[23]

The unemotive acting style also contributes vitally to the overall measured pace of the film. This, along with the long takes, static set-ups, and sparing camera movements, imposes on the film the kind of deliberate speed that encourages the viewers to attend more closely, to work actively at interpreting. Like Krapp reading the novel, we read the film "one shot at a time," savoring each detail. The languorous pace also mirrors one of the themes of the story: Effi engages in the affair with Crampas in part out of boredom. The restrictions of the society of the petty nobility are stultifying, especially for such a free-spirited young woman as Effi. Insensitive viewers take this slow pace as part of an overall flatness of the film,[24] but they fail to grasp that this tedium, like all the other features of stylization in the film, operates not only as a distancing device but also as a thematically significant element.

In addition to relying on long and medium-long shots to keep the viewer at a distance, Fassbinder uses another visual device to achieve an alienation effect: that of shooting scenes through various partial obstructions like nets, gauzes, grillworks, bushes, steam vapor, veils, or lace. This technique is particularly effective at moments of intimacy and at emotional peaks—in short, at moments when characters are most vulnerable and in greatest danger of losing control and revealing themselves. The eye of the camera is thus not all-seeing, nor can we ever penetrate the characters fully; there is always some barrier which prevents us from identifying with a character, which keeps us aware that we are looking *at* them, not *with* them. Even at the emotional high point of the film, when Effi denounces Innstetten and breaks down (into tears),

[23] Hughes and Riley, op. cit., p. 16.

[24] Viewers' impatience with the pacing of the film is perhaps best accounted for by one of Robert Bresson's lapidary observations: "Condemned are the films whose slowness and silences are confused with the slowness and silences of the theater." *Notes sur le Cinematographe*, Paris, Gallimard, 1975, p. 112. The translation is mine.

when the camera moves in for the tightest close-up of the film, she is shot through the ornately carved back of the chair she is sitting in.

Finally, among the devices in the film which both distance and engage the viewers, perhaps the most striking is the use of mirrors. Throughout his films Fassbinder has shown a particular attachment to this device:

> I have always had a special relationship to mirrors because they break open a scene between the people in the shot, and at the same time we can concentrate on a certain point; they bring the focus back to what is important. It happens simultaneously.[25]

In *Effi Briest* this device is carried to an extreme; mirrors are ubiquitous, sometimes substituting for direct shots of the characters, sometimes presenting faces where the positive image gives us only their backs, sometimes showing a second (or multiple) image of what is already visible directly. But they always give us the image at one remove; they add another level of alienation to the already mediated images of the film so that what we see is not the thing in itself but the reflection, and what is reflected is the outward appearance, the form. Even where a mirror might be expected to show us the reaction of a character whose face would otherwise be hidden from the direct view of the camera, as in a conversation (contrasted to the Hollywood reverse-angle shot), the opacity of the characters (derived from the static poses and the underemotive acting style) nevertheless still forces us to work at understanding. Nor do the mirrors always present a completely faithful reflection of the "reality" within the film. Characters sometimes appear to be directly opposite each other as they converse, but in fact they are in different depth planes—it is only by virtue of a mirror that the images seem to be face to face. Several shots actually trick us by relying on our predisposition to take the film image as an accurate rendering of reality and then revealing, through the movement of the camera or a character, that our initial interpretation was an illusion or at least a distortion. The mirrors can produce accurate reflections of an external reality, but our comprehension of that reality requires a continuous conscious effort—and, on occasion, revisions.

[25] Hughes and Riley, op. cit., p. 14.

Like the other stylizing devices of the film, mirrors also have thematic functions. Effi and Innstetten are often seen checking their outward appearances in mirrors and making the small corrections necessary to ensure that they present socially acceptable "faces." Without these means for keeping watch on herself, as on the beach or in the carriage with Crampas at night, Effi is in great danger of deviating from the rigidly prescribed social conventions. Without the inner resources of strength of an Innstetten, she needs external supports and checks to restrain her impulsiveness.

While the mirrors in themselves do not provide completely reliable or perspicuous reflections of the characters, they are also emblematic of the broader means of indirection by which characters—particularly Effi—are delineated. Although we have Effi's own speeches and actions to tell us that she is ambitious, vain, snobbish, and superstitious, as well as affectionate, spontaneous, innocent, and free-spirited, her nature is also revealed as she is mirrored in the eyes of the other characters. The fact that she is attracted to the "outsiders" like Gieshübler, Roswitha, and Trippelli is ultimately a positive sign, for they are sympathetic characters, and they clearly like her for her admirable qualities.

Fassbinder's stylization extends beyond the devices and techniques which serve in part to distance the audience. The film is not heavily symbolic, but the symbols that do appear subtly reinforce thematic elements of the story. Fassbinder retains the Chinaman from the novel, a vague presence from the past which the superstitious Effi feels is constantly hovering in the background. As in the novel, we hear about him only as an ominous presence. Absent from the film are the other unsettling furnishings in the Innstetten home in Kessin: the hanging shark and the crocodile. Fassbinder's significant innovation in the residences in both Kessin and Berlin is the omnipresence of marble statues, often of children. Like the shadowy figure of the Chinaman, which, as Crampas observes, Innstetten is using to "educate" Effi indirectly—he remarks that "a ghost like that is as good as a cherub with a sword" (Chapter 16)—the statues are always there, always watching. And Trippelli reinforces this feeling of being under constant observation: "Everywhere, one is being watched, from left and right, in front and in back" (Chapter 11). More than just ominous presences, the statues are constant guardians: immobile like the rest of the static compositions, rigid like the unyielding social conventions, cold like the unemotional ideal of this society, but watching to prevent a misstep. One statue which reappears makes an even further apt allusion: The statue of a maiden pouring water from an urn with a goose by her side calls to mind the fairy tale from Grimm of the goose-girl, a story of a princess who, after leaving home to be married, suffers because of her passivity and immature carelessness.

The music which Fassbinder uses very sparingly also fits in subtly with the themes of the film. The motif is from Camille Saint-Saens's *Havanaise for Violin and Orchestra*, and the sweetness of the solo violin in part reinforces the romantic nature of the story. But the motif is ultimately bittersweet, for it combines melancholy with the sweetness as the harmony shifts subtly from major to minor and back to major again. Moreover, the gentle rhythmic imbalance between the basic duple meter in the orchestral accompaniment and the slightly conflicting triple rhythms in the solo part reinforces the vague sense of disquiet which we feel throughout.

Fassbinder's film is extraordinarily faithful to both the spirit and substance of Fontane's novel, but its pervasive commitment to cinematic stylization makes it a striking work in its own right and truly one of the masterpieces of the New German Cinema. Through a complex of devices which keep us distanced from the story, he engages us in an ongoing process of creating a text. Thus, in insisting that "the audience should continue to work, as in reading a novel,"[26] Fassbinder has given us a "writerly" text which we must re-produce as we view it.

[26] Ibid., p. 16.

PETER HARCOURT

ADAPTATION THROUGH INVERSION
Wenders's *Wrong Movement (1974)*

freely based on Wilhelm Meister's
Apprenticeship *by Johann Wolfgang Goethe*

Johann Wolfgang Goethe (1749–1832) was in his day the complete man of letters. Never satisfied with anything he produced, he continuously rewrote many of his own texts, striving to incorporate into them a greater complexity of insight. He aspired after a totality of knowledge which was impossible to achieve. The idealism of his cosmological ambitions was frustrated by his keen observation of the inconsistencies of human life. *Wilhelm Meister's Apprenticeship* (1795–96), which like *Faust* preoccupied Goethe for many years, combines in its final version the philosophical quest of *Faust* with the sensitivity to relationships and the yearning for idealized, romantic love of *Elective Affinities*. Like much of Goethe's work, this book is curiously modern. While seeking wholeness, it depicts disintegration. It is no wonder that it should have appealed to both Peter Handke and Wim Wenders, and that when they both became artists collaborating on a variety of projects, they would do something about this particular text.

> Such are always the beginnings of the scenic art. The rude man is contented if he see but something going on, the man of more refinement must be made to feel, the man entirely refined desires to reflect.[1]

I would like to thank Christopher Faulkner for helping me to disentangle some of the conceptual knots in an early draft of this article, and Barbara Harris for helping me to understand the original German more closely.
[1] Goethe, *Wilhelm Meister's Apprenticeship and Travels*, translated by Thomas Carlyle, London, Chapman & Hall, 1874, Vol. II, Book iii, p. 74. All references are to this edition.

The films of Wim Wenders, like Goethe's works, provide material for reflection. They are films to think with. Whether his more personally conceived, black-and-white road movies like *Alice in the Cities* (1974) and *Kings of the Road* (1976) or his adaptations in color from the work of other writers—*The Goalie's Anxiety at the Penalty Kick* (1971, Peter Handke), *The Scarlet Letter* (1972, Nathaniel Hawthorne), and *The American Friend* (1977, Patricia Highsmith)—there is no single meaning derivable from them. They can be most disturbing when they seem most playful (*Friend*) and most complex when they seem most simple (*Alice*). They are full of disruptions, and there is no uniformity of tone.

In *Alice in the Cities*, for example, there are those meditative moments which occur between the scenes—quiet images accompanied by a pentatonic guitar motif as if in imitation of a Japanese koto. These moments lend a Zen-like, Ozu-derived contemplativeness to this otherwise most accessible and "naturalistic" of his movies. Even *The Scarlet Letter*, which Wenders himself doesn't value, is interesting in this respect. Perhaps *because* of the problems he encountered shooting this tale of puritanical New England Protestants in Catholic Spain with an international cast, there is a similar complexity of tone.[2] Senta Berger's Hester combines with the Italian histrionics of Lou Castel's Dimmesdale and the extraordinarily sensuous performance of Yella Rottlander's Pearl to turn this adaptation somewhat on its head—rather as Buñuel did with *Robinson Crusoe*. While watching *The Scarlet Letter*, we can never be too sure where our sympathies are or whether we are witnessing presentation or parody.

As in many other Wenders films, as in much of Handke, and as in the original Goethe, *Wrong Movement* (1974) is structured around the concept of a journey. It works through displacements, through a series of castings-off. In this way, the narrative acquires a dimension of allegory. It becomes a search—for something that is absent, for some alternative, for something more.

Goethe's original Wilhelm, disillusioned by love, sets out in search of other values. He throws himself into theater—especially into Shakespeare and more particularly *Hamlet*. He is constantly active, continually playing a leadership role. The Handke-Wenders

[2] See Jan Dawson, *Wim Wenders*, translated by Carla Wartenberg, Toronto, Festival of Festivals, 1976, p. 7.

I know I shall love you
very much one day

Like the original Goethe novel by which it was inspired, Wim Wenders's *Wrong Movement* is structured around the concept of a journey. Wilhelm (Rüdiger Vogler) explains to Therese that he must move on.

Wilhelm, on the other hand, while he also sets off on a journey, responds to life passively. People group round him and tell him things. Perhaps they are attracted by that wry, one-sided smile that Rüdiger Vogler lends to the part, to that charmingly detached quality that allows his acquaintances to interpret his indifference as curiosity.[3] Like Shakespeare's Hamlet, however, he cannot bring himself to act.

Thus, both texts, inscribing different values, address themselves to the present. How does one live in the present? How does one relate to others? What is the value of art and the meaning of love? What are the values by which one must live?

As much a critique of the novel as a rewriting of it, *Wrong Movement* is an adaptation through inversion. Goethe's energetic quest for wholeness is answered in Handke and Wenders by a withdrawn passivity, a sense of hopelessness when faced with the complexities of contemporary life. While Wilhelm failed to

[3] See Henry Welsh, "Wim Wenders, Cinéaste de la Subjectivité," *Jeune Cinéma 94* (Paris), April 1976, pp. 27–28.

achieve his wholeness, he could still believe in it because he perceived the problems as personal, and personal problems are amenable to personal solutions.

For Handke and Wenders, however, the situation is more complex. For them, the problems are both cultural and political and therefore not so amenable to merely personal solutions. Hence the sense of apathy that enervates Wilhelm on the personal level. He feels that there is nothing he can do about these problems. He can't even write about them.

Wenders's adaptation through inversion is apparent in the general tone of the film, which emerges as perhaps his most complex creation. If Handke's influence is everywhere, so, hauntingly, is Goethe's. Part of the complexity in this particular film stems from the allusive play with the literary tropes conventional in Goethe's day but less familiar in ours. This playfulness distances us from the film, blocking easy access. *Wrong Movement* thus contains ironies which cannot be derived from the film itself.

One obvious example: Writing in the eighteenth century *and* in German, Goethe was permitted by the codes of narrative exposition to have his characters deliver extended monologues as if in conversation. In *Wilhelm Meister's Apprenticeship*, some of these monologues go on for pages—sometimes for chapters! As new characters are introduced, they define themselves by their stories. While we could relate this structuring device to a kind of self-involvement, to the kind of egotism that, arguably, is characteristic of so much of classic German thought,[4] it would be a misreading of the text—or at least an ahistorical reading for a modern audience—to take this characteristic as a signifier of alienation. Nowadays, however, conversational codes are far more naturalistic; thus, the device of the monologue which we find in both Handke and Wenders does suggest alienation—not only similar to Brecht's *Verfremdungseffekt*, which distances us from the text, but also much like Marx's *Verdinglichung*, the sense we can have in our urbanized world of feeling more like *things* than like people.

Of course, Handke too writes from within a narrative tradition. His own suppression of psychological analysis and naturalistic dialogue is paralleled at times in Heinrich Böll and stands on the shoulders of Robbe-Grillet and the narrative innovations brought

[4] See George Santayana, *Egotism in German Philosophy*, London, J. M. Dent & Sons, 1939.

about in the late fifties by the *nouveau roman*. In the cinema, moreover, this same device of the extended monologue acquires the force of italics. Because film tends toward naturalistic representation, in which people on the screen pretend to be speaking like people in real life, characters who speak in monologue appear as highly theatrical or "denaturalized."[5]

In *Wrong Movement*, as new characters are introduced and explain themselves through their stories, the monologues create a comic effect initially. The characters all seem strange, detached both from the people they are talking to and from the world they inhabit. They talk less to others than out of some kind of inner necessity.[6] This absence of verisimilitude not only suggests psychological alienation (*Verdinglichung*) but also creates aesthetic estrangement (*Verfremdungseffekt*). The characters, while remaining characters, are transformed into signifiers: They become part of the many elements that make up the structure of the film, which strives toward a signification which, as in Goethe, is not easy to pin down. The use of this technique is a break with the art of the past, certainly of the recent past. The classic bourgeois novel provided reassurance, at least on the surface, offering an obvious meaning to cling to. It defined the boundaries of its imaginary world.

At the beginning of his journey in Wenders's film, Wilhelm opens up one of the books that his mother has packed for him—Eichendorff's *Diary of a Good-for-Nothing*. He begins to read: "My father's mill-wheel was splashing merrily and snow dropped from the roof and sparrows twittered and created a racket. . . ." This is exactly the kind of "naturalistic" writing that Handke has renounced, that the sophisticated taste of the twentieth century no longer receives as plausible, and that in his desire to be a writer Wilhelm himself will never achieve. The fictional world that Wilhelm inhabits is less confident than Eichendorff's. The Handke-Wenders world is full of the dislocations of irrational encounters, encounters that do not form part of a classical narrative exposition that has a beginning, a middle, and an end.

---

[5] For an analysis of this characteristic, see Peter Harcourt, *Six European Directors*, Harmondsworth, Penguin Books, 1976, pp. 228–229.
[6] For a further development of this point, see Noureddine, Ghali: "Wim Wenders," In *Cinéma '76* (Paris) No. 216, December 1976, pp. 23–32.

What is it that keeps men in continual discontent and agitation? It is, that they cannot make realities correspond with their conceptions, that enjoyment steals away from among their hands, that the wished-for comes too late, and nothing reached and acquired produces in the heart the effect which their longing for it at a distance led them to anticipate (II, ii, 68).

As in Goethe, *Wrong Movement* begins with a reference to a failed love relationship, but it is handled elliptically. It doesn't seem important. It is more a plot device, for basically, through the opening moments of the film, we see Wilhelm as trapped. He breaks the window of his bedroom, as if desperate to get free. As he cycles off one day from the town of Heide in Schleswig-Holstein toward the North Sea,[7] the images are of energetic movement, reinforcing the need to get away.

He is dominated by his mother who seems to understand his problem better than he does: "don't lose that unrest and discontent of yours," she says to him before giving him money and putting him on a train. "You'll need it for your writing." Wilhelm wants to be a writer, but what can he write about? He doesn't like people, and, as we learn later on, he doesn't particularly notice things. How, then, can he write? That is, apparently, what he is trying to find out.

Like Goethe's Wilhelm (though far more succinctly), in the course of his journey he encounters several characters who are presented in unconventional ways.

Most unusual is the train conductor. "A terrible thing happened to me today," the character begins, without invitation. He then goes on to explain to Wilhelm and his two companions, Laertes and Mignon, that he had left his house that morning wearing unmatching socks and had forgotten his umbrella. He is impatient at Wilhelm's suggestion that, since it hadn't rained, it didn't really matter. The conductor is talking about propriety, about the ordered universe of the good old days. When he exchanges with Laertes a military salute, we receive our first hint that these two men might have a common past.

Even the major characters are presented indirectly. They appear as images before Wilhelm actually meets them or, as with Laertes, as a trace of his presence before he actually appears. Wilhelm

---

[7] The location is identified in the published screenplay. See Peter Handke, *Falsche Bewegung*, Frankfurt-am-Main, Suhrkamp Verlag, 1975, p. 7.

notices three drops of blood on a seat in the train. They are from his nosebleed, Laertes finally explains; his nose bleeds, he claims, because he remembers the past: "Maybe I'll tell you about it at breakfast tomorrow."

Wilhelm first sees Therese as a woman on the platform when they are changing trains at Hamburg-Altona. He watches her from his window as she looks out at him from hers. She is on a train adjacent to his, also going to Bonn. As the two trains pull out, hers gradually assumes a more accelerated and more elevated route, while Wilhelm strains his neck to keep sight of her until she finally disappears from view.[8] "The woman that created such longing in you," says Laertes as he tells Wilhelm who she is. Laertes knows her from her appearances on television, especially in Chekhov— another "old-fashioned" writer. Although Laertes seems to be suffering from his memory of the past, as if it were a kind of punishment, he is also aware of the present.

Mignon, the other companion, is presented rather oddly as well. To begin with, she is mute (or at least finds no reason to talk).[9] The dark hair and deep-brown eyes of Nastassja Nakszynski's embodiment of her suggest a creature from another country, even from another world. She seems immediately "in love with" Wilhelm, yet she is curiously tied to Laertes. They are both "artistes," as he explains: He plays the harmonica, and she is an acrobat. Her way of thanking Wilhelm for paying for their train tickets is to walk on her hands.

The world that Wenders presents is upside down. There is a sense of traveling forward toward the future yet with many references to the past. Chekhov, Eichendorff, and even Flaubert have been alluded to,[10] and Laertes actually suffers from his memory. Wilhelm seems to be trying either to ignore his memory or at least to postpone the responsibilities of having to deal with it.

Earlier in the film, when his mother is seeing him off, he can't

[8] This moment refers back to the closing helicopter shot of the train in *Alice in the Cities*, a shot which in turn leads to the opening helicopter shot of *Wrong Movement*—a connection of which Wenders is quite conscious. See "Entretiens avec Wim Wenders," *Cinéma '76* (Paris), No. 216, December 1976, pp. 33–48.
[9] Goethe's Mignon is somewhat androgynous when first presented but very agile and athletic (Vol. II, Book iv, p. 76). Also, frequently, she is mute.
[10] The other book that Wilhelm's mother packed for his travels was Flaubert's *L'Éducation Sentimentale*.

bring himself to deal with the experience. "I would remember her better later," he says to himself. "In some other place." And later in the film when they reach Bonn, he places a phone call to Therese, but he doesn't answer the return call. "I wanted to know her voice which I hoped was like her gaze," he mutters. "Afterwards, I'd write it down in detail." Of course, he never does.

At this stage of the film, while the ultimate significance of all these details may still largely elude us, the authority of the presentation gives us confidence that eventually meaning will emerge. Wenders is most skillful in handling his materials. The characters' faces keep dissolving into images of landscapes or shots of rails flying by, speeding Wilhelm on his way toward some new sort of life. What he will encounter, we are yet to find out.

> He in whom there is much to be developed will be later in acquiring true perceptions of himself and the world. There are few who at once have thought and the capacity of action. Thought expands but lames; action animates, but narrows. (VIII, v, 234)

Once in Bonn, Therese makes contact with Wilhelm, and another character joins this little band of seekers. This is Bernhard Landau, a poet, whose writings express extreme disgust with himself and his body. In a magnificent performance by the ubiquitous Peter Kern, Bernhard laments the distance that he feels divides him from the rest of the world.

In an important sequence, the band of companions sets out to find Bernhard's uncle, a man who initially wanted to be a composer and who therefore suffers from being a capitalist. "People like that are the right sort of capitalists," Bernhard explains as they drive off into one of those extraordinarily luminous evening skies that cinematographer Robbie Müller has so frequently created for Wenders.

They arrive at the wrong house and find the wrong capitalist. He welcomes them nevertheless, as he was just about to shoot himself. In Goethe's text, Wilhelm's band of players was frequently taken up by nobility that would house and feed them and thereby sponsor their theatrical art. In Handke-Wenders's world, of course—a world basically dominated by the marketing motif—art is supported by capitalism; yet here we have a very curious capitalist indeed.

To begin with, he inhabits a world that is surreal in its decrepitude. There are holes in the walls, a garden chair serves as furniture in the living room, an iron is still sitting on an ironing board in an alcove upstairs—no doubt a leftover from the capitalist's wife, who killed herself a short time before. Also, if throughout the first four books of Goethe's *Wilhelm Meister's Apprenticeship* there were constant discussions of art, in *Wrong Movement* we have in this sequence merely the empty flickerings of a television set. While it is constantly there in the capitalist's living room, it is a set without an image, and it is wrapped in polythene. The presence of art in Goethe is answered by its absence here. Goethe's sense of fullness has given way to emptiness.

Like the other characters in the film, the capitalist defines himself by his monologues. More particularly, he offers two disquisitions on loneliness—the first to all the group, the second later on to Wilhelm alone. The first one concerns his belief that loneliness doesn't exist. One simply simulates it by aping what are received as the signifiers of loneliness. One sits alone outside on the porch with the appropriate expression on one's face. People passing by then look on as if at a lonely person. This is what he does, the capitalist explains: "It makes me feel reborn. It gives me a sense of security."

This disquisition, absurd in its context, is central to the world of Peter Handke. It is central to what might be called the "disassociated sensibility" that, on the psychological level, informs so many of his characters. It is equally prominent in, for example, *Short Letter, Long Farewell* (1972) and in *The Goalie's Anxiety at the Penalty Kick*, which Handke wrote in 1970 and Wenders filmed the following year. In all these works, and especially in *Wrong Movement*, the isolated monologues take on a philosophical thrust. What is the relationship between private feelings and our inherited social codes, especially the codes of language? This seems to be what the capitalist is talking about. Perhaps this is why Mignon never speaks. She doesn't want to falsify reality by reducing it to language, by saying the same sorts of things that other people say. In those big brown eyes of hers there seems to be wisdom. She looks like she knows something.

As for Wilhelm, *er mochte Schriftsteller werden* ("he wants to be a writer"). But how can one become a writer if one cannot find a language appropriate to one's feelings, if the words available have been used up by others in the pursuit (possibly) of false ideals? This question is present even in Goethe, and it is central to any serious writer working today.

The capitalist's second disquisition locates the problem of loneliness more specifically in culture. He presents his ideas in historical and political terms. People are lonely, he explains, especially the Germans, because they have not been permitted to acknowledge their own fear—their *Angst*, as the original German puts it. They have been taught to behave with fortitude and courage with such insistence that they have never come to know who they really are. In Germany, he explains, more than anywhere else, "philosophy could be used as an ideology so that the criminal methods required to overcome fear could be legalized. Fear was considered vain and shameful." This fear of acknowledging fear has helped to create what he calls "all the dead souls of Germany."[11] "I refuse to overcome my fear," he concludes, as he drives a ballpoint pen into the palm of his hand, deeply, until it bleeds.

When the capitalist goes up to bed, Wilhelm picks up the blood-stained pen and produces in his notebook a kind of Japanese hieroglyph—perhaps the most meaningful thing we see him write because it acknowledges a relationship between the capitalist and Wilhelm. Bypassing the codes of language, Wilhelm transfers the blood of the capitalist into his own text. Through the ancient tribal ritual of blood brotherhood—*Blutbruderschaft*—Wilhelm thus acknowledges his own fear.

—

> It is our ambiguous dissipating education that makes us uncertain: it awakens wishes, when it should be animating tendencies; instead of forwarding our real capacities, it turns our efforts towards objects which are frequently discordant with the mind that aims at them (VIII, iii, 209).

Wrong Movement is full of intricately executed sequences. There is the breakfast scene after the evening with the capitalist in

[11] This "fear of fear" is an idea obviously very close to Wenders. Rüdiger Vogler mentions it in *Alice*; echoing Roosevelt's declaration of war after the attack on Pearl Harbor, Wenders has Dennis Hopper say much the same thing in *The American Friend*: "There is nothing to fear but fear itself."

which all the participants share the experience of their dreams—all except Mignon, who finds dreams ridiculous, and Bernhard, who has forgotten his. This is also the moment when Laertes, through his song about Rosenthal, begins to reveal himself as a Jew killer —a Jew killer who might still be one if politics would allow it.

The following scene is the consummation of Wenders's cinematic choreography. All our traveling companions wander up a mountain road. The characters regroup constantly, forming themselves around Wilhelm in order to share their stories with him. Throughout it all, Bernhard, a big man, carries a tiny red parasol —another oddly surrealistic detail. We can hear the sound of rifle shots in the distance, and Mignon and Therese whistle together Beethoven's "Ode to Joy."

Bernhard and Wilhelm talk about art as Wilhelm and Laertes had earlier talked about politics. Wilhelm can't write politically, he explains, because it seems so insincere. Yet it was through writing that he discovered the need for politics. "If only politics and poetry could be united," Wilhelm concludes. "That would be the end of longing and the end of the world," replies Laertes, rather out of character. Desire would cease to exist, and peace and calm would reign.

As if to reinforce this Zen-like idea, Wenders ends this walk into the heights with a close-up of Therese and Wilhelm talking together. Beneath them, many miles below, a tiny boat on the Rhine passes between their faces. This is reminiscent of Ozu, where the image of a boat or train suggests the sense of something passing, of something moving away.[12]

Bernhard then remembers his dream about the capitalist being threatened and harassed. They all run down the hill to find him hanging in his foyer. The group moves on. Bernhard deserts them without explanation, and they return to town to Therese's apartment, where there is excrement in the lobby and graffiti on the elevator walls.

Inside the apartment there is also a television set. This set, however, can produce an image—a sequence, in fact, from the Jean-Marie Straub-Daniele Huillet film *The Chronicle of Anna*

---

12 Wenders has frequently acknowledged the influence of Ozu, both on his style and on his handling of characters. See Jan Dawson, *Wim Wenders*, New York, Zoetrope, 1977, p. 10.

Magdalene Bach (1967). This reference might suggest that television is not entirely an empty experience. It might suggest, however fleetingly, the ideal of continuity of life through art which plays such a large part in the Goethe original. Certainly, Therese's talk, while ironing, about the artificiality of the theater refers back to Goethe. Why cannot the theater include everything, she seems to be asking.[13] But Wilhelm is only partly listening to her. He is working on a story of a kindly man who is incapable of pity. "I believe it will turn out political," he says.

It is, of course, the story of himself. He wants to kill Laertes for his treatment of the Jews, but he is incapable even of that. While crossing the Main on a ferry, he tries to push Laertes overboard, but loses his courage. When Laertes' nose begins to bleed again, Wilhelm offers him a tissue and Laertes gets away.

~

> He who only tastes his error, will long dwell with it, will take delight in it as in a singular felicity: while he who drains it to the dregs will, if he be not crazy, find it out (VI, ix, 187).

As stated earlier, Wim Wenders's *Wrong Movement* is a film that will not reduce itself to a single interpretation. Meaning—signification—would reside in the intersection of the various possible readings: formal, historical, cultural, and psychological. However, since every work of art is, at least in part, about other works of art, I should like to suggest that the presence of Goethe as a constant frame of reference, sometimes as a conscience, invites a reading of this film in terms of allegory—in terms of parable, in fact.

From this perspective, both Laertes and the capitalist would seem tied to the past. Both are in part responsible for, yet are suffering from, the sins of Nazi ideology—indeed, from an idealism that goes far back into Germany's philosophical past, with its traditional discontent with the terrestrial world. This restlessness is central to the thinking of Goethe—perhaps one of the major reasons why Handke and Wenders wanted to rewrite this particular Goethe text.

[13] In Goethe, discussions of art are everywhere, especially throughout the first four books. But see especially the discussion of fencing and Wilhelm's desire to make it more "realistic" for his production of *Hamlet* (Vol. IV, Book v, p. 196).

The capitalist has some insight, but it is not strong enough to prevent his suicide. Laertes, on the other hand, is locked into images of how the world ought to have been. He remembers the solidarity he felt, as a Nazi youth, singing round the campfires, feeling superior to the rest of the world. He sees himself as a self-flagellating martyr for the Nazi cause. When we last see Laertes, he is running away into a field. He disappears from the film, but his presence lives on in contemporary Germany.

Mignon, by extrapolation, might refer to the future. She is sensuous but mute. She possesses an inner wisdom. She rejects the hateful elements that occur in her world. She blocks her ears when Laertes speaks against Jesse Owens, the black American Olympic champion, and she turns away from Bernhard Landau when he recites his poem of self-disgust. She is trusting and undemanding. She receives Wilhelm into her bed with no expectation of either continuity or explanation.[14] Until the intervention of Wilhelm (perhaps his most constructive act), she was dependent on Laertes —that is, on the past. But as Wilhelm agrees with Therese, "she'll have to get used to being alone." The future of Germany must free itself from a dependence on these past ideals about how life ought to be. It will have to trust its senses and find a new voice. Meanwhile, it must be silent.[15]

Bernhard Landau also deserves his place within this tentative, allegorical grid.[16] He might be seen as German art as it is valued abroad—that is to say, not much at all. Through the Western world, France and the United States are the cultural imperialists. Apart from music, which more often than not is Austrian, German art, and especially German literature, is comparatively little

[14] In Handke's screenplay, Wilhelm initially leaves Mignon, approaches Therese's door, hesitates, and then returns to Mignon. *Falsche Bewegung*, op. cit., p. 47.
[15] Locked within his idealistic thinking, Goethe has to kill his Mignon off. She wastes away, as was the convention of that time, from a love for Wilhelm unnoticed by him (VIII, iii, 210). Goethe's Wilhelm must leave the world of terrestial love for far higher things!
[16] Although there is no Bernhard Landau in Goethe, there are a number of incidents that might have inspired his being. See especially Philina's impatience with buccolic songs: "O that I might never hear more of nature, and scenes of nature! . . . There is nothing in the world more intolerable than to hear people reckon up the pleasures you enjoy . . ." (II, iv, 85). This is the exact opposite of what Bernhard gives us in his poem.

known. Perhaps for the time being, that is as it should be. Tainted by its complicity in the atrocities of the Nazi regime, German literature and philosophy have been somewhat discredited. Many contemporary Germans welcome this devaluation. When driving off to find his uncle, Bernhard explains to his friends: "I've never amounted to much. I hope I'll stay that way." He doesn't want to be influential. He is resigned to being unrecognized because he feels himself unlovely.

The role of Therese is harder to characterize. A blend of many women in Goethe, she seems to strike the right balance between art and life. In this way she embodies what Wilhelm is seeking, but he is unable to deal with her. She is a loving, thoughtful person who is also an artist. At the same time, especially as she is incarnated by Hanna Schygulla, she is a full-bodied woman who also makes demands. Unlike Mignon, she wants Wilhelm to either help her or leave her. She is what a woman could really be if men were not so involved with their own insecurities. As things now stand, with men so uncertain, she will have to live alone.

Finally, there is Wilhelm—the kingpin of our story. He is more like Goethe's Wilhelm than one might imagine. "An adventurer who shies from adventure,"[17] he is the idealist turned inward, the idealist *manqué*. Discontented with life as he has experienced it, he is incapable of responding to life directly. He strives to deal with life retrospectively with the hope of turning it into art. "One day," he says to Therese toward the end of the film, "I know I'll really love you." But not now. There are things he has to do.

Wilhelm is a man who yearns to live in a more halcyon world: the world of an imagined past, the world created by the fictions of Eichendorff and Flaubert. This would be a world that, whatever the difficulties, might be free from *Angst*. There would not be the same incapacitating split between the world of thought and the world of action, between culture and language—indeed, between politics and poetry. It would be a world of less self-consciousness, a world not requiring the fear of perpetual postponement. "I'd like to write something as essential as a house or an evening glass of wine," he says at one time to Laertes. "More essential, in fact." In a less divided world, by writing he might be able to provide some-

[17] John Fell, "The Wrong Movement." *Film Quarterly*, Vol. XXXII, No. 2, Winter 1978–79, p. 49.

thing useful, something that people could share. But this is a world that no longer exists.

Unlike Handke's screenplay, the film implies that without such a world, Wilhelm might never be able to write. Handke's text suggests that all this passivity, this detached observation, was necessary to give Wilhelm that charge of "erotic insight" that would finally get him going. Wenders's film, on the other hand, seems far more negative.[18]

As in both Goethe and Handke, Wenders's Wilhelm ends up alone in the heights of the Alps. But what for Goethe signified transcendence and for Handke detachment, for Wenders signifies defeat and isolation. As Bernhard recognized about himself at the end of his long poem, Wilhelm too is in a "bell jar," cut off from experience by his own thought processes and by his striving for an art he is unable to achieve.

What am I doing up here? he asks himself. Why did I tell my friends that I had to continue my travels through Germany? "It was only an excuse. I really just wanted so much to live my stupid life alone." His back is toward the camera as he delivers this final monologue. "Why did I threaten the old man," he continues, "instead of listening to his tale? I felt I had missed out somehow and was still missing out with every new movement." As he speaks these final words, Wenders superimposes the title in bright red letters across the screen—*Falsche Bewegung* (*Wrong Movement*).

If the ending of the film seems negative, if Wilhelm is incapable of transforming the details of his life into the affirmation of art, paradoxically, it is from these same details that Wim Wenders, helped by Peter Handke, has created this extraordinary film.

---

[18] The passionate self-questioning that ends this film is entirely Wim Wenders's. It is absent from Handke's screenplay. On the contrary, in Handke as Wilhelm is standing on the mountain, the sound of the wind gradually gives way to the sound of a typewriter getting louder and louder—not unambiguously positive (for it would be an offscreen sound), but potentially so nevertheless. *Falsche Bewegung*, p. 81.

WILLIAM R. MAGRETTA & JOAN MAGRETTA

STORY AND DISCOURSE
Schlöndorff & von Trotta's *The Lost Honor of Katharina Blum (1975)*

from the novel by Heinrich Böll

When Volker Schlöndorff was asked to comment on the relationship between his film, *The Lost Honor of Katharina Blum* (co-directed with his wife, Margarethe von Trotta, in 1975), and Heinrich Böll's 1974 novel,[1] he answered: "We never considered whether it was a literary adaptation."[2] The reply seems at first highly disingenuous, considering that so many of Schlöndorff's films have been adaptations: *Young Törless* (1966, from Robert Musil), *Michael Kolhaas* (1968, from Heinrich von Kleist), *Coup de Grâce* (1977, from Marguerite Yourcenar), and most recently *The Tin Drum* (1979, from Günter Grass). But Schlöndorff goes on to explain that in making *Katharina Blum* the question wasn't

> how to transpose to the screen what is in the book, but how to transpose to the screen what there is in reality, and that Böll treated in his book. Both of us refer to a common point of departure which is reality, and we think about it in one way for the book, in another for the film.[3]

Despite the vagueness of the last clause, the distinction is crucial: It is not Böll's treatment of his material that Schlöndorff wants to

© copyright 1981, William R. Magretta and Joan Magretta
[1] Heinrich Böll, *Die verlorene Ehre der Katharina Blum oder: Wie Gewalt enstehen und wohin sie führen kann*, Köln, Verlag Kiepenheuer & Witsch, 1974.
[2] Marcel Martin, "Entretien avec Volker Schlöndorff," *Écran*, No. 46, April 1976, p. 65. The translation is ours.
[3] Ibid.

adapt, but the material itself, the kernel of meaning at the core of the novel.

The "reality" that Schlöndorff invokes appears, first of all, to reside in what the Anglo-American critical tradition has called the "themes" or "meanings" of the work. In actual practice, however, the reality that Schlöndorff-von Trotta represent in the film is more broadly the story contained in the narrative—what is variously termed *histoire, fabula,* or *récit* in contemporary narrative theory and which encompasses "the content or chain of events (actions, happenings), plus what may be called the existents (characters, items of setting)."[4] This basic, underlying level of story is crucially distinguished from the discourse (*discours, sjužet,* or *raconté*), the actual expression or the form in which the story is realized. "In simple terms, the story is the *what* in a narrative that is depicted, the discourse the *how*."[5]

The story of Katharina Blum is simple, powerful, and, in the words of Böll's narrator, "brutal." Blum, a decent and respectable young housekeeper, attends a party on the eve of Carnival, where she meets a young man named Ludwig Götten. They fall in love at first sight and spend the night at Katharina's apartment; after telling her he is wanted by the police, Götten manages to elude them with Katharina's help. Furious that Götten has escaped, the police treat the innocent Katharina as if she were a vile accomplice in undefined terrorist acts. Thus begin several days of the most abusive interrogation by the police and vicious slander by a scandal-mongering popular newspaper called the *News*; Katharina's life is destroyed by the brutal lies of the press, and in particular an unscrupulous reporter named Tötges. Just four days after this incredible affair begins, Katharina calmly murders Tötges and turns herself over to the authorities.

For Böll and Schlöndorff-von Trotta, this story is the obvious vehicle for basic themes. First, it reveals the witch-hunt mentality in contemporary Germany, the pervasive fear of terrorism which is used to justify the violation of civil liberties. In 1972, Böll himself was defamed by the media, and his house was searched by police after he apparently did little more than urge that terrorist Ulrike

[4] Seymour Chatman, *Story and Discourse: Narrative Structure in Fiction and Film*, Ithaca, Cornell University Press, 1978, p. 19.
[5] Ibid.

Meinhof be given safe conduct and a fair trial (as opposed to the lynch justice advocated by the Springer press).[6] Neither Böll, in life or in fiction, nor Schlöndorff-von Trotta encourage terrorist violence. They are, however, concerned with the growing repressiveness of the state. What Schlöndorff says about his film applies as well to Böll's novel—it isn't about what we usually think of as terrorism, but "about the everyday terrorism of institutions . . . the combined machinery of the press, of the judiciary, of the police administration and, formed by them, public opinion."[7]

Another major idea embodied in the story is the way the media create and control reality. The novel repeatedly juxtaposes what characters say with the gross distortions printed in the *News*. Tötges's reckless and irresponsible abuse of language—which he cynically calls "helping simple people to express themselves"—is contrasted with Katharina's scrupulous care to render her history with the utmost precision. In novel and film, Katharina refuses to sign the police deposition unless it maintains the crucial distinction she insists upon between a man's *Zudringlichkeit* ("advances") and his *Zärtlichkeit* ("tenderness"). The question is far from trivial for Böll, who regards the use of language as a moral and political act. As Theodore Ziolkowski notes, Böll has repeatedly underlined the moral responsibilities of writers to their language: "Anyone who deals with words, he warns, must be fully aware of the power they bear."[8]

Even the ways names are used exemplify the different attitudes toward language and toward characters. Thus, Tötges addresses Katharina familiarly and contemptuously with the diminutive *Blumchen*. The film takes this cue from the novel and constructs a fully developed pattern of naming. Katharina's memory of Götten begins significantly with his gentle words, "Your name is Katha-

[6] Böll's embroilments are presented at greater length in Frank Grützbach (ed.), *Heinrich Böll: Freies Geleit für Ulrike Meinhof*, Köln, Verlag Kiepenheuer & Witsch, 1972; Theodore Ziolkowski, "The Inner Veracity of Form," *Books Abroad*, No. 47, Winter 1973, pp. 17–24; and Jack Zipes, "Political Dimensions of *The Lost Honor of Katharina Blum*," *New German Critique*, No. 12, Fall 1977, pp. 75–84. (Zipes reports that "since 1971, over 800,000 people have been investigated and interrogated by a special police force" [p. 76].)

[7] Volker Schloendorff, "De Toerless à Katharina Blum," *Jeune Cinéma*, No. 94, April 1976, p. 11. The translation is ours.

[8] Ziolkowski, op. cit., p. 22.

Blornas and Else Woltersheim. Thus, near the end of the narrative a series of chapters tells us what becomes of the main characters after the incident, much in the manner of the epilogues of nineteenth-century novels.

Schlöndorff-von Trotta choose a more straightforward chronological rendering of the story, employing one of the traditional resources of entertainment films—suspense. Furthermore, their rendering exploits the broad appeal of the archetypal Hitchcockian situation: the innocent bystander suddenly caught in a nightmare intrigue. Abandoning Böll's subtitle, and saving his corrosive epigraph[11] for the *end* of the film, Schlöndorff-von Trotta engage us first in the story, not the discourse. The only departures from chronology are two flashbacks of Katharina with Ludwig at Else's party, and a police film of Götten made that same night. If the film is more rigorous in its time frame than the novel, it also takes a more narrow focus on Katharina, omitting Böll's postscript accounts of the other characters. By maintaining this focus on Katharina and on the actual chronology of events, the film engages the audience more directly, invites a more active participation, and makes a greater, more immediate emotional impact. Our concern is with the unfolding of events, with the ongoing actions of real characters.

To our earlier observation that Böll engages us through our curiosity to understand the *why* of the story must be added an equally compelling engagement with the mediating presence of the narrator. The narrator-as-character is highly elusive and problematic, and we never know with any certainty just who he is. Through him, Böll's presentation of the story is complex, illustrating the full spectrum of narrative possibilities from the "documentary" use of written records such as the police transcripts, in which the "author" functions as a collator or editor (what Chatman terms "non-narrated representation"[12]), through the other extreme of self-conscious narration, in which the narrator comments not only on the story but on the discourse itself. Despite these

---

[11] "The characters and action in this story are purely fictitious. Should the description of certain journalistic practices result in a resemblance to the practices of the *Bild-Zeitung*, such resemblance is neither intentional nor fortuitous, but unavoidable."

[12] Chatman, op. cit., pp. 146–262.

shifting perspectives, we are constantly aware of the narrator's mediating function. We become as involved with him, and with his strategies for telling the story, as we do with the story itself; stated in another way, his presence distances us from the raw emotional potential of the story, engaging us intellectually in a complex web of discourse ironies. Only an inattentive reader would be taken in by the "objective" dossier format and the narrator's protestations of scrupulous objectivity, for although we ultimately side with him, he often reveals himself to be gossipy, opinionated, subjective, pedantic, fussy, and exasperatingly obtuse.

Although there is no narrator in the film, it would be an over-simplification to regard what we see as an "unmediated" story. Like the novel, the film achieves an interesting tension between distancing and engagement. At the most obvious levels, we are involved in the unfolding of events (the "what next"), the passage of time, and the character of Katharina. Our access to her is more direct and more intimate than in the novel: We actually *see* her throughout the film, while she is never directly described in the novel; her meeting with Ludwig is given in subjective flashback as *her* memory, whereas in the novel the only first-person accounts we have are her formal depositions. The love story is thus presented lyrically and romantically in the film, whereas Böll's narrator treats it with a mild sneer. What the film loses in narrative intricacies and verbal wit, it gains in direct emotional impact. But there is also a complex distancing at work in the film. If Böll's narrator is often chillingly ironic, Schlöndorff-von Trotta produce a "cool" effect through the repeated motif of scenes shot in icy-blue lighting or in cold institutional settings like the police head-quarters and the hospital. Despite the titles which announce the arrival of each new day, thus suggesting a kind of documentary "realism," there are elements of stylization that make the familiar world seem strange: the garish, almost nightmarish unreality of the Carnival setting (exploited more fully in the film than in the novel, partly because of the nature of the film image—the setting is always *there*), the repressiveness of space (through repeated shots of corridors, elevators, bars, caged stairways, and opaque windows), and the eerie musical score by Hans Werner Henze, one of the leading contemporary composers of Europe.

This music, one of the film's great virtues, is atonal—that is, it does not depend on the traditional oppositions of consonance and dissonance, of tension and resolution, and on the comforting stability of a recognizable tonal center. Thus, it is unsettling since we can't perceive readily what we usually think of as a structure or an organization. Without the movement toward the satisfying moment of resolution in a cadence, we feel left up in the air and distraught.[13] Henze has scored the music in part for conventional instruments, but he emphasizes their full range of tonal colors, especially in glissandos and flutter tonguings; in addition, he uses a flexatone—a kind of musical saw which produces a high-pitched, biting, vibrating sound with a particularly chilling tremolo effect. These tonal colors, with the emphasis on untraditional timbres, endow the music with an additional unreal, disorienting quality, making it serve as another form—albeit subtle—of terrorism.

All this is not to say that the music is completely formless, however. The texture of the music varies crucially: The relatively open, spare textures reinforce our uneasiness; the full textures, which at times almost saturate the musical space, heighten our emotions. Perhaps the most remarkable effects are the intensification of tension produced by the rising pitches and dynamic levels at the most critical moments, most notably as Tötges enters Katharina's apartment for the fatal "interview" and as the publisher of the *News* delivers his egregiously self-serving funeral oration. In each case, the almost unbearable tension is broken—but scarcely resolved—not by a cadence but by silence.

Although the music heightens our feelings of unreality, thus serving to mirror Katharina's experience of estrangement, it is also often integrated more closely into the sound track when it shades off into sounds of the real world. Thus, as Katharina drives to Sträubleder's country place, where Ludwig has been hiding out and where she will see the monstrous forces assembled for his capture, the music blends into the siren of a police caravan which passes her on the road.

If the many elements of visual and aural stylization remind us that film can be as subtly mediated as fiction, the necessarily more direct presence of characters in film (a subject to which we will

[13] This atonality is the musical analogue for the frustration of Böll's narrator, who complains in the end that he is unable to achieve "harmony" and "integration" (p. 133) in his account of the story.

return) has led in this case to a vital structural change, one owing a good deal to an essentially dramatic aesthetic: The character of Tötges appears more fully as Katharina's real adversary. In the novel he is hardly ever directly present; we see the results of his actions, we read his articles and the report of his death, but it is only in the final chapter that we actually "see" him in Katharina's first-person account: "I could see right away what a bastard he was, a real bastard. And good-looking, too. What people call good-looking" (p. 137). In the film Tötges is often on-screen; we actually see him and Beizmenne exchanging documents, while the novel only tells us that "there were certain important details for which he [Beizmenne] had to thank reporters from the *News*" with their "flexible" and "unconventional" methods of operation (p. 118). This transposition is characteristic of the greater dramatic concentration of the film, in which Katharina is pitted against her principal tormentors, Tötges and Beizmenne. Whereas the novel deliberately passes over the obvious dramatic climax of the story—Katharina's murder of Tötges—since "the outcome is known" (p. 122), Schlöndorff-von Trotta heighten the climax by having Tötges urge Katharina to exploit her notoriety by selling her story. This more complete realization of Tötges as a character also sharpens situational ironies, only some of which are implicit in the novel: that Tötges portrays Katharina as a slut, a term clearly more appropriate for his sexual behavior than hers; that although the public perceives Tötges as a hero and Katharina as a villain, our perceptions are the opposite; that although Tötges "murders" Katharina's mother, he publicly blames Katharina, while she openly accepts her responsibility for his death; and that although Katharina is immediately missed (the Blornas can't even make a good cup of coffee without her), we see at Tötges's funeral that he has been instantly replaced by another unsavory clone from the *News*, one who, incidentally, shows no more respect for Tötges's mother than Tötges had shown for Mrs. Blum.

Even with the basic restructuring of the story, which met with Böll's approval,[14] Schlöndorff-von Trotta have made what would

[14] In the *Écran* interview previously cited, Schlöndorff indicates that even when Böll was writing *Katharina Blum* he had in mind that someday it would be filmed. Schlöndorff reports that Böll agreed with their idea to tell the story chronologically and that he was especially helpful in "concretizing"

generally be considered a "faithful" adaptation of the book; that is, they preserve the story more or less intact, adding little and leaving little out. There are only two completely invented sequences in the film, the first of which is the meeting between Sträubleder and Katharina, dishonestly engineered by the Dominican father. His quotation from Marx about the alienating property of gold (also added in the film), which originally cast suspicion on Katharina, now seems ironic as Father Urbanus "betrays" Katharina into Alois's hands, clarifying connections implicit in the novel between institutions of power, here capitalism (and academia) and the church. An effective long shot at the end of the sequence pits the tiny red van of Katharina, Else, and Konrad against the endless line of black Mercedes limousines parked in front of the monastery. The "natural" sound of church bells modulates into the unsettling Henze music.

Before the film's epilogue (Tötges's funeral), there is a very brief but important "invented" scene: the underground meeting of Ludwig and Katharina as each is being led by a squadron of guards. For a moment, they break free and embrace, but they are quickly separated by their jailers. The appeal of this scene is directly emotional, reminding us that, in a sense, Katharina's only crime was falling in love. The brutal separation of the couple in this dark, enclosed space (the harsh repressiveness is emphasized by the clanging of metal barriers and the echo of footsteps) provokes our direct sympathy with the victims. In the novel, no meeting occurs, and it is instead our critical faculty that is engaged, as Böll's narrator archly reports that Katharina, considered a "model prisoner,"

> is to be transferred to the commissary where, however (so one hears), she is most unenthusiastically awaited: there is dismay on the part of both administration and inmates at the reputation for integrity that precedes her. . . . Thus we see that integrity . . . is not desired anywhere, not even in prisons, and not even by the administration (p. 129).

---

the characters, correcting the initial tendency of Schlöndorff-von Trotta to make the authorities too old. ("We saw them as our fathers," says Schlöndorff. "He made us understand that today *we're* the fathers" [p. 65].) Böll agreed immediately with Schlöndorff-von Trotta that Angela Winkler was perfect for the part of Katharina.

In addition to these completely "invented" scenes, certain story events which Böll's narrator only mentions or treats obliquely but does not describe directly are rendered more extensively in the film. Here, as in any source study, our examination of what a director chooses to render helps us discover the emphasis of his version. Tötges's "interview" with Mrs. Blum is a good example. Böll's narrator begins by asserting that Tötges was responsible for Mrs. Blum's death, but then, in going on to consider the actual event further, he becomes preoccupied with the difficulty of ascertaining whether the interview ever took place: Tötges claims (or boasts) that it did, but he must justify his having (mis)quoted Mrs. Blum in his article; the hospital authorities are perhaps "denying what ought not to have happened" (p. 105). Finally, since Tötges claims to have used "the simplest trick in the book" (p. 104), disguising himself as a painter, the narrator cautions us to withhold judgment because "the honor of the German craftsman must not be besmirched" (p. 106). But his scrupulous attempts to cast doubt on Tötges's responsibility are excessive, and thus we suspect them. And the mode of discourse here tends to convey a more general comment about the way people are always out to defend their selfish interests. There is no indirection in the film, which "shows" this scene with shocking swiftness. With no preliminary establishing shot, the sequence opens abruptly with a close-up two-shot of the helpless Mrs. Blum lying in bed, plastic pipes through her nose, and Tötges's face pressed alongside hers on the pillow. "How does a mother feel faced with that?" he asks cruelly, pointing to his own screaming headlines in the *News*. The scene is horrifying, and as Tötges leaves in disgust, tearing off the surgical gown he has used as a disguise (linking him with the policemen we have seen putting on disguises), we are shown the bank of electronic devices that are monitoring Mrs. Blum's body. The effect is directly chilling.

Another scene the film "shows" and the novel only mentions is Ludwig's capture by the police; rather, what is shown is Katharina's arrival at the scene *after* he has been taken away. The distinction is important because as its rendering makes clear, Schlöndorff-von Trotta are not interested in the potential for exciting spectacle that such moments usually provide, but rather in presenting Katharina's growing alienation from the oppressive world around her.

We are struck first by the ever-present swarm of reporters and by the ludicrous display of military machinery and personnel—enough to carry out a small invasion—all in pursuit of one man. Katharina wanders around the scene as if unable to get her bearings, and she is almost run over by an armored car (as earlier the Blornas were threatened by a street-washing machine—the film's imagery consistently suggests the menace of modern technology). It is the final shot of this sequence that merits special notice. As the Henze score replaces completely all natural sound, we watch Katharina walk steadily away from us across a barren field. Vehicles cross the frame going in all directions; a helicopter takes off. The effect of all this random, disorderly movement and the absence of natural sound is disorienting. Yet despite the confusion of planes and directions, Katharina Blum maintains a straight course. Her isolated, black figure gradually but steadily recedes in the extreme distance at the rear of the frame.

There are, finally, significant differences between scenes as they are fully reported in the novel and as they are realized in the film. These differences are primarily a function of the different characteristics of the media employed, the most striking of which is the greater immediacy and specificity of the film image. That is, film is essentially presentational, concentrating on showing (corresponding to Plato's mimetic function) rather than telling or recounting (the diegetic function). This necessarily gives film a greater determinacy in representing scenes, what phenomenologists call *Bestimmtheit*, as contrasted to the relative indeterminacy (*Unbestimmtheit*) possible in accounts in prose narratives. The result is, as Christian Metz states, a greater "impression of reality."[15] While the novelist may choose how much detail and which details to use in presenting a scene—that is, he may select only the details relevant for the meaning(s) he wishes to communicate—the film image must have (or appear to have) all the details that would be present in reality. The initial storming of Katharina's apartment is a good case in point. In the book, the narrator tells us that

> Beizmenne was beginning to lose both his patience and his nerve, and a detachment of eight heavily armed police officers broke into

[15] Christian Metz, "On the Impression of Reality in the Cinema," in *Film Language: A Semiotics of the Cinema*, translated by Michael Taylor, New York, Oxford University Press, 1974, pp. 3–15.

the apartment, storming it with the most intensive precautionary
measures, searched it, but found no trace of Götten (p. 18).

The film drops the first clause since (1) we don't yet know who
Beizmenne is, and (2) it is the kind of authorial comment about
the story which the film eschews. It is in the rendering of the rest
of the sentence that the greater specificity of the film image plays a
crucial role. The helmeted guards in military uniform look more
like invading aliens from another planet—or even like terrorists
themselves—than like the forces of law and order. Silhouetted in
the cold, blue predawn light, the men appear dark, sinister, and
terrifying. For those who object to the film's heavy-handed treatment of the police as villains, it is worth noting that the uniforms
are authentic, purchased from the same firm that supplies them for
the police. The "intensive precautionary measures" we see become
ridiculously grotesque because in the midst of them, the camera
pans from the troops perched on an outside ledge to the harmless
Katharina, alone at her breakfast table in a white bathrobe. To
show the "storm and search" not only requires more discourse
time than the bare report of the novel, thus emphasizing the event,
but also requires greater specificity—in this case, the effect is violent, brutal, and frightening. The "search," for example, involves
not only the tearing apart of Katharina's orderly apartment, but a
humiliating probe of her body by Policewoman Pletzer, who then
has the effrontery to tell Katharina how nicely she has "fixed up"
her bathroom.

This kind of story irony is generally more characteristic of the
film than the discourse ironies we have noted in the novel. However, another scene reported in the novel and presented in the
film—the interrogation of Else Woltersheim—shows that Schlöndorff-von Trotta can exploit both kinds of irony. Else's protest to
the authorities about their questionable methods and aims follows
in the film (but not the novel) Tötges's illicit exchange of information with Beizmenne, and in particular his news that Else's father
was a Communist. This juxtaposition (in fact, an overlapping,
since the scenes are linked by a sound bridge) of her complaint
with the very practice she is complaining about obviously stresses
a basic story irony. But more effective here is the mode of presentation. As Else pleads movingly for human decency and dignity,

she is ignored in a cluttered frame. Not only do Hach and Korten sneeringly dismiss her charges, but they and others walk rudely in and out of the frame. The camera stays on Else, trying to hear her out, but as she speaks, Beizmenne walks between her and the camera, momentarily blocking our vision. This gesture, and the general clutter of the whole scene, epitomizes the appalling insensitivity of the interrogators. When Else finally asks Hach and Korten what, exactly, they are investigating (they have just asked about her father), they rudely leave the frame, leaving the distressed Else alone, and we hear Hach's disdainful reply, "Let the state decide."

A scene which effectively demonstrates the greater immediacy of the film is Katharina's destruction of her apartment. The chapter in the novel, consisting of only three short paragraphs, begins as follows:

> It is, surely, astonishing that neither Miss W. nor Konrad B. was astonished when, with no thought of intervening in any way, they watched Katharina walk to the little bar in her living room, take out one bottle each of sherry, whiskey, and red wine and a half-empty bottle of cherry syrup and, with no visible sign of emotion, throw them against the immaculate walls, where they smashed and spewed their contents (p. 80).

The catalogue of items thrown, followed by similar lists in the next paragraph of items thrown in the kitchen and then in the bathroom, is ironic, a mark of the kind of excessive objectivity of the narrator that calls attention to him rather than to what he is describing. What kind of person, we must ask, can he be to note at a time like this that the cherry syrup had been opened previously? The chilling depersonalization of this style, also used in the equally ironic catalogue of Katharina's obscene mail in the preceding chapter, becomes the focus of our response to the event. If the prose draws our attention to the narrator and to a list of nouns (the objects thrown), the film rivets us on the total image of Katharina, the deliberateness of her action, and the image of her apartment, which changes by increments as each bottle hits the wall and leaves its ugly mark. Although this is an instance in which a scene from the novel is "performed" fairly directly on film, the different impact of the two versions is unmistakable. The wry indirection of the novel is transposed into the terrifying directness of the film.

Although some will inevitably bemoan what is lost in the adaptation, we shouldn't undervalue what has been gained. Film's greater immediacy and specificity of setting is exploited brilliantly in the murder of Tötges. In one of the film's most impressive shots, as Katharina sits erect and calm in a straightback chair awaiting Tötges's arrival, the wreckage of her life is visible all around her. The hideous blotches on the wall, reminiscent of a similar setting in Antonioni's *Red Desert* (1964), share the frame with Tötges as he makes his obnoxious proposals to her. Thus, the earlier scene in which Katharina destroys her apartment, with all its potent associations, is in a sense *present* in this one.

Although it is often thought that novels require greater reader participation than do films, because they at least demand that we visualize scenes,[16] the opposite seems true in one of the most crucial moments of both narratives—the interrogation of Katharina about her excessive driving. Böll's narrator interprets the action as he reports it, telling us that all those present, as well as Katharina, were "shocked" and "fascinated" by Beizmenne's calculations. He tells us that it "seemed" as if Katharina wasn't angry, but that instead "she was trying to figure out where and when she had driven why and where to" (p. 49). And finally, before Katharina's uninterrupted first-person transcript cited by the narrator and performed in the film, we are told that there was a feeling in the room of having "penetrated an intimate secret of Katharina Blum" (p. 49).

In watching this scene in the film, we must ourselves perform the interpretation; we must "read" the event before us just as the narrator has in the novel. We are able to do this by attending not only to the languages of words, gestures, and facial expressions but also to the cinematic languages of framing and shot distance. As the initial question is asked, a crowded but composed five-shot places Katharina in the midst of her interrogators. The camera moves closer to her, eliminating the stenographer and Beizmenne

[16] For example, as astute a critic as Leon Edel maintains that novels make us "active and imaginative readers" whereas films reduce us to "inert picture watchers." "Novel and Camera," in John Halperin (ed.), *The Theory of the Novel: New Essays*, New York, Oxford University Press, 1974, p. 188.

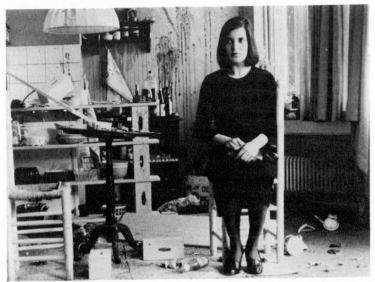

The Lost Honor of Katharina Blum is based on the Heinrich Böll novel
of the same name. Here Angela Winkler, who plays the title role, sits surrounded by the wreckage of her life as she awaits the unscrupulous
Tötges. *Photo courtesy of Museum of Modern Art*

from the foreground and Korten from the right, leaving a two-shot
of Katharina at center frame and Hach behind her and to the right.
He then walks out of the frame, and the camera moves yet closer
to Katharina until her face fills the left side of the frame and she
turns her head and looks to her left, not *at* anything but toward a
masked space. The shifts in composition, in shot distance, and in
the direction of Katharina's gaze all signal the privacy of this
moment. It is clear that her account of her solitary drives is not so
much an explanation as it is a self-discovery. The privileged moment comes to an end when, referring to the lonely women who
get drunk in front of their television sets, she turns her head and
looks straight at us again, saying that "that scares me." While the
novel has told us that those present were "surprised or embar-
rassed . . . as if for the first time Blum had revealed something
personal and intimate" (p. 51), the film simultaneously evokes the
emotion and the interpretation from us directly.

The scene is also an important index of the nature of the story,
and it takes us back to the remark of Schlöndorff's with which we

began. The "reality" at the heart of both novel and film is not only the crucible of terrifying events but the compelling and complex character of Katharina that emerges from it. Those who wish to turn these narratives into political tracts and, having done so, then fault them for oversimplifying have been blind not only to the richness of the discourses but to the subtleties of the story itself. In both versions, the enduring humanity and dignity of Katharina Blum is the mystery—and the miracle—at the story's core. In their film, Schlöndorff and von Trotta have been faithful to the essential humanism of Heinrich Böll.

BIRGITTA STEENE

FILM AS THEATER
Geissendörfer's *The Wild Duck (1976)*

from the play by Henrik Ibsen

Next to *A Doll House* and *Hedda Gabler, The Wild Duck* must be Ibsen's most popular play. Written in 1884, it dramatizes the story of a petit-bourgeois Norwegian family, the Ekdals, and sets forth the theme of the life lie which was to be summed up half a century later by T. S. Eliot in his poem *Burnt Norton*: "Human kind cannot bear very much reality." Ibsen himself realized that with *The Wild Duck* he had departed radically from earlier drama (including his own) in which the hero(ine) had strength and stature even in defeat. The Ekdal household is headed by the weak and sentimental Hjalmar Ekdal, who lives on the pipe dream that he is one day going to produce a remarkable invention which will bring fame and riches to his family. Into the contented Ekdal home comes Gregers Werle, Hjalmar's friend from his student days, whose father has been instrumental in setting up Hjalmar in the photography business and has arranged for Hjalmar's marriage to Gina Hansen, a former maid in the Werle household. Gregers is a fanatic who sees truth telling as his mission in life. He proceeds to reveal his father's brief involvement with Gina before her marriage. Hjalmar's ego is hurt; he rejects Gina and Hedvig, the Ekdals' teenage daughter. Desperate, the girl kills herself.

There are to date five screen adaptations of *The Wild Duck,* the most recent being Hans Wilhelm Geissendörfer's *Die Wildente* (1976). In a brief article on film versions of Ibsen's work, the Norwegian novelist Karsten Alnaes dismisses *Die Wildente* as "merely filmed theater" and calls the film noteworthy primarily "because of the fine performance of Bruno Ganz as Gregers

Werle."[1] But Geissendörfer's film is indeed what it purports to be: an *adaptation* of *The Wild Duck* rather than a filmed stage performance, an adaptation revealing the director's awareness of the different conventions that rule the stage and the screen, and attempting to circumvent the restrictions of the stage without losing the drama's essential quality of a living-room tragedy—a story of small insignificant people whose trapped lives are defined by the narrow spatial boundaries of their home.

Most of the time the camera is in front of and behind the stage, revealing it and hemming it in rather than expanding it beyond the space seen or suggested by the play. When Geissendörfer shoots Gregers's return from his walk with Hjalmar in the backyard of the Ekdals' apartment, the camera goes outside, not in order to demonstrate its spatial freedom but as part of a psychological and narrative logic: Hedvig has just been sent out of the house by Hjalmar, which in turn enables Geissendörfer to show the cruel discrepancy between Gregers's excitement at having accomplished his mission and Hedvig's sadness at having been rejected by her father as a result of it. When Ibsen employs "the miracle of the curtain"[2] between acts IV and V to account for the lapse of time between Hjalmar's flight from home and his return after a drinking session with Relling, Ekdal's medical neighbor, Geissendörfer inserts a tavern sequence and transposes from the Ekdal living room to the bar the major confrontation between Relling and Gregers as the latter arrives in search of Hjalmar. The sequence is not so much an addition to the play as an attempt to use a cinematic convention (the cut to a new locale) instead of a theatrical one (the curtain fall).

One of the key questions in any filmed version of a stage drama is the extent to which the filmmaker should accept the physical limitations of the theater. There is no absolute rule to be applied in this matter. Alnaes's sweeping judgment of Geissendörfer's *Die Wildente* was based on a biased notion that the theater possesses an aesthetic absolute to which the cinema can never come close, an

---

[1] Karsten Alnaes, "Footlights to Film," *Scandinavian Review*, Vol. 66, No. 4, December 1978, p. 71.

[2] The phrase is André Bazin's, in "The Theater and the Cinema," *What is Cinema?* translated by Hugh Gray, Berkeley, University of California Press, 1967, pp. 76–124.

all-too-common view among people evaluating the two art forms.

But as André Bazin suggests, a filmmaker has only to define the dramatic circumference of his adaptation in such a way that we accept its verisimilitude, its natural realism, and he or she will be completely free to remain faithful to many if not all the theatrical conventions employed by the playwright.[3] Bazin is arguing both against the literalness with which "canned theater" preserves the physical layout of the stage and against the conscious, technical use of a camera which tries at all costs to break the boundaries of the stage. He demonstrates how a filmed version of Jean Cocteau's drama *Les Parents Terribles* (1948) is successful precisely because the director realizes the importance of the claustrophobic atmosphere of the play and deliberately deprives himself of the use of a multiple setting and shots of exterior nature.

To film an Ibsen drama like *The Wild Duck* presents an analogous but more complex problem. The often stuffy Ibsenite living room, clearly defined by strict nineteenth-century middle-class behavior, suggests a circumscribed world, one in which the freedom of the individual may easily be curtailed and in which the roaming spirit must delude itself and resort to daydreaming and fantasy or else remain frustrated and unfulfilled. But a (often self-destructive) release from the bourgeois bonds, existing as a sad homage to the human imagination, is almost always present as a potential in Ibsen's plays and is often postulated in the use of space that is more suggestive than fully visualized. For instance, in *A Doll House* Helmer's study, to which he, Dr. Rank, and Krogstad have access, is never entered by Nora so that we become aware, throughout the drama, of a male-oriented social world that is completely closed to her. The inner room in *Hedda Gabler*, of which we can glimpse only the portrait of Hedda's father on the wall, becomes both the real and symbolic space where Hedda can ultimately seek her freedom-in-death from the dull and restrictive world of Tesman and Judge Brack.

In Ibsen's drama, then, the space beyond the main stage often constitutes as large a part of the psychological action as the arena where the actual events are performed. To film an Ibsen play must therefore be an extraordinary challenge to the filmmaker, since

[3] *Ibid.*

Ibsen's work is rooted in his juxtaposition of a clearly defined, limited space in which the often drab lives of the characters unfold and the real—yet largely invisible—space that exists behind a closed door or a drawn curtain, space often wrought with mystery for both characters and audience.

The attic in *The Wild Duck* is an actual part of the Ekdals' apartment. But in Ibsen's meticulous stage directions it is separated by a curtain from the living room and studio area, where all the main action takes place. All the members of the Ekdal household except Gina will at some time or another pull the curtain aside to catch a glimpse of the wild duck, the attic's supreme inhabitant. But Ibsen's visualized action never takes place *in the attic*. That remains a realm which is much talked about in the drama but never actually shown, never seen by the audience as an objective reality. Because this hidden world is not seen, its multiple meanings, suggested indirectly by the different characters, can be shared by the audience, which is free to adopt the point of view of any or all the members of the Ekdal household.

In filming *The Wild Duck,* Geissendörfer opts for bringing the camera, and thus the audience, into the attic. He recreates it before our eyes with all its nooks and corners and barnyard animals. This approach immediately poses a major problem: How is he to suggest the metaphorical meaning of the wild duck? The literalness of the cinematic image, projecting just an ordinary duck, threatens to destroy its poetic implications in Ibsen's drama. Wisely enough, Geissendörfer cuts almost all symbolic allusions to the injured fowl in the text and relies instead on the total *mise-en-scène* of the attic to reveal the bird's mysterious connection to the Ekdal family.

Geissendörfer sets the action in the attic on three separate occasions, presenting it through the eyes of all the main characters: Hedvig, Hjalmar, Old Ekdal, and Gregers. We first enter the attic shortly after Gregers's arrival at the Ekdals'; the presentation of the attic to the viewers is also Gregers's introduction and response to it. The second sequence in the attic depicts Hjalmar and his father as they go hunting for rabbits in preparation for Hedvig's birthday. In the play, Hjalmar and Old Ekdal's dependency upon the attic as an escape from their personal doldrums and professional failure is clear enough, but their actual hunting for rabbits receives of necessity only a passing reference in the text. Geissendörfer, on the other hand, creates a whole new farcical sequence in which the two men appear quite ludicrous—dangerously so, for they are supposed to be childish people but not looneys—as they simulate a real big-game expedition, testing the wind and the distance to and size of their prey (a rabbit). By and large this sequence fails because Geissendörfer's portrayal here of the two men seems somewhat inconsistent with his less ironic view of them in the rest of the film, in which he deliberately plays down Ibsen's depiction of Hjalmar as a conceited and ridiculously melodramatic character and of Old Ekdal as a hopeless drunkard.

The third time Geissendörfer sets the action in the attic occurs towards the end of the film, when Hedvig goes there to kill herself. Both this sequence and the first attic episode represent a shift in space rather than a complete addition to the original play in that the director transfers Ibsen's dialogue from the studio and living room to the attic.

Every time Hjalmar and Old Ekdal are about to enter the attic, Hedvig asks to come along. The attic is not an area where she goes alone or without permission. When she does so at the end of the film, it means that she is breaking a parental rule and has cut herself off from her family in a desperate response to her father's rejection.

To Hedvig the attic is an archetypal world defined by the poetic phrase *på havsens bunn* ("at the bottom of the sea"), a reference to the dark depths from which the wild duck has been rescued. The attic is also a magic extension of the Ekdal living quarters, a half-forbidden or unexplored ground which she enters with her father and grandfather as if she were about to set out on a marvelous adventure. Geissendörfer's first presentation of the attic brings out the sense of mystery that the Ekdals (with the exception of Gina) attach to the place; it opens to us like a dark cave lit up gradually in a warm glow of light. The family advances in hushed silence and speaks to Gregers in subdued voices, until the spell is broken by young Werle's clumsy overturning of a tin pail, a foreshadowing of his shattering of the Ekdals' fantasies and illusions later in the film.

Gregers Werle is instantly intrigued by the attic: Having been shown its marvels and having been told the story about the wild duck—how it was shot by Old Werle and rescued by his "clever dog"—he expresses his wish to stay with the Ekdals. From Ibsen's play, we know that Gregers sees himself as "a clever dog" who is going to save the sinking Ekdal family. In the film, we understand little by little that the attic appeals to him because of its symbolic potential. Gregers is a person who needs to abstract reality; he metamorphoses the attic into a place where, through Hedvig's sacrifice of the wild duck, his father's victims are going to be born again. But when Hedvig kills herself rather than the duck, it is because, unlike Gregers, she does not believe in vicarious sacrifices and symbolic acts. If she has been rejected, she and not the duck must die. She commits her suicide in the place where now dwells the wounded bird with which she identifies strongly.

Because Hedvig's death is an act of genuine despair and not a staged sacrificial rite, it seems wrong of Geissendörfer to present it as he does: with a great deal of stylized pathos. Only if we see Hedvig's death with Gregers's distorted vision can we accept the sentimentality of the scene: the slow, visually calculating camera, and the beams of light filtering through the window and enveloping Hedvig in a *gloria celestis* as she stands with the wild duck in her arms, looking into the light from above. This is precisely how we imagine that Gregers would like to picture Hedvig's last moments: in a solemnly cliché-ridden pose. The problem is, however, that the scene is not photographed from Gregers's point of view, since he is not present in the room, but from the point of view of the objective camera. In the final analysis, one suspects therefore that Geissendörfer has not intended this part of the third and last attic sequence as a biting dig at Gregers but as a genuinely moving depiction of a child's preparations for dying. If so, the scene fails because of its melodramatic perspective.

One might contrast this scene with the equally pathetic deathbed vignette with which the sequence and the film close. Hjalmar Ekdal is seen kneeling with Hedvig in his arms, his big phlegmatic body enfolding her until she becomes little more than a small object that completes his round figure. Hulking and humming the tune he has played earlier on his flute (or is it a few bars from Sibelius's "The Dying Swan at Tuonela," which has been heard earlier in the sequence?),[4] Hjalmar is rocking the dead child while

---

[4] The choice of musical accompaniment could hardly be more appropriate, with the melody of the dying swan reinforcing the playwright's and the director's intention to relate Hedvig to the injured duck.

the camera tracks back to Gregers and Dr. Relling. When the camera cuts again to Hjalmar's bulky figure on the floor, wallowing in melodramatic self-pity, we know that his display of emotion is a form of sentimentality that only a Gregers would mistake for moral purging and that Dr. Relling will deflate with his psychological perceptiveness.

It is amazing how much of one's response, positive or negative, to Geissendörfer's film emanates from his handling of the attic world. One of his real strokes of genius in adapting *The Wild Duck* for the screen is his ability to make the attic and the living-room world of the Ekdals reinforce each other. It is important for our understanding of the full impact of Gregers's destructive pathos that we sense the attic both as a compensation for the dreary life of the Ekdals and as an expression of their ability to bring magic and love into their world. Hedvig, for instance, may identify with the wild duck, but she also sees it as a living thing needing her affection. As with so many children, she expresses her own emotional needs through a defenseless animal. Hjalmar and his father may escape from daily responsibilities into the attic, but their ultimate reason for going there is to bring joy to Hedvig.

Geissendörfer is aware of Ibsen's attempt to suggest that the two men belong more in the make-believe world of the attic than in the realm of business and finance. This reflects their weakness, which may have caused Old Ekdal's troubles in the past and which makes Hjalmar's verbal promises totally unreliable. In the scene after the dinner party with Consul Werle, when Hjalmar has forgotten to fulfill his promise to Hedvig to ask the Consul for some delicacies to take home with him, Geissendörfer ingeniously shows how Hjalmar tries to cope with the child's disappointment. In what seems a marvelous streak of intuition, Hjalmar resorts to a magic game. A close-up shot shows his hand fluttering in spellbinding motions to the accompaniment of a swishing, mysterious sound, as if Hjalmar were about to conjure forth real samples of the menu.

But Hjalmar cannot transform the piece of paper enumerating the dishes served at the dinner into a real sampling of the delicacies on the Werle table. Hedvig, lured momentarily into Hjalmar's make-believe game, can only be disappointed by the outcome, for unlike all the mysterious paraphernalia in the attic, Hjalmar's magic has no foundation in an existing world. Put differently, Hjalmar and Old Ekdal are men of fantasy but not real magicians.

Hjalmar's failure in this scene to create a magic in which Hedvig can trust—the way she apparently trusts in his invention—is a perceptive addition by Geissendörfer to the play. It helps crystallize in purely visual terms the fact that Hjalmar's flaw is his charming ability to draw magic circles around his being.

We see another example of this in the scene in which Hjalmar shows Gregers his would-be invention. The room where this remarkable gadget is to materialize contains nothing but an empty table. But Hjalmar describes his role as inventor and family provider to Gregers, guiding him through the world of his home and talking in a whispering voice, as if he had some big secret to share which could be divulged only in greatest confidence. In fact, Hjalmar's inflated view of himself becomes so obvious in this scene that Geissendörfer does not need the reinforcement of Hjalmar's sentimental speech pattern—a central feature in Ibsen's verbal text—to point out the flaws in his personality.

For the most part, Geissendörfer stays close to the original text throughout *Die Wildente*. Except for the hunting sequence and the opening segment of the film (discussed below), he writes no new text. His verbal cuts are relatively few; besides those referred to earlier, the following seem the most noteworthy:

1. Omission of the play's exposition
2. Omission of Gina's and Hedvig's small talk
3. Omission of Mrs. Sörby's conversation with Gina
4. Omission of Gregers's negative references to himself
5. Toning down of Hedvig's outburst when Hjalmar leaves the family
6. Omission of Relling and Gregers's verbal confrontation about the life lie

Ibsen's play opens with an offstage dinner party speech by Old Werle, which is heard and commented on by two eavesdropping servants, Pettersen and Jensen. The speech is in honor of Mrs. Sörby, Werle's housekeeper whom he intends to marry. Pettersen and Jensen make a passing reference to Werle's amorous escapades in the past. Their gossip is interrupted by the unexpected arrival of Old Ekdal, Werle's former business companion, who is now doing copying work for him after having served a prison sentence for criminal timber transactions. It is obvious that Old Ekdal's arrival on the scene is inappropriate. His shabby appear-

ance contrasts with the formal and festive atmosphere of the dinner party. Old Ekdal is an intruder, an embarrassing reminder of
the past that Old Werle would rather forget.

In Geissendörfer's film, the opening point of view is still that of
the two servants, one of them attentively waiting and the other
casually reading the newspaper. The dinner party has not yet
begun; Pettersen and Jensen are not divulging any inside information about Consul Werle. Their function as a "spying" chorus, an
age-old stage function for servants which provides the audience
with the play's exposition, is changed in the film version: The
director uses Pettersen and Jensen as the camera eye, passive ob-
servers of a street scene outside Consul Werle's patrician home. As
it turns out, the two servants are unwittingly waiting for Nemesis
to strike, *i.e.,* for the arrival of Gregers Werle, the Consul's son,
who is coming home after twelve years in the mines up at Hoidal,
where Old Ekdal used to be supervisor. From the moment the
carriage pulls up with the Consul's son, the focus is on Gregers
Werle. We know nothing yet about the Werle-Ekdal past.

By shifting the role of intruder from old Lieutenant Ekdal to
young Werle, Geissendörfer largely ignores Ibsen's emphasis on
the Werle past. From the beginning, the film becomes a story in the
now about a revengeful son and fanatic who hates his father and
whose arrival breeds disaster and tragedy. Gregers Werle's destructive idealism is certainly explicit in Ibsen's play, but there it is
juxtaposed to Old Werle's past: By the time father and son meet,
we know about the former's philandering and his manipulative
business transactions and are ready to question his easy dismissal
of Gregers's dead mother as a "neurotic." To Ibsen, Old Werle is
not necessarily innocent, even though the law has pinned the crime
on his former partner, Old Ekdal. To Geissendörfer, on the other
hand, Gregers's father is an imposing and formidable figure and a
person of great dignity. To add to his prestige Geissendörfer has
his title changed from *grosserer* (approximately "merchant") to
Consul.

What Geissendörfer does with the father-son motif in *The Wild
Duck* seems very Germanic and very Freudian: He transforms
"Consul" Werle into a paternalistic semigod and Gregers Werle
into a son with a mother fixation. The first shot of the Consul,
which opens the third sequence, depicts him rising like a divinity in

a glow of light at the end of a long formal dinner table. And while Ibsen only hints at Gregers's love for his deceased mother, Geissendörfer has him carry along a framed picture of her, which is the first thing he unpacks both when he arrives at his father's house and later when he takes up his abode with the Ekdals. During his first man-to-man talk with Hjalmar Ekdal, whose "honor" he is determined to resurrect, Gregers looks at a family album which has a picture of his mother on the front page. She becomes the ubiquitous presence behind all his actions.

No doubt, one can see *The Wild Duck* as an Oedipal conflict of classic dimensions, a psychological revenge drama in which the father's power and will remain patriarchally strong despite his aging and oncoming blindness, and the son's unresolved sexual conflict manifests itself in his bitter rejection of the father and in a religious zeal that demands the purging of Hjalmar and Gina Ekdal's marriage and the sacrifice by young Hedvig of the wild duck, the token of paternal abuse.

In keeping with his interest in the father-son motif, Geissendörfer elaborates on Hjalmar's relationship to Old Ekdal in two specific instances, neither of which receives more than a passing reference in Ibsen. At the dinner party at Consul Werle's, Hjalmar sees his father emerge through a door in the library and, ashamed, quickly turns his back on him. Gregers upbraids him for denouncing his father and for not taking a stand, a view in keeping with Gregers's opinion that sons are responsible for the deeds of their fathers.

In a second instance, Geissendörfer adds a whole sequence to the original play (the hunting sequence). As a symbolic analogy to the Gregers-Old Werle relationship, the sequence no doubt intrigued Geissendörfer: Here are a father and son sharing their joy at an innocent "outing" and making preparations to celebrate Hedvig's birthday, a sharp contrast to the lack of rapport between Gregers and his father. But here also is an event which in its bungling childishness helps set the stage for Hedvig's death from the same pistol used to shoot the rabbit. And finally the hunt forms an ironic parallel to Gregers's hunt of defenseless victims in the Ekdal family.

The father-child syndrome is also a central element in Gregers's unctuously paternalistic relationship to the Ekdal family. His ap-

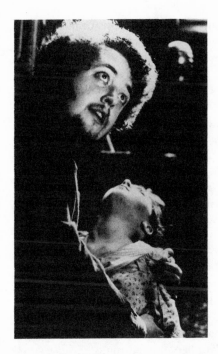

Hedvig (Anne Bennent) is only a child of twelve in Geissendörfer's film version of *The Wild Duck*. Here Hjalmar (Peter Kern) cradles her in his arms in a pathetic deathbed vignette following her suicide with Old Ekdal's pistol. *Photo courtesy of New Yorker Films*

proach to Hedvig has little of the spiritual sibling sympathy one senses so strongly in Ibsen's drama. Rather, he becomes a patriarchal substitute for the will-less Hjalmar. As such, he plants the idea of sacrifice in Hedvig's mind after visiting her at her evening prayers, and he expresses his disapproval when she almost retracts her vow in the clear light of the following morning.

Gregers's role as moralistic parent figure is put in sharper relief by Geissendörfer's making Hedvig, superbly acted by Anne Bennent, two years younger than in Ibsen's play. In the film Hedvig is a child of twelve rather than a young girl entering puberty. This makes Gregers's insistence upon her sacrifice even more grotesque and his physical rapprochement more ominous. So strong seems his attraction to her that it is difficult not to regard his two visits to her bedroom—both of them additions to the play—as those of a potential child rapist. Possibly Geissendörfer's intentions were to suggest not only Gregers's repressed emotions but also Hedvig's generous soul, for he lets the girl reciprocate Gregers's embrace when he breaks down at her bedside and, sobbing, kisses her hysterically. However, Hedvig's innocence only seems to increase the obscenity of Gregers's behavior, making it difficult to draw the line between his psychological abuse of the girl and a barely suppressed sexual violation of her.

Such a reaction to Gregers and Hedvig's relationship is quite possibly colored by the fact that Geissendörfer's *Die Wildente* pushes Ibsen's play in a male chauvinist direction, a debatable trend in view of Ibsen's emphasis on the women's strength in *The Wild Duck*. Geissendörfer's opening sequence sets the patriarchal tone when Pettersen shows his awesome respect for Consul Werle and suggests that Gregers's impromptu invitation of Hjalmar Ekdal to his father's dinner will be an unwelcome move to Werle senior.

The ensuing dinner sequence solidifies the mood of male dominance in the Werle household, but in addition Geissendörfer changes Ibsen's conception of Gina Ekdal as well as of Mrs. Sörby. In the original play they are two strong-willed and action-oriented women, but in the film Mrs. Sörby becomes little more than a competent hostess who brings comfort to the Consul in his old age. Ibsen, on the other hand, assigns her an important confidential scene with Gina and gives her an opportunity to suggest the real basis of her relationship with Werle, namely, mutual trust and truthfulness, *i.e.,* the very opposite criteria of Gina and Hjalmar's marriage. In the film Mrs. Sörby and Gina, these two Ibsenite matriarchs, never meet. In fact, while Mrs. Sörby is explaining to Hedvig and Gregers (in the backyard of the Ekdal home) why she will marry Consul Werle, the camera cuts briefly to the Consul's formidable figure as he sits waiting in his carriage. Instead of a tête-à-tête between two resilient women, Geissendörfer presents Mrs. Sörby in a confessional scene, with the male authority figure hovering in the background.

Gina Ekdal's role as portrayed by Jean Seberg seems far more delicate and much less dynamic than what Ibsen suggested. Ibsen's Gina is a very robust and prosaic woman who walks with a waddle (like a duck!) and keeps a close eye on Hjalmar. She is a strong maternal person who puts up with his fantasies and indolence as if he were a child throwing temper tantrums. But she knows he is a good-for-nothing. More importantly, in the original play a strong mother-daughter bond exists between Gina and Hedvig. Ibsen gives us a feeling that together these two women tolerate what they see as Hjalmar's weak nature, because he seems clever and smart to them and represents a society that neither has ever known. To them Hjalmar is what the attic is to Old Ekdal and his son: a realm where the impossible can exist unchallenged and half-fulfilled. Hjalmar's invention is the dream that sustains the family in their drab life, just as the attic is a playground that keeps Hjalmar and Old Ekdal from falling into ennui and despair.

In *Die Wildente,* Gina's whole attention is directed toward Hjalmar. Hedvig hardly exists for her, except as someone who can be ordered out into the kitchen to fetch food trays. In Ibsen, Gina pays attention first and foremost to the child, and though the domestic bond between Gina and Hedvig is based on traditional women's roles, it harbors great emotional strength, none of which comes through in the film. Gina seems to lose her self-control when Hjalmar confronts her with her past; after that she can do little more than fuss around him like an anxious lover afraid of being jilted. Whether owing to cultural bias or to personal prefer-ence, Geissendörfer tones down the mother-daughter relationship and focuses only on the father-child syndrome.

Throughout the film, the dramatic entrances are made by men. Visually, Mrs. Sörby's visit has a strong impact only because she arrives with the Consul in his splendid carriage. This is in keeping with a rhythmic pattern in the film, which builds each major se-quence around the male-intruder motif. The visitor or messenger is often announced by a jarring doorbell, followed by an abrupt cut that calls attention to itself and breaks the cozy or formal atmo-sphere of the occasion. In the third sequence, for instance, Old Ekdal interrupts the dinner party at Consul Werle's. In Ibsen's play, Old Ekdal emerges as a crushed man who causes a minor nuisance by his unexpected arrival but who behaves in an apolo-getic and subdued manner. In the film, although Old Ekdal exits with an apology and a bow, Geissendörfer turns his visit into a real challenge for the Consul by having the camera single out the two men in the crowded room. During what seems like a silent eternity, they engage in a psychological tug-of-war. When Old Ekdal bows out as the loser, his exit has a great deal more dignity than in the play, an interesting twist that seems in line with the film's patri-archal bias and results in Old Ekdal playing a much more suppor-tive role to Hedvig than in Ibsen's drama.

The intruder motif is varied subtly from sequence to sequence.

In the second sequence the role is performed by the messenger Pettersen as he delivers Gregers's invitation and asks Hedvig to give it to her father; he thus interrupts the accepted routine of life in the Ekdal family, in which Gina takes care of the photography business and Hjalmar spends his days resting on the living-room couch, fantasizing about his invention. Soon this domestic scene will change. The next time (in the fourth sequence) the camera takes us into the Ekdal household, Hjalmar has just returned from the Consul's party, where he has been made the butt of ridicule by some of the other guests. Back home, after some bragging and a flare-up of bad temper, Hjalmar is coaxed into his old self by Hedvig's offering to bring him beer and his flute. The melodious flute solo performed by Hjalmar in a half-professional stylized pose on the steps leading into the attic—with the two women as an admiring public—seems to restore the family harmony. When the mood is shattered by the abrupt arrival of Gregers, the director can suggest that the visitor is indeed an intruder who destroys Hjalmar's performance, which is both an artificial act and a genuine source of joy to the Ekdals.

From then on, other visitors will simply reinforce Gregers's role of nemesis. The Consul's unexpected call interrupts a breakfast at which Dr. Relling, sharing Gina's herring salad with the decadent theologian Molvik, has asked Gregers if he does not appreciate participating in a genuine family gathering. Gregers, as always intent upon his mission of truth and revenge, can see nothing but "a bog of foul air" in the Ekdal marriage. At that moment Old Werle rings the doorbell. On the stage the timed irony of such a visit would seem like a forced symbolic interruption, the sign of the manipulative technique of the well-made play. But on the screen the irony works better because the camera can cut and shift the focus to the new arrival at the moment he interrupts the action in the Ekdal living room. Some of the oldest conventions of the cinema—the crosscut and parallel shots, and the shift of space and locale through editing—create a "natural" simultaneity and verisimilitude that alleviate our distrust at too many coincidences. Geissendörfer's adaptation of *The Wild Duck* is an excellent example of how a changing camera perspective can help suspend our disbelief when Ibsen's events seem too perfectly arranged.

We can see how crucial cutting and change of space are to our acceptance of coincident events if we compare the handling of Old Werle's arrival to Hedvig's suicide toward the end of the film. Her pistol shot rings out at the very moment that Hjalmar accusingly fantasizes about his child ignoring her family for those who can offer her more material comfort in life. Again, in Ibsen's drama the timing seems too precise, the bitter irony too obvious. Hedvig's death threatens to become a symbolic event rather than the final desperate act of a rejected child. The film adaptation underscores this.

Geissendörfer's earlier handling of Ibsen's irony of coincidence shows that he does not feel bound to adopt Ibsen's stage technique. Rather, his presentation of Hjalmar's denouncement at Hedvig's moment of death seems dictated by the thematic thrust of his adaptation. Geissendörfer's *Die Wildente* is a tragedy of *paternal* failure, imagined or real. In the breakfast sequence Geissendörfer shifts the focus to Old Werle; in the suicide scene he ignores Hedvig and stresses Hjalmar's fatal role by zooming in on his face and letting him utter right into the camera his unfair surmise of Hedvig's ungratefulness to her family.

André Bazin—quoting Sartre—claims that one of the basic differences between the stage and the screen is that "in the theater the drama proceeds from the actor, in the cinema it goes from the decor to man."[5] This reversal of the dramatic flow would make the *mise-en-scène* of crucial importance in a film adaptation of a stage play, a fact that can be observed in Geissendörfer's development of all the characters but especially perhaps of Gregers Werle.

In Ibsen's drama Gregers makes several verbal allusions to himself as a Christ figure or an exceptionally unlucky person, someone who is singled out to be "the thirteenth man at the table" or has to carry a heavy cross. Geissendörfer cuts all such metaphorical references in Gregers's speech. Instead, young Werle's self-imposed asceticism and zealous sense of mission are suggested by placing him, when he is alone, in the sparsely furnished room in the Consul's house and in the equally frugal-looking room he rents from the Ekdals. Neither room is part of Ibsen's stage design. Both stand in marked contrast to the other rooms in the two houses: to the formal opulence of the Consul's room and the rich red tones of

[5] Bazin, op. cit., p. 79.

the Ekdal studio or the cluttered coziness of their attic. When we see Gregers with the Ekdal family, he is never placed at the oblong table next to the red sofa that is the focal gathering point in the living room. On several occasions Geissendörfer emphasizes Gregers's separateness from the Ekdals by employing a different lighting for them, surrounding the family with soft reflections from kerosene lamps and Gregers's figure with a direct cold, grayish light.

Gregers's personality seems indeed to emanate from the decor to the man. When he enters his room in his father's house, the camera includes a shot of a crucifix on the wall. Such a decoration is unthinkable in an upper-middle-class Scandinavian context (as is the frugality of the room, which looks more like a whitewashed German country *Gasthaus*), a cultural idiosyncracy that one can see as a breach in ethnic realism but also as the director's deliberate creation of a symbolic *mise-en-scène*. Later, after Gregers has moved in with the Ekdals, his role as crusader is made visually explicit when he stands against the arch-formed window in his room, as though in front of a church window, and touches his fingertips in a preacherlike gesture. Accompanied by organ music and hardly able to contain his excitement at the prospect of "saving" Hjalmar from his illusions, Gregers tells his startled friend: "We two must go for a long walk." Because of the visual context, the words take on an ominous symbolic ring: Unknowingly, it is the Golgotha of the innocent victim Hedvig that Geissendörfer's Gregers is beginning to map out.

Geissendörfer's emphasis on the *mise-en-scène* may also explain why he omitted Ibsen's discussion of the life lie; it is a verbal abstraction that sums up the main characters' response to reality. On the screen that response can be suggested visually through the juxtaposition of actor and details in the *mise-en-scène*, including scenes taking place in the attic. A verbal exchange between Relling and Gregers would become almost a tautology under those circumstances.

When Bazin speaks about a movement from decor to actor on the screen, he sees this as a manifestation of the basically realistic nature of the cinema and lauds it as a sign of the film medium coming into its own, breaking with the stylized conventions of the theater play. Geissendörfer's use of the *mise-en-scène* seems to contradict this assumption, however. Some of the most stunning placements and movements of his actors within the *mise-en-scène* are very studied and carry implications far beyond realistic film-making. In Gregers and Hjalmar's brief encounter in Gregers's room, the decor clearly carries the symbolic weight of verbal entendre on the stage. The realism lies in the prosaic language: "We two must go for a long walk, Hjalmar." But the extended meaning of those words lies in the stylized *mise-en-scène*.

At times (as in the example above), Geissendörfer uses the *mise-en-scène* successfully to amplify the often pruned language. At other times, one gets a feeling that he is carried away with his own visual ingenuity so that a particular shot becomes too self-sufficient and the actor's role in it not altogether motivated. One such case is a stunning shot of Gina as she sits in the shaded living room when Hjalmar returns from his walk with Gregers. She is dressed in black as compared to the somewhat lighter shades of her clothing earlier. Questions of motivation immediately present themselves: Why is Gina in mourning? Why has she pulled the curtains and withdrawn into the dark? The fact that these questions demand to be answered suggests that the psychological realism of the character and all the symbolic overtones of the *mise-en-scène* do not harmonize. The shot of Gina posing as it were in the studio is of course extremely intriguing, suggesting her connection with photography, the family's source of income. Now she is no longer the photographer taking pictures of clients; she is herself an object in a darkroom, exposed to Hjalmar's camera eye, its lens opened by Gregers Werle.

But Gina's pose lacks a psychological *raison d'être* and points out how difficult it is to achieve a balance between character realism and visual symbolism on the screen. The above-mentioned scene seems suspect because Geissendörfer has not shown much interest in Gina earlier in the film; hence, she remains a nonentity to us, and the visually impressive shot of her comes off as a director's somewhat self-indulgent comment on a character rather than the natural expression of the character's conscious or unconscious drive.

By and large, Geissendörfer's adaptation of *The Wild Duck* shows that a filmmaker with artistic intelligence and perceptiveness can translate into filmic terms the visual potential that is part of every great theater text. My reservations about *Die Wildente* are mostly connected with Giessendörfer's treatment of the women: Gina's submissiveness, Hedvig's melodramatic death, Mrs. Sörby's role in the shadow of the Consul. In the final analysis, however, *Die Wildente* has many outstanding features: the creative use of the *mise-en-scène*; the imaginative presentation of visual and sound elements, which capture the metaphorical texture of Ibsen's deceptively prosaic language and amplify the psychological focus chosen by the director; and the camera's sensitive registering of a piece of highly professional screen acting.

ALAN SPIEGEL

THE CINEMATIC TEXT
Rohmer's *The Marquise of O . . . (1976)*

from the story by Heinrich von Kleist

During the early seventies, one of the milder irritants of my moviegoing life was the way in which the films of Eric Rohmer kept dropping out of mind. First they were there; then, with speed, stealth, and apparent finality, they weren't. Nor did they leave any traces, just a leafy annoyance at one's incapacity to worry about their disappearance. I suppose I really should have tried to care a bit more: A lot of serious moviegoers were making such a fuss about these films, and it wasn't hard to see what much of the fuss was about. Rohmer *was*, after all, someone to admire. There was obviously taste, discipline, intelligence, and witty seriousness in almost everything he did.[1] Few other contemporary directors worked so well within a methodology of limitation; few labored within the self-imposed astringencies of craft with such unlabored assurance, such fur-slippered comfort; few deployed the frame and the internal cut with such economy and exactness of placement. And films like *Claire's Knee* (1970) and *Chloe in the Afternoon*

[1] Eric Rohmer was born in 1923 in Nancy, France, and apart from making films, has been a film critic, an author (*Hitchcock*, with Claude Chabrol), and an editor of *Cahiers du Cinéma*. Since 1950 he has created different kinds of films for different purposes—shorts, documentaries, educational films for French television—most of this work never shown in this country. From 1962 to 1972 he wrote and directed the six films (known as the *Six Contes Moraux*) on which his international reputation has been based. The first two in this series—*La Boulangère de Monceau* (1962) and *Le Carrière de Suzanne* (1963)—have not been released here. The others are *La Collectioneuse* (1968), *Ma Nuit Chez Maud* (*My Night at Maud's*; 1969), *Le Genou de Claire* (*Claire's Knee*; 1970), and *L'Amour, l'Apres-Midi* (*Chloe in the Afternoon*; 1972). In 1976 he made the *Die Marquise Von O . . .* (*The Marquise of O . . .*) from a story by Heinrich von Kleist, and in 1978 *Perceval le Gallois* (*Perceval*) from the medieval romance by Chrétien de Troyes.

(1972) were so cunningly shaped, so delicately proportioned, so much all of a piece. As narrow as their premises might be, they fulfilled those premises with the intellectual rectitude of an algebraic solution and the moral rectitude of a kept promise.

My problem, however, began with the premises themselves: all that elegance of means pledged to what seemed such niggling ends; complications of gentle irony, always sophisticated and amusing but also too careful and meeching, almost donnish in their self-congratulatory pawkiness and their penchant for smiles too sly and jokes too tiny, boneless, and well-behaved. I found the Rohmer protagonists smug and prissy with finicky deliberation, lay clerics performing pirouettes of cerebration and hesitation about whether to sleep with this girl, or where, when, and how to touch that one's knee. And as the films went on, these swanky little problems, instead of expanding outward through allusion, symbol, or poetic suggestion, seemed only to become more pinched and shriveled until finally the characters themselves, their sensible presences, seemed to dissolve amid the vapors of introspection. Self-analysis kept corroding the visible so that by the end, you were left with the dry ice of a few aphorisms and the passing flutter of *pensées creuses*; it was a little like seeing ghosts. No director of Rohmer's stature seemed to make it so hard for you to remember what his characters looked like.

These judgments of Rohmer's work were based on the films I had seen before the appearance of *The Marquise of O . . .* in 1976. I present them here not at all as the kind of public indictment that hopes to create or even reflect a consensus but rather as a personal confession that hopes to provide a context for a modified turnabout, an awakened interest, and a current preference neither to press nor to revise early estimates, but simply to hold them in suspense, to keep the matter open. While I don't feel especially repentant nowadays, I do feel a good deal less complacent about my chronic amnesia *vis-à-vis* Rohmer's films.

With *The Marquise of O . . . ,* Rohmer was suddenly there for me in a way he had never been before, and this time there was to be no putting him out of mind. This one film gave me such rich, friendly, and unexpected pleasure that, as often happens in such cases, I felt perfectly willing to see again all the other Rohmer films and think them through a second time. And as also often happens in such cases, I have as yet done nothing of the kind, old prejudices having the tenacity of first loves. Instead, I have returned to *The Marquise of O . . .*, and after each viewing—such is its charm—continue to experience the same surge of guilt and good will toward its maker, and continue to do nothing about it, as well as continuing to find this film (perhaps mistakenly) a sort of free-standing loner, one of the loveliest, tenderest, most gracious and sagacious works of its decade, a humorous and decorous enchantment from end to end, an uninsistent treasure.

Unlike Rohmer's other films, it was not based on a story of his own making. This time Rohmer drew upon the work of Heinrich von Kleist, one of the heroes of German romanticism and one of the front-rank literary men of the nineteenth century. It was Kleist whom Thomas Mann described as "one of the greatest, boldest, and most ambitious poets Germany has produced; a playwright and storyteller of the very first order; a man unique in every respect, whose achievement and career seemed to violate all known codes and patterns."[2]

On the face of it, this large-spirited and disruptive artist may not represent the most predictable choice of collaborators for Eric Rohmer. But then one has only to read Kleist's story to see what must have seized Rohmer's initial interest. One finds there, among many other things, a reflection of Rohmer's own concern for hidden motive, psychic evasion, terraced irony, svelte talk, and carefully groomed and quarantined suburban spaces (gardens, parlors, vestibules, bedchambers, and dining rooms). Though Kleist rarely describes the faces and figures of his characters or the rooms in which they sit, he flanks and infiltrates their numerous conversations with squads of precise and intimate detail of posture and gesture that make these conversations right enough for the cinema and precisely right for the kind of cinema Rohmer admires and, of course, practices. On the other hand, the style and subject matter of Kleist's story are still sufficiently different from Rohmer's previous films to effect a refreshing and gratifying sea change in his work—a greater vitality of character, a more opulent visual surface, a richer and more conflicted moral and social texture, and

[2] Thomas Mann, "Kleist and his Stories," preface to *The Marquise of O . . . and Other Stories*, translated and edited by Martin Greenberg, Frederick Ungar, New York, 1973, p. 5.

throughout, a finer, warmer, denser, and more varied range of emotion.[3]

After living with his "moral tales" for almost twenty years (first written as prose fiction, then translated to the screen), Rohmer felt he had exhausted this content and was ready to try something else. "Also I wanted to perfect myself as a director," he told a *New York Times* interviewer (October 22, 1976). "As a writer, my universe is very limited . . . and by directing other texts, I have an opportunity to work with types of action that I am not capable of writing." Rohmer went to Kleist, then, in order to renew his art, expand his subject matter, and develop ("perfect" himself) as an artist. I think it is fair to say that the results accomplish not only these aims but something else as well, something quite special. Again, Rohmer: "It wasn't simply the action I was drawn to, but the text itself. I didn't want to translate it into images or make a filmed equivalent. I wanted to use the text as if Kleist himself had put it directly on the screen, as if he were making a movie." To this end, this French director spent four years learning German in order to film the text in its original language with a cast of German actors. (Imagine Renoir learning Russian to film *The Lower Depths*; 1936). Furthermore, he has made a film that shadows its literary counterpart with unprecedented scruple, often word for word and gesture for gesture, so that, aside from some slight additions, deletions, one reshuffling, and one medium-sized transformation (more of this later), most of what you see and hear on the screen finds either its exact match, close approximation, or logical verbal precedent in the original text. If this film had no other virtue—though it has many and greater—it could still stand as a matchless act of devotion and thoroughness that one literary-

---

[3] I feel this to be true not only of *The Marquise of O . . .* but of Rohmer's next film, *Perceval*, which has an adventurous structure, the sweetest of colors, a twinkling use of hands and arms, one charming digression, and all sorts of attractive flashes, but is finally only a scholar's *jeu d'esprit* and a much lesser work than the previous adaptation. The trouble here isn't that Rohmer's intelligence and inventiveness are any less in evidence—in fact, they were never more prominent—but that Chrétien's twelfth-century tale, traced faithfully as it is, remains firmly sealed off in its period—indeed, the film seems as fey, curious, remote, intermittently opaque, and, to a modern eye, as intermittently balmy as its literary counterpart. The same meticulous fidelity, however, applied to the nineteenth-century Kleist reveals not only a child of its time but one of our own.

minded artist has performed for another, and in this respect, a model of the adapter's art and a measure by which to gauge similar aesthetic transactions past and future.

But to say this, all of this, is to say only the least of it. It would hardly serve the originality of this work to leave the impression of yet another "faithful adaptation," even one a little more faithful than the others. Anyone can recall, and not without pleasure, any number of respectful and respectable films whose decencies are substantially those of a tributary kind, gestures of self-abnegation haloed by historical and cultural sanction and the immemorial glow of a literary classic—Lean's *Oliver Twist* (1947), Dickinson's *Queen of Spades* (1949), Heifitz's *The Lady with the Dog* (1959), etc.—loyal retainers whose worthiness lives in and derives from snug bondage to a master who rules by remote control and leaves tips. By contrast, Rohmer hasn't only "served" Kleist— he has, in fact, swallowed him whole. He has made by way of Kleist's written text his own cinematic text—no other term for it—one that achieves a style and form independent of Kleist. Certainly no book, and certainly no ordinary film, it extrapolates freely from both forms. Throughout his physical structure, Rohmer underscores those devices which have joint affiliation and legitimacy in both film and literature: Title cards frequently provide not only background information but blueprint instructions to be doubled by a subsidiary image; recurrent slow-fades-to-black beat time between short scenes (this in violation of the high velocity and headlong impetus of Kleist's prose), as if turning a page or accounting for blank spaces between chapters of print; midway, an unannounced and anonymous voice-over butts in to bridge a transition between events, complicating the fact that the first two-thirds of the story is recited in flashback by a different narrator, a very visible but unnamed tavern gossip (Kleist engineers his own flashback more directly through omniscient narration). But, most important, at the core of Rohmer's presentational manner resides the primacy of the spoken word in film, analogous to but obviously very different from the written word in a book—that is, the power of the spoken word to shape and direct the image that embodies it, to charge the image with the rigor and grace of abstraction, to sail the image into regions of thought and feeling often invisible to the eye but delectable to the mind.

Seeing for Rohmer is primarily an act not of observation but of understanding. This means that in order to understand Rohmer's story, the viewer must "watch," pay attention to exactly what the characters are saying, and in this way become a "reader" of the film. This in principle should not be hard to do, but in practice many people are not prepared to do it because they are accustomed to movies that present the drama in terms of action, not of conversation. In Rohmer's films, however, the central action is usually the conversation itself, and in this particular film, after the initial scenes (oblique aspects of a citadel under siege), the conversation tends to be fairly continuous. But Rohmer teaches you to understand that what matters most in this film—as in *any* film —is not how much talk there is but whether the talk is worth paying attention to. He teaches you to understand that when you say a film is "talky," what you really mean is that the talk you hear—even if there isn't a lot of it by clock or word count—is trite or dull or gross, not worth your time and attention.[4] Talk that is witty or brilliant or revealing is never "talky," no matter how much there is of it, and this sort of talk *moves* quickly; you like keeping up with it and work to do so. This talk has the energy and animation and the spellbinding charm of things in motion—like a car taking a corner on two wheels or the parabola of a pie en route to an eye—things worth looking at in a motion picture. One of the things you are keenly aware of in this film is that when talk is good, it is photogenic—one of the integral and expressive means that a film director may employ to tell his story without fear of being thought "uncinematic."

You will also note that Rohmer uses the spoken word in both the usual way—to convey information, attitudes, and feelings— and in a particularly formal way. He does what other serious film artists have done when trying to impose a unifying logic on a hybrid medium that seems to push out in so many different aesthetic directions (literary, theatrical, plastic, photographic) at once: He raises one aesthetic component to the status of a dominant (as in music) and coordinates all the other components

---

[4] In a similar manner, when we describe a film as "stagy," we really mean that the director doesn't know how to use space, how to arrange actors and objects in a natural and expressive way within the varied planes of a given setting; thus, a play on the stage can also be "stagy," but good ones never are.

around it in a contributory fashion. Just as the Russian directors in the twenties italicized montage and the American silent clown italicized the kinetic intelligence of his own body, Rohmer italicizes language as an organizing norm, a *point d'appui,* a kind of signature key (music again) that far from ignoring the "purely visual" components—camera, cut, prop, physical movement—clarifies and distinguishes them through spare and concentrated usage. One way he ensures the formal dominance of language is by asking you to listen to a lot of it; another way is to ask the actors, as he does here, to speak their lines in a relatively dry, measured, slightly stiff, slightly affectless way, as if they were putting quotation marks around their words, and as if these words existed slightly apart from them and the story they were in and issued from some other source. In spite of frequent emotional outbursts—plenty of tears, blushes, and angry faces—the actors often seem to be "reading," not acting in the customary sense (another aspect of the "cinematic text"). This stylized manner of speaking—and you can find even more austere versions of it used to different ends in the films of Rohmer's countrymen, Godard and Bresson—is of course dramatically right for the stiff-backed civilities of Kleist's social and military elite. But it also endorses language as a discrete, self-perpetuating, partly undigested element of design, one that streams alongside the dramatic action at a fractionally different tempo.

This cool and starchy delivery keeps you attuned to the ebb and flow of the words as such, and conserves and protects the emotion embodied in them, releasing it slowly and with considerable *politesse,* arousing your feelings obliquely but abidingly through the intelligence rather than directly through the viscera. As against certain well-known methods of naturalist and expressionist film and theater that exhaust their effects through jackhammer repetition of direct emotional assaults, Rohmer's controlled "readings" sacrifice the self-consuming fire of conventional "expressivity" for the regulated perdurable heat of a deliberate form built to weather the elements.

The manner is measured, the subject matter is not; the control, the dry reserve, and the stored resonance keep elegant check on the odd and turbulent narrative events. The story may not be the boldest or most ambitious of Kleist's work—it is among the earliest of his tales, written in 1808, three years before he committed suicide at age thirty-four—but it is in almost every other way a small masterpiece. For this reason, you can be assured that the following brief resumé of the plot is especially barbarous.

The marquise, a young widow of the highest character and principle, with several children, mysteriously and absurdly finds herself pregnant without the slightest notion of how or why, or most puzzling, who. She announces her condition in the newspaper and asks the unknown father to come forward and identify himself. Here the tale drifts back a few months to an attack on the citadel commanded by her father during which a member of the opposition, a brave and impetuous Russian count, also of the highest character, saves her from rape at the hands of his men. Some time after, the count reappears at her home and proposes marriage. The abruptness of the offer stuns the marquise and her parents, who send the strange and attractive young man away with a promise to consider his offer. At this point, what has been a suspicion for several months becomes a certainty: The marquise is pregnant. She is banished from the home, but shortly after her advertisement appears, her parents—now convinced of her innocence and in the teeth of a scandal—bring her back in two remarkable reconciliation scenes. The count returns, but this time in answer to the request made in the newspaper: On the night of the siege, after she had fainted from exhaustion, he himself had taken advantage of her. The marquise flees in horror from the man she once thought to be an "angel" but now considers a "devil." They are married but live apart while the count patiently courts her all over again. One year after the birth of their son, and after the gift of the count's will leaving his fortune to the child and its mother, he is finally and joyfully embraced by his wife, and they celebrate a second wedding, "happier than the first."[5]

Most readers seem to agree about the entrancements of this work, but few come together over its meaning. It is characteristic of Kleist's vision that it can be read in opposite ways at once. The tale is both charmer and baffler, both noble and ironic, cynical and idealizing, something of a fairy tale and something of its op-

[5] Heinrich von Kleist, "The Marquise of O . . ." in *The Marquise of O and Other Stories,* translated by David Luke and Nigel Reeves, Penguin, New York, 1978, p. 113. Subsequent reference to this edition will appear in the text.

posite. (One early judge deemed it a work "of great moral dignity." Thomas Mann thought it "crassly realistic."[6]) Kleist's moral and philosophic stance plants itself firmly at the center of mystery and paradox, of yoked antinomies and swift somersaults of logic and behavior. *The Marquise of O . . .* locks together savior and rapist, angel and devil, pregnant widow and immaculate virgin, loving devotion and guilty conscience, lofty ideals and hysterical repression; that is, a world of romantic heroism and one of abrasive psychology, a world long gone and one still present.

Rohmer's film, however, is somewhat different: The Kleistian letter, as already noted, has been followed wherever possible, but the spirit has been modulated gently but appreciably. The play of paradox and irony is eminently present, but the clash of opposing forces is everywhere less urgent and divisive; gone too is that "unconditional striving" that Goethe deplored but we now admire in Kleist. As against Rohmer's blendings and equilibrations, the scale of Kleistian contradiction is more extreme and exacerbated, at once more idealizing and more unreasonable, more exalted and more neurotic. His style is harder, faster, and frostier than Rohmer's, his transitions more abrupt, his climaxes more vehement, his syntactical gait—the famous long, long sentences autocratically marshaling mobs of parenthetical and dependent clauses, bristling antagonists clenched in an iron fist—more anxious and precipitous. For instance, when the count rescued the marquise from her assailants, "he smashed the hilt of his sword into the face of one of the murderous brutes, who still had his arm around her slender waist, and the man reeled back with blood pouring from his mouth; he then addressed the lady politely in French, offered her his arm . . ." ("The Marquise of O . . ., pp. 69–70) and so on. The distance here between violence and civility pivots around a semicolon (as it does in the original German). In Rohmer, the scuffle takes place in the middle distance in a single shot; there is no sword hilt, no bloody mouth, no close-up, no conversation. The attackers disperse into the darkness, and the count helps the marquise to her feet. The scene is staged effectively; Kleist's antithesis is present in the action, but the cool stasis of the camera angle has softened the edges of its oppositions. The following example, how-

[6] Mann, op. cit., p. 20.

ever, is more than a detail: Upon being escorted to safety, the marquise faints, and it is clear from Kleist's presentation that the count takes her immediately. In Rohmer, after administering a sleeping potion (this change, according to the director, to satisfy the credulity of a modern audience), the count leaves, waits, then returns later that evening to satisfy his desire. The change isn't an egregious one, but it's characteristic of the film's general ambience; Rohmer's hero is more calculating and self-conscious than Kleist's, that is, more like a Rohmer hero.

I'm talking about differences now, not diminishments. It is only fitting that despite his expressed intentions, Eric Rohmer hasn't resisted the perfectly natural (and artistic) impulse, conscious or unconscious, to be himself. His project really isn't the fanciful (and impossible) one of turning himself into Kleist, but the realistic (and attainable) one of rendering Kleist's language, motif, and dialectic in his own careful, tender, wry, and sophisticated way. Collateral to his special treatment of Kleist's language, his visual style derives from the neoclassical art of Kleist's period, an art of clarity, simplicity, reasoned symmetry, and boxlike perspective— qualities not precisely analogous to Kleist's grave tumult but obviously deeply sympathetic to Rohmer's temperament and personal assessment of his subject.[7] And this art has inspired Rohmer to some of his loveliest colors, compositions, and stagings. His visual pallette is one of great delicacy, airiness, and serenity, a restful buoyancy of Empire tonalities (off-white and ivory, pearl-gray, turquoise, sea and midnight green, and occasionally deep-shadowed royal reds). Following neoclassical tradition, he stylizes the movements of his actors in terms of line so that their bodies stand free and clear of the surrounding space and secure their own visual rhythm. When the rapists, for example, seize the marquise, she rises (wonderfully) on her slippered toes, throws her head back,

[7] Rohmer doesn't imitate, he alludes: There is the ghost of David's *Madame Récamier* (the marquise reclining on her couch); a posture from Fuseli's *The Nightmare* (on the night of the rape, a dreaming marquise turning in her bed with raised knee and arms outstretched behind her head); a bit of set design from Fragonard's *The Bolt* (the disciplined negligence of the red velvet canopy above the bed in the citadel); a canvas studied by Rohmer's actors; and figural reference to the portraiture of Ingres and the court painting of Goya (tight shots of the marquise and her family, singly and in groups, seated in direct frontal position; sometimes a scarf, a cloak, or a mantilla tracing the line of a female arm and furled about a crooked elbow).

Using a visual style derived from the neoclassical art of Kleist's period, Rohmer in *The Marquise of O . . .* sees to it that the body of actress Edith Clever stands clear of the surrounding visual space. *Photo courtesy of New Line Cinema*

and arches her chest outward—a posture midway between a straining, feathered thing trapped in flight and a figurehead on the prow of galleon. Or even more remarkable, when the doctor sarcastically informs her of her pregnancy, the marquise rushes toward the camera from deep space, pauses frame left, wavers, then veers sharply to the right and in one motion flings herself toward the couch and slips to one knee, face in hands, trunk, nape, and head flowing into a single, continuous curve of grief—an ironic Niobe on an ancient frieze. Naturalistic gestures keep flowering in this sudden way into abstract ones: Rohmer's articulation of plastic form characteristically transforms singular motions into enlarged, clarified, classical shapes that have the power of generalizations, of publicly recognizable expressions of private emotion, of sensual, pictorial appeals to intellectual concepts.

The compositional strategy here is so orderly that any disruption of its pliant geometry becomes doubly expressive, a toned-down version of Kleistian shock. Once you get used to a recurrence of stable, rectilinear designs—particularly the frequent scroll-like arrangements of figure and furniture in a single line along the frontal plane parallel to the lens, as in a bas-relief—any movement to and from deep space or along the diagonal becomes notably stressful (as in the abortive escape from the citadel, an oblique trek of the marquise and her party into a darkening funnel of space). Once you accept the equipoise of a stationary camera and the medium-full shot as a norm, any single cut to a long view or a close-up (like the face of a languid servant announcing the name of the count in answer to the advertisement) or any single tracking motion (the camera advancing toward the count like an accusatory finger before his rape of the marquise) restores a thrilling resonance to these primary techniques that lesser directors usually neutralize through overuse.

These orderings and disorderings, harmonies and arrestments, are more than a matter of good "conservative" filmmaking; they are central to Rohmer's reading of Kleist, the formal correlatives of the tension between an idealized shaping of experience and the unreasonable and uncontrollable surgings within experience itself. Rohmer has understood that the problem posed by Kleist's tale does not depend upon the identity of the "unknown" father, that the tale is emphatically not a whodunit. Both story and film make it abundantly clear at the outset (through a number of pointedly unsubtle hints) that it is the count alone who is responsible for the marquise's dilemma.[8] The real problem—and the film's rich humor hinges upon this—is why the marquise and her family take so long to realize what has been made plain to the audience almost all along, why they continue to overlook not just the most obvious suspect, but for all intents and purposes the *only* suspect. "The count," cries the marquise (in the film), "is above reproach." Her exalted version of the world will filter experience only in terms of

[8] One of the film's very few vague and indecisive gestures is the shot of the young servant Leopoldo staring at the marquise in the cellar after her rescue (not in Kleist). Since neither the stare nor any similar visual insinuation recurs, Leopoldo's claim on our suspicions seems rather equivocal. Rohmer may simply have wanted to establish his presence early to prepare us for the mother's use of him in her plan to test the marquise's innocence.

inflationary and absolutist categories; thus, she persists in viewing the count as a figment of high romance—first as "angel" only, then "devil" only. Her happiness at the end is predicated on her acceptance of "angel" and "devil" conjoined in a single spirit, of paradox and human complication, of a full humanity. She is neither dolt nor naif, but rather unyieldingly high-minded. Her problem then is one of epistemology, and the narrative itself becomes a critical inquiry into the contradictory nature of a romantic (even quixotic) ordering of experience.

It is to Rohmer's credit that he does not make the marquise and her family *too* rigid; they are kind, courteous, hospitable, and dignified; the marquise herself has great charm. But they are also insular, overcivilized, and stiff with attenuated principle, and the film associates them with insulated interiors (slammed doors, walled barriers), fastidious geometric groupings (pyramids, rectangles, etc.), and most concretely, with the sedentary position. Rohmer depicts their removal from reality by means of a wonderful touch (not in Kleist): We first see mother and daughter at the beginning of the siege seated in a chamber of the citadel, their figures in profile, their heads bent, caught in a kind of trancelike slumber, a family of Sleeping Beauties. Suddenly there is the sound of an explosion, and a plume of smoke waves across the upper half of the image—both women snap to attention. A bit later, the morning after the rape, there is another crack of gunfire, and the sleeping marquise also bolts upright in her bed (as outside a firing squad dispatches her would-be assailants). This "explosive" reality, the world "outside," is the domain of the count, and he is associated with abrupt intrusions, segregated spaces (in his conversation with the family, he is often framed alone), and illegal entries (he is first seen in the attack on the citadel, jumping off a wall against a fiery sky; later he jumps another wall when he breaks in upon the marquise at her country estate). Everytime he bursts in upon them, the family reacts with shock and disbelief; invariably they start back in their chairs, and invariably someone rises (usually the father, who then asks the count to "sit down"). Everytime he takes leave of them, either immediately or shortly thereafter, the marquise changes her residence (three times actually, from the citadel to the town to the country and back to the town) as if to reconstitute her position against him and fortify

herself all over again. Each time the family regroups, and each
time the insistent Russian comes at them. His allegorical function
is of course to shake them from their "trance," to stir them to deep
passion; their function, on the other hand, is to accommodate him
to their lives, to "civilize" him (make him "sit down"). At the
final fadeout, he enters the world of the marquise by joining her on
the couch, and she enters his by throwing her arms about his
neck.

He not only compels the marquise to reach out to him, but just
as important, his impetuous, even improper behavior teaches the
members of her family how to reach out to each other. It is the
count's pivotal adventure with the "swan" that summarizes the
central experience of the characters (transposed by Rohmer from
the middle of Kleist's story to the end of the film to give it climactic significance). The count tells the marquise how as a boy he
watched a swan swimming about and threw mud at it, how it dived
beneath the surface of the waves and then rose up again washed
clean by the water, and how he then knew he was in love with the
swan. The tale is a parable of how the count's initial lust has
turned to love, a Black Forest variant of the orthodox Christian
"fortunate fall" that conceives sin as a prelude to grace and
wounding as necessary to healing. (The fall and rise of the swan
translates graphically into the many falling and rising gestures that
occur throughout the film; often, the marquise protests her innocence on her knees, and in the latter third of the work, mother,
father, and count "go down" before her and beg forgiveness.)
Each of the major characters defiles either another or himself, and
in so doing achieves emotional release and discovers in himself
fresh and hitherto-unknown reserves of courage, love, and devotion. A raging father threatens his daughter with a pistol and
throws her out of his house before weeping and taking her on his
knee. A cunning mother lies to her daughter to test her innocence
before falling at her feet in contrition. And the marquise herself
makes a glowing virtue of her shame by choosing the condition of
an "outcast" and electing to raise her fatherless, unborn child in
defiant solitude beyond the protective bounds of family and com-
munal sanction.

In this respect, The Marquise of O . . . is a great family romance
and particularly marvelous in its depiction of the reunion of the

family triad on a plane of "higher innocence." The reconciliation of mother and daughter—with the mother kneeling to the daughter, the daughter to the mother, and both rising together amid happy tears—is a magnificent one in both film and book. And the reconciliation of father and daughter, and then all three reunited at the table (the return of the prodigal child to the equally prodigal parents), is in Kleist a scene of shocking bliss. The mother rejoices to discover the father "kissing his daughter's mouth in indescribable ecstasy," and when she leads them to the table, they follow "like a pair of betrothed lovers" (pp. 107–108).

After reading this extraordinary passage with its amalgam of disturbing and joyous, incestuous, and ennobled emotion, some may feel that the same scene in the film, wonderfully affecting though it may be, is by comparison a bit coarse-grained, smarmy, and sentimental. Some may feel that by planting a young girl in the lap of an elderly, white-haired gentleman and having him eagerly kiss her mouth, Rohmer turns his audience into voyeurs. Kleist's medium, of course, is the abstract one of language, and we don't actually see anything in the physical sense; the graphic and material crust of the scene has been burnt away, leaving us to imagine it in the mind's eye. A lover of Kleist may feel that Rohmer—despite all his appeals to the literary and the verbal—simply by making any kind of a film out of this story has restored the material crust and presented to the eye what should be left to the mind alone.

I would not deny the truth of this (it is to some degree true of any film of any novel), but neither do I really want to endorse it. If one knows and admires the scene in Kleist, one is bound to find something to complain about in Rohmer's treatment of it. But if one only knows the scene in Rohmer, one would be pressed to imagine many things as moving or as gratifying. Kleist's tale is one of the great ones, but Rohmer's film is a pleasure too, a qualitatively different kind of pleasure, but one that only the most compartmentalized of minds would disvalue.

In order to *understand* a movie, we want to know everything we possibly can about it, everything about Rohmer's film and everything about its source. But in order to *judge* the quality of a movie, we finally and frankly need only the movie. Whether a film has been faithful or unfaithful to the original novel has finally little or nothing to do with its success or failure as a film. One's emotion at a film is unique; you won't get this emotion from any other film, and you won't get it from the story or play the film was based on. And it is indivisible; you don't start parsing its causes while it is happening. (It hardly matters that after this emotion has been spent, we learn that it was produced not by something Rohmer had done but something that was done by Kleist, or perhaps the cameraman, Nestor Almendros, or perhaps the superb actress, Edith Clever). As it happens, Rohmer has shown enormous respect for Kleist, but what must finally matter even more is the respect he has poured into his film. And even if he had loved Kleist less in order to love his film more, that love too would have gone to the right place.

MICHAEL WOOD

THE CORRUPTION OF ACCIDENTS
Buñuel's *That Obscure Object of Desire* (1977)

from the novel The Woman and the Puppet
by Pierre Louÿs

Spain, "*cette terre encore primitive,*" had a certain vogue in France in the nineteenth century, from Mérimée to Gautier, and from Debussy to Ravel. It meant, usually, Granada and Seville, orange trees, boleros, secret gardens, southern nights, gypsies, guitars, castanets, and abrupt, capricious passions unknown to the colder civilizations of the north. It meant dark-eyed, dark-haired beauties, to the point that a character in Flaubert's *Éducation Sentimentale* (1869) can claim to be tired of them: "*Assez d'Andalouses sur la pelouse!*" ("Enough, Andalousian women on the lawn!"). The hero of Pierre Louÿs's *La Femme et le Pantin*, (*The Woman and the Puppet*), published in 1898, is so entirely caught in this dusky Iberian fantasy that he regrets never having had a blond mistress, inadvertently suggesting a title to Luis Buñuel as he does so: "I will never have known the pale objects of desire." Buñuel's *Cet Obscur Objet du Désir* (*That Obscure Object of Desire*; 1977) is described as "*inspiré par*" Louÿs's novel.

La Femme et le Pantin is a late, elegant, slightly febrile contribution to the mythology. Mérimée's (and Bizet's) Carmen becomes Concha, and she is very young, almost an anticipation of Lolita. She is a virgin, that dream of possessive Don Juans, that mirage of a girl who would be neither a whore nor your wife nor the wife of somebody else: undiscovered country. She flaunts her

The material used here appeared in a different form in the *New York Review of Books* (February 23, 1978). Reprinted with permission. Copyright © 1978, Nyrev, Inc.

virginity in front of Don Mateo, the hapless, aging hero of this story; offers it to him and holds him at bay since she knows he can't have what he wants without simultaneously losing it. She undresses in front of him but won't sleep with him; gets into bed with him but is wearing an intricate, impenetrable corset. At this moment the mirage becomes nightmare, and the corset signals the end of Mateo's youth because he thinks all women now, for him, will wear such corsets, or will want to: "That corset, that barrier between love and me, it seemed to me that from then on I would see it on all women . . .".

The nightmares multiply. Concha dances nude for a group of tourists, her virginity still intact but somehow scattered. She makes love to someone else before Mateo's horrified eyes, her virginity given to a handsome young fellow who is everything Mateo is not, or is no longer. Mateo beats her, and this, it turns out, is what she wanted all along. She grovels in delight and confesses she was faking with the young man, solely to torment Mateo. This unlikely story happens to be true. Mateo takes her, and the two embark together on a long life of misery and mutual torture—Concha inventing infidelities, and sometimes actually performing them, so that Mateo will knock her about when she comes home. But if she likes punishment, Louÿs says, she also likes the crime, not for the pleasure it gives her but for the pain it causes others: "Her role in life ended there: to sow suffering and watch it grow." All of this, in one form or another, finds its way into Buñuel's movie, along with a great deal of verbatim quotation from the Louÿs text.

As masculine terror sprung to life, as a figment escaped from Mateo's shaky psyche, Louÿs's Concha is very persuasive. As a woman, of course, she is merely a familiar scapegoat, bearing the blame for all the male anxieties which victimize her, and *La Femme et le Pantin,* unfortunately, is more interested in the scapegoat than the terror. Indeed, it identifies the terror only to pile it up on the scapegoat. Mateo's beating Concha is a particularly murky subject in this context. In one sense, this is Concha's greatest victory and Mateo's greatest humiliation: A Spanish gentleman, a royalist and a romantic, is forced, repeatedly, to hit a woman—the disgrace is far worse than anything else that happens to him. Yet even the phrasing I've just used shows what a strange proposition this is. It's not happening to him, it's happening to her, and beneath the subtle issue of broken masculine honor lies a crude and ugly old doctrine: Women can be kept in their place only by force; what's more, they like it that way.

Buñuel has long admired the work of Pierre Louÿs, especially his *Trois Filles et Leur Mère,* a delicately pornographic book much cherished by André Breton and the Surrealists. For a powerfully original moviemaker, Buñuel works relatively rarely from original scripts. Of his thirty-two films, only eleven are *not* based on previously existing works, and those eleven are full of allusions and borrowed themes. Even *Los Olvidados* (1950), Buñuel says with a smile, lifts part of its plot from *Rigoletto.* What this means is that Buñuel tends to *find* his films—in novels, plays, jokes, news stories, old anecdotes—rather than making them up. He cuts away and/or replaces everything that is not to his purpose, but he generally retains a great deal of his source—this is the case even with *Belle de Jour* (1967), a novel by Joseph Kessel which seemed to Buñuel stale and faded but tempting because of the film hiding in it, rather as figures hide in the sculptor's stone. *La Femme et le Pantin,* I gather, did not seem stale or faded to Buñuel, but it was still only a beginning for a film; the film had to be freed, so to speak, from the text.

Buñuel wrote a script based on the Louÿs novel for a French producer in 1957. The film must have been thoroughly freed, since the producer, according to Francisco Aranda, gave up the project as being "pure Buñuel," not an adaptation of Louÿs at all. A version of the novel, using its title and starring Brigitte Bardot, was directed by Julien Duvivier in 1959.

But Buñuel, even then, had an illustrious predecessor. Joseph von Sternberg's *The Devil Is a Woman* (1935)—the last film he made with Marlene Dietrich, the end of a series which contained *The Blue Angel* (1930), *Morocco* (1930), *Dishonored* (1931), *Shanghai Express* (1932), *Blonde Venus* (1932), and *The Scarlet Empress* (1934)—was also based on the Louÿs novel. And it was "pure Sternberg" in a way which makes Buñuel's film seem almost fanatically faithful to the book. Perhaps I may add, for what it's worth, that in Buñuel's *Simon del Desierto* (1965) the devil *is* a woman, played by Silvia Pinal.

Sternberg's film offers crowds, a carnival, masks, silhouettes, Rimsky-Korsakov; complicated, constricting sets, all blinds and shutters and fragile, slatted doors; torrential rain, umbrellas, a duel in a downpour, the climate and atmosphere of a universal, nameless tropic; and above all Dietrich, the lucid, calculating, spectacular monarch of all this. Dietrich looks about as Spanish as the Snow Queen. Concha here ceases to be a child or a sadist and becomes simply a remarkable woman who likes power and is entertained by weakness in others. No question of virginity here— she has another lover and shows him to Don Mateo (here called Don Pascual). Money, important in Louÿs, is essential in Sternberg; that is why Dietrich is bothering with her puppet-admirer at all. She needs the funds he provides.

She is regally, cynically insincere. "As I write this," she says, "my heart is bleeding, and my eyes are filled with tears." She is not writing, she is dictating to a scribe; her eyes are clear and dry, she wears a faint pout of contempt, and her heart, we may be sure, is unscratched and all her own. "That woman," Don Pascual says later, in a line which von Sternberg (or Dos Passos, who receives a writing credit) ought to have resisted, "has ice where others have a heart." And in one wonderful moment, where the whole cruel myth flashes out, she is fussing with her hair, abstracted, busy, indifferent. Her distraught admirer says, "Concha, I love you. Life without you means nothing." Dietrich, without turning her head or ceasing to dab at her hair, says in her slightly metallic voice, "One moment, and I'll give you a kiss. . . ."

What men seem to want in this fantasy is not to be ill-treated but to be ignored. The turn in the myth comes when Concha is shown to have a warm heart after all. A duel is added to the Louÿs story. Don Pascual, an excellent shot, able to put a bullet through the corner of a playing card at some distance, doesn't even fire in defense of his life; he is hurt; and Concha, touched by such perfect devotion, leaves his rival and returns to spend the rest of her days with her damaged and aging but victorious hero.

At least, this is what the plot says. Dietrich's face and manner say something else altogether more oblique and interesting. When she visits her wounded lover in the hospital, he is still angry and refuses her the forgiveness she asks. He growls, "Are you going, or do I have to call one of the orderlies?" She says, "I'm going," moves to the door, opens it, looks at the figure on the bed, pretends to close the door, but stands there contemplating what we

Buñuel's film adaptation of
Louÿs's *The Woman and
the Puppet* was called *That
Obscure Object of Desire*
and made use of two Con-
chas. The first, played by
Carole Bouquet, enters the
life of Mathieu (Fernando
Rey) with roses. The sec-
ond Concha (Angela Mo-
lina) is a more sultry type.

are supposed to realize is her changed life. Now she knows how much he loves her, her icy heart has thawed, and she's decided to come back to him for keeps. But we can't really *see* any of this. Dietrich in close-up looks like Dietrich, not like a woman whose heart is thawing. She looks remote, intelligent, amused, beautiful, poised, and scheming. She is doing sums in her head, grinning delicately as she ponders what is worth what. This shot, held for a long time, makes nonsense of what the movie wants to say, but it is unforgettable. Dietrich, in the midst of this messy mythology, reclaims her privacy and makes her own choices. It's just that we don't know what she chooses, or why. Rita Hayworth, later, was able occasionally to get something of this effect on the screen. But one never felt she was *really* making choices, and she couldn't prevent the mythology from spilling over into her life.

The descendant of Dietrich (and Bardot) in Buñuel's version of the Louÿs novel, when he finally got to make it, was to have been Maria Schneider. Early in the shooting she was replaced not by another woman but by *two* women, Carole Bouquet and Angela Molina, who play Concha in alternating appearances: the first French, quiet, slender, mocking, perhaps cruel; the second Spanish, sultry, dark, dull, and no sort of actress at all. The reasons for this trick are no doubt playful rather than profound, and the general, floating effect is splendid. The terrible Concha—the *femme* who used to be so *fatale*—is reduced to a series of switches; she is now one girl, now the other, and the lovelorn Don Mateo (here a dapper Frenchman called Mathieu Fabert, played with wit and fussy charm by Fernando Rey) doesn't even notice the difference. Not only that, the *film* doesn't notice the difference. Both girls are called Concha, live in the same places, wear the same (or nearly the same) clothes, have the same mother, and have the same voice on the sound track. Only moviegoers, trained to attend carefully to appearances, to look for the actress behind the role, see any of this. The message of the trick, insofar as it has a message beyond its discreet intention to unsettle audiences a bit, is sly and double. Women, it suggests, are such abstractions for men that it doesn't matter what they look like as long as they are properly attractive, show up in the right places, and answer to the right names. Furthermore, men are actually interested in only one part of a woman's anatomy—the dark object of desire, which is one meaning of the French title of the movie—so no wonder the rest of her body and her life is out of focus.

Still, we shouldn't overread this improvised joke. Jokes in Buñuel, for reasons I shall return to, are generally part of a war on excesses of meaning. The twin Conchas do not represent different aspects of a single woman, or shifting perceptions of her by Mateo-Mathieu. The alternation between the actresses is governed by a careful avoidance of significance. But this elusive, vanishing heroine—vanishing repeatedly from Mathieu's life, vanishing constantly into her own other avatar—does help us see the distance which separates Buñuel from both von Sternberg and Louÿs. Buñuel's Concha is a projection of masculine terror too, but she is not a scapegoat, and she is not an incarnation of icy indifference. When she says she is not interested in money, or that she hates what she is doing to Mathieu as much as he does, we believe her, or almost. She says the same thing in Louÿs and is unmistakably lying. In Buñuel she is not *unmistakably* anything, and even her mystery is different from Dietrich's. Dietrich is mysterious because she has her reasons, which the film knows nothing of; Bouquet and Molina are mysterious because they don't really make up a person at all, merely a subtle sketch of a person, blurred by Mathieu's clinging needs. For Buñuel, both men and women are trapped in their desire and are to be observed with an uninterfering lucidity which is itself a form of compassion.

But men are what he knows about; men and their dreams, their anxious longing for the Conchas of the world. The more one sees Buñuel's film, the more clearly it becomes a film about Mathieu. Of course, even dreams have histories, and even the joke of using the two actresses is clouded by an old prejudice since together the girls seem to offer a picture of the perfect man-eater: French and ironic, Spanish and steamy, all rolled into one by the zigzagging of the viewer's (and director's) mind. Toward the end, when Mathieu follows Concha to Seville, the film lapses into a rather dutiful rehearsal of Louÿs's material, which loses both Louÿs's and Buñuel's most interesting preoccupations in the process. Concha is now plainly witch and tormentress, dances nude for the tourists, fornicates on the floor in front of Mathieu, is beaten, and follows Mathieu back to Paris. There is very little mystery or subtlety here, very little more than the worn stereotype of a woman ruining a poor old chap who simply wanted to get into bed with her. I don't know whether Buñuel lost interest in his film or fell himself into the mythology he had played with so brilliantly for the film's first hour.

Pauline Kael (*The New Yorker,* December 19, 1977) was right to speak of the "relaxed virtuosity" of Buñuel's late films, beginning with *Le Charme Discret de la Bourgeoisie* (1972), and she may have been right to speak of serenity. Certainly Buñuel was less angry by then than he had been in *Los Olvidados* and *El Angel Exterminador* (1962). But he has always been serene in one sense—able to treat excruciating subjects as if they belonged to someone he knew rather well, but was not himself—and the precise quality of the late films is very hard to describe. *Cet Obscur Objet du Désir*, for example, returns us very directly to *Viridiana* (1961) and *Tristana* (1970): same immaculate actor, Fernando Rey, in all three cases; same obsessive problem—the encroaching, enclosing desire of an older man for a younger woman. In *Viridiana* the woman refuses the man, and he commits suicide. In *Tristana* she accepts him, and they live meanly ever after, she ensnared in her inescapable hatred for him, he crippled and aged by his never-ending desire for her. In *Cet Obscur Objet,* the girl neither rejects nor accepts the man, and they seem set up for a life of cruelty and feuding close to that of *Tristana*. Of course, we can't simply attribute all this anxiety to Buñuel, but he surely understands it, and into the most beautiful of the Sevillian scenes of this late film he drops the information, passed on to Mathieu by his misogynist manservant, that someone or other is in the habit of calling women "sacks of excrement."

That doesn't sound too serene. On the other hand, the complicated joke lurking in the genealogy of *Cet Obscur Objet* suggests fairly relaxed notions, at least about some matters. This is a displaced Spaniard's film based on a dilettante Frenchman's novel about Spain—a situation reflected in the film itself by Buñuel's turning Louÿs's Spanish central character into a Frenchman, but then having him played by a Spaniard and dubbed, for good measure, by yet another Frenchman. Buñuel has not lived in Spain since 1936, and has shot only two films and part of a third in Spain since then.

The self-parody in *Cet Obscur Objet* also suggests a reasonably equable view of a past career. In *Viridiana* a girl lectures an older man on his concern for others—he dips a stick into a water butt and fishes out a bee before it drowns. A young man seduces an older woman, and the camera cuts away brusquely to a cat pouncing on a rat. There is a certain impatience in these images, and they are too clumsy to be thought of as artful symbolism. But they do mean what they seem to mean, and they are not jokes. In *Cet Obscur Objet*, Mathieu tries to buy Concha from her pious mother; when the mother asks him if he intends to marry her daughter, we hear a loud, sudden click. A moment later the manservant comes in, takes a patently rubber mouse out of a trap, and mutters words to the effect that this one won't be running around at night any more. A few scenes later, in a bar, there is a fly in Mathieu's drink, and the waiter says he's pleased that they've finally caught it. Both images reflect Mathieu's pursuit of Concha, obviously, although the mouse in the trap appears also to be a picture of Mathieu's idea of marriage; for that matter, he is closer to drowning in his feelings than she is. But the principal effect is simply comic: an allusion to *Viridiana*, if we remember it; a gag about Buñuel's mannerisms, or perhaps about the whole question of meaning in movies, if we don't.

One of the chief tensions in all Buñuel's films, part of his legacy from Surrealism, is that between the lives people live and the stories they tell, or to put it slightly differently, between the things that happen and the meanings that people ascribe to them. At the heart of Surrealism is a flight from meaning, a yearning for pure, unarranged chaos. But every gesture we make, every speech, every object we point a finger or a camera at, is already part of a universe of discourse, enrolled in a grammar of associations and exclusions. The most we can hope for is to pry a few words or objects loose for a moment, suspend briefly the long dominion of significance. Buñuel approaches this problem in different ways in different films, and one of the reasons Carole Bouquet is so good in *Cet Obscur Objet* is that she joins a whole company of Buñuel enigmas, bids for chaos that wobble back toward meaning. She is not simply another icon of woman-as-mystery.

In spite of the anxiety that kicks up from the central theme at times, *Cet Obscur Objet* feels relaxed because Buñuel here, as in his last few films, is less worried, more amused by the inevitable

THE CORRUPTION OF ACCIDENTS

victory of interpretation over life. Why does a man cross the screen carrying a sack early in the film? Why does the same man, transplanted from Seville to Paris, appear again, carrying what seems to be the same sack? Why does Mathieu show up in one scene carrying this sack? Why does he take it with him when he goes out to dinner? Why does it appear in the window of a shop in a Paris arcade? Does it have anything to do with the sacks of excrement already mentioned? I don't think these questions need an answer. What is important is to understand how the possibility of a meaning for this sack *spoils* its gratuitous presence in the film as an *objet trouvé (et retrouvé)*: an obscure objet of the kind André Breton scoured Paris for in *Nadja*. The very possibility of a meaning ruins a certain form of freedom, and it is this ruin and this freedom which Buñuel wishes us to contemplate. He offers neither nostalgia nor wisdom, but an engaging practical example of the art of accepting defeat without learning to expect it.

Accidents in Buñuel, a Surrealist manifesto in support of *L'Age d'Or* (1930) said, "remain uncorrupted by plausibility." They do, until they are swallowed up in stories, which are always agents of the plausible. We all love stories, and no one more than Buñuel. Yet stories carry the disease of meaning in a particularly virulent form, and Buñuel's task has often been to peddle stories while keeping them from signifying.

In Louÿs and von Sternberg, Mateo (Pascual) told his story to a young man as a warning against Concha, an attempt to save him from her wiles. The moral was that such warnings always go unheard—in these matters no one's experience counts but our own. The story's meaning was clear enough, but its usefulness was in doubt. In Buñuel's films, there is no young man to be warned, even in vain. Mathieu is telling his story to a group of traveling companions on a train because they want to know why he has just poured a bucket of water over a young woman's head. "You will agree that it's better to soak someone than to kill them," he says, and then regales them with his yarn—Concha, of course, is the girl he's just drenched, "the worst of women," he insists.

This is a parody of narrative convention—travelers settling in for a long trip, all French, all neighbors and friends of friends, happy at the prospect of a juicy tale—but it does prop up the narrative of the film. What happens is that the story told and the story in the telling just can't be thought of together. After Mathieu ends his account of the night of the corset, for example—we have just seen Concha naked in his arms, wearing her gruesome piece of tightly knotted armor—suddenly we are back in the train compartment, watching Mathieu tell his tale. His adult hearers are all agog, and two children stand in the doorway, eager for more. The adults then notice the children and send them away, and Mathieu apologizes gracefully, modestly: "And yet I don't think I said anything improper or indiscreet. . . ."

There is no way in which Mathieu's evident sincerity can be made to correspond to the spicy story he is recounting. How can he have told it properly, discreetly? The feat is unimaginable, not meant to be imagined. What we must imagine instead is a yawning, comic gulf between experience and all renderings of it.

Stories are often a form of explanation, as Mathieu's is, and explanations are among Buñuel's favorite targets. "There are no accidents in the unconscious," a dwarf psychologist says in *Cet Obscur Objet,* paraphrasing Freud. But all the dwarf is saying is that Mathieu, having lost Concha and having sworn that he never wanted to see her again, went to Seville because he knew that was where Concha came from. Everyone understood that already, even Mathieu; the dwarf's pleased smile at his own expertise (he is a professor of psychology who gives "private lessons") is a mockery of knowingness.

But there is an element in the film that cannot be reclaimed by a story or recuperated for meaning, and that is a persistent, recurring terrorism, as frequent in Seville as it is in Lausanne or the French countryside. A car is blown up, a taxi is stolen, a power plant is bombed, men are shot in the street; characters speak of kidnappings, hijackings, guerilla activities; the film ends in an explosion which recalls the mushroom cloud at the close of Orson Welles's *The Trial* (1962).

At first, I thought all this was in part an elegant "translation" of the fireworks in Louÿs's novel, which is set in Carnival time in Seville. The notion seems (and is) fussy, but it is not fussier than finding a hint for a title in a phrase like *"ces pâles objets du désir."* I was certainly reluctant to accept the heavy-handed suggestion that appeared to be skulking in these images and events: political repression, like sexual repression, leads to explosion and nightmare. True enough, but a reduction of both politics and sexuality to far too simple a scheme.

Finally I came to feel that terrorism in the film represents an unmanageable normality, a world in which chaos as well as meaning could turn into tyranny. The terror is erratic, uncoordinated, uninterpretable, launched from right and left, a jumble of initials and nonsensical factions, horribly familiar, and part of daily life. A car explodes in Seville; Mathieu frowns, looks at his watch, irritated by the delay: Sudden death has become a traffic jam. Another character remarks that all this stuff—ransom, exchange of hostages, and so on—will soon be on the sports pages of the newspapers. And in this untidy form, terrorism is the world's incursion into the coherence of Mathieu's obsession, an envoy from contemporary reality, and a reminder that there are accidents everywhere—even, no doubt, in the unconscious. Buñuel, always one of the clearer-headed of the Surrealists, understands, of course, that accidents uncorrupted by plausibility may be truly terrifying and the reverse of what we actually desire.

Even so, we cannot welcome their corruption. *Cet Obscur Objet du Désir*, like most stories, finds out where it is going, even though it wanted to go nowhere. It becomes a film that can't continue, can't end, and can't go back to its beginning. Having taught us to suspect all explanations, it explains itself unconvincingly. When Mathieu pours the bucket of water on Concha, the gesture is funny and unforeseen. When she later appears with a bucket of water and pours it on him, we see not only her revenge but also the stealthy return of reliable meaning. Buckets of water make perfect sense if they are part of a ritual, steps in a dance of insult. They, and things like them, can almost be predicted, and all Buñuel's films finish, or should finish, when they start to look so plausible.

Notes on the Contributors

DUDLEY ANDREW, Associate Professor of Comparative Literature, heads the film division at the University of Iowa. He has published *The Major Film Theories* and *André Bazin* with Oxford University Press.

PETER BRUNETTE teaches English and film at George Mason University and has written for film journals including *Film Quarterly*, *Film Criticism*, and *Cineaste*. He is working on a book on Roberto Rossellini.

BERNARD F. DICK is Professor of English and Comparative Literature at Fairleigh Dickinson University, Teaneck-Hackensack. He has published critical studies of William Golding, Mary Renault, and Gore Vidal as well as the film text *Anatomy of Film*. He is completing a book to be entitled *Lillian Hellman and Film*.

CHARLES EIDSVIK teaches film in the Drama department of the University of Georgia. He has published a book, *Cineliteracy* (1979), with Random House and has contributed articles to *Literature/Film Quarterly* and *Film Comment*.

JOHN L. FELL is Professor of Film at San Francisco State University. He is the author of *Film and the Narrative Tradition* (1974), *Film, an Introduction* (1975), and *A History of Films* (1979).

LINDLEY HANLON is Assistant Professor and Deputy Director of the Film Program at Brooklyn College of the City University of New York. She has published and lectured on French film, the avant-garde, and the theory and structure of narrative.

PETER HARCOURT currently teaches in the Film Studies Program at Carleton University, Ottawa. He is the author of *Six European Directors* and has published widely in journals such as *Film Quarterly*, *Film Comment*, and *Sight and Sound*.

ANDREW HORTON is Chairman of the Film Department at Brooklyn College. He has contributed articles to a variety of journals including *Cineaste*, *Literature/Film Quarterly*, and the *Journal of*

Popular Film. He is completing a book, *Comparative Cinema: Multi-national Approaches to Film.*

NEIL D. ISAACS is the author of fourteen books including *Fiction into Film: A Walk in the Spring Rain* (with Rachel Maddux's novella and Stirling Silliphant's screenplay). He is Consulting Editor on Film Books to The University of Tennessee Press, and an editoral board member for *Literature/Film Quarterly.*

MARSHA KINDER is Professor of Literature and Film at Occidental College. She co-authored *The Self and the Cinema: A Trans-Formalist Perspective* (1979) and *Close-Up: A Critical Perspective on Film* (1972), is a member of the editorial board of *Film Quarterly* and *Quarterly Review of Film Studies.*

T. JEFFERSON KLINE is Professor of French and Chairman of the Department of Modern Foreign Languages and Literatures at Boston University. He is the author of *André Malraux and the Metamorphosis of Death* (1973) and has published articles on Bertolucci in the *International Review of Psycho-Analysis* and other journals.

IRA KONIGSBERG is a Professor of English at the University of Michigan and teaches courses in literature and film. His books include *Samuel Richardson and the Dramatic Novel* (1968), *Critical Thinking* (co-edited, 1968), and *The Classic Short Story* (edited, 1971). He has completed a book on *Narrative Technique,* has begun a dictionary of cinematic terms for Macmillan, and will complete Yan Barna's biography of Erich von Stroheim.

BEN LAWTON is Assistant Professor of Italian literature and film in the department of Foreign Languages and Literatures at Purdue University. He is editor of *Film Studies Annual* and has published a number of articles on Italian literature and cinema. He is finishing a book on Italian neorealism.

JOAN MAGRETTA is the Director of the English Program at Transylvania University, where she teaches literature and film. Her work has appeared in *Film Quarterly,* *Literature/Film Quarterly,* *Studies in the Novel,* and *The Nathaniel Hawthorne Journal.*

WILLIAM R. MAGRETTA is an Assistant Professor of English at the University of Kentucky, where he teaches linguistics, semiology, and narrative analysis. His articles have been published in *Literature/Film Quarterly,* *Genre,* and *Film Quarterly.*

STUART Y. MCDOUGAL teaches modern literature and film at the University of Michigan. He is the author of *Ezra Pound and the Troubadour Tradition* and numerous articles on literature and film.

RUTH PRIGOZY is Associate Professor and former Chairperson of English at Hofstra University. She has published a variety of articles on Fitzgerald, Hemingway, and the modern novel, and has co-edited an anthology of short stories for Macmillan.

ALAN SPIEGEL is a member of the English faculty of the State University of New York at Buffalo, where he teaches courses in film and literature. He is the regular film critic for *Salmagundi* and author of *Fiction and the Camera Eye*, published by the University of Virginia Press.

BIRGITTA STEENE is Professor of Scandinavian and Comparative Literature at the University of Washington and Director of the University Cinema Studies Program. She is the author of a study of Ingmar Bergman and August Strindberg, and has contributed articles on film and modern drama to numerous journals.

ALAN WILLIAMS teaches in the Film Division at the University of Iowa. His articles on cinema have appeared in *Film Quarterly*, *Quarterly Review of Film Studies*, *Wide Angle*, and *Yale French Studies*. His *Max Ophuls and the Cinema of Desire* will be published by Arno Press under their "Dissertations on Film" series.

MICHAEL WOOD is Professor of English and Comparative Literature at Columbia University. He is the author of *Stendhal* (1971) and *America in the Movies* (1975), and is currently at work on a book on Luis Buñuel.

Sources for Films Listed
in Film Credits and Filmography

ACB
Art Cinema Booking Service
1501 Broadway
New York, New York 10036
(212) 947-2445

AUD
Audio-Brandon Films
34 MacQuesten Parkway South
Mount Vernon, New York 10550
(914) 664-5051
    or
1619 North Cherokee
Los Angeles, California 90028
(213) 463-0357
    or
3868 Piedmont Avenue
Oakland, California 94611
(415) 658-9890
    or
8400 Brookfield Avenue
Brookfield, Illinois 60513
(312) 485-3925

BI
Bauer International
19 North Bridge Street
Somerville, New Jersey 08876
(201) 526-5656

BUD
Budget Films
4590 Santa Monica Blvd.
Los Angeles, California 90029
(213) 660-0187

CIV
Cinema 5

595 Madison Avenue
New York, New York 10022
(212) 421-5555

CON
Contemporary Films/McGraw-
    Hill Films
Princeton Road
Hightstown, New Jersey 08520
(609) 448-1700
    or
1221 Avenue of the Americas
New York, New York 10020
    or
828 Custer Avenue
Evanston, Illinois 60202
(312) 869-5010
    or
1714 Stockton Street
San Francisco, California 94133
(415) 362-3115

COR
Corinth Films
410 East 62nd Street
New York, New York 10021
(212) 421-4770

CWF
Clem Williams Films, Inc.
2240 Nobleston Road
Pittsburgh, Pennsylvania 15205
(412) 921-5810
    or
5424 W. North Avenue
Chicago, Illinois 60639
(312) 637-3322

FI
Films Incorporated
35-01 Queens Blvd.
Long Island City, New York 11101
(212) 937-1110
        or
4420 Oakton Street
Skokie, Illinois 60076
(312) 676-1088
        or
offices in Atlanta, Boston, Dallas,
    Hollywood, Salt Lake City, and
    San Diego

HUR
Hurlock Cine World
13 Arcadia Road
Old Greenwich, Connecticut
    06870
(203) 637-4319

IVY
Ivy Films/16
165 W. 46th Street
New York, New York 10036
(212) 765-3940

JAN
Janus Films
745 Fifth Avenue
New York, New York 10022
(212) 753-7100

NLC
New Line Cinema
121 University Place
New York, New York 10003
(212) 674-7460

NYF
New Yorker Films

43 West 61st Street
New York, New York 10023
(212) 247-6110

SWA
Swank Motion Pictures
201 South Jefferson Avenue
St. Louis, Missouri 63166
(314) 534-6300

TWF
Trans-World Films
322 South Michigan Avenue
Chicago, Illinois 60604
(312) 922-1530

TWY
Twyman Films
329 Salem Avenue
Dayton, Ohio 45401
(513) 222-4014

UA
United Artists Sixteen
729 Seventh Avenue
New York, New York 10019
(212) 245-6000

WHO
Wholesome Film Center
20 Melrose Street
Boston, Massachusetts 02116
(617) 426-0155

WSA
Warner Brothers
Non-Theatrical Division
4000 Warner Blvd.
Burbank, California 91503
(213) 843-6000

Film Credits

Film Title	*La Symphonie Pastorale*
Date	1946
Producer	Films Gibe
Director	Jean Delannoy
Screenplay	Jean Aurenche and Pierre Bost (from the novel by André Gide)
Photography	Armand Thirard
Music	Georges Auric
Cast	Michele Morgan (Gertrude)
	Pierre Blanchar (Jean Martin, Pastor)
	Line Noro (Amelie, his wife)
	Jean Dessailly (Jacques)
	Andrée Clement (Piette)
	Louvigny (M. Castelan)
	Rosine Luguet (Charlotte)
	Albert Glade (Paul)
Length	105 minutes. Black and white.
Rental	Budget; Wholesome Film Center (subtitled)
Film Title	*Journal d'un Curé de Campagne* (*Diary of a Country Priest*)
Date	1951
Producer	Robert Sussfield and U.G.C.
Director	Robert Bresson
Screenplay	Robert Bresson (from the novel by Georges Bernanos)
Photography	Leonce-Henry Burel
Music	Jean-Jacques Grunewald
Cast	Claude Laydu (Priest)
	Nicole Maurey (Louise)
	Nicole Ladmiral (Chantal)
	Marie-Monique Arkell (Countess)
	Jean Riveyre (Count)
	Serge Bento (Mitonnet)
	Jean Danet (Olivier)
Length	116 minutes. Black and white.
Rental	Audio-Brandon
Film Title	*La Ronde*
Date	1959
Producer	Sacha Gordine

Director	Max Ophuls
Screenplay	Jacques Natanson and Max Ophuls (based on the play by Arthur Schnitzler)
Photography	Christian Matras
Music	Oscar Strauss
Cast	Simone Signoret (The Streetwalker)
	Anton Walbrook (The Raconteur)
	Simone Simon (The Parlormaid)
	Danielle Darrieux (The Married Women)
	Odette Joyeux (The Shopgirl)
	Isa Miranda (The Actress)
	Serge Reggiani (The Soldier)
	Daniel Gelin (The Student)
	Fernand Gravet (The Married Man)
	Jean-Louis Barrault (The Poet)
	Gérard Philipe (The Count)
Length	97 minutes. Black and white.
Rental	Janus Films (subtitled)

Film Title	*Les Liaisons Dangereuses 1960*
Date	1959
Producer	Les Films Marceau-Cocinor
Director	Roger Vadim
Screenplay	Roger Vadim, Roger Vailland, and Claude Brulé (from the novel by Choderlos de Laclos)
Photography	Marcel Gignon
Music	Thelonious Monk and Jack Murray (pseudonym)
Cast	Gérard Philipe (Valmont)
	Jeanne Moreau (Juliette)
	Jeanne Valerie (Cécile)
	Annette Vadim (Marianne)
	Simone Renant (Madame de Volanges)
	Jean-Louis Trintignant (Danceny)
Length	
Rental	None

Film Title	*Zazie dans le Métro (Zazie)*
Date	1960
Producer	Louis Malle, through Nouvelles Editions du Film
Director	Louis Malle
Screenplay	Louis Malle and Jean-Paul Rappeneau (from the novel by Raymond Queneau)
Photography	Henri Raichi
Music	Florenzo Carpi
Cast	Catherine Demongeot (Zazie)
	Philippe Noiret (Gabriel)
	Antoine Roblot (Charles)

Hubert Deschamps (Turandot)
Annie Fratellini (Mado P'tits-Pieds)
Clara Marlier (Albertine)
Vittorio Caprioli (Trouscaillon, alias Pedro-Surplus)
Length   85 minutes. Color.
Rental   New Yorker Films (subtitled)

Film Title	*La Ciociaria* (*Two Women*)
Date	1961
Producer	Carlo Ponti
Director	Vittorio De Sica
Screenplay	Cesare Zavattini (from the novel by Alberto Moravia)
Photography	Gabor Pogany
Music	Armand Travajoli
Cast	Sophia Loren (Cesira)
	Jean-Paul Belmondo (Michele)
	Eleonora Brown (Rosetta)
	Raf Vallone (Giovanni)
	Renato Salvatori (Florindo)
	Carlo Ninchi (Michele's father)
	Andrea Checchi (Fascist)
Length	105 minutes. Black and white.
Rental	Audio-Brandon Films (dubbed and subtitled versions)

Film Title	*Jules et Jim* (*Jules and Jim*)
Date	1961
Producer	Marcel Berbert and Les Films du Carosse/Sedif
Director	François Truffaut
Screenplay	François Truffaut and Jean Grauault (from the novel by Henri-Pierre Roché)
Photography	Raoul Coutard
Music	Georges Delerue
Cast	Jeanne Moreau (Catherine)
	Oscar Werner (Jules)
	Henri Serre (Jim)
	Marie Dubois (Therese)
	Vanna Urbino (Gilberte)
	Boris Bassiak (Albert)
	Sabine Haudepin (Sabine)
	and the voice of Michel Subor
Length	104 minutes. Black and white.
Rental	Janus Films (subtitled)

Film Title	*Le Mépris* (*Contempt*)
Date	1963
Producer	Georges de Beauregard, Carlo Ponti, and Joseph E. Levine

Director	Jean-Luc Godard
Screenplay	Jean-Luc Godard (from the novel *Il Disprezzo* [*A Ghost at Noon*] by Alberto Moravia)
Photography	Raoul Coutard
Music	Georges Delerue (Italian version, Piero Piccioni)
Cast	Brigitte Bardot (Camille Javal)
	Michel Piccoli (Paul Javal)
	Jack Palance (Jeremy Prokosch)
	Fritz Lang (Himself)
	Giorgia Moll (Francesca Vanini)
	Jean-Luc Godard (Assistant Director)
Length	99 minutes. Color.
Rental	Audio-Brandon (subtitled)

Film Title	*La Religieuse* (*The Nun*)
Date	1966
Producer	Georges de Beauregard
Director	Jacques Rivette
Screenplay	Jean Gruault and Jacques Rivette (from the novel by Denis Diderot)
Photography	Alan Levent
Music	Jean-Claude Eloy
Cast	Anna Karina (Suzanne Simonin)
	Micheline Presle (Mme de Moni)
	Liselotte Pulver (Mme de Chelles)
	Francine Bergé (Sister St. Christophe)
	Christine Lenier (Mme Simonin)
	Francisco Rabal (Dom Morel)
	Wolfgang Reichmann (Father Lemoine)
	Catherine Diamant (Sister St. Cécile)
	Yori Bertin (Sister St. Thérèse)
	Jean Martin (M. Hébert)
Length	140 minutes. Color.
Rental	Macmillan Films (subtitled)

Film Title	*Blow-Up*
Date	1966
Producer	Carlo Ponti
Director	Michelangelo Antonioni
Screenplay	Michelangelo Antonioni and Tonino Guerra; English dialogue in collaboration with Edward Bond (from the short story by Julio Cortázar)
Photography	Ray Parslow
Music	Herbert Hancock
	"Stroll On" featured and conducted by the Yardbirds
Cast	David Hemmings (Thomas)
	Vanessa Redgrave (Jane)

Sarah Miles (Patricia)
John Castel (Bill)
Peter Bowles (Ron)
Jane Birkin (The Blonde)
Gillian Hills (The Brunette)
Harry Hutchinson (The Old Man)
Verushka, Jill Kennington, Peggy Moffitt, Rosaleen Murray, Ann Norman, Melanie Hampshire (The Models)
Julian Chagrin and Claude Chagrin (The Tennis Players)

Length	110 minutes. Color.
Rental	Films, Inc.

Film Title	*Fellini Satyricon*
Date	1969
Producer	Alberto Grimaldi
Director	Federico Fellini
Screenplay	Federico Fellini and Bernardino Zapponi (from the "novel" by Petronius)
Photography	Giuseppe Rotunno
Music	Nino Rota, Ilhan Mimaroglu, Tod Dockstader, and Andrew Rudin
Cast	Martin Potter (Encolpius)
	Hiram Keller (Ascyltus)
	Max Born (Giton)
	Fanfulla (Vernacchio)
	Salvo Randone (Eumolpus)
	Mario Romagnoli (Trimalchio)
	Magali Noel (Fortunata)
	Alain Cluny (Lichas)
	Capucine (Tryphaena)
	Joseph Wheeler (The Suicide)
	Tanya Lopert (The Emperor)
Length	127 minutes. Color.
Rental	UA 16 (subtitled)

Film Title	*Une Femme Douce* (*The Gentle Creature*)
Date	1969
Producer	Parc Film/Marianne Production
Director	Robert Bresson
Screenplay	Robert Bresson (from the story "The Gentle Creature" by Dostoevsky)
Photography	Ghislain Cloquet
Music	Purcell and Jean Wiener
Cast	Dominique Sanda (She)
	Guy Frangin (He)
	Jane Lobre (Anna)
	Dorothée Blank

	Claude Ollier
Length	87 minutes. Color.
Rental	New Yorker Films (subtitled)

Film Title	*Tristana*
Date	1970
Producer	Robert Dorfmann, Epoca Film-Talia Film (Madrid), Selenia Cinematografica (Rome), and Les Films Corona (Paris)
Director	Luis Buñuel
Screenplay	Luis Buñuel and Julio Alejandro (from the novel by Benito Pérez Galdós)
Photography	José F. Aguayo
Cast	Catherine Deneuve (Tristana)
	Fernando Rey (Don Lope)
	Franco Nero (Don Horacio)
	Lola Gaos (Saturna)
	Jesus Fernandez (Saturno)
	Antonio Casas (Don Cosme)
	Jose Calvo (Bell Ringer)
Length	98 minutes. Color.
Rental	Audio-Brandon (subtitled)

Film Title	*Die Angst des Tormanns beim Elfmeter* (*The Goalie's Anxiety at the Penalty Kick*
Date	1971
Producer	Filmverlag der Autoren (Munich) and Österreichischer Telefilm (Vienna)
Director	Wim Wenders
Screenplay	Wim Wenders (from the novel by Peter Handke)
Photography	Robbie Müller
Music	Jürgen Knieper
Cast	Arthur Brauss (Josef Bloch)
	Kai Fischer (Hertha Gabler)
	Erika Pluhar (Gloria T.)
	Libgart Schwarz (Anna)
	Marie Bardischewski (Maria)
Length	101 minutes. Color.
Rental	Bauer Films (subtitled)

Film Title	*Il Decamerone* (*The Decameron*)
Date	1971
Producer	Franco Rossellini for PEA (Produzioni Europee Associate s.a.s.)
Director	Pier Paolo Pasolini
Screenplay	Pier Paolo Pasolini (from *The Decameron* by Boccaccio)
Photography	Tonino Delli Colli

Music	Pier Paolo Pasolini with Ennio Morricone
Cast	Franco Citti
	Ninetto Davoli
	Jovan Jovanovic
	Vincenzo Amato
	Angela Luce
	Giuseppe Zicaina
	Gabriella Frankel
	Vincenzo Cristo
	P. P. Pasolini
Length	105 minutes. Color.
Rental	New Yorker Films (subtitled)

Film Title	*Il Conformista* (*The Conformist*)
Date	1971
Producer	Maurizio Lodi-Fe
Director	Bernardo Bertolucci
Screenplay	Bernardo Bertolucci (from the novel by Alberto Moravia)
Photography	Vittorio Storato
Music	Georges Delerue
Cast	Jean-Louis Trintignant (Marcello)
	Stefania Sandrelli (Giulia)
	Dominique Sanda (Anna)
	Pierre Clementi (Lino)
	Gastore Moschin (Manganiello)
Length	108 minutes. Color
Rental	Films Incorporated (subtitled)

Film Title	*L'Horloger de Saint Paul* (*The Clockmaker*)
Date	1973
Producer	Raymond Danon
Director	Bertrand Tavernier
Screenplay	Jean Aurenche and Pierre Bost (from the novel *The Clockmaker of Everton* by Georges Simenon)
Photography	Pierre William Glenn
Cast	Philippe Noiret (Michel Descombes)
	Jean Rochefort (Commissaire Guiboud)
	Jean Denis (Antoine)
	Julien Bertheau (Edouard)
	Yves Afonso (Bricard, policeman)
	Jacques Hilling (Costes)
Length	105 minutes. Color.
Rental	Joseph Green (subtitled)

Film Title	*Effi Briest*
Date	1974

Producer   Tango Film
Director   Rainer Werner Fassbinder
Screenplay   Rainer Werner Fassbinder (from the novel by Theodor
                Fontane)
Photography   Jurgen Jurges and Dietrich Lohmann
Music   Camille Saint-Saens
Cast   Hanna Schygulla (Effi Briest)
                Wolfgang Schenck (Baron von Innstetten)
                Ulli Lommel (Major Crampas)
                Karlheinz Bohn (Wüllersdorf)
                Lilo Pempeit (Frau Briest)
                Herbert Steinmetz (Herr Briest)
                Ursula Stratz (Roswitha)
                Irm Hermann (Johanna)
                Hark Bohm (Gieshübler)
Length   140 minutes. Black and white.
Rental   New Yorker Films (subtitled)

Film Title   *Falsche Bewegung* (*Wrong Movement*)
Date   1974
Producer   Solaris Film (Munich)
Director   Wim Wenders
Screenplay   Peter Handke (freely based on Johann Wolfgang
                Goethe's novel *Wilhelm Meisters Lehrjahre*)
Photography   Robbie Müller
Music   Jurgen Knieper
Cast   Rüdiger Vogler (Wilhelm Meister)
                Hanna Schygulla (Therese)
                Hans Christian Blech (Laertes)
                Peter Kern (Landau)
                Nastassja Nakszynski (Mignon)
                Ivan Desny (Industrialist)
                Marianne Hoppe (Wilhelm's mother)
                Elisabeth Kreuzer (Janine)
Length   103 minutes. Color.
Rental   Bauer Films (subtitled)

Film Title   *Die Verlorene Ehre der Katharina Blum* (*The Lost Hon-
                or of Katharina Blum*)
Date   1975
Producer   Eberhard Junkersdorf for Paramount-Orion/WDR/Bio-
                skop Film (Munich)
Director   Volker Schlöndorff and Margarethe von Trotta
Screenplay   Volker Schlöndorff (from the novel by Heinrich Böll)
Photography   Jost Vocano and Peter Arnold
Music   Hans Werner Henze
Cast   Angela Winkler (Katharina Blum)

Mario Adorf (Beizmenne)
Dieter Laser (Werner Tötges)
Heinz Bennent (Dr. Blorna)
Hannelore Hoger (Trude Blorna)
Harald Kuhlmann (Moeding)

Length	106 minutes. Color.
Rental	Films, Inc. (subtitled)

Film Title	*Die Wildente (The Wild Duck)*
Date	1976
Producer	Bernd Eichinger, Solaris-Film Production in cooperation with Sascha-Film and WDR
Director	Hans W. Geissendörfer
Screenplay	Hans W. Geissendörfer (from the play by Henrik Ibsen)
Photography	Robbie Müller
Music	Nils Janette Walen
Cast	Peter Kern (Hjalmar Ekdal)
	Jean Seberg (Gina Ikdal)
	Bruno Ganz (Gregers Werle)
	Anne Bennent (Hedwig Ekdal)
	Martin Floerchinger (Old Ekdal)
	Heinz Bennent (Relling)
	Heinz Moog (Consul Werle)
Length	105 minutes. Color.
Rental	New Yorker Films (subtitled)

Film Title	*The Marquise of O . . .*
Date	1976
Producer	Janus Films (Frankfurt), Artemis (Berlin), Les Films du Losange (Paris), and Gaumont (Neuilly)
Director	Eric Rohmer
Screenplay	Eric Rohmer
Photography	Nestor Almendros
Cast	Edith Clever (Marquise)
	Bruno Ganz (Count)
	Peter Luhr (Father)
	Edda Sieppel (Mother)
	Otto Sander (Brother)
Length	102 minutes. Color.
Rental	New Line Cinema

Film Title	*Cet Obscur Objet du Désir (That Obscure Object of Desire)*
Date	1977
Producer	Serge Silberman
Director	Luis Buñuel
Screenplay	Luis Buñuel, with Jean-Claude Carrière

Photography	Jean Harnois
Cast	Fernando Rey (Mathieu Fabert)
	Carole Bouquet and Angela Molina (Concha)
Length	100 minutes. Color.
Rental	Films Incorporated (subtitled)

Selected Filmography: European Film Adaptations from Literature— 1943–Present

The list of films that follows is arranged alphabetically by director. Although not all the films are masterpieces, and some may be thoroughly undistinguished, all the directors are worthy of note—some are major, others minor, but none are obscure. Gathering this material has been difficult. The information is scattered, and sources often disagree about details. We made no attempt to settle such discrepancies or to be exhaustive in our listing. Nevertheless, we hope we have given some sense of the role adaptation has played in the work of these interesting European directors. Films discussed in this volume are not included.

Director *Film (country, date)* *Length, B&W or color*	*Literary source*	*Rental* *source(s)*
ALLEGRET, MARC *Lady Chatterley's Lover* (France, 1957) 98 min. B&W	from the novel by D. H. Lawrence	AUD, BI
ALLIO, RENÉ *The Shameless Old Lady* (France, 1965) 94 min. B&W	from the short story "Die unwürdige Greisin" by Bertolt Brecht	TWY
ANGELOPOULS, THEODORE *Thiasos (The Traveling* *Players)* (Greece, 1975)	based in part on the *Oresteia* of Aeschylus	
ANTONIONI, MICHELANGELO *Le Amiche (The Girl* *Friends)* (Italy, 1955)	from "Tra Donne Sole" in *La Bella Estate* by Cesare Pavese	
AUTANT-LARA, CLAUDE *Le Diable au Corps* (France, 1947) *Occupe-toi d'Amélie*	from the novel by Raymond Radiguet from the play by	

(France, 1949)	Georges Feydeau	
Le Blé en Herbe	from the novel by	
(France, 1954)	Colette	
Le Rouge et le Noir	from the novel by	IVY
(France, 1954)	Stendhal	
146 min. Color		
The Gambler	from the novella by	AUD
(France, 1958)	Fyodor Dostoevsky	
102 min. B&W		
The Count of Monte Cristo	from the novel by Alex-	
(France, 1961)	andre Dumas, *père*	
Le Meurtrier (*Enough*	from the novel by Pa-	AUD
Rope)	tricia Highsmith	
(France, 1965)		
104 min. B&W		

BERGMAN, INGMAR

The Magic Flute	from the opera by	FI
(Sweden, 1975)	Mozart	
134 min. Color		

BERTOLUCCI, BERNARDO

Before the Revolution	based on *The Charter-*	NYF
(Italy, 1964)	*house of Parma* by	
115 min. B&W	Stendhal	
Partner	partly based on "The	NYF
(Italy, 1968)	Double" by Fyodor	
112 min. Color	Dostoevsky	
The Spider's Strategem	from the story "The	NYF
(Italy, 1970)	Theme of the Traitor	
97 min. Color	and the Hero" by Jorge	
	Borges	

BRESSON, ROBERT

Les Dames du Bois de	from *Jacques le*	CON
Boulogne	*Fataliste* by Denis	
(France, 1944)	Diderot	
90 min. B&W		
Pickpocket	loosely based on *Crime*	NYF
(France, 1959)	*and Punishment* by	
75 min. B&W	Fyodor Dostoevsky	
Mouchette	from the novel by	NLC
(France, 1966)	Georges Bernanos	
80 min. B&W		
Four Nights of a Dreamer	from "White Nights" by	NYF
(France, 1971)	Fyodor Dostoevsky	
83 min. Color		

BROOK, PETER
    Moderato Cantabile   from the novel by   SWA
    (France, 1960)   Marguerite Duras
    93 min. B&W

BUÑUEL, LUIS
    Robinson Crusoe   from the novel by   TWY
    (Mexico, 1952)   Daniel Defoe
    Abismos de Pasión   from *Wuthering Heights*
    (Mexico, 1953)   by Emily Brontë
    Nazarin   from the novel by   AUD
    (Mexico, 1958)   Benito Pérez Galdós
    92 min. B&W
    Diary of a Chambermaid   from the novel by   IVY
    (France, 1964)   Octave Mirbeau
    76 min. B&W
    Belle de Jour   from the novel by   HUR
    (France, 1966)   Joseph Kessel
    100 min. Color

CACOYANNIS, MICHAEL
    Electra   from the tragedy by   UA
    (Greece, 1963)   Euripides
    110 min. B&W
    Zorba the Greek   based on the novel by   FI
    (Greece-USA, 1964)   Nikos Kazantzakis
    142 min. B&W
    The Trojan Women   from the tragedy by   SWA
    (USA, 1971)   Euripides
    105 min. Color
    Iphegenia at Taurus   from the tragedy by
    (Greece, 1977)   Euripides

CARNÉ, MARCEL
    Les Portes de la Nuit   from the novel *Le Ren-*
    (France, 1946)   *dez-Vous* by Jacques
                            Prévert
    La Marie du Port   from the novel by
    (France, 1950)   Georges Simenon
    Thérèse Raquin (*The*   from the novel by   AUD
      Adultress)   Émile Zola
    (France, 1953)
    106 min. B&W
    Trois Chambres à Man- from the novel by
      hattan   Georges Simenon
    (France, 1965)

CHABROL, CLAUDE
    Web of Passion (*Leda*)   based on the novel *The* AUD

(France, 1959)	*Key to Nicholas Street*	
101 min. Color	by Stanley Ellin	
The Road To Corinth		
(France, 1967)	based on a novel by	
Just Before Nightfall	Claude Rank	
(France, 1971)	from the novel *The*	COR
100 min. Color	*Thin Line* by Edward	
	Atiyeh	

CLAIR, RENÉ

Porte des Lilas	from the novel *La*	AUD
(France, 1957)	*Grande Ceinture* by	
	René Fallet	

CLÉMENT, RENÉ

Les Jeux Interdits (*Forbid-*	from the novel by	JAN
den Games)	François Boyer	
(France, 1952)		
90 min. B&W		
Monsieur Ripois (*Knave of*	from the novel *M.*	
Hearts)	*Ripois et la Nemesis* by	
(France, 1954)	Louis Hemon	
Gervaise	from *L'Assomoir* by	BUD
(France, 1957)	Émile Zola	
116 min. B&W		
Barrage contre le Pacifique	from the novel by	
(France, 1958)	Marguerite Duras	
Plein Soleil (*Purple Noon*)	from the novel *Talented*	AUD
(France, 1961)	*Mr. Ripley* by Patricia	
115 min. Color	Highsmith	

CLOUZET, HENRI-GEORGES

Manon	from *Manon Lescaut*	TWF, CON
(France, 1949)	by Abbé Prevost	
90 min. B&W		
The Wages of Fear	from the novel by	AUD, BI
(France, 1953)	Georges Arnaud	
138 min. B&W		

COCTEAU, JEAN

Beauty and the Beast	from the version by	JAN
(France, 1946)	Mme Leprince de	
90 min. B&W	Beaumont	
Les Parents Terribles	from Cocteau's play	JAN
(France, 1948)		
Orpheus	from Cocteau's one-act	CON, JAN,
(France, 1949)	play	BI
94 min. B&W		

COSTA-GAVRAS
Z	from the novel by	CIV
(France-Algeria, 1968)	Vassilis Vasilikos	
135 min. Color		

DASSIN, JULES
Rififi	from the novel by	BI
(France, 1954)	Auguste le Breton	
115 min. B&W		

DELANNOY, JEAN
Dicu a Besoin des Hommes	from the novel by
(France, 1949)	Henri Queffélec

DE SICA, VITTORIO
Miracle in Milan	based on the novel by	JAN
(Italy, 1951)	Cesare Zavattini	
95 min. B&W		
The Condemned of Altona	from the play by Jean-	FI
(Fox, 1962)	Paul Sartre	
114 min. B&W		
Marriage Italian Style	from *Filumena Martu-*	AUD
(Italy, 1964)	*rano* by Eduardo di	
102 min. Color	Filippo	
The Garden of the Finzi-	from the novel by	CIV
Continis	Giorgio Bassani	
(Italy, 1970)		
103 min. Color		

DREYER, CARL
Vredens Dag (*Day of*	from the play *Anne*	ACB, CON,
Wrath)	*Pedersdotter* by Hans	COR, BI
(Denmark, 1943)	Wiers-Jenssen	
98 min. B&W		
Ordet (*The Word*)	from the play by	CON, COR
(Denmark, 1954)	Kaj Munk	
126 min. B&W		

FASSBINDER, RAINER WERNER
The Bitter Tears of Petra	from Fassbinder's play	NYF
Von Kant		
(Germany, 1972)		
124 min. Color		
Wildwechsel (*Jail Bait*)	based on the play by	NYF
(Germany, 1972)	Franz Xaver Kroetz	
99 min. Color		
Despair	adapted by Tom Stop-	NYF
(Germany, 1978)	pard from the novel by	
119 min. Color	Vladimir Nabokov	

FELLINI, FEDERICO
Toby Dammit (in *Spirits of the Dead*) (along with segments by Malle and Vadim) (France, 1969) 118 min. Color — from the story "Never Bet the Devil Your Head" by Edgar Allan Poe — WHO

FRANJU, GEORGES
La Tête contre Les Murs (France, 1958) — from the novel by Hervé Bazin

Les Yeux sans Visage (France, 1959) — from the novel by Jean Redon

Thérèse Desqueyroux (France, 1962) 107 min. B&W — from the novel by François Mauriac — ACB, CON

Thomas L'Imposteur (France, 1965) 94 min. B&W — from the novel by Jean Cocteau — ACB, CON

GEISSENDÖRFER, HANS
Die Gläserne Zelle (*The Glass Cell*) (Germany, 1979) 93 min. Color — from the novel by Patricia Highsmith

GODARD, JEAN-LUC
Les Carabiniers (France, 1963) 78 min. B&W — loosely based on the play by Benjamino Joppolo — NYF

Masculin/Feminin (France, 1966) 103 min. B&W — loosely based on the stories "La Femme de Paul" and "Le Signe" by Guy de Maupassant — SWA, COR

Pierrot le Fou (France, 1966) 110 min. Color — loosely based on the novel *Obsession* by Lionel White — CON, COR

GORETTA, CLAUDE
The Lacemaker (Switzerland, 1977) 108 min. Color — based on the novel by Pascal Lainé — NYF

HANDKE, PETER
The Left-Handed Woman (Germany, 1976) — based on Handke's novel

HERZOG, WERNER
Woyzeck (Germany, 1979) — from the play by Georg Büchner

MALLE, LOUIS

Les Amants (The Lovers) (France, 1958) 90 min. B&W	from *Point de Lende-main* by Dominique Vivant and Baron de Denon	JAN
Le Feu Follet (The Fire Within) (France, 1969) 108 min. B&W	from the novel by Pierre Drieu la Rochelle	NYF
William Wilson (in *Spirits of the Dead*) (along with segments by Fellini and Vadim) (France, 1969) 118 min. Color	from the story by Edgar Allan Poe	WHO

MELVILLE, JEAN-PIERRE

Les Enfants Terribles (France, 1949)	from the novel by Jean Cocteau	JAN, COR
Léon Morin, Prêtre (France, 1961) 117 min. B&W	from the novel by Béatrix Beck	ACB, CON
L'Aimé des Ferchaux (France, 1962)	from the novel by Georges Simenon	
Le Deuxième Souffle (France, 1966) 125 min. B&W	from the novel by José Giovanni	AUD
L'Armée des Ombres (France, 1969)	from the novel by Joseph Kessel	

OPHULS, MAX

Letter From An Unknown Woman (USA, 1948) 80 min. B&W	based on the story by Stefan Zweig	BUD
Le Plaisir (France, 1952) 95 min. B&W	based on three stories by Guy de Maupassant	BI
The Earrings of Madame De . . . (France, 1953) 105 min. B&W	from the novel by Louise de Vilmarin	CON, ACB, COR
Lola Montès (France, 1955) 100 min. Color	from the story by Cécil St.-Laurent	AUD

PASOLINI, PIER PAOLO

The Gospel According to	from the Bible	AUD

St. Matthew
(Italy, 1964)
136 min. B&W

Edipo Re (*Oedipus Rex*) (Italy, 1967)	from Sophocles	
Medea (Italy, 1971) 110 min. Color	based on Euripides	NLC
The Canterbury Tales (Italy, 1971)	from Chaucer	

RENOIR, JEAN

Diary of a Chambermaid (USA, 1946) 81 min. B&W	from the novel by Oc- tave Mirbeau and the play by Heuse, Lorde, and Noces	IVY
The Golden Coach (France, 1953)	from the play *Le Car- rosse de Saint-Sacre- ment* by Prosper Merimée	
The Elusive Corporal (France, 1962) 90 min. B&W	from the novel by Jacques Perret	CON

ROHMER, ERIC

Six Moral Tales: *La Boulangère de Monceau* (1962) *La Carrière de Suzanne* (1963) *La Collectionneuse* (1967) *My Night at Maud's* (1968) *Clair's Knee* (1969) *Chloe in the Afternoon* (1972)	All derived from tales by Rohmer, although the tales weren't pub- lished until after the films appeared	
Perceval le Gallois (France, 1978) 140 min. Color	from the romance of Chrétien de Troyes	NYF

ROSSELLINI, ROBERTO

Giovanna d'Arco Al Rogo (Italy, 1954)	from the play by Paul Claudel	
Vanina Vanini (*The Betrayer*) (Italy, 1961)	from *Chroniques Ital- iennes* by Stendhal	

SCHLÖNDORFF, VOLKER

Young Törless (Germany, 1966)	from the novel by Robert Musil	NYF

87 min. B&W
Michael Kohlhaas   from the story by
(Germany, 1969)   Heinrich von Kleist
Coup de Grâce   from the novel by
(Germany, 1977)   Marguerite Yourcenar
The Tin Drum   from the novel by
(Germany, 1979)   Günter Grass

SJÖBERG, ALF
Miss Julie   from the play by   BUD
(Sweden, 1951)   August Strindberg
87 min. B&W

STRAUB, JEAN-MARIE
Machorka-Muff   based on "Haupt-   NYF
(Germany, 1962)   staedtisches Journal"
18 min. B&W   by Heinrich Böll
Not Reconciled   from *Billiards at Half-* NYF
(Germany, 1965)   *Past Nine* by Heinrich
51 min. B&W   Böll
Othon   from the play by   NYF
(Germany, 1969)   Pierre Corneille
83 min. Color
History Lessons   from a play by   NYF
(Germany, 1973)   Bertolt Brecht
88 min. Color
Moses and Aaron   the opera by Arnold   NYF
(Germany, 1975)   Schoenberg
105 min. Color

TAVERNIER, BERTRAND
Let Joy Reign Supreme   based in part on the   COR
(France, 1974)   novel *The Regent's*
120 min. Color   *Daughter* by Alexandre
                                  Dumas

TRUFFAUT, FRANÇOIS
Shoot the Piano Player   from the novel *Down*   JAN
(France, 1960)   *There* by David Goodis
84 min. B&W
Fahrenheit 451   from the novel by   CWF
(USA, 1966)   Ray Bradbury
112 min. Color
The Bride Wore Black   from the novel by   UA
(France, 1968)   Cornell Woolrich
107 min. Color
Mississippi Mermaid   from the novel *Waltz*   UA
(France, 1969)   *into Darkness* by Wil-
110 min. Color   liam Irish

The Wild Child (France, 1970) 85 min. B&W	from the memoir by Jean Itard	UA
Two English Girls (France, 1972) 108 min. Color	from the novel by Henri Roché	JAN
The Green Room (France, 1978) 94 min. Color	based on themes from "The Altar of the Dead" and "The Lesson of the Master" by Henry James	

VADIM, ROGER

Metzengerstein (in *Spirits of the Dead*) (along with segments by Fellini and Malle) (France, 1969) 118 min. Color	from a story by Edgar Allan Poe	WHO

VISCONTI, LUCHINO

Ossessione (Italy, 1942)	based on *The Postman Always Rings Twice* by James Cain	AUD
La Terra Trema (Italy, 1948) 162 min. B&W	inspired by the novel *I Malavoglia* by Giovanni Verga	AUD
Senso (Italy, 1954) 125 min. Color	from a novella by Camilla Boito	AUD
White Nights (Italy, 1957)	based on the story by Fyodor Dostoevsky	
Rocco and His Brothers (Italy, 1960) 175 min. B&W	from the novel *Il Ponte della Ghisolfa* by Gio- vanni Testori	AUD
The Leopard (Italy, 1963) 161 min. Color	from the novel by Giuseppe Lampedusa	FI
The Stranger (France, 1968) 104 min. Color	from the novel by Albert Camus	FI
Death in Venice (USA, 1971) 130 min. Color	from the novella by Thomas Mann	WSA
The Innocent (Italy, 1978)	from the novel by Gabriel d'Annunzio	

WENDERS, WIM
    The Scarlet Letter   from the novel by   BI
    (Germany, 1973)   Nathaniel Hawthorne
    94 min. Color

    The American Friend   based on the novel   NYF
    (Germany, 1977)   *Ripley's Game* by
    127 min. Color   Patricia Highsmith

ZEFFIRELLI, FRANCO
    Romeo and Juliet   from Shakespeare's play FI
    (British-Italian, 1967)
    138 min. Color

Selected Annotated Bibliography

The critical tradition concerned with the process of adaptation from literature to film is slight at best. A few works, however, deserve mentioning for those who wish to understand more fully both film and literature and the relationship between the two. An excellent place to begin would be James Goodwin's review of the field in his article "Literature and Film: A Review of Criticism," *Quarterly Review of Film Studies*, Vol. 4, No. 2, Spring 1979, pp. 227–246.

Books

Beja, Morris. *Film and Literature*, New York, Longmans, 1979. An introductory classroom text covering twenty-five adaptations as well as "literary" films such as *Wild Strawberries*. Useful only on the most elementary level.

Bluestone, George. *Novels into Film*, Berkeley, University of California Press, 1966 (reprint of 1957 edition). The pioneering book on the subject, which begins by pointing out the limitations of converting material from a verbal language to a visual one and then proceeds to map out the territory where they converge. As our introduction states, his observations are clearly in need of revision, expansion, and questioning.

Bresson, Robert. *Notes on Cinematography*, translated by Jonathan Griffin, New York, Urizen Books, 1975. In line with Roland Barthes and others, Bresson expresses a practicing filmmaker's view of cinema as a form of "writing."

Eidsvik, Charles. *Cineliteracy*, New York, Random House, 1978. A textbook with a helpful general chapter on "Cinema and Literature" in which Eidsvik discusses the clash and similarities between modernist literature and cinema, which has tended toward popular "fantasizing about the past."

Eisenstein, Sergei. *The Film Sense*, translated by Jay Leyda, New York, Praeger, 1947. Eisenstein's essay on the influence of Charles Dickens on D. W. Griffith helps us see clearly how early cinema learned from literary sources and structures.

Kawin, Bruce. *Mindscreen: Bergman, Godard, and First Person Film*, Ithaca, Cornell University Press, 1972. Kawin's study is a close examination of how film narrative has, in the hands of Bergman and Godard, become a complex art form capable of representing points of view that previously seemed limited to fiction.

McConnell, Frank. *The Spoken Seen: Film and the Romantic Imagination*, Baltimore, Johns Hopkins University Press, 1975. Emphasizing the narrative nature of film and literature, McConnell explores film as an outgrowth of a romantic perspective. He points to the similarity between film and fiction as media for expressing complicated and challenging representations of "internal fantasy and external constraint in our experiences of life" (p. 38).

————. *Storytelling and Mythmaking: Images from Film and Literature*, New York, Oxford University Press, 1979. Relying heavily on Northrop Frye's categories of literature, McConnell goes further here than in his earlier study to suggest both the similarities and differences between film and literature as they apply to the traditions of epic, romance, melodrama, and satire. Narrative in film and fiction is discussed in terms of archetypes.

Richardson, Robert. *Literature and Film*, Bloomington, Indiana University Press, 1969. Richardson successfully argues against McLuhan that film literacy reinforces and expands literary literacy, but his coverage of adaptation is too brief to be of importance.

Robbe-Grillet, Alain. *For a New Novel: Essays on Fiction*, translated by Richard Howard, New York, Grove Press, 1965. Robbe-Grillet, who writes and directs films as well as publishes novels, points out the cinematic influence (primarily the emphasis on the visual) that has been so evident in the *nouveau roman* in Europe and America.

Ropars-Wuilleumier, Marie-Claire. *De la Littérature au Cinéma: Genèse d'une Écriture*, Paris, Armand Colin, 1970; and *L'Écran de la Mémoire: Essais de Lecture Cinématographique*, Paris, Seuil, 1970. These, as our introduction has suggested, are the most helpful works on the subject yet published. Ropars-Wuilleumier, building on concepts from Roland Barthes and Christian Metz, clearly shows that filmmakers since World War II have become increasingly concerned with problems of language and narration, topics that until now have been more often associated with novelists and poets.

Sontag, Susan. *Against Interpretation*, New York, Dell Books, 1972. Sontag holds that there are more useful analogies which may be drawn between cinema and the novel than between cinema and theater, most especially the fact that both cinema and fiction can present us with a work that is "absolutely under the control of the director (writer) at every moment."

Spiegel, Alan. *Fiction and the Camera Eye: Visual Consciousness in Film and the Modern Novel*, Charlottesville, University of Virginia Press, 1976. Spiegel provides a clear focus on narrative and the breakdown of narrative in modern fiction and film.

Wagner, Geoffrey. *The Novel and the Cinema*, Cranbury, N.J., Fairleigh Dickinson University Press, 1975. Discussed here are a variety of European films, which Wagner explores in terms of how director-writers have made use of the capabilities of film to go beyond the limitations of fiction.

Articles

There are many articles on specific films that have been adapted from specific sources. A few more theoretical pieces would include the following:

Dick, Bernard. "Authors, Auteurs, and Adaptations: Literature as Film/Film as Literature," *Yearbook of the American Comparative and General Literature*, No. 27, 1978, pp. 72–76. Dick emphasizes the differences between film and literature as follows: "(1) in film the laws of verisimilitude are relaxed; (2) the visual has priority over the verbal; (3) mythic associations are more readily formed in film than they are in literature; (4) film authorship, where one person assumes credit for a collective effort, is unique."

Eidsvik, Charles. "Toward a 'Politique des Adaptations,' " *Literature/Film Quarterly*, Vol. 3, No. 3, 1975, pp. 255–263. Eidsvik argues convincingly that adaptation should not be viewed as a semibastardized form of art but rather as an opportunity for even greater artistic and popular achievement.

Schneider, Harold W. "Literature and Film: Marking out Some Boundaries," *Literature/Film Quarterly*, Vol. 3, No. 1, 1975, pp. 30–44. Schneider's article is a practical work on how to set up a fruitful film-literature program in universities, but the examples he chooses to discuss suggest the flexibility of film narrative and the wide range of approaches to adaptation that have developed over the years.

—Andrew Horton

Index

Walbrook, Anton, 41, 42, 43, 45, 47, 48, 50
Wedding Dance (Brueghel), 219
Weekend (Godard), 200
Weightman, John, 50
Welles, Orson, 94, 136, 145, 339
Wenders, Wim, 188–202, 263–77
Whale, James, 117
"White Nights" (Dostoevsky), 158
Wild Duck, The (Geissendörfer), 295–312
  the attic in, 298–301
  father-son motif in, 303–4
  women in, 306–7
Wild Duck, The (Ibsen), 295–312
Wilder, Thornton (*Our Town*), 40*n.*
Wilhelm Meister's Apprenticeship (Goethe), 263–72, 274–77
Williams, Charles, 131
Winkler, Angela, 287*n.*

Wittgenstein, Ludwig (*Tractatus*), 66
Woman and the Puppet, The (Louÿs), 329–36, 338–39
Wrong Movement (Wenders), 5, 263–77
  as parable, 274–77

Young Törless (Schlöndorff), 278
Yourcenar, Marguerite, 278

Zavattini, Cesare, 78, 83
Zazie dans le Métro (Malle), 5, 63–77
  critique of French society in, 73–75
  and Hollywood traditions, 68–70
Zazie dans le Métro (Queneau), 63–75, 77
Ziolkowski, Theodore, 280